WHAT WRITERS KNOW

The Language, Process, and Structure of Written Discourse

EDITED BY

MARTIN NYSTRAND

Department of English
University of Illinois at Chicago Circle
Chicago, Illinois

 1982

ACADEMIC PRESS
A Subsidiary of Harcourt Brace Jovanovich, Publishers
New York   London   Toronto   Sydney   San Francisco

Figure I.2, pp. 12 and 13: From "The earliest precursor of writing," Schmandt-Besserat, Denise, copyright June 1978 by Scientific American, Inc. All rights reserved.

Chapter 2 is a revised and expanded version of a paper entitled "Using Readability Research to Investigate Writing," published in *Research in the Teaching of English*, Vol. 13, No.3, October 1979:231-242.

Tables 2.1 and 2.2, pp.62 and 63, were previously published in Millar and Nystrand, "The Language Trap," *English Journal*, 1979,*68* (3), 36-41. Table 2.3 on p.71 is a revised version of another table that appeared in the same article.

ACADEMIC PRESS, INC.
111 Fifth Avenue, New York, New York 10003

United Kingdom Edition published by
ACADEMIC PRESS, INC. (LONDON) LTD.
24/28 Oval Road, London NW1 7DX

Library of Congress Cataloging in Publication Data
Main entry under title:

What writers know.

Includes bibliographies and index.
1. Written communication. 2. Rhetoric. 3. Psycho-
linguistics. 4. Sociolinguistics. 5. Speech acts
(Linguistics) I. Nystrand, Martin.
P211.W45 1981   001.54'3   81-19146
ISBN 0-12-523480-5   AACR2

PRINTED IN THE UNITED STATES OF AMERICA

82 83 84 85   9 8 7 6 5 4 3 2 1

To Nancy, who has waited far too long

Contents

╱ INTRODUCTION

Rhetoric's "Audience" and Linguistics' "Speech Community": Implications for Understanding Writing, Reading, and Text   1

Martin Nystrand

PART I
THE LANGUAGE OF WRITTEN DISCOURSE

CHAPTER **4**

Defining Thematic Progressions and Their Relationship to Reader Comprehension   87

Barbara S. Glatt

CHAPTER **5**

Context as Vehicle: Implicatures in Writing   105

Marilyn M. Cooper

CHAPTER **6**

Children as Writers: The Beginnings of Learning to Write   129

Robert A. Gundlach

CHAPTER **10**

Explorations in the Real-Time Production of Written Discourse

269

Ann Matsuhashi

CHAPTER **11**

✓ Speech–Act Theory and Writing

291

Martin Steinmann, Jr.

✓ CHAPTER **12**

What Writers Need to Know That They Don't Know They Need to Know

325

John B. Black, Deanna Wilkes-Gibbs, and Raymond W. Gibbs, Jr.

CHAPTER **13**

Learning to Revise: Some Component Processes

345

Elsa Jaffe Bartlett

CHAPTER **14**

Writing and Learning in School Settings   **365**

Arthur N. Applebee

List of Contributors

Numbers in parentheses indicate the pages on which the authors' contributions begin.

ARTHUR N. APPLEBEE (365), Stanford University, School of Education, Stanford, California 94305

ELSA JAFFE BARTLETT (345), Department of Neurology, New York University Medical Center, New York, New York 10016

ROBERT DE BEAUGRANDE (211), Department of English, University of Florida, Gainesville, Florida 32611

CARL BEREITER (173), Department of Applied Psychology, Ontario Institute for Studies in Education, Toronto, Ontario M5S 1V6, Canada

JOHN B. BLACK (325), Department of Psychology, Yale University, New Haven, Connecticut 06520

JAMES BRITTON (149), Goldsmith's College Professor of Education Emeritus, University of London, London, SE14 6NW, England

MARILYN M. COOPER (105), Department of English, University of Southern California, University Park, Los Angeles, California 90007

RAYMOND W. GIBBS, JR. (325), Department of Psychology, Yale University, New Haven, Connecticut 06520

BARBARA S. GLATT (87), Department of English, University of Illinois at Chicago Circle, Chicago, Illinois 60680

HILLEL GOELMAN (173), Department of Psychology, York University, Downsview, Ontario M3J 1P3, Canada

ROBERT A. GUNDLACH (129), Department of Linguistics, Northwestern University, Evanston, Illinois 60201

ANN MATSUHASHI (269), Department of English, University of Illinois at Chicago Circle, Chicago, Illinois 60680

MARTIN NYSTRAND (1, 57, 75), Department of English, University of Illinois at Chicago Circle, Chicago, Illinois 60680

MARLENE SCARDAMALIA (173), Department of Psychology, York University, Downsview, Ontario M3J 1P3, Canada

MARTIN STEINMANN, JR. (291), Department of English, University of Illinois at Chicago Circle, Chicago, Illinois 60680

MICHAEL STUBBS (31), Department of Linguistics, University of Nottingham, University Park, Nottingham NG7 2RD, England

DEANNA WILKES-GIBBS (325), Department of Psychology, Yale University, New Haven, Connecticut 06520

Preface

In the first edition of *Psycholinguistics* (1971), Dan Slobin commented that the Harvard–M.I.T. breakthroughs in cognitive psychology and language of the early 1960s promised insights into the nature of the human mind. In the completely rewritten second edition of 1979, he notes how things have changed in 20 years of research: The psycholinguistic study of the mind now promises insights into the nature of human language.

The study of language is indeed alive—not just research on the nature of language per se, but especially research on the many forms, purposes, and contexts of its use. Moreover, the focus of this research is increasingly on the forms, uses, and processes of *written language*. Linguists and psychologists, for example, have become interested in problems of texts and discourse. Psychologists and anthropologists have become interested in the structure and nature of narrative. Scholars of all sorts have become deeply involved in issues related to public documents in society. All these strands of research point far beyond the sentence in the investigation of language: The common denominator here is written discourse—its structure and use, plus the ways in which it is learned. Investigation of the language and structure of written discourse is essential to the study of texts, stories, and public documents for the simple reason that most sustained texts in English are written, not spoken.

The current state of writing research is not unlike linguistics in the wake of Chomsky's revolution in 1957. There is curiosity about children learning to write and read, for example, that is reminiscent of interest in children's acquisition of speech in the early 1960s. There is renewed interest, too, in the systemic character and internal logic of language forms, especially texts. Above all, there is a clear sense in all this research that important new insights about language are imminent—that the research gap, for example, between language comprehension and language production, as well as between reading and writing, is about to be narrowed, if not entirely closed. Writing research is an exciting, emerging area of inquiry—rapidly expanding and increasingly multidisciplinary.

There are some important differences, however, between psycholinguistics in the early 1960s and current writing research. There are many new experimental methodologies, plus some old ones which have been put to profitable use in this new venture (many are included in this volume). Moreover, there is new interest in the social context of language use and the language functions associated with these uses. Indeed, it may be argued that written language has become interesting to social scientists largely because of interest in the problems and contexts of language use: Spoken and written language do not differ in terms of grammatical constructions (Wardhaugh, 1969) or lexicon (Miller, 1951) available to users, though these resources are deployed very differently both in proportion and complexity in various ways of writing and speaking (Joos, 1962; see Smith, 1975, for discussion).

Indeed, writing research is in such an active state of change that during the 10 months in which the present volume was written, it became necessary to change the subtitle from *Studies in the Psychology of Writing* to *The Language, Process, and Structure of Written Discourse.* The contents of this volume are very comprehensive; they deal not only with the psychology of writing but also with the language of written discourse, the social functions of written language, and the structure of written discourse.

What Writers Know: The Language, Process, and Structure of Written Discourse focuses on the unique features of written language by investigating what writers know and nonwriters must learn in order to write. The contributors bring to bear many important methods and concepts from psychology, linguistics, rhetoric, and artificial intelligence to investigate this knowledge. They seek to clarify relations between writer and reader, writer and text, and text and context, as well as to characterize writing adequately in terms of these relations—that is, to show how requirements of context, text, and reader affect and constrain writers in their tasks. In many cases, the investigators seek to distinguish written language and writing from other forms and uses of language such as speech and reading, hence offering a characterization of writing as writing.

This book is written for researchers, graduate students, advanced undergraduates, and many educators concerned with the special problems of writing and written language. It will also be useful in courses in cognitive psychology, applied linguistics, the philosophy of language, rhetoric,

educational measurement, the linguistics of literacy, and English education.

REFERENCES

Joos, M. *The five clocks.* International Journal of American Linguistics Monograph Number 28
(1962).
Miller, G. A. *Language and communication.* New York: McGraw-Hill, 1951.
Slobin, D. I. *Psycholinguistics.* (1st ed.). Glenview, Illinois: Scott, Foresman, 1971.
Slobin, D. I. *Psycholinguistics.* (2nd ed.). Glenview, Illinois, Scott, Foresman, 1979.
Smith, F. The relation between spoken and written language. In E. H. Lenneberg & E.
Lenneberg (Eds.), *Foundations of language development: A multidisciplinary approach* (Vol. 2).
New York: Academic Press, 1975. Pp. 347–360.
Wardhaugh, R. *Reading: A linguistic perspective.* New York: Harcourt Brace Jovanovich, 1969.

Acknowledgments

I have received help and comments in many forms from many people during this project. I have many debts to pay, if only through acknowiedgment.

A primary debt is to Richard Buchanan, Bob Gundlach, and Martin Steinmann, Jr., without whose support, suggestions, and frequent disagreements this work could never have been undertaken or completed.

Another primary debt is to all the contributors—one of the finest and most professional groups of scholars I have ever known.

The next debt is to many readers whose suggestions and comments on various drafts were always generous and constructive: Arthur Applebee, Robert de Beaugrande, Michael Brown, Margaret Himley, Kyoko Inoue, Ann Matsuhashi, John Mellon, Carol Serverino, and Michael Stubbs.

Yet another debt is to all my students, who have taught me far more than they suspect.

The Graduate College Research Board of the University of Illinois at Chicago Circle provided me with a key research leave which allowed me to devote myself full time to this project in its last months.

The final debt is to my wife, Nancy, and our family and friends, particularly Gerald and Helen Androne, for their continuous companionship, support, and generosity. Much of my own writing was done in the calm and serenity of the Craven Farmstead in Plymouth Township, Wisconsin.

To all these individuals, thank you.

Rhetoric's "Audience" and Linguistics' "Speech Community": Implications for Understanding Writing, Reading, and Text

Martin Nystrand

INTRODUCTION

Despite their respective preoccupations with speakers—good speakers and native speakers—both rhetoric and linguistics have always had someone else lurking in the background. For rhetoric, this significant other is **audience;** for linguistics, it is **speech community.** Neither audience nor speech community is very well defined. Roughly, rhetoric's audience is the group the speaker or writer hopes to influence by argumentation (Perelman & Olbrechts-Tyteca, 1969, p. 19) while linguistics' speech community is any group sharing knowledge and rules-of-use of a common language (cf. Hymes, 1974). Audiences are concrete and can be (*a*) conversation partners, (*b*) groups of listeners assembled to hear particular speeches, or (*c*) readers sharing some common interest with the writer in a particular argument. By contrast, a speech community is an amorphous collectivity made up not just of those listeners or readers attending a particular text for a particular purpose, but theoretically all potential speakers, listeners, conversants, writers, and readers—in short, ALL LANGUAGE USERS WHO MIGHT CONCEIVABLY INTERACT WITH EACH OTHER THROUGH LANGUAGE, though not necessarily a particular text.

Rhetoric's audience is the concrete focus of deliberate speech acts (see Steinmann, this volume). Saussure describes these *actes de parole* as "wilful and intellectual" (1959, p. 14); the speaker–writer seeks to persuade or

WHAT WRITERS KNOW
The Language, Process,
and Structure of Written Discourse

otherwise move the audience. Individual speakers rarely move or modify their speech communities in any sense, however; this collectivity exists like an institution "outside the individual" and "only by virtue of a sort of contract signed by the members" (Saussure, 1959, p. 14). Indeed, THE SPEECH COMMUNITY ACTS ON THE INDIVIDUAL who, as a learner, becomes a fluent native speaker through a process of socialization, that is, by becoming a member of the "tribe" (cf. Hymes, 1967). By interacting first with "that little coterie of people who constitute his meaning group" (Halliday, 1978, p. 1) and then perhaps with a more remote and potentially far more wide-ranging speech-qua-writing community (Berry, 1958; Stubbs, 1980; Vachek, 1973), the individual comes to know tacitly the significant differences and regularities that make up his spoken and written language.

A text that is effective from the point of view of rhetoric because of its power to affect a particular audience is interesting to linguistics for what it reveals, ALONG WITH MANY OTHER TEXTS, about the language resources that speakers and writers draw on in realizing the aims of discourse. Hence, while rhetoric properly examines the effects of texts on audiences, linguistics focuses on the irreversible and indelible effects that the collective whole has on the individual as a user of language. Rhetoric looks at **speeches,** linguistics considers **speech.**

The **rhetorical study of audience** may be defined, then, as the investigation of writers' plans and goals, taking into account the ways in which writers locate all available means for achieving particular effects on readers, plus causal relations between effective texts and such effects. The **linguistics of writing,** by contrast, is the examination of the effects of readers, as speech community of the writer, upon writers and the texts they compose. It is true, of course, that audiences often affect their speakers: Good speakers sense when they are being effective and when they are not and make the necessary adjustments. It is also true that individuals occasionally affect their speech communities; indeed, having done so is a major distinguishing characteristic of many popular culture heroes. Nonetheless, the main focus of rhetoric is the effects that speakers and writers hope to have on particular audiences in the form of particular speeches, while the main focus of linguistics is the effects that the speech community has generally on language users in the form of speech.

These two orientations toward the speaker's significant other have very different, albeit complementary, implications for understanding writing and language production in general. Obviously any particular text is simultaneously rhetorical and linguistic in character. Hence, my distinction is analytic, contrasting the **structure of discourse** with the **resources of language for discourse.** In effect, these orientations represent different points of departure for the study of writing, entailing different premises and generating very different lines of inquiry into the nature of writing, reading, and text. The purpose of this chapter is to look closely at the ideas of audience in rhetoric and speech community in linguistics, teasing out respective implications for understanding writing behavior and written language. My purpose here is not to analyze particular rhetorical stances nor to examine various speech communities but rather to consider the implications of these concepts for the study of writing. How do the fundamental notions of audience and speech community shape our ideas about writing? What kinds of questions do these orientations suggest? And what aspects of writing fall outside the scope of each?

One final, general note by way of introduction. My intent here is nothing so ambitious as a comprehensive survey of important competing points of view in rhetoric and linguistics. Rhetoric certainly focuses on more than audience, and linguistics is far more readily defined by interests other than speech community. The idea of speech community has mainly and seriously interested only a few sociolinguists, including recently Fishman, Gumperz, Hymes, and Halliday. Indeed, "to interpret linguistic processes from the standpoint of the social order," as Halliday notes in *Language as Social Semiotic* (1978, p. 3) is to move away from consideration of language per se. Hence I deliberately juxtapose these two focuses, not because I wish to review or explain rhetoric and linguistics (something I clearly do not do), but only because their joint consideration raises a good many critical questions about the nature of writing. There are easily as many discussions of writing in rhetoric that gloss over language as there are discussions of language in linguistics that gloss over writing. However, the identity and nature of the speaker–writer's significant other is a common concern for both rhetoricians and linguists: Rhetoricians say most about language when they turn to audience, and linguists say most about written language when they turn to speech community and the social aspects of language use. More often than not, they say different things, but careful consideration of this common ground is very suggestive for the study of writing. Hence, I have chosen to juxtapose rhetoric's AUDIENCE and linguistics' SPEECH COMMUNITY as a useful way of organizing and focusing many key issues in current writing research, which itself is becoming increasingly interdisciplinary.

RHETORIC'S AUDIENCE

In the beginning, rhetoric saw audience as that particular group of listeners subject to the speaker's influence. Whether rhetoric was the Sophists' pleading causes successfully, Plato's helping others understand truth and justice, or Aristotle's observing in any given case the available means of persuasion, the audience was a concrete and immediate fact for orators, a very real concern for students of rhetoric, and a critical factor for theoreticians of discourse. Indeed, the main task of rhetoric historically has been formalization of the means and principles whereby speakers and writers mobilize arguments as vehicles of influence.

The importance of audience as a concept in rhetoric is especially conspicuous in "rhetorics" where it is absent and nowhere more apparent than in deleterious forms of writing instruction which proceed without reference to actual readers. During the eighteenth and nineteenth centuries, the rise of the popular press along with efforts to secure mass literacy in British and American schools fostered a decline of oratory along with a concomitant rise of writing as the primary mode of rhetoric in these societies. A major effect of this shift was an abstraction of audience. This abstraction was partly due to differences between spoken and written language: Compared to orators, who can never escape the concrete fact of their ever present listeners, writers must often be reminded of their readers. Far more important, however, were programs of mass literacy as they developed in nineteenth-century American schools. These programs intensified this abstraction by stylizing and reifying the writer's audience. Young writers were regularly urged to "speak agre[e]ably to the common usage of the tongue" and admonished to drop "mean and sordid" usages: "polite and elegant speakers distinguish themselves by their discourse, as persons of figure do by their garb; one being the dress of the mind, as the other is of the body [Ward, 1759, p. 308; cited in Douglas, 1976, p. 109]."

One may charitably argue that this emphasis came about partly because of needs to standardize composition curricula in the interests of mass literacy. That is, to teach large numbers of children to write, teachers created "manageable" lesson plans and adopted streamlined textbooks— prototypical "developmental" curricula—which in effect treated writing as a series of discrete forms to master rather than situations of influence to manage. Education on a large scale was only part of the problem, however. Far more important were meritocratic pressures of upward social mobility that stereotyped the audience and purposes of writing in particular ways—ways moved less by argument, reason, and illocution and more by style and certain desired perlocutionary effects associated with the polish and trappings of social class (cf. Douglas, 1976). Writing was openly presented to students as a kind of "proper talk"—an important outward sign of a presumed inner grace: "educated man."

The end result of these developments, R. Young (1978) notes, has been a rhetoric characterized by "emphasis on the composed product rather than the composing process; the analysis of discourse into words, sentences, and paragraphs; the classification of discourse into description, narration, exposition, and argument; the strong concern with usage (syntax, spelling, punctuation) and with style (economy, clarity, emphasis); the preoccupa-

tion with the informal essay and the research paper; and so on [p. 31]."
Indeed, writing in the absence of a rhetorical context is not really discourse;
it is the bloodless, academic exercise of essay-making, dummy runs (Britton, Burgess, Martin, McLeod, & Rosen, 1975; Dixon, 1967), and pedagogical artifacts such as the five-paragraph theme—in short, a degeneration of rhetoric (cf. Perelman & Olbrechts-Tyteca, 1969).

Essential to rhetoric, then, is a notion of audience as person or persons whom the speaker or writer hopes to influence. Even if the writer's audience is necessarily more diffuse and remote than the speaker's always present listener, the writer nonetheless has a sense of whom he or she hopes to influence—the piece is for certain individuals more than others; and the readers will in fact be that group sharing a common interest in the writer's argument.

In short, rhetoric deals properly with the structure of discourse—as Booth puts it, "balance among three elements that are at work in any communicative effort: the available arguments about the subject itself, the interests and peculiarities of the audience, and the voice, the implied character of the speaker [1963, p. 139]." This focus inevitably leads to questions about the effects of texts on readers, as well as to analyses of texts and writing with this end in mind: What distinguishes an effective text? See Steinmann; and Black, Wilkes-Gibbs, and Gibbs (this volume). What must a writer know to compose one? See Steinmann; Black, Wilkes-Gibbs, and Gibbs; and Cooper (all in this volume). How do writers compose them? See Scardamalia, Bereiter, and Goelman; Matsuhashi; and Beaugrande (all in this volume). How do good writers differ from poor ones? See Bartlett (this volume). What indeed are all the available means of persuasion? And how do writers go about locating such means? What are the respective roles and relations of writers and readers in actual discourse? See Nystrand, "The Structure of Textual Space" (this volume).

These questions lend a strong teleological character to rhetorical descriptions—a case of the end or result explaining the means. Hence, the composing process is mobilization of those means likely to effect a plan and yield good results. This is the design and intent of Cicero's sequence **invention, arrangement, style, memory,** and **delivery,** as well as contemporary echoes in cognitive models: Bruce, Collins, Rubin, and Gentner's (1978) stage model of **discovering ideas, manipulating ideas, producing text,** and **editing text;** and Hayes and Flower's (1980) process model of **generating ideas, organizing ideas,** and **translating ideas into text.** In all these schemes, including these newest of rhetorics, writing presents the writer with the problem of evoking a certain state of mind in the reader (Black, in press) or otherwise achieving some goal. It is this final cause that has historically motivated and organized virtually all rhetorical descriptions of writing.

THE STRUCTURE OF DISCOURSE VERSUS THE
RESOURCES OF LANGUAGE FOR DISCOURSE

While the structure of discourse is clearly central to the concerns of rhetoric, analysis or description of the resources of language for written discourse is not. Indeed, discourse schemes often obscure the role of language in the process. Many discussions of writing as discourse simply make no mention of language at all. And when language is not ignored, it is often ancillary to cognitive processes. Hence, language production is characterized as "the verbal rendition of thought" or "the execution of speech plans" or "the translation of propositional content from long-term memory into acceptable sentences" (see Clark & Clark, 1977, Chapters 6 and 7 for a thorough review of this literature). But what is this process of translation? How indeed are ideas "formatted" or "converted into text"? One is tempted to respond with the obvious and tautologic: "by writing them," "by turning them into acceptable written sentences," but how writers might do this, of course, is precisely what any account of writing must explain.

If rhetoric is a matter of invention, arrangement, and delivery; or— updated in current parlance—generating, organizing, and translating ideas into text, then it is precisely at the point of translation that things become interesting for the study of writing for it is presumably here that spoken and written discourse part company and researchers are most likely to find out about the unique character of writing. Surely Olson (1977) and Hirsch (1977) are right to note the scribal and discourse conventions that make writing different from speech. Yet these differences must be more than noted; they must be explained. How does the written language work? See Stubbs (this volume). Specifically how does language function as an element of written discourse? See Nystrand, "An Analysis of Errors in Written Communication" (this volume). What language resources do writers draw on in realizing the aims of discourse? See Glatt (this volume). How do fluent writers differ from beginners (clearly a different question than how good writers differ from poor ones)? See Bartlett; Britton; Gundlach; and Scardamalia, Bereiter, and Goelman (all in this volume). What do WRITING RHETORS know that SPEAKING RHETORS (pleaders and orators) never needed to learn? See Scardamalia, Bereiter, and Goelman (this volume). Would it be hard or easy for an accomplished but illiterate orator to become an effective essayist? And finally the hardest question of them all, requiring answers to all the others: What kinds of knowledge do teachers need to address? See Applebee (this volume). How indeed shall we describe this activity whereby writers make things known?

If speech and writing are both forms of discourse differing only in "translation formats" and "mapping procedures," then learning to write does not involve learning a new communication system altogether, but merely modifying an existing one by transferring and channeling a language system already acquired from one medium (speech) into another (writing). This Bloomfieldian premise seems to underlie many forms of writing instruction which, bizarrely, encourage writers to develop their "ears," for example, checking spellings by "listening" to what the letters "say" and punctuating according to where the "voice" pauses (e.g., *Webster's Seventh New Collegiate Dictionary*, 1963, p. 1193). If written discourse differs from spoken discourse in more than mapping procedures and translation formats, however, this conclusion may not follow. These issues take on special significance if it can be shown, as I think it can, that THE RESOURCES OF DISCOURSE ARE NOT ANCILLARY TO COGNITION BUT ACTUALLY SHAPE THE POSSIBILITIES FOR AND HENCE THE CONDUCT OF DISCOURSE ITSELF.

The point here is that questions about language functioning fall outside the scope of investigations that focus exclusively on the structure of discourse. Writing is almost always discourse (discounting a lot of school writing, of course), but discourse is not always written: The two are related asymmetrically. Language, after all, is not an aim of discourse; language is the *sine qua non* of discourse. Hence, there is more to writing research than the study of written discourse processes.

Full characterization of writing, then, will not only deal with writer purposes, strategies, plans, goals, and so on, but also the resources of the written language for discourse. Too often the latter have been neglected. This neglect is both attudinal and procedural; in both cases it is a priori. There is the attitude, for example, that the language aspects of writing are uninteresting (merely the "superficial etiquette of getting thoughts down on paper" compared to the main business of thinking [McPherson in Sawyer, 1977]) reinforced by the dominant assumption—at least in the English-speaking world (Mathews, 1966)—that writing is not really language but speech written down. Writing has been thought to differ from speech mainly in ways too trivial to be of interest to rhetoric (or linguistics), whose real business is the art and skill of making good speeches and effective arguments. Perelman and Olbrechts-Tyteca (1969) acknowledge the differences between spoken and written discourse in passing, for example, but choose to skip over these differences—and consequently the character of written language as it bears on the problems of discourse—"for reasons of technical convenience, and in order not to lose sight of the essential role played by audience . . . . [And since] it is frequently forgotten that this applies to everything written as well," they choose to dwell not on "whether or not the presentation is spoken or written, or distinguish between formal discourse and the fragmentary expression of thought [pp. 6–7]."

One way to investigate the process whereby ideas become written text is to control for ideas and vary the mode of production: observing someone make the same point in an essay, a television editorial, and a speech; or comparing dictating and writing. Such investigations have been conducted by Gould (1980) and Scardamalia, Bereiter, and Goelman (this volume). The results are very revealing. First, speaking and writing are so very different that controlling one for the purposes of experimental comparison inevitably distorts the other somewhat (dictating is not entirely representative of speaking). Furthermore, a discourse scheme such as generating, organizing, and translating ideas into text reveals no significant differences between oral and written text production: Effective production, for example, shows more planning than ineffective production WHATEVER THE MODE. Since there clearly ARE significant differences between spoken and written discourse and between spoken and written language production, we can only conclude that there is more to writing than goals, plans, and task-related knowledge; and that these differences are beyond the scope of analytic frameworks focusing on goals, plans, and so forth. In effect, generating, organizing, and translating ideas into text tell us about discourse—about writing as a means to an end, but very little about the language of written discourse, that is, the nature of the means themselves. With all their empirical power, these categories will not tell us what effective essayists know that accomplished orators and pleaders never needed to learn. To understand the language of written discourse, we must look to another set of variables, namely, the social functions of language (Stubbs, this volume) and the production variables of writing (Scardamalia, Bereiter, & Goelman, this volume).

WRITTEN LANGUAGE FUNCTIONING

It might seem that little of importance is at stake here; a certain kind of information slips by about, say, handwriting and scribal conventions, but nothing of serious consequence regarding the conduct of discourse or the organization of writing processes. In my view, the opposite is the case. The neglect of language "in the interests of discourse" is indefensible in rhetoric as well as linguistics in view of the fundamental role that written language resources play in defining the possibilities and shaping the conduct of written discourse. There are two points to be made: first, in language generally, FORM FOLLOWS FUNCTION at least as much as ideas; and second, THE FUNCTIONS OF WRITTEN LANGUAGE ARE VERY DIFFERENT FROM THOSE OF THE SPOKEN. As a consequence, an adequate understanding of writing must take these differences into account. Moreover, understanding writing requires looking at the writer's speech community as much as the audience.

Form Follows Function

Language is as it is largely because of what it is required to do for its users. Halliday (1978, pp. 21–22) notes the following general functions:

1. Language has to interpret the whole of our experience, reducing the indefinitely varied phenomena of the world around us, and also of the world inside us, the processes of our own consciousness, to a manageable number of classes of phenomena: types of processes, events and actions, classes of objects, people and institutions, and the like.

2. Language has to express certain elementary logical relations like 'and' and 'or' and 'if', as well as those created by language itself such as 'namely', 'says' and 'means'.

3. Language has to express our participation, as speakers, in the speech situation; the roles we take on ourselves and impose on others; our wishes, feelings, attitudes and judgments.

4. Language has to do all these things simultaneously, in a way which relates what is being said to the context in which it is being said, both to what has been said before and to the 'context of situation'; in other words, it has to be capable of being organized as relevant discourse, not just words and sentences in a grammar-book or dictionary.

In addition, LANGUAGE HAS TO ESTABLISH AND MAINTAIN **communicative homeostasis,** i.e., reciprocity and common understandings between conversants. This is equally true for all aims and modes of discourse. As Rommetveit notes, "Human discourse has its basis in some pre-established social reality [1974, p. 101]"; and when speakers move beyond this shared and taken-for-granted world, "the language used will be subject to new demands if [conversants] are to continue to understand one another [Applebee, 1978, p. 7]." In terms of function, language is interesting not as (*a*) knowledge of rules governing production (competence informing production), or as (*b*) the expression of semantic content, or as (*c*) the translation of ideas into acceptable and appropriate sentences or other text formats, or as (*d*) the achievement of some desired effect on receivers. The functional analysis of language highlights mainly the **resources of language** (cf. Halliday, 1978) FOR ESTABLISHING AND MAINTAINING SHARED UNDERSTANDINGS BETWEEN CONVERSANTS IN PARTICULAR **contexts of situation** (cf. Firth, 1950; Malinowski, 1923); and its use or occurrence is therefore an ACTIVITY INVOLVING APPROPRIATE WAYS OF GETTING ON IN PARTICULAR SPEECH COMMUNITIES. These ways-of-speaking take the form they do largely because of conversants' or users' **need to function** in particular situations.

Himley (Note 1) has proposed a scheme showing how this need to function manifests itself in various forms of writing. She shows (Figure 1) how text and context covary with situations of use—how "Exit" signs and notes addressed to the milkman, for example, are likely to be very cryptic (or "exophoric" [cf. Gregory & Carroll, 1978]) since the context of such requests is clear for both parties. The scripts (cf. Schank & Abelson, 1977) for these texts *in situ* are reasonably straightforward. That is to say, "Much of what is said relates in an important way to what is not said. . . . The more knowledge two people share, the less they need to talk about it [Gregory & Carroll, 1978, pp. 51–52]." By contrast, written requests in the relative absence of reciprocal understanding between conversants—say a formal complaint to the milk company about poor delivery along with a request

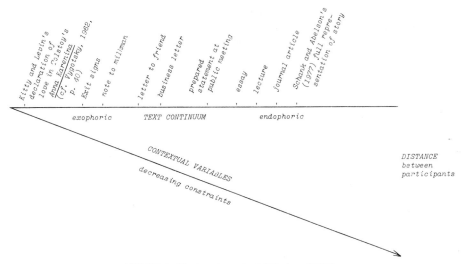

FIGURE 1. Text and context (Himley, 1980).

for improved service; or a follow up complaint plus request for help addressed to the State Commerce Commission (with carbon copy to the milk company)—all these texts must be far more explicit and self-contextualizing (or "endophoric" [cf. Gregory & Carroll, 1978]) if all parties involved are to act appropriately. Clearly, any text will serve its communicative function if and only if the participants tag it onto a common set of unstated perspectives, categorizations, and premises. Hence, a cryptic note will suffice for the person who regularly delivers the milk but not for either the milk company or the commerce commission.

Any text—spoken or written—is never simply or even primarily a matter of translating thoughts into well-chosen words; and language production, whether spoken or written, is never entirely ancillary to cognition, coming as it were "after the ideational fact." More than anything, language is an activity motivated by users' needs to make things known in particular ways for particular purposes and to establish and maintain common understandings with other conversants; and the form of a particular text is always determined as much by the conversants' need to function in these situations as it is by whatever it is they wish to express. In describing "message structure," Rommetveit (1974) notes that "what is made known can ... *not* be described in terms of any autonomous propositional content. ... Message structure must instead be conceived of as a particular pattern of nesting ["free" or new information onto "bound" or given information], generated in an interplay of tacit and verbally induced presuppositions on the one hand and semantic potentialities on the other [p. 92]."

If language-as-speeches is the expression of thought in acceptable text formats, it is no less, as speech, the realization of meaning in particular contexts of use.

Many models of **language production** are some variation of the following model:

$$\text{SPEAKER'S THOUGHTS} \longrightarrow \text{TEXT}$$

To this model, we may juxtapose a model of **motivated language activity:**

$$\Delta\text{KNOWLEDGE} \longrightarrow \text{TEXT}$$

where ΔKNOWLEDGE represents any discrepancy in conversants' assumptions, premises, and knowledge at some point in time when they share some common interest in these assumptions, premises, and knowledge.

Written and Spoken Language Serve Very Different Functions

That form follows function has major and profound implications for understanding written and spoken forms of discourse since WRITTEN AND SPOKEN LANGUAGE SERVE VERY DIFFERENT FUNCTIONS FOR USERS. Occasionally, literate individuals can choose to write a letter or pick up the phone, but in most cases there is no choice (see Stubbs, 1980). For example, I could but would not respond in writing to the person standing at my door; I could but would be ill-advised to sell my house to a stranger on the verbal understanding that the buyer would pay me $2000 a month for the next 30 years; and I could but would never make an oral—or for that matter mental—shopping list beyond more than a couple of items. Written and spoken language FUNCTIONALLY COMPLEMENT each other in this respect (cf. Vachek, 1973). Significantly, any literate person always chooses speaking or writing appropriately. Consequently, adequate descriptions of literacy must include not only rules-of-use regarding the spoken and written **codes** but also rules-of-use involved in "switching" back and forth between spoken and written language **modes** (cf. Haas, 1970).

Written and spoken language are in fact governed by different norms:

The SPOKEN NORM of language is a system of phonically manifestable language elements whose function is to react to a given stimulus (which, as a rule, is an urgent one) in a dynamic way, i.e., in a ready and immediate manner, duly expressing not only the purely communicative but also the emotional aspect of the approach of the reacting language user.

The WRITTEN NORM of language is a system of graphically manifestable language elements whose function is to react to a given stimulus (which, as a rule, is not an urgent one) in a static way, i.e., in a preservable and easily surveyable manner, concentrating particularly on the purely communicative aspect of the approach of the reacting language user [Vachek, 1959; cited in Vachek, 1973, pp. 15–16].

The special functions of written language are especially clear when the historical origins of literacy are examined. Writing apparently first developed "as a novel application late in the fourth millenium B.C. of a recording system that was indigenous to western Asia from early Neolithic times [8500 B.C.] onwards [Schmandt-Besserat, 1978, p. 59]." According to Schmandt-Besserat, farmers in the Zagros region of Iran (Tepe Asiab and Ganj-i-Dareh) first kept track of their herds and crops in Neolithic times with a system of clay tokens (see Figure 2). The Neolithic tokens antedate both Chinese idiograms and Maya hieroglyphs, the first by 6000 and the second by 5000 years. The tokens are clearly abstract in their notation, suggesting that writing was genuinely symbolic from the start, not pictographic as is commonly assumed (e.g., Gelb, 1963). This simple system of record keeping eventually developed to serve the more complicated accounting needs of burgeoning trade networks, crafts specializations, and

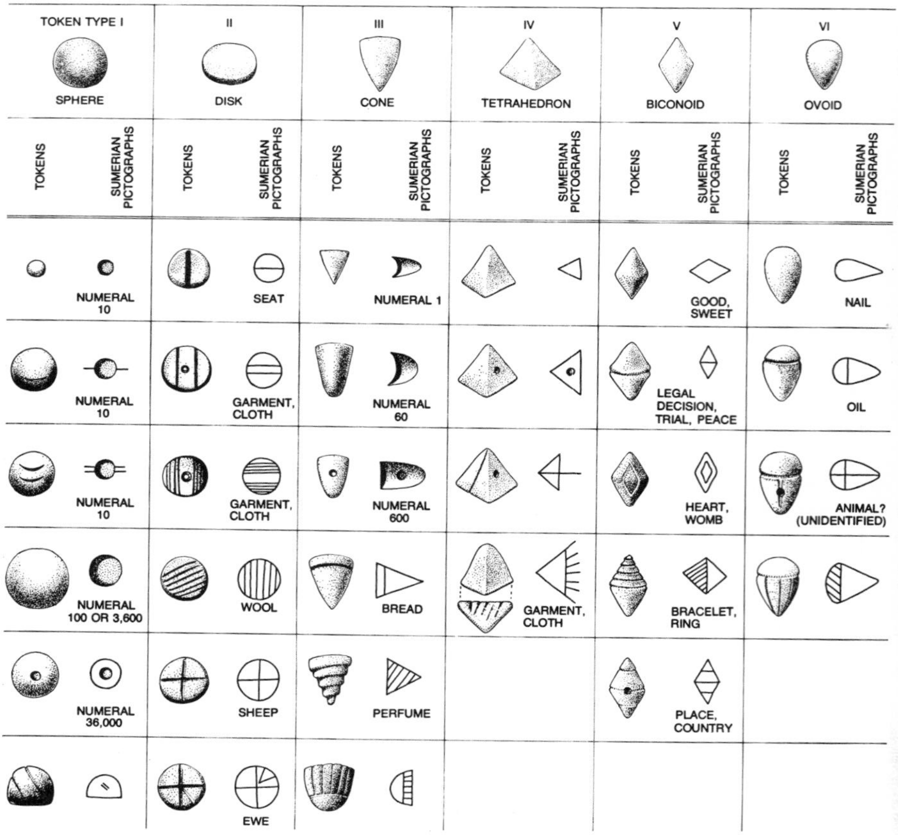

FIGURE 2. Clay token types.

government functions (e.g., collecting taxes) which came about with the
rise of cities in western Asia early in the Bronze Age, between 3500 and
3100 B.C. At about this same time, shippers made yet another innovation
when they included with shipments appropriate numbers of representative tokens sealed in egg-shaped clay casks called *bullae*. These casks
served, in effect, as bills of lading and shipping both and secured shipments for buyers, who upon delivery could open the unbroken casks and
know that what was delivered was the same as what was shipped. Shippers soon developed a system of notation to show ON THE OUTSIDE OF THE
CASKS the number and types of tokens inside. Inevitably, shippers did
away with the tokens altogether yet retained the *bulla* notations. In time,
this system of secondary symbolism was adapted from clay casks to clay
tablets and eventually to the much simpler and more convenient medium
of paper. Schmandt-Besserat concludes, ''The substitution of two-

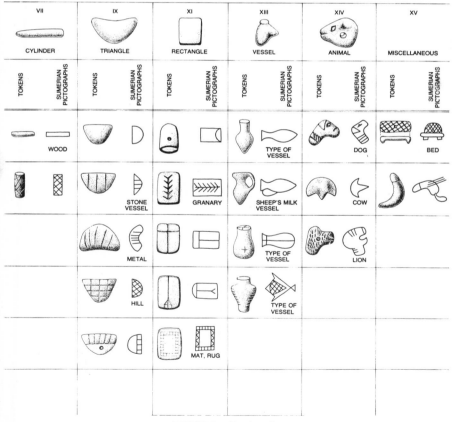

FIGURE 2. *Continued.*

dimensional portrayals of the tokens for the tokens themselves would seem to have been the crucial link between the archaic recording system and writing [p. 59]." The study clearly suggests that writing (and perhaps reading too) developed, if not actually started, in response to the record-keeping needs of societies distinguished first by the exigencies of agricultural planning and then by the complexities of trade and commerce. Plato was no doubt correct in *The Phaedrus* when he noted that writing fosters forgetting, but he could not have anticipated the important social uses of such "forgetting": Writers can depend on lists and texts to record and store information they otherwise would need to keep track of in other ways. As Stubbs (1980) notes, writing systems assist and extend the limits of natural memory; they facilitate history making; and they foster critical inquiry by making thought and knowledge public and available to more people for a longer period of time than speaking can. In short, writing serves and fosters certain civil functions that inevitably arise when societies develop special needs for certain kinds of information processing, needs having mainly to do with trade, commerce, law, and government.

Linguistic form is intimately related to language function in the same general way Piaget has shown that biological and cognitive functions are related to their respective structures. About the latter two, Piaget (1970a) notes:

> To sum up, order structures do seem at the outset (from the DNA stage) to be inherent in every biological organization and in its functioning. At the other end, order structures are produced by thought, but a thought which also is ordered in its functioning. Between these two extremes are found all the intermediary stages, and the parallelism between these and inclusion structures could be described in greater detail. Here again we are confronted with a fundamental isomorphism between biological and cognitive structures [p. 166].

The functional analysis of writing extends this analysis to include social as well as biological and cognitive structures. Hymes (1974) notes that "social function gives form to the ways in which linguistic features are encountered in actual life. This being so, an adequate approach must begin by identifying social functions, and discover the ways in which linguistic features are selected and grouped together to serve them [p. 196]." In all cases—biological, cognitive, and social—structures develop as organisms, individuals, and societies adapt in response to respective needs; in each case, the need to function in particular ways fuels development of forms and structures effectively serving these functions. Language is the way it is because of what it must do for its users; and the psychology of writing, like Piaget's psychology of intelligence, is largely the individual's adaptation to certain environmental requirements. In the case of writing, these requirements result from the social environment, namely, the writing community (Berry, 1958; Stubbs, 1980; Vachek, 1973; see also Stubbs, this volume).

WRITERS' SPEECH COMMUNITIES

Speech communities differ essentially from audiences, I have noted, in the relationship the speaker has to each. Speakers seek to persuade, move, or otherwise affect their audiences by means of particular speech acts, but speakers rarely move, change, or otherwise affect their speech communities. Instead, the participation of native speakers and fluent writers in particular speech communities is testimony to the principle that the speech community acts on the speaker. (Actually, individual speakers and writers are always members of many more than one speech community, but this important distinction does not affect the fact that becoming a member of any speech community ALWAYS involves learning the ways-of-speaking of the group in question.) These distinctions may seem complicated by the fact that the writer's audience, compared to the speaker's, is relatively diffuse and hard to know with any precision. Indeed, writers may easily address many readers they will never meet—even individuals who will be born long after they themselves have died. In so far as a speech community is an abstract collectivity, one may be tempted to conclude that the writer's diffuse audience, unlike the speaker's always present conversant or group of listeners, is in fact the speech community of the writer. That is to say, the writer's speech community might be taken to be all eventual readers. Such a conclusion misses the most fundamental distinction between an audience and a speech community, however—namely, that speakers address their audiences (diffuse, eventual, or present) THROUGH PARTICULAR TEXTS but become members of their speech communities by learning the ways-of-speaking of these groups, and especially the POTENTIAL FOR MAKING MANY TEXTS. An audience always shares some particular concern with the speaker on the occasion of some particular speech act; by contrast, members of a speech community are not ever required, either by rule or definition, to actually interact with each other. Indeed, they may very well NEVER speak or write to each other; the point is that they COULD EFFECTIVELY SO INTERACT IF REQUIRED since they know the ways-of-speaking of the group. They can greet each other appropriately; they can ask for and offer information; they can express agreement or disagreement; they can get others to shut the door; they can persuade the milk company to resume its deliveries; and so. Indeed, some can "speak" to each other in ways so specialized that, were they actually to meet other members of these specialized communities, they might not be able to talk with each other: The international academic community, for example, is largely an English print community.

Individuals become members of particular speech communities by learning what counts as ways-of-speaking for the group of users in question. Investigating written language functioning, as opposed to the structure of discourse, consequently focuses on the effects that readers, collectively the writer's speech community, have on individuals as writers and the texts they compose. In particular, investigation of written language functioning focuses on written language norms to understand the effects that readers have on writers, whose texts must clearly reflect these norms if they are to communicate. Clearly, such focus on tacit knowledge and language functioning is very different from rhetorical inquiries that focus on the effects that writers hope to have on their readers by means of deliberate speech acts.

Halliday (1978) draws this distinction quite sharply: "Just as the view of language as knowledge, which is essentially an individual orientation, can be used to direct attention outwards, through such concepts as the speech act, towards language in society, so the essentially social interpretation of language as behavior can be used to direct attention onto the individual, placing him in the human environment, ... and explaining his linguistic potential, as speaker-hearer and writer-reader, in these terms [p. 11]." The first inquiry into individual speech acts raises questions about writing as speeches, that is, individual writers' means to particular ends such as the persuasion of readers. By contrast, inquiry into the writer's linguistic potential raises questions about speech or the means themselves—"the full set of verbal means available to persons [as] members of a speech community [Hymes, 1974, pp. 170–171]"—and especially about how any aim of discourse can be achieved by composing texts.

Written language—this "set of verbal means available" to writer–readers—is best understood as a shared synchronous system (cf. Saussure, 1959) or equilibrated structure (cf. Piaget, 1970b), that is, that system of resources which writers draw on in particular ways-of-speaking. The possibility of writer–reader communication owes necessarily to the character of the written language for any group of writer–readers as a stable system of signs, or schematized possibilities. This requirement for structure and system applies generally to any meaning group (see Nystrand, "The Structure of Textual Space," this volume), with examples including not only spoken and written language, whose structures are determined by a criterion of acceptability in the respective speech communities; but also other systems of communication such as "the alphabet of deaf-mutes, symbolic rites, polite formulas, military signals [Saussure, 1959, p. 16]," and scientific inquiry, taken broadly as discourse, where there is "no standard higher than the assent of the relevant community [Kuhn, 1962, p. 94]." It is precisely the character of written language—like any language—as a stable system of signs that results in what many have termed its "transparency" for users, enabling them to read and write texts, while limiting non-writer–readers to seeing and copying them. In effect, written language is the unnoticed ground upon which writers cut the figure of their meaning.

The written language is like the spoken in this fundamental way: On the one hand, the features that define its character and promote its functioning are determined largely by the social fact of its collective use, that is, the community of users; on the other hand, the individual act is informed by the social fact. Written language is "the system of graphical means employed for the purpose of producing written utterances acceptable in the given language community [Vachek, 1973, p. 9]." Hence, the special relations that define written language functioning and promote its meaningful use (i.e., foster conditions of reader meaning) are wholly circumscribed by the systemic relations that obtain in the speech community of the writer.

As members of their speech communities, then, writers not only have working knowledge of appropriate **conditions of reader meaning** (*la langue*) but also knowledge of relevant **ways-of-speaking** (*la parole*), in this case "quickly and distinctly to the eyes" of fellow writer–readers (Frinta, 1909, p. 36; cited in Vachek, 1973, p. 13).

On Knowing Conditions of Meaning in the Community

The conditions of meaning in any speech community are enhanced as the context of any sign, event, or utterance is elaborated according to the possibilities allowed by the group. My wife understands my *Want one?* and I understand her cryptic nod perfectly at 5 p.m. (but not at 10 a.m.), for example, because this exchange takes place in the highly constrained ritual of drinks-before-dinner—an intimate and late-afternoon speech community of two. Generally, information about an event or statement (x or p) increases as the constraints upon x or p increase. This is true because any increase in constraint upon x (that is, elaboration of x's context) allows the elimination of many possibilities regarding x. We can never know any particular datum or x in and of itself; a contextless nod, for example, is utterly ambiguous. We go about both knowing things and making them known by relating them to other, comparable things. In other words, relationships are significant only if they are made—indeed CAN be made—in the context of a particular system or framework, such as the ritual before dinner at my home, an unequivocally established *sous-entendu du discours* (Ducrot, 1973, p. 8 cited in Rommetveit, 1974, p. 25).

We gain knowledge by discarding possibilities, not adding them. Mainly, we learn about things by finding out what they are NOT—testing, as it were, those least probable hypotheses which Popper (e.g., 1959) calls "best" because, when unsubstantiated, they enable us to exclude many, many possibilities in a single stroke (Piaget, 1970b, p. 84). As Saussure notes, the significance and value of any particular thing is "in being what the others are not [1959, p. 117]."

Saussure is only one of many scholars to make this general distinction. A few other examples are from history of science, commonsense knowledge, and perception:

a. **History of science.** For Kuhn (1962), the gaze of scientists is clearest in the context of paradigms, that is, the particular conventions governing conduct of inquiry in the various disciplines.

b. **Commonsense knowledge.** For social phenomenologist A. Schutz (1967), commonsense knowledge is distinguished by discrete "finite provinces of meaning," each distinguished by its own set of rules which lend consistency and significance to experience—domains such as gossiping with friends, playing games, mailing letters. Collectively, such activities make up "the funded experience of life," the "sedimented structure of the individual's experience"—in short, the discourse of daily life.

c. **Perception.** For many psychologists (e.g., Ames, 1952; Bruner, 1951; Köhler, 1971; Neisser, 1976; Piaget, 1969, 1970b), perception is an organized transaction between the organism and environment in which the organism probes the environment within the context of certain expectations. The brain guides the senses "as a searchlight" (Popper, 1972, cf. Bruner, 1951) employing what Neisser (1976) calls "anticipatory schemata."

Conditions of Meaning

From these diverse studies we understand more clearly the conditions of meaning which were first articulated by Saussure in his 1906 lectures on language:

1. One understands the SIGNIFICANCE of any given term not in the positive content of the term but rather the PLACE OF THE TERM IN A SYSTEM OF INTERDEPENDENT TERMS. I know x in the context of y and z; I know apples in the context of oranges, peaches, and pears; I know 3 in the context of $1-n$; I know the experimental group in the context of the control group; and I know you in the context of many past encounters.
2. The MEANING or value of a given term derives solely from the TENSION GENERATED BY THE SIMULTANEOUS PRESENCE AND CONSTRAINT OF OTHER TERMS IN THE SYSTEM. As with an equation, these terms constrain each other reciprocally.
3. CONCEPTS are defined "not by their positive content but negatively by their relations with other terms of the system. Their most precise character is in being what the others are not [Saussure, 1959, p. 117]."
4. The CONDITIONS OF MEANING are above all a CONGRUENCE OF OPPOSING, RELATIVE, AND NEGATIVE TERMS—in short, a system of relevant constraints. Knowledge is a matter of **contrastive categorization.**
5. The system of constraints operating in any speech community exists by TACIT AGREEMENT—"a sort of contract signed by members of the community [Saussure, 1959, p. 14]."

As a consequence of the contractual, social nature of these constraints, what is made known by any particular statement can be assessed only by relating "*what is said* in a systematic fashion to *what in each situation is tacitly and reciprocally presupposed* [Rommetveit, 1974, p. 104]."

What is said has two sorts of context relevant to its meaning: the linguistic (*la langue*) and the situational (*les sous-entendues*). At 5 p.m., the linguistic context permits me to say to my wife, *Want one?* but not *One want what* or *Est-ce que tu want ein chose bitte?* On the other hand, the situational context permits me to open with *Want one?* but not *Don't you agree?* or *Good morning* or *Colorless green ideas sleep furiously still, dear.*

Here are some of the ways in which what is written is constrained by these respective contexts:

Linguistic Constraints

1. I may write *nowhere* but not *nowhere* . As Saussure (1959) notes, "The value of letters is purely negative and differential. . . . The only requirement is that the sign[s used for particular letters] not be confused . . . with the signs used for [the other letters]. . . . Values in writing function only through reciprocal opposition within a fixed system that consists of a set number of letters [pp. 119–120]."

2. I may write *nowhere* for *nowhere* but not *now here* or *no where* .

3. I may write (in English) linearly from left to right in multiple and progressive sequences, that is, from top of the page to bottom, but not from right to left, bottom to top.

4. I must confine my script to the page I am writing on.

5. I may indicate relationships among ideas and statements by indenting (including **paragraphing** and **listing in columns**) and punctuating.

6. I may spell *fish*, but not *ghoti* as proposed by George Bernard Shaw (Stubbs, 1980, pp. 51–53), or *ffish* or *phish* (Haas, 1970, p. 57n in Stubbs, 1980, p. 53).

7. I may not randomly alter scripts, for example, θεός ate Персианова .

Situational Constraints

1. I am constrained by "superordinate genre conventions" (Steinmann, 1981). For example, I will not generally include spurious details in fiction. As Steinmann (1981) explains, "Whenever the doorbell rings at 221b Baker Street, the caller not only is interesting—'a wild-eyed and frantic young man, pale, dishevelled, and palpitating' ("The Adventure of the Norwood Builder"), say—but occasions a series of Holmesian deductions [p. 254]." For the same reason, I will not begin technical reports *in medias res* ("Once upon a time . . ." [Applebee, 1978]).

2. I am constrained by my readers' knowledge or lack of it. Hence, I may write unsigned, *Nothing today, thanks* to the person who delivers my milk, but not to the milk company. I may reasonably ask attorneys, but very few patients, to read and sign currently used consent-to-perform-surgery forms (Cassileth, Zupkis, Sutton-Smith, & March, 1980). Clark and Haviland

(1977) call this constraint the **given-new contract:** "The speaker agrees (a) to use given information to refer to information she thinks the listener can uniquely identify from what he already knows and (b) to use new information she believes to be true but is not already known to the listener."

Generally, situational constraints take precedence over linguistic constraints, and higher-level linguistic constraints take precedence over lower-level linguistic constraints. Hence, an otherwise illegible scrawl may well be readable if the reader has a good sense of the writer's basic gist. Also, many linguists have shown (e.g., Wilks, 1972) and some have taken great delight in showing (e.g., Robinson, 1975) that many of Chomsky's original examples of grammatical-but-meaningless sentences, such as *Colorless green ideas sleep furiously,* are meaningful when adequately contextualized: the sentence is a line of verse from a poem about contemporary urban life or a description of part of a dream or the punchline from some intricate joke. Part of the writer's problem is knowing how to use the resources of the written language adequately to constrain the reader and leave no doubt about *les sous-entendues* or anything else. Bartlett (this volume) has researched one aspect of this problem.

Writers' Ways-of-Speaking

If the conditions of meaning are a system of constraints involving juxtaposition or counterpoint of elements, meaning proper is the mind's resolution of tension among these elements, tension created by the constraints. The character of the mind is to find wholes and relations, not isolated fragments and particulars. The phenomenon of meaning is, in short, the mind's transformation of particulars into a coherent, organized whole. This transformation is indeed the essence of any interpretive act (see Nystrand, "The Structure of Textual Space," this volume), and such schematizing activity manifests itself at all levels of experience: We listen to notes but hear music, we view patches of pigment but see images, we look at words but find meanings. The phenomenon of meaning is this gestalt-like transformation whereby the knower resolves tensions and oppositions among the particulars of experience. Colloquially, we know this experience as *click, putting two and two together, Eureka!*—though the activity is far more common and regular than Archimedes' proverbial and momentous experience in thèbath. The process is at work at all levels of knowing, from scientists probing the salient features of the universe to children learning the distinctive features of their language.

The activity is Piaget's assimilation, "the source of that continual relating, setting up of correspondences, establishing of functional connections . . . [Piaget, 1970b, p. 71]." To assimilate is to make sense of things—to relate the unfamiliar to the already known, to fit elements of experience into existing cognitive structures. Indeed, comprehension cannot occur EXCEPT in a context of schematized possibilities. This is why a totally foreign language is jibberish or noise, while the words of one's native tongue are wholly transparent.

If the conditions of meaning are a system of **constraints,** the fundamental principle of meaning itself is **assimilation.** The former is a set of **systemic relations** obtaining in **social groups,** while the latter is a **psychological process.** In any system of signs such as writing, these principles are mutually dependent. Hence, writer inscriptions and texts are significantly shaped by readers' needs for assimilation, or comprehension. Conversely, reader comprehension is significantly governed by writers' inscriptions, or textual constraints. In this way, opposed, relative, and juxtaposed elements of text are transformed into positive information and meaning by the reader.

As an equilibrated structure, written language is a thoroughly reversible system for its users. Writers can effect all manner of changes in a text. They can cross out and rewrite. Writers and readers both can review texts and find new meanings. Readers can write to writers and so become writers themselves. The number of changes that can be made in any text is indefinite. Yet none of these transformations alters the written language system itself at any given point in time. Transformations of text inevitably "engender elements that belong to the system and preserve its laws [Piaget, 1970b, p. 14]."

The possibility of communication between writers and readers, then, owes entirely to the character of writing for the participants as a stable, autonomous system of signs, or schematized possibilities. "We speak here deliberately of a system," Vachek notes, "not a mere inventory . . .: each grapheme belonging to that system is mainly characterized by being different from the other graphemes of that system [1973, p. 9]." Other research supporting the systemic character of written language includes Albrow (1972), Venesky (1970), C. Chomsky (1970), and Stubbs (1980). The systemic character of written language is indeed intuitively obvious from the quality of transparency that characterizes its use for both readers and writers. As Polanyi and Prosch (1975) point out, fluent readers do not SEE words and texts, they READ them. It is precisely the character of writing as a stable system of signs that results in its transparency for fluent readers. Just as readers focus through the printed word onto the meaning of the text, writers too have a peculiar, subsidiary awareness of their pens: They know them where they touch paper, not hand. Mainly, they pour themselves into their work unaware of the pen altogether, concerned only with the sense they must make. Only those beginners and strangers who do NOT participate in this system of interdependent meaning-relations that is the written language are limited to seeing and copying words, unable to read and write them. That the system itself does not intrude upon, but is wholly subsidiary to the consciousness of the participants clearly demonstrates the character of writing for writers and readers as a stable, autonomous system of signs.

Both reader and writer seek to make sense—the one OF print, the other IN print. More fundamentally, each presupposes the sense-making capabilities of the other. Writers do not convey or transcribe their thoughts, they speak to their readers by management of relevant and distinctive orthographic features, a task that may properly be called compositional. While meaning is in the reader, then, the conditions of meaning and the possibilities for communication are in the text: The writer puts them there. To write is to create conditions of written meaning and reader comprehension—to compose texts that, independent of the writer's actual, immediate presence, will speak to relevant readers. Lucidity is less a property of the text per se and more the reader's actualization of a semantic potential—a condition experienced by readers when writers suggest well. Like a drama, any well-crafted text is both RESULT OF AND OCCASION FOR the constructive processes of the mind.

E. H. Gombrich notes in *Art and Illusion* (1960) that the artist "cannot copy a sunlit lawn, but he can suggest it [p. 38]." The painter inquires not into the nature of the physical world but rather "into the nature of our reactions to it. He is not concerned with causes but with the mechanisms of certain effects. His is a psychological problem—that of conjuring up a convincing image despite the fact that not one individual shade corresponds to what we call 'reality' [1960, p. 49]." *Mutatis mutandis*, composing in any medium entails an investigation of the "beholder's share." The composer must learn the possibilities and limitations of the medium, arranging pigments, notes, and words in appropriate ways-of-speaking so that viewers, listeners, readers—indeed, members of any meaning group—might find images, music, messages—in short, meaning.

To create conditions of meaning, speakers and writers "sculpt" their respective speech streams. Indeed, language functioning is largely characterized by the rules and constraints operating in users' elaborations and segmentations of their language. A major difference between writers' and speakers' ways-of-speaking, for example, is due to the fact that, while both spoken and written language are produced in time, the written language must also operate in space. J. Goody (1968) puts it this way: "The importance of writing lies in its creating a new medium of communication between men. Its essential service is to objectify speech, to provide language with a material correlative, a set of visible signs. In this material form speech can be transmitted over space and preserved over time; what people say and think can be rescued from the transitoriness of oral communication [pp. 1–2]." While many salient aspects of the writing process are time-related (see Matsuhashi, Beaugrande, both in this volume), many of the factors that actually constrain production relate to the fact that the resulting text itself is partly a spatial construct. Writers' ways-of-speaking are consequently subject to the following constraints on elaboration and segmentation:

I. Elaborations

A. **Graphic Elaborations**
   1. *Cursive.* Writers combine four possible segment-strokes (bars, hooks, arches, and loops) to form letters according to well-defined rules (Eden, 1961).
   2. *Graphemic.* "Rules governing the use of . . . graphemes (including graphotactic rules) in the given language community have clearly a normative character within that community, and any use contrary to these rules is felt as contrary to the norm and evaluated either as a mistake or, in some specific circumstances, as a case of intentional deviation, prompted by some functional motive . . . [Vachek, 1973, p. 9]."

B. **Orthographic Elaborations.** Spelling is governed by rules which make certain combinations permissible and others unlikely or impossible (Haas, 1970; Stubbs, 1980; Venezky, 1970).

C. **Syntactic Elaborations.** Writers, like speakers, make "a wide range of decisions about syntactic formatting," including such *"optional* mappings" as sentences (Beaugrande, 1980, p. 11). Writers, more than speakers, employ sentences as a standard grammatical format (Beaugrande, personal communication).

D. **Lexical Elaborations.** Skilled writers elaborate potentially troublesome parts of texts according to the terms of the given-new contract and the general requirements for semantic coherence. These elaborations are carefully keyed to those terms and concepts which are critical to reader comprehension; their purpose is to "buttress" the text in precisely those spots that threaten common categorizations and reciprocity between writer and reader (Nystrand, Note 2), in effect providing explicit bridges (cf. Haviland & Clark, 1974) between precisely those propositions whose relations readers might otherwise miss. For one aspect of this problem, see Bartlett (this volume).

II. Segmentations

A. **Graphic Segmentations.** Writers reliably leave spaces between words whereas speakers more typically pause within words.

B. **Text Segmentations.** Writers, more typically than speakers, not only elaborate but also segment discourse into conventional sentence formats. Writers also signal conceptual shifts through paragraphing and indenting (Rodgers, 1966) and categorization through columns and lists.

CODA

By this point, it should be clear that when rhetoric has focused on audience, it has underscored certain psychological aspects of writing in the same way that linguistics, when it has focused on speech community, has touched on the social aspects. The perspectives are complementary: The one starts with the writer and moves out to the audience; the other starts with the group and moves in on the individual. The one looks at speeches and the structure of discourse; the other looks at speech and the resources of language for discourse.

When composing is studied under the rubric of audience, the central issue is how ideas become text: Inquiry starts with the writer's thoughts and investigates the processes whereby these thoughts become manifest as text. The research problem is typically characterized in terms of WRITER KNOWLEDGE AS IT BEARS ON THE PROBLEM OF GENERATING AND TRANSLATING THOUGHTS INTO TEXT. The text itself is the vehicle for these thoughts, and the audience is the receiver.

By contrast, linguistics' speech community portrays the writer as someone who becomes a member of some meaning group by learning its ways-of-speaking and, as a result, is able to interact linguistically with its members. While "the study of language as knowledge is an attempt to find out WHAT GOES ON INSIDE THE INDIVIDUAL'S HEAD [Halliday, 1978, p. 13; emphasis added]," the study of language as interaction is an attempt to find out WHAT GOES ON LINGUISTICALLY IN GROUPS. The central issue in the latter is how individuals become members and maintain their membership; the research question is identification and analysis of "the ways of speaking in the community, together with the conditions and meanings of their use [Hymes, 1974, p. 200]." From this social perspective, a text is not so much a vehicle for individual expression and influence as much as it is a social mechanism—strictly speaking the sociolinguistic means—for establishing and maintaining reciprocity and mutual understandings among members of particular speech communities.

Halliday (1978) contrasts these two general perspectives on language as **intraorganism** and **interorganism** paradigms. It is "possible to investigate language from the standpoint of the internal make-up of that organism: the brain structure, the cerebral processes that are involved in its speaking and understanding, and also in its learning to speak and to understand [p. 10]." But it is also possible to investigate language as "the means whereby people interact. . . . There is an intra-organism perspective on language as well as an inter-organism [p. 10]." "In other words, instead of looking at the group as a derivation from and extension of the biologically endowed mental power of the individual, we explain the nature of the individual as a derivation from and extension of his participation in the group. Instead of starting inside the organism and looking outwards, we can adopt a Durkheimian perspective and start from outside the organism in order to look inwards [p. 14]."

The formulation of writing as individuals addressing audiences inspires neo-Platonic descriptions of writing and language production. As the translation of thought, a text can never totally capture the thoughts which it must "mirror" in expression. A text is "an incomplete or misleading expression of the [textbase . . . which] completely expresses the ideas that a speaker or writer has in mind [Kintsch, 1974, p. 11]." Adequacy of expression, then, is assessed in terms of this "textbase"—the writer's thoughts—and fullness of meaning is equated with explicitness of text (e.g., Olson, 1977).

Can language production begin elsewhere than with the speaker/writer's thoughts? Perhaps not, but CONCEPTIONS of language production certainly can. The formulation of writing as participation in a speech community, for example, highlights language as THE LINGUISTIC REALIZATION OF THOUGHT IN PARTICULAR SITUATIONS OF USE—something very different from its translation into hard copy. The translation of thought into text implies the **manifestation of a semantic content** whereas the realization of thought implies the **actualization of a semantic potential.** The first description highlights the writer's task as first finding something to say and then finding a way to say it (in acceptable sentences and according to established conventions of written discourse). The second description highlights the writer's task as one of drawing effectively on the resources of language in order TO SET IN MOTION THE POSSIBILITY OF MEANING; like electricity, there is potential, but there is no arc of meaning till some reader completes the circuit. The formulation and functional analysis of writing as participation in a speech community highlights the resources available to writers for creating the textual potential for such arcs. Creating texts and composing are not fully understood "after the ideational fact." Writing is nothing less than the main semantic event—the very activity whereby writers make things known.

REFERENCE NOTES

1. Himley, M. Text and context: A dynamic interaction. Chicago: University of Illinois at Chicago Circle, 1980. ERIC document ED 193 640.
2. Nystrand, M. Elaborating and buttressing: A writer-reader interaction model of readability. Unpublished technical report and paper given at the 1981 Convention of the College Conference on Composition and Communication, Dallas, March 26, 1981.

REFERENCES

Albrow, K. H. *The English writing system: Notes towards a description.* London: Longmans, 1972.

Ames, A. Accommodation, convergence, and their relation to apparent distance. *Journal of Psychology,* 1950, *29,* 195–217.

Applebee, A. N. *The child's concept of story: Ages two to seventeen.* Chicago: University of Chicago Press, 1978.

Beaugrande, Robert de. *Text, discourse, and process: Toward a multidisciplinary science of texts.* Norwood, N.J.: Ablex, 1980.

Berry, J. The making of alphabets. In J. Fishman (Ed.), *Readings in the sociology of language.* The Hague: Mouton, 1968.

Black, J. Psycholinguistic processes in writing. In S. Rosenberg (Ed.), *Handbook of applied psycholinguistics.* Hillsdale, N.J.: Lawrence Erlbaum, in press.

Booth, W. The rhetorical stance. *College Composition and Communication,* 1963, *14,* 139–145.

Britton, J. Burgess, T., Martin, N., McLeod, A., & Rosen, H. *The development of writing abilities (11–18).* London: MacMillan Educational, 1975.

Bruce, B., Collins, A., Rubin, A., & Gentner, D. *A cognitive science approach to writing. Technical Report No. 89.* Urbana: Center for the Study of Reading, 1978.

Bruner, J. S. Personality dynamics and the process of perceiving. In R. Blake & G. Ramsey (Eds.), *Perception—An approach to personality.* New York: Ronald Press, 1951.

Cassileth, C., Zupkis, R., Sutton-Smith, K., & March, V. Informed consent—Why are its goals imperfectly realized? *The New England Journal of Medicine,* 1980, *302,* 896–900.

Chomsky, C. Reading, writing and phonology. *Harvard Educational Review,* 1970, *40,* 287–309.

Clark, H., & Clark, E. *Psychology and language: An introduction to psycholinguistics.* New York: Harcourt Brace Jovanovich, 1977.

Clark, H., & Haviland, S. E. Comprehension and the given-new contract. In R. O. Freedle (Ed.), *Discourse production and comprehension.* Norwood, N.J.: Ablex, 1977. Pp. 1–40.

Dixon, J. *Growth through English.* Urbana: National Council of Teachers of English, 1967.

Douglas, W. Rhetoric for the meritocracy. In R. Ohmann, *English in America: A radical view of the profession.* New York: Oxford University Press, 1976. Pp. 97–132.

Ducrot, O. *Dire et ne pas dire. Principes de semantique linguistique.* Paris: Herman, 1972.

Firth, J. R. Personality and language in society. *The Sociological Review,* 1950, *42,* 1950.

Frinta, A. *Novočeská výslovnost [Modern Czech pronunciation].* Prague: Akademie, 1909.

Gelb, I. J. *A study of writing.* Chicago: University of Chicago Press, 1963.

Gombrich, E. H. *Art and illusion: A study in the psychology of pictorial representation.* Princeton: Princeton University Press, 1960.

Goody, J. Introduction. In J. Goody (Ed.), *Literacy in traditional societies.* New York: Cambridge University Press, 1968.

Gould, J. D. Experiments on composing letters: Some facts, some myths, and some observations. In L. W. Gregg & E. R. Steinberg (Eds.), *Cognitive processes in writing.* Hillsdale, N. J.: Lawrence Erlbaum, 1980.

Gregory, M., & Carroll, S. *Language and situation: Language varieties and their social contexts.* London: Routledge and Kegan Paul, 1978.

Haas, W. *Phono-graphic translation.* Manchester: Manchester University Press, 1970.

Halliday, M. A. K. *Language as social semiotic: The social interpretation of language and meaning.* Baltimore: University Park Press, 1978.

Haviland, S. E., & Clark H. What's new? Acquiring new information as a process in comprehension. *Journal of Verbal Learning and Verbal Behavior,* 1974, *13,* 512–521.

Hayes, J. R., & Flower, L. Identifying the organization of writing processes. In L. W. Gregg & E. R. Steinberg (Eds.), *Cognitive processes in writing.* Hillsdale, N.J.: Lawrence Erlbaum, 1980.

Hirsch, E. D., Jr. *The philosophy of composition*. Chicago: University of Chicago Press, 1977.

Hymes, D. Linguistic problems in defining the concept of "tribe." In J. Helm (Ed.), *Essays on the problem of tribe. Proceedings of the 1967 annual spring meeting of the American Ethnological Society*. Seattle and London: American Ethnological Society, 1967. Pp. 23–48.

Hymes, D. *Foundations in sociolinguistics: An ethnographic approach*. Philadelphia: University of Pennsylvania Press, 1974.

Kintsch, W. (Ed.). *The representation of meaning in memory*. Hillsdale, N.J.: Lawrence Erlbaum, 1974.

Köhler, W. *The selected papers of Wolfgang Köhler*. Edited by Mary Henle. New York: Liveright, 1971.

Kuhn, T. S.   *The structure of scientific revolutions*. Chicago: University of Chicago Press, 1962.

Malinowski, B. The problem of meaning in primitive languages. Supplement 1 to C. K. Ogden & I. A. Richards, *The meaning of meaning*. London: Kegan Paul, 1923.

Mathews, M. M. *Teaching to read: Historically considered*. Chicago: University of Chicago Press, 1966.

Neisser, U. *Cognition and reality: Principles and implications of cognitive psychology*. San Francisco: W. H. Freeman, 1976.

Olson, D. R. From utterance to text: The bias of language in speech and writing. *Harvard Educational Review*, 1977, 47, 257–281.

Perelman, C., & Olbrechts-Tyteca, L. *The new rhetoric: A treatise on argumentation*. Translated by J. Wilkinson and P. Weaver. Notre Dame and London: University of Notre Dame Press, 1969.

Piaget, J. *The mechanisms of perception*. London: Routledge & Kegan Paul, 1969.

Piaget, J. *Biology and knowledge: An essay on the relations between organic regulations and cognitive processes*. Chicago: University of Chicago Press, 1970. (a)

Piaget, J. *Structuralism*. Translated and edited by C. Maschler. New York: Harper & Row, 1970. (b)

Polanyi, M., & Prosch, H. *Meaning*. Chicago: University of Chicago Press, 1975.

Popper, K. R. *The logic of scientific discovery*. New York: Harper & Row, 1959.

Popper, K. R. *Objective knowledge: An evolutionary approach*. London: Oxford at the Clarendon Press, 1972.

Robinson, I. *The new grammarians' funeral: A critique of Noam Chomsky's linguistics*. London: Cambridge University Press, 1975.

Rodgers, P. A discourse-centered rhetoric of the paragraph. *College Composition and Communication*, 17, 1966, 2–11.

Rommetveit, R. *On message structure*. New York: Wiley, 1974.

Saussure, F. de. [*Course in general linguistics*]. Edited by C. Bally and A. Sechelaye in collaboration with A. Riedlinger. Trans. by W. Baskin. New York: The Philosophical Library, 1959.

Sawyer, T. Why speech will not totally replace writing. *College Composition and Communication*, 1977, 28, 43–48.

Schank, R., & Abelson, R. *Scripts, plans, goals, and understanding: An inquiry into human knowledge structures*. Hillsdale, N.J.: Lawrence Erlbaum, 1977.

Schmandt-Besserat, D. The earliest precursor of writing. *Scientific American*, 1978, 238, 50–59.

Schutz, A. *Collected papers, Vol. I: The problem of social reality*. Edited by M. Nathanson. The Hague: Martinus Nijhoff, 1967.

Steinmann, M. Jr. Superordinate genre conventions. *Poetics*, 1981, 10, 243–261.

Stubbs, M. *Language and literacy: The sociolinguistics of reading and writing*. London: Routledge & Kegan Paul, 1980.

Vachek, J. Two chapters on written English. *Brno Studies in English*, 1959, 1, 7–38.

Vachek, J. *Written language: General problems and problems of English*. The Hague: Mouton, 1973.

Venezky, R. L. *The structure of English orthography*. The Hague: Mouton, 1970.

Ward, J. *A system of oratory delivered in a course of lectures*. London, 1759.

Webster's seventh new collegiate dictionary. Springfield, Mass.: G. & C. Merriam Company, 1963.

Wilks, Y. A. *Grammar, meaning, and the machine analysis of language*. London: Routledge & Kegan Paul, 1972.

Young, R. E. Paradigms and problems: Needed research in rhetorical invention. In C. R. Cooper & L. C. Odell (Eds.), *Research on composing: Points of departure*. Urbana: National Council of Teachers of English, 1978.

THE LANGUAGE OF WRITTEN DISCOURSE

Chapter 1

Written Language and Society: Some Particular Cases and General Observations

Michael Stubbs

Europeans and Americans may . . . feel that it is somehow
"natural" that writing should be evaluated more highly than
speech; although a little thought will make it clear that this
category is by no means universal—Lesley Milroy, 1980, pp.
98–99

SOME PECULIARITIES OF WRITTEN LANGUAGE

A peculiar feature of some academic articles is that it is not certain who their audience is going to be. If the articles are on topics of potentially wide, general interest (such as reading and writing), they are likely to be prepared with ill-defined social groups in mind, such as teachers, researchers, or the man in the street. This problem is acute in an international collection of articles on written language, where many different nationalities and many different disciplinary perspectives are likely to be represented, among readers and authors: practicing teachers, educational researchers, psychologists, sociologists, and linguists—all with different assumptions and interests, and probably not even agreeing on what reading and writing mean.

This chapter is a revised and expanded version of a paper presented to the fifth national conference of the Australian Reading Association in Perth, Western Australia, in August 1979, and due to be published in volume 2 of the conference proceedings.

WHAT WRITERS KNOW
The Language, Process,
and Structure of Written Discourse

Some academic articles, in particular those published in specialist journals, are of course written for a relatively small, well-defined, and homogeneous group of fellow professionals, who are actively working in some academic specialism: say, acoustic phonetics, low-temperature physics, or the study of Old Norse. This in itself causes confusion. Readers with a general interest in the area may try to read such articles and find them impenetrable, because they were not designed for general readers in the first place. This may not often happen in most specialized areas. But it often happens when readers with a general interest in some aspect of language try to read articles on linguistics that were primarily intended for fellow academic linguists.

I raise these problems at the outset of this article, not only because they touch on practical problems faced by authors in a collection such as this one, but because these problems point to peculiar features of written language in general. Spoken language is usually addressed to particular individuals, but written language only has very marginal functions of this kind: notes to the milkman and postcards to grandmother. The vast bulk of printed material has no well-defined addressee. It will often have a mythical social group in mind as an audience: beginning teachers, working mothers, sociology students, the educated layperson. But once language has been written down, it has to stand on its own, strangely institutionalized and decontextualized. Writers are uncertain what they can assume their readers know, and readers are usually unable to ask the writer for clarification. These are features of written language that often cause problems for children learning to read and write.

Conference papers are even more peculiar, in that they are a strangely mixed mode: written down, with a view to being spoken aloud, and hopefully designed at this stage for oral presentation. Like written language, they are likely to be condensed, highly edited, with a high information load and low redundancy. But listeners cannot use the kinds of comprehension strategy they can with written language. They cannot reread unclear sections or skip sections they know already; they are condemned to follow the speed of spoken presentation. The spoken version may suffer from having been composed on paper; the version later written up for publication may suffer from having been adapted from an oral presentation.

In this chapter, I want to discuss reading and writing as sociolinguistic activities. They are obviously psychological activities, involving the processing of visual information and various kinds of problem solving. But they are also linguistic activities; people read and write meaningful language. And they are activities that serve particular social functions in different communities.

It is possible to think of the problem of 'what writers know' within such a framework. It then becomes clear that writers must have knowledge of the wider writing community in which their written product becomes an artifact. This involves sociocultural knowledge of, for example, the high value that is placed on written language, particularly formally published language, by the Western academic community. However, these values are not universal, as I shall show in the following.

SOME INTRODUCTORY ANECDOTES

Since I am not sure of the disciplinary background of my readers—in fact, since I am not at all sure precisely for whom I am writing—I would like to try and create a small amount of context by mentioning very briefly half a dozen recent personal incidents, which have led me in various ways to think about the different roles that written language serves in modern societies, and the different relationships it may have with spoken language.

Recently, I was waiting for a train in a station in a city in the English Midlands (Leicester), and noticed a poster advertising an estate agent. The poster was written in three versions: in three non-Roman scripts, and presumably in different Asian languages, with no English translation. Even as a professional linguist, I could identify only two of the scripts, and none of the languages with any certainty, although I could guess what a couple of them probably were.

Some time ago, I had to attend a barmitzvah in a synagogue in London. Being a fairly traditional synagogue, the service was conducted throughout in Hebrew, except for the sermon in English (for which I was grateful). Even though I had a bilingual prayer book, I could not follow the progress of the service. This was not very surprising, but what surprised me rather more was that many of the congregation seemed unable to follow it either, and were constantly asking each other what page we were at in the book.

I used to do some adult literacy tutoring. On one occasion, one of my pupils rang me at home, and the telephone was answered by someone else in the house who took a message. When they passed on the message, they asked me who had telephoned: I said it was one of my pupils. They looked surprised and said: "But he sounded quite normal."

I once asked this particular pupil how he managed to get along in everyday life, without being able to read—something I could hardly imagine. He explained that he just has a strategy for most contingencies. He had a friend who always filled out his tax-return. If he went to a restaurant, his girl friend always ordered the meal from the menu. Since he could not read a telephone directory, he would ring directory enquiries and say it had been stolen from the telephone booth. He said he had no real problems. He wanted to learn to read, incidentally, because he wanted a driving license for heavy good vehicles, and needed limited literacy for this purpose.

Another of my adult literacy pupils was an agricultural worker from the northeast of Scotland, on an involuntary stay in the south, in prison. His accent and dialect were so marked that I had real difficulty understanding him in conversation for several months. I had no problem, however, understanding him when he was reading aloud to me, since he then switched sharply into a variety of standard Scottish English very close to my own. He had no difficulty in understanding my standard English, of course, since he was familiar with such a variety from radio, television, the education system, and so on.

One final incident. When the renowned British broadcaster Wilfred Pickles died in March 1978, interesting facts were revealed about his work for the BBC during World War II. Pickles was well-known for his Yorkshire (northern English) accent. In the early 1940s, when it was feared that Germany might invade Britain, he was moved to London to read the news on radio. The reason, which was not advertised at the time, was that it was felt that the Germans might be able to imitate a southern English accent and mislead people with false news broadcasts but they would not be able to imitate a Yorkshire accent. Pickles was popular in the south, but in the north, people complained that they sent their children to school to learn to talk properly, only to have them hear the BBC news being read with a local regional accent.

These incidents are all commonplace in themselves, but they could be multiplied ad infinitum from other everyday observations. And they raise a large number of questions about the role that written language plays in society: what it means to be literate in a multilingual society; the changing and increasing demands on literate members of modern societies; the different attitudes toward literacy in different social groups; the peripheral part that literacy plays in many people's lives; the concept of partial literacy, in one or more languages, for restricted purposes; the confusion in many people's minds between literacy and intelligence, or between literacy and normality; the complex relations between written language and standard spoken language; the prestige and stigma associated with different regional and social varieties of language; the social and educational forces that maintain the standard language. I think such examples show already, therefore, that any coherent theory of reading and writing cannot be purely psychological. For questions of individual psychology may be swamped by powerful social attitudes concerning regional and national values, group solidarity, and so on.

THE RELATION OF SPOKEN AND WRITTEN LANGUAGE

Written language cannot be fully analyzed in isolation from spoken language. There are cases (further discussed later, see page 52) where a person may be able to read a language (for example, a dead language such as Latin or Sanskrit) that they cannot speak. But in general our understanding of written language clearly draws on our knowledge of the corresponding spoken language and on our linguistic competence in general. It is obvious that reading and writing are not merely psychological activities, involving the visual interpretation of word and letter shapes, but that this interpretation involves linguistic knowledge.

One thing that is central to any theory of literacy is an understanding of the relation between spoken and written language. Unless we know what this relation is, we do not know what it is that children learn when they learn to read, since we do not know the relation between the spoken language that they bring to school and the written language that they learn there. This is perhaps obvious, and it is something that is being taken into account more and more in the preparation of basal readers for young children.

What is rather less obvious perhaps is that the relationship between spoken and written language is not well understood. It is easy to assume, in fact, that there is one set of relationships that can be easily stated. But if we look at the place of written language in different societies at different times, we find that many different relations are possible.

I will take three types of case in Britain that show that the linguistic diversity of industrialized countries is often underestimated, and that the relation between spoken and written language may vary widely. I will take examples from the Gaelic-speaking community in northwest Scotland, working-class communities in Belfast in Northern Ireland, and various examples from immigrant communities; and make various more general points on the basis of these examples.

Some of the geographical, historical, and social facts in what follows may seem of purely local interest, and rather a long way from the immediate concerns of the nature of written language. But this is because I wish to argue that such local facts are crucial, if we wish to understand the relationship between spoken and written language in different communities. The gist of the argument is that we require an ethnography of reading and writing, and although this had been proposed by scholars (e.g., by Basso, 1974) the required fieldwork has hardly been started.

GAELIC IN SCOTLAND

I will take first the case of Gaelic-speaking Scotland. (Some of the facts cited in the following are from MacKinnon, 1977, the first substantial sociolinguistic study of an area of the Scottish Gaidhealtachd; others are from Thomson, 1976, and from my own observations.) There are around 80,000 Gaelic–English bilinguals in Scotland, with no remaining monolinguals, except among the very young, or a few very old women in the most remote districts. The men have traditionally been very widely traveled and have therefore been bilingual with English. A large number of

Gaelic speakers live in the industrial city of Glasgow in the center of the country. But when one refers to Gaelic-speaking Scotland, one is usually thinking of the Gaelic-speaking community that is concentrated on the islands off the northwest coast of Scotland. This is a day's drive plus an hour in the ferry from Glasgow and Edinburgh, and around 600 miles from London—not far in absolute distance, but a long way in psychological terms from the Westminster parliament in London; the area has very low priority for British politicians. Unemployment is the highest in Britain: around 25%. And educational opportunities are very poor. The only institution of higher education in the whole of the Highlands and Islands area is one technical college. Even the Scottish Nationalist Party only formulated a policy on Gaelic in 1974. Given the failure of attempts at Scottish devolution, and the decline of SNP Members of Parliament at Westminster in the 1979 general election (which voted in the Conservative Thatcher government) this fact is of little practical importance in any case.

Gaelic in Scotland has been retreating under pressure from English for a thousand years. Around A.D. 1000, Gaelic was probably spoken over the whole of Scotland, although there is some dispute over this. By the 1300s, English was already the normal language in central areas of the country. In the 1700s, Gaelic was still the normal language of the Highlands. But in the second half of the eighteenth century, the collapse was dramatic. A major demographic fact about the area is its continuing depopulation. The serious depopulation started in the mid-eighteenth century, when the Highland clan system collapsed after the Battle of Culloden in 1745. This was the battle in which Prince Charles Edward Stuart (Bonny Prince Charlie or The Young Pretender) so mismanaged things, that the Highlanders were defeated in less than half an hour. The collapse led to large-scale emigration, mainly to North America.

All in all, this was a very unromantic period of Scottish history—the romantic picture of the kilted Scotsman being largely a later creation of authors such as Sir Walter Scott. In deliberate attempts to dismantle the clan system, Highlanders were forbidden to wear tartan, carry arms, or play the bagpipes. There was also continuing official condemnation of Gaelic. For example, in 1872, the Education Act (Scotland) made no reference to Gaelic. And as late as the 1930s pupils in the Scottish islands were punished for speaking Gaelic in school. One punishment was to wear the maidecrochaidh, a stick on a cord, worn around the neck. (The same device was used in schools in Wales for pupils caught speaking Welsh.) The device was passed from pupil to pupil, to whoever was caught, and the pupil left wearing it at the end of the day was beaten.

Given this thousand year history of decline, it is amazing that Gaelic is still as vigorous as it is. But it is still the everyday language in the Outer Isles, with up to 90% of the population fully bilingual in some areas. On the mainland, Gaelic is hardly heard at all: partly due to very strong norms of politeness, which forbid Gaelic to used in front of English-speaking tourists. On the Inner Isles, tourists can often hear Gaelic spoken, by listening to men in the public bar of pubs (not the lounge bar!). On the Outer Isles, Gaelic can be heard almost anywhere.

One of the major theoretical problems for sociolinguistics is this often unexpected capacity of low-prestige languages to survive what appears to be the relentless pressure of major world languages. We require therefore an explanation of how Gaelic has managed to survive so well, and this requires some further basic sociological and demographic data. The social organization of the Scottish Outer Isles is very unlike most of the rest of Britain. They comprise rural crofting and fishing communities, with no true middle class. The community is very strongly religious and Sabbath observance is absolute. In almost all the islands, the religion is Presbyterian, Calvinist, and austere; this is a central factor in the maintenance of Gaelic. Late marriage, after the age of 30 or 40, is normal. And this late marriage and continuing depopulation, leads to a low birth rate, and to an aging and declining population. The young often leave to get a good education on the mainland or to find work. The maintenance of the language is helped by the nature of the traditional communal society and by its geographical isolation.

In schools in the northwest of Scotland today, initial literacy is taught in Gaelic where appropriate. But English is the official language, and Gaelic rapidly becomes a subject on the curriculum, comparable to geography or mathematics or whatever. Despite the high level of language maintenance, and the fact that literacy in Gaelic is general, very little written Gaelic is in evidence. There are, for example, almost no bilingual roadsigns. I have only ever seen two in the Highlands and Islands area (on Skye), and I suspect that they are for the benefit of tourists. I have also seen a Bank of Scotland (in Tarbert, Harris) with a redundant Gaelic sign: *Banca na h'Alba*). This is simply not an issue, in contrast to the situation in Wales, for example, where people have been jailed over the question of bilingual roadsigns.

It would be easy to assume, in fact, that the situations of Scottish Gaelic and Welsh in Britain would be very similar. But they differ in significant respects. Welsh has official status in Wales and is required by law to be used alongside English for various purposes. Gaelic has no official status in Scotland at all. Wales has developed a system of bilingual schools, but there is nothing comparable in Scotland. And it is evident in general that the speakers of Welsh and Scottish Gaelic have very different attitudes toward their languages. Even with situations that are superficially so similar—two Celtic languages spoken in different areas of Britain—the relation of these languages to English cannot be taken for granted. There is, simply, no language dimension to Scottish politics, as there is in Wales.

In the Scottish Islands, even notices in shops about local events are in

English. There are probably two reasons for this. First, it caters for some people who are literate only in English; the young acquire literacy in Gaelic at school and the old learned on the Gaelic Bible, but some middle-aged people have missed out. Second, it caters for the English-speaking incomers: the minority who are nevertheless the ones who are active in local politics and in charge of the committee structure on the islands. The norms of politeness are such that incomers are not required to learn Gaelic. (It is much more important that they observe the Sabbath.) English is therefore the language of committees and bureaucracy. It is possible, in principle, to use Gaelic in matters of business, politics, and law, but impossible in practice, since documents are in English, there are few Gaelic-speaking lawyers, and so on.

A factor in the inevitable decline of Gaelic is therefore that English is being used in more and more domains, particularly those that require institutionalized written language, such as business and commerce, law, technology, and tourism. One other very simple factor in Gaelic literacy is that, as with all minority languages, there is only a small market for books. Printing and publishing are uneconomic, with small print-runs, which push up the prices of books and restrict the market even further. Arguably there are far too many books published in English, but not enough in Gaelic.

To summarize, factors contributing to the decline of Gaelic are: high emigration; an aging and unbalanced population; the break up of the Gaelic-speaking area, now spread across many different islands with poor communications between them; the number of English-speaking incomers; the lack of official status for the language; and the increasing use of English in technical and bureaucratic domains. The shift of English is therefore geographical, social, and functional. Factors contributing to the maintenance of Gaelic include not only rather obvious ones such as the geographical, social, and functional. Factors contributing to the maintenance of Gaelic include not only rather obvious ones such as the geographical isolation of the area. They include also factors that are not immediately apparent to outsiders, because they involve the local values system, which revolves around the traditional communal society and religious beliefs.

WRITTEN LANGUAGE AND INSTITUTIONALIZED COMMUNICATION

The relationship between written language and bureaucracy, which I have pointed to briefly before, is an important one. Many of the functions of written language depend on its ability to create durable and accurate records. These recording or storage functions are obvious enough to us as fluent and practiced readers, but they were not obvious, for example, to the early printers. It was about a hundred years after the invention of movable type before books were regularly printed with page numbers, yet only then could they be fully exploited for reference and the easy retrieval of information (McLuhan, 1960). And it is a common experience that beginning readers have to be taught explicitly to exploit the permanence of written text. Children have to learn to process written text in ways not possible with spoken language: to read faster or slower depending on the purpose of reading, to reread, skim read, use indexes, and so on. At a higher level, it is a common complaint that students often have no idea how to exploit the information storage potential of big libraries. This is not surprising, since modern library systems are very complex, involving different systems of cataloguing and indexing, systems of abstracting services, and computer-assisted search systems relating different libraries across the world. The investigation of methods of indexing or abstracting articles, for example, is now no longer concerned merely with rather crude attempts at picking out key words. It is drawing on recent ideas about formal representation of the discourse structure of written texts (Hutchins, 1978).

The storage functions of written language lead, of course, to its central role in running any modern organization, from a small business to a state. And the bulk of written material has institutional, administrative, and bureaucratic functions.

As an international language, English has unique roles in the worldwide recording and transmission of information, in business and commerce, science and technology, education, and government. Not only is English the native language for some 400 million people. There are millions more who use English as a second language in areas such as India, West Africa, and Malaysia, where governments have retained English as an auxiliary language of wider communication after independence. There are still more millions who have learned English as a foreign language for various purposes. These figures lead to other startling statistics on the role of written English in conveying and recording information. It is estimated that 75% of the world's mail is in English (Strang, 1970, p. 73) and that 50% of the world's scientific literature is in English (Quirk et al., 1972, p. 4).

It is possible to compare the world's languages in a very general way, by comparing their utilization in writing. Ferguson (1962), in a widely quoted taxonomy, proposes four levels of utilization: **WO**—no use, that is the language has no writing system; **W1**—normal written purposes; **W2**—use for reporting original research in the physical sciences; **W3**—use for translations and resumes of scientific work in other languages. This taxonomy obviously requires to be made finer grained for some purposes, but the general point is clear.

Consider the following more detailed examples of the relationship between written English and other languages. If we want to understand fully how written English works, we cannot study it in isolation, but have to look at the relations between it and other writing systems. It is obvious, first of all, that there is a striking correspondence between the major writing systems in use in the world, and major political and religious blocs: Roman, Cyrillic, Arabic, Chinese. We need therefore the concept of the wider writing community (Berry, 1968) within which a writing system is used.

One feature of English spelling is that it often differentiates native words from foreign borrowings. For example, *llama* is recognizably foreign. There is a rule of English spelling that words do not end in -*i:* words which do are recognizably foreign, for example, *ski, pi, khaki, timpani,* and so on. Further, there is a growing international vocabulary shared by a large number of languages, especially in fields such as politics, sport, science and technology. Often such words are recognizable in a wide range of languages precisely because the spelling is NOT too closely related to the different pronunciations. An understanding of the writing conventions of one language therefore requires a study of its relations with other languages that are culturally important to the speakers.

I emphasize these peculiar facts about written English for two reasons. First, they mean that English puts enormous pressure on minority languages with which it comes in contact. For example, Scottish Gaelic is maintained to an impressive degree at the level of everyday life in a traditional community, but is increasingly restricted in the functions it serves outside local life. This is one of the ways in which a language dies. The incoming language takes over more and more of its functions. Second, when we investigate the functions that written language serves in the real world, we find that many of them are institutionalized and depersonalized, and clearly beyond the needs and experience of children. It would be quite impossible, for example, to explain most of the points I have just made about the worldwide distribution of English to young children learning to read. Young children, in a rather literal sense, have no need of written language, and this constitutes a great teaching problem. Several of the points I have made about the uses of written English in bureaucratic and technological areas, are also beyond the experience even of older students [see also Gundlach, chapter 6, this volume.]

MORE ON THE RELATION OF SPOKEN
AND WRITTEN LANGUAGE

A common view of the relation between spoken and written language might be diagramed as follows:

Both spoken and written language show stylistic variation from formal to informal. Spoken language shows more variation than written. It ranges from the formal language of lectures and speeches to casual and intimate conversation between individuals who know each other well and share background knowledge. Written language shows relatively less stylistic variation, since it is used predominantly for rather formal purposes. Casual written language, such as personal letters between individuals, are a relatively minor use when compared with the massive amount of formally published material that characterizes modern industrial societies. The written and spoken scales overlap. In other words, more formal spoken language is more similar to written language. Some styles of formal spoken language are of course based closely on written language. For example, a lecture may be based on written notes. But spoken language is rarely if ever as formal as the most formal written language of public notices, legal documents, and the like.

It has even been suggested that styles of language can be ranged along a single, linear continuum from casual to formal, and that this continuum simply ignores the distinction between spoken and written English. Labov (1966, 1972a, and elsewhere) in a large number of well-known studies, has collected speech data by recording speakers in different social settings: casual conversation, interviews, reading connected texts, and reading lists of words. In research in the United States, mainly in New York, he has found that informants' language shifts consistently in a single direction along this linear stylistic continuum, which could be diagramed in this way:

formal ↑	reading lists of words
WRITTEN │	reading connected text
SPOKEN │	interview style
casual ↓	casual conversation

Labov argues that there is a single linear measure of the amount of attention which speakers pay to their speech, and that as the social situation becomes more formal, this monitoring increases, and the style changes.

It is tempting to regard this model of a linear continuum as a theoretical statement about the relation between spoken and written language. However, it is, first of all, a statement about people's reactions to different kinds of language: how they READ lists of words, for example. And, second, the correct interpretation would seem to be that the linear relation is not a necessary statement about the relation between spoken and written language, but an empirical finding that holds for Labov's New York data, but which does not hold everywhere. It seems, in fact, that this continuum depends on speakers being highly literate and therefore having a particular view of the relation between spoken and written English.

Consider further what may happen to the diagram if one adds (still in a highly simplified way) the distinction between standard and nonstandard spoken language, and attempts to show how these three dimensions interact: formal versus casual; spoken versus written; and standard versus nonstandard. One kind of relationship could be diagramed as follows:

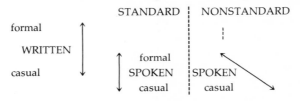

All written language is on the standard language side of the line. This represents the norm for contemporary English, rather than being literally true. That is to say, nonstandard written English, in dialect poetry for example, is very much the exception rather than the rule. And often when nonstandard English is written, in novels for example, it is between quotation marks, as the written repesentation of spoken English. In other words, there is a special relationship between writing and the standardization of the language. Standardization almost necessarily implies writing. Full standardization implies deliberate codification by generations of printers, publishers, dictionary makers, grammar book writers, schoolteachers, and the like. Further, there is stylistic variation within nonstandard dialects of any language, just as there is within spoken standard dialects. But this style-shifting will often involve dialect shifting, toward the standard dialect in more formal social situations.

Since the standard versus nonstandard distinction is also related to the social class stratification of modern societies, all this might also imply a linear model of another kind: that people often aspire to be like people above them in the social class scale; and that they often aspire to SPEAK like them. The basic notion is therefore of a single prestige norm, where there is a correlation between middle-class language, standard language, written language, and stylistically formal language. However, although this model fits some cases, including what one might roughly refer to as Western

middle-class society, it does not fit all societies, as the next case sudy shows.

ENGLISH IN BELFAST

As a second case study of the different place that literacy and written language may play in communities, I would like to discuss very important sociolinguistic work that has been done in Belfast, in Northern Ireland, by James and Lesley Milroy. (Milroy, 1980; Milroy & Milroy, 1977, 1978; Milroy & Margrain, 1978). They have done detailed fieldwork in lower working class communities in decaying inner city areas in Belfast. Like tight-knit working class groups elsewhere, the local community networks they have studied are relatively self-contained and isolated from the upwardly mobile mainstream society. In fact, the groups studied might best be regarded as being marginal: outside the industrial class structure, rather than occupying the lowest position within it (Milroy, 1980, pp. 74–75). They are closed communities, characterized by multiplex networks, in which people interact in more than one capacity: that is, a man's neighbor is likely also to be a kinsman and a fellow employee. Being relatively isolated from mainstream society, such communities appear to impose their own linguistic norms on their members. There is evidence, for example, that they are relatively unaffected by, and ignorant of, the norms of standard English.

The Milroys have collected extensive data on how written and spoken language are perceived in these Belfast working class communities. They carried out the same kind of procedure as Labov, recording people in casual and formal interaction, and in reading tasks. But they propose that reading is perceived as quite a different activity from conversation. They found predictable style shifting from casual to formal conversation. But this direction of shift was not always maintained in reading out lists of words. Here the style often shifted back to a vernacular style of pronunciation.

Many of their informants were illiterate or semiliterate: able only to read the three-letter words on the lists. Many other informants simply refused to read connected texts at all. They said they never read anything aloud normally, excepting possibly instructions on a can of food; they sometimes argued that it is wrong to read aloud what someone else has written, since it is wrong to take on someone else's role in this way. They were happy to read lists of unconnected words, and did this rapidly, with a characteristic rhythm and rise–fall intonation: *bag, bad, rag, stab*. It seems that, for these informants, reading aloud is a speech event that is partly outside the norms that govern other speech events. It might not even be recognized as a speech event at all. The informants do not normally do it, and will do it only with embarrassment, if at all. The view of speaking and reading as lying on a stylistic continuum may apply only to confident, highly literate speakers.

More generally, the Milroys argue that not all language communities have a single, easily identifiable prestige norm. The notion of a single norm, in which formality, written medium, and middle class standards coincide, is a product of middle-class European and American societies, but is not universal.

In other work, Labov (1972b) has warned against the bias introduced into linguistics by the fact that most linguists are white, middle-class, socially and geographically highly mobile individuals, who are not members of any natural speech community. The Milroys are pointing out that Labov himself has been misled by this bias in some of his own work.

Finally, the Milroys' work provides a detailed study of a case where a low-prestige language has shown an unexpected capacity to resist the relentless pressure of a standard language. They point (e.g., Milroy, 1980, p. 178) to the close-knit network structure of the community as an important mechanism of language maintenance.

ATTITUDES TO WRITTEN LANGUAGE IN OTHER COMMUNITIES

It would be possible, of course, to find in other communities totally different beliefs again about the value of reading aloud. For example, there are many places, particularly in the Middle East where children are taught to read aloud a foreign language that they do not understand at all, because of the religious significance of the language (Ferguson, 1971). Such teaching at least used to be common in synagogues in Britain, although the practice is probably changing. Learning to read aloud in Hebrew can be a formidable task if there is no understanding of the language, since in the scrolls Hebrew is written unpointed, with no indication of the vowels.

Different cases of this kind imply very different cultural beliefs about what is meant by literacy and the functions that it can serve. Goody (1968) presents papers on what he terms "restricted literacy" in many countries. He points out that, although many peoples have been in contact with written language over the past 2000 years or more, most of them have only been marginally affected. This is still the case with many people in the world. There are fewer and fewer countries left in which people do not have access to written language in some form. But individuals may not have access to literacy in their own language or dialect.

In addition, there are now many reports available of the high value that is given to oral traditions in many parts of the world by social groups who stand outside the mainstream middle-class culture (Bauman & Sherzer, 1974; Labov, 1972b; Opie & Opie, 1959). As Milroy (1980) argues, the view that written language is to be more highly valued than spoken language, is not a generally held belief, but a belief that has particular historical roots in Western culture.

In this article, due to my ignorance of other cultures and other writing systems, I am only able to discuss a few cases of the functions of written language in different social groups in Britain. Although Britain might appear superficially rather homogeneous, I am arguing that there is unexpected diversity even there. I could make my case much stronger if I were competent to discuss more exotic cases involving, for example, Eastern languages which use writing systems very different from ours (e.g., Chinese).

Many of our ideas about language in general and about written language in particular have not only the middle-class bias discussed previously, but a more general Western bias. This has occasionally been pointed out. For example, J. R. Firth's theories of nonsegmental, prosodic phonology were explicitly influenced by his knowledge of Indian languages with their various writing systems. And Bugarski (1970) has discussed in general terms the ways in which Western linguistics has been biased by the particular segmental analysis of language foisted on us by our alphabetic and word-based writing system.

LITERACY IN MULTICULTURAL BRITAIN

As I have shown already, there is often unexpected diversity in the native British population. Sociologists often give the impression that Britain is all rather homogeneous, and often seem to think that they may as well do their fieldwork in London or the big English cities. They seldom seem to get as far as Scotland or Ireland. However, the major source of linguistic diversity in contemporary Britain is the recent immigration into London and the big urban conurbations in the Midlands, such as Birmingham, Nottingham, and Leicester. The whole linguistic configuration of many areas of Britain has changed radically in just 20 years. There are not even accurate statistics on the languages spoken by immigrants, since Census figures refer only to country of birth: and this can only give a very rough indication of language for someone coming from a multilingual country such as India or countries in West Africa. Questions about racial, ethnic, and linguistic origins are clearly questions about very sensitive areas, and there has been a great deal of debate over whether such questions should be asked in the 1981 British census (HMSO, 1978; Saunders, 1978).

Since the whole linguistic configuration of large areas of Britain has changed profoundly since the period of large-scale immigration in the 1960s, it is unfortunate, but understandable, that both politicians and educators are often ignorant of the facts and issues involved. Of course, even census data on the language backgrounds of immigrants would not reveal how immigrant groups actually use different languages.

The first major report on the teaching of English in England was the Newbolt report published in 1921 (HMSO, 1921). It simply makes no reference at all to any language other than English. A more recent and very influential report is the Bullock report published in 1975 (HMSO, 1975). It does discuss the problem, although it refers rather coyly to "children of families of overseas origin," and is very sparse on statistics. The Bullock report also supports the principle of bilingual education, but it does not specify what is meant by this or how it might be put into practice. An estimate (Campbell-Platt, 1976) of the most widely spoken immigrant languages in Britain, in descending order, is:

Punjabi, Urdu, Bengali, Gujerati, (i.e., northern Indian languages), Polish, Italian, Greek, Spanish, and Cantonese or Hakka.

To this could be added (from Rosen, 1980), in alphabetic order this time:

Afrikaans, Arabic, French (including French creoles), Hausa, Igbo (West African languages), Japanese, Malay, Maltese, Persian, Portuguese, Pushtu (Iranian), Sinhalese (from Sri Lanka), Serbo–Croat, Swahili, Tagalog, Tamil (from Southern India), Twi (from West Africa), Turkish, Yoruba, and others.

It is now common for teachers in some English cities to have classes where native English-speaking children are in a minority. Nursery and infant classrooms in schools in English cities are now among the most linguistically varied and interesting environments to be found anywhere.

A large number of children in Britain's ethnic minorities now attend evening or weekend classes outside the school system, in their mother tongue. Little is known about the extent of such provision, or how effective it is (but see Saifullah Khan, 1976, 1978, 1980, for discussion). Classes are held in these languages, at least:

Arabic, Chinese, Greek, Gujerati, Hebrew, Hindi, Hungarian, Italian, Latvian, Polish, Punjabi, Spanish, Ukrainian, and Urdu.

Such classes are also held in other countries: for example, one estimate for Australia (Grassby, 1977) is that 100,000 children attend such ethnic schools in 25 languages. There are many motivations for this demand for instruction in the mother tongue. Children may be more fluent in English than the parents, and the parents are worried about being able to communicate with their children. The parents may plan to have the children marry within the community in the native country. They may fear forced repatriation, or wish to return home at some time. Or there may be parental pride in the language and culture. Or there may be religious reasons.

Few teachers have much idea of the existence of such schools; nor do they generally have any knowledge of the mother tongues of their pupils or the implications of acquiring literacy in these languages. This is not surprising, given the linguistic complexity involved. At least a couple of dozen languages are involved, if we are talking of the situation in London and the urban conurbations in the English Midlands, and several different writing systems, including:

Arabic, Chinese, Cyrillic, Devanagari, Greek, Gurmukhi, Hebrew, Urdu.

The linguistic complexity in a single case may be considerable. For example, Punjabi speakers from Pakistan, will write their language in the (Perso–Arabic) Urdu script (not the Gurmuhki script which is used in the Punjab). Their religious book, the Quran, is learned in Arabic. In schools in Birmingham, Punjabi teaching has been organized for some children by Asian members of staff (Chapman, 1976), but parents are not always in favor. They argue that their children would be wasting less time if they were learning English. In addition, English-medium education is prestigious. They may nevertheless send their children to mosque evening classes to learn Arabic. In addition, it is quite possible for someone to speak Punjabi and English fluently, but to be literate only in English.

A problem now is that many immigrant children opt for the language of their peers, and refuse to use their mother tongue at all, even with parental encouragement. For example, Wiles (1979) documents the case of an immigrant boy, who lived in India until he was 4 years old. His preferred language was Bengali, which was the language of his father and friends, but he was also in contact with Hindi and English. At the age of 4:2 (4 years, 2 months), he was in Britain, clearly recognizable as a foreign speaker of English. At the age of 4:6 he was attending a play group in West Sussex, and had acquired some local accent features. At age 5, he was in a primary school in north London. The West Sussex features were giving way to London features. By now he was reluctant to speak Bengali, despite parental encouragement, and English was clearly his dominant and preferred language. It is an important sociolinguistic finding that the peer group is usually the most powerful influence on children's language. Children grow up talking like their friends, and not like their parents (cf. Labov, 1972b). This fact should, of course, be exploited in classroom teaching, as it is more and more in the development of types of collaborative learning.

THE STATE OF THE ART

I will finish with some brief comments on the state of the art in research on literacy and on written language. Concentrated research on reading has been underway since the end of the nineteenth century. In Britain, the

Education Acts of 1870 and 1872 made the first requirements of universal literacy for schoolchildren, and set off a large amount of research. There are several terms and concepts that appear to have a modern ring to them, but have been used for a long time. The term "congenital word blindness" was first used as long ago as 1896, for example, in the *British Medical Journal* (Morgan, 1896). Despite a hundred years of research, we would have to admit, however, that there is nothing even approaching a coherent theory of reading and writing.

It is a generalization, but a fair generalization, to say that the dominant approach to reading over this period has been an experimental psychological approach. Reading has tended to be seen as a perceptual process involving the recognition of word and letter shapes, eye span, eye movements, and so on. It has again been known since the nineteenth century that, in reading, the eyes move in a jerky fashion (Javal, 1897).

Again it is a generalization, but a fair one, that research on reading has tended to ignore various things. First, it has often been ignored that what is read is language. People generally read meaningful texts, and texts are linguistically organized. Competent readers can, of course, read nonsense syllables if they are required to do so, for example, as part of a test; and this ability has to be accounted for. But, by and large, readers settle down with a good book, and not with a string of nonsense syllables. We have to distinguish, therefore, between a peripheral activity that readers can perform in response to a special request, and the activity of reading that readers engage in naturally. This distinction is important for several reasons. It is at the center of many disputes over just what "reading" means. Is it what fluent readers do naturally?; what they can, in principle, do?; what young children should be taught to do?

The fact that readers usually read connected meaningful text is, of course, not ignored in all research. It is central to approaches that take reading to be a "psycholinguistic guessing game," to use Goodman's phrase (Smith, 1973). And the real uses to which reading is put have been emphasized by researchers such as Lunzer and Gardner (1978) who have investigated the way in which children actually handle written material in real classrooms.

Second, the relation between spoken and written language has often been ignored. Not always, of course: There are some excellent reading schemes that begin very explicitly from the child's own spoken language. One example is the British *Breakthrough to Literacy* scheme (Mackay *et al.*, 1970). More accurately perhaps, the relation between spoken and written language may now be taken for granted and regarded as uncontroversial. But as I have illustrated, the relationship between spoken and written language differs in unexpected ways in different cultures.

Third, there has been a tendency to ignore the social functions of written language: the reasons why people read and write. Again, as I have shown, this cannot be predicted, but needs to be studied within different communities.

The neglect of such topics is partly the fault of linguists. Due to particular historical reasons, twentieth-century linguistics has given priority to spoken language. This has been partly a reaction against previous language study, in which spoken language was despised and literary language was regarded as the high point of linguistic development. One apotheosis of this view was represented by Dr. Johnson in the Preface to his famous dictionary of 1755. He took a view, which is still often held today, although often not as explicitly or clearly stated as he expressed it: Spoken language is "wild and barbarous jargon" that has to be given order by being "reduced to an alphabet."

The high value attributed to written language continued throughout the period when the study of classical languages took precedence over the study of English and other modern European languages in Europe and America. However, a significant change began to take place at the end of the nineteenth century. This was the period in which several different trends came together, not least the invention of mechanical ways of recording speech, and led to the development of phonetics as a serious academic discipline in England. There had been a long history in England of interest in different forms of speed writing and shorthand. Generally these were based on the conventional orthography. But Isaac Pitman's system, published in its first form in 1837, was based on a new analysis, and was fundamentally phonemic in the way it related directly to spoken English. A. J. Ellis, along with Pitman, was interested in questions of spelling reform, and published important work on phonetics in 1847. Further influential work on representing spoken language was Bell's ideas on 'visible speech,' published in 1867. This used symbols that were conventionalized diagrams of the vocal organs. The system was used by Henry Sweet (the model for Professor Higgins in Shaw's play *Pygmalion*) who published important work on phonetics and the theory of transcription in 1877 and 1890. And the Phonetic Teachers Association (later to become the International Phonetic Association) was founded in 1886. Practical mechanical methods of recording speech were only becoming available during this period. Edison's phonograph was first demonstrated in 1877. Disc records did not become available until years after that. Radio spread in the 1920s and convenient, portable tape recorders were not available till the 1940s.

As a result of these various advances, a significant shift took place towards the study of spoken language in England. In the United States, a shift toward studying spoken language also occurred, in particular after 1900, although in the United States, other factors contributed to this study. A major factor was the intensive study of American Indian languages. These languages were often on the point of dying out and required to be recorded as rapidly as possible. They were, of course, largely unwritten

languages, and they were despised as being primitive. A lot of effort therefore went into showing how complex they were, and we find aggressive
statements by American linguists asserting the primacy of spoken language.

The most famous statement is probably Bloomfield's (1933, p. 21) that
"Writing is not language, but merely a way of recording language by
means of visible marks." Such comments are, as I say, understandable in
view of the intellectual climate of the time. On a charitable interpretation,
Bloomfield's statement is very ambiguous. On a literal interpretation, it is
both muddled and simply false. That 'writing is not language' is true only if
we assume that 'writing' here refers to one medium in which language
may be realized. The same is true of speech, of course: Speech is not language. But written language is language. The statement is ambiguous insofar as it fails to distinguish explicitly between language as an abstract
underlying system, and the different media in which language may be
realized. However, the second half of the statement is wrong in its implication that the recording has no effect on the language: writing is not
"merely" a record.

Just to emphasize that such attitudes have not really changed even now,
consider this statement from Trudgill, a leading British sociolinguist, which
is more or less a paraphrase of Bloomfield's statement, with the added
confusion of the claim that spoken language comes first and is then recorded by being written down. "Writing is parasitic upon speech in that it
is simply a way of recording the spoken language in an enduring visual
form (Trudgill, 1975, p. 20)." To see how the debate continues, one might
also look at R. A. Hall, Jr.'s review of Josef Vachek's book on *Written
Language* (Hall, 1975; Vachek, 1973). Hall was one of the American linguists
who was most vociferous, in the 1940s and later, in defense of nonprescrip-
tive attitudes to nonstandard and unwritten language. The result of views
such as Bloomfield's was the virtual abandonment of the study of written
language in mainstream American linguistics from the 1920s to the present.
It is also simple to check just how few references there are to written
language or literacy in most contemporary textbooks on theoretical linguistics and sociolinguistics. Only a few individuals, such as Martin Joos and
Dwight Bolinger, published the occasional article on problems of written
language. In contemporary Chomskyan linguistics, the focus of interest is
now on the nature of human language. It is not interested in the relations
between spoken and written language. Two main strands of linguistic
work on written language have, however, continued. One strand has been
work by European linguists, working mainly in Prague. The main name
here is Josef Vachek. Second, there is the enormous amount of work on
creating writing systems for unwritten languages done by the missionary
linguists working with the Summer Institute of Linguistics. (See
Gudschinsky, 1976, for a review of this work.)

I do not think it is special pleading, however, to argue that the study of language does have particularly awkward problems associated with it, which are not encountered in other scientific pursuits. Linguists constantly have to decide whether to study particular languages or human language in general, and also whether to study language (or A language) or its realizations in speech or writing. The first distinction has been referred to as the difference between first- and second-order theories (Sampson, 1975). First-order theories are theories, descriptions, or grammars of particular languages. They tend to give prominence to idiosyncracies, and on what makes, say, English different from Eskimo. Second-order theories are theories of the nature of human language. They are theories of linguistic universals, of ways in which all human languages are alike, and ways in which they differ as a whole from, say, animal communication systems. Other sciences do not have this problem, but all linguistic descriptions are distorted in some way by having to make a choice between concentrating on what is unique to a language or on what is universal. (Stubbs and Berry, 1980, discuss this in more detail with reference to a particular current debate in English grammar, about whether features of the English verb should be described in a way that brings out the idiosyncratic behavior of English verbs or which relates the description of English to universal grammar.)

The second distinction is between a language and the medium in which the language is realized. The medium will usually be speech or writing, but could also be, for example, manual signing for the deaf. One could study the relation between the medium and the language (e.g., whether a writing system is consistently alphabetic–phonemic, morphophonemic, or syllabic), or differences between the syntax of spoken and written English, or such problems. Or one can write a grammar of a language with no reference to its realization, since the grammar of written and spoken English is, after all, largely shared.

In practice, the two distinctions are often related to each other, although as far as I can see, they are logically independent. Thus an interest in the second-order theory of linguistic universals often goes along with a lack of interest in the particular realizations of a language. Chomsky, for example, is interested in linguistic universals and never discusses the relations between spoken and written language. Bloomfield, on the other hand, is especially interested in particular exotic languages, and concentrates on their spoken versions (although this is due mainly to practical, not theoretical, reasons; and, as I have said before, he does not give a satisfactory account of the relation between the spoken and written language).

The shifts of interest between written and spoken language can also be seen in shifts of fashion in foreign language teaching, which has often been influenced by current trends in linguistics. The traditional **grammar-translation** method was based firmly on written, and usually literary, language. This approach was perfectly understandable and appropriate, insofar as it was long used for teaching dead classical languages, such as Latin and Greek. It has always been more evident, with reference to learning foreign languages, that written and spoken language can be kept separate, at least for some purposes. It makes perfect sense to say of someone: He has a reading knowledge of German, or whatever, but cannot speak it. And if the language in question is a language that is no longer spoken and is studied primarily for its literary or historical interest (for example, Latin, Greek, Old English, or Sanskrit), then there is no obvious alternative to the grammar-translation method.

However, by the 1920s it was becoming evident that teaching grammatical rules explicitly and translating written texts from one language to the other, was less appropriate for modern languages. The grammar-translation method began to be replaced by the **direct method,** which advocated learning by hearing the spoken language. Bloomfield and American structuralist methods, together with behaviorist psychology, led to **audiolingual** methods, most obviously represented in many language laboratory courses. Here, the emphasis is on the spoken language. In extreme forms of language laboratory drills, nothing is explained explicitly to the learners. They are expected to repeat over and over again the model on the tape, and to induce the correct patterns. The behaviorist–structuralist approach assumes that skill in handling the written language comes after, and is dependent on, command of the spoken language.

More recently there has been interest in teaching READING ABILITY in foreign languages, with or without teaching ability in the spoken language. This has been related especially to the teaching of English for special purposes, for example, teaching English for scientific and technological purposes. This approach has seemed particularly appropriate with older learners where it is possible to foresee their communicative needs. For example, they may be university science students in the Middle East or India who need to be able to read scientific papers.

CONCLUDING COMMENTS

One comment about research: A sociolinguistic theory of literacy will have to be based on a great deal of observation of the uses to which written language is put in a wide range of social settings. These uses are by no means always obvious to outsiders, since they may differ widely in different communities, and the kind of observational and ethnographic work required has hardly been started. And one comment about teaching practice: A major principle in teaching any language skills is that work should, as far as possible, have some genuine communicative purpose. The kind of understanding of the many different functions of reading and writing which I have discussed, should therefore also underlie such teaching.

This chapter is tidily packaged, as is the convention for written academic articles, between headings, subheadings and references. However, this cannot disguise the fact that the argument is often rather formless, jumping between details of Scottish geography, the history of linguistics, English spelling, and so on. This is because I have tried to argue that a coherent theory of written language must be much less narrowly based in its facts than many studies in the past. I have dealt in more detail elsewhere (Stubbs, 1980) with some of the topics that I have dealt with scantily here. But I am only too aware that my own knowledge is narrowly restricted, and that I have said almost nothing at all, for example, of the different kinds of writing systems and their uses in other parts of the world. Such a range of reference will be necessary if we are to have the basis for a general, second-order theory of the universal characteristics of written language. At present we can do little more than document some surprising local idiosyncrasies.

"What writers know" is always different when they finish writing a book or article, from when they started. I know from personal experience that formulating ideas in written language changes those ideas and produces new ones. But problems writers have include deadlines, and a less formless argument will have to wait. What readers know when they come to the end of a chapter may or may not be the same as when they started!

REFERENCES

Basso, K. The ethnography of writing. In Bauman & Sherzer (Eds.), *Explorations in the ethnography of speaking*. London: Cambridge University Press, 1974. Pp. 425–432.

Bauman, R., & Sherzer, J. (Eds.) *Explorations in the ethnography of speaking*. London: Cambridge University Press, 1974.

Berry, J. The making of alphabets. In J. A. Fishman (Ed.), *Readings in the sociology of language*. The Hague: Mouton, 1968. Pp. 737–753.

Bloomfield, L. *Language*. New York: Holt, 1933.

Bugarski, R. Writing systems and phonological insights. *Papers of the Chicago Linguistic Society*, 1970, 453–458.

Campbell-Platt, K. Distribution of linguistic minorities in Britain. In *Bilingualism and British education: The dimensions of diversity*. London: Centre for Information on Language Teaching, 1976. Pp. 15–30.

Chapman, R. D. Bilingualism in Birmingham. In *CILT*, 1976, pp. 74–77.

CILT *Bilingualism and British education: The dimensions of diversity*. London: Centre for Information on Language Teaching, 1976.

Ferguson, C. A. The language factor in national development, *Anthropological Linguistics*, 1962, 4, 23–27.

Ferguson, C. A. Contrasting patterns of literacy acquisition in a multilingual nation. In W. H.

Whiteley (Ed.), *Language use and social change*. London: Oxford University Press, 1971. Pp. 234–253.

Goody, J. (Ed.) *Literacy in traditional societies*. London: Cambridge University Press, 1968.

Grassby, A. J. Linguistic genocide. In E. Brumby & E. Vaszolyi (Eds.), *Language problems in Aboriginal education*. Western Australia: Mount Lawley College of Advanced Education, 1977. Pp. 1–4.

Gudschinsky, S. C. *Literacy: The growing influence of linguistics*. The Hague: Mouton, 1976.

Hall, R. A., Jr. Review of J. Vachek, *Written Language*. *Language*, 1975, *51*, 461–464.

HMSO *The Teaching of English in England*. London: His Majesty's Stationery Office, 1921.

HMSO *A Language for life*. London: Her Majesty's Stationery Office, 1975.

HMSO *1981 census of population*. London: Her Majesty's Stationery Office, 1978.

Hutchins, W. J. The concept of 'aboutness' in subject indexing. *Aslib Proceedings*. 1978, *30*, 172–181.

Javal, E. Essai sur la physiologie de lecture. *Annales d'Oculistique*, 1897, *82*, 242–453.

Labov, W. *The social stratification of English in New York City*. Washington, D.C.: Center for Applied Linguistics, 1966.

Labov, W. *Sociolinguistic patterns*. Philadelphia: University of Pennsylvania Press, 1972(a).

Labov, W. The linguistic consequences of being a lame. In W. Labov, *Language in the inner city*, 1972(b). Pp. 255–292.

Labov, W. *Language in the inner city*, Philadelphia: University of Pennsylvania Press, 1972(c).

Lunzer, E., & Gardner, K. (Eds.) *The effective use of reading*. London: Heinemann, 1978.

Mackay, D. *et al*. *Breakthrough to literacy: Teacher's manual*. London: Longmans, 1970.

MacKinnon, K. *Language, education and social processes in a Gaelic community*. London: Routledge & Kegan Paul, 1977.

McLuhan, M. (1960) The effect of the printed book on language in the sixteenth century. In E. Carpenter & M. McLuhan (Eds.), *Explorations in communication*. London: Cape, 1970. Pp. 125–135.

Milroy, J., & Milroy, L. Belfast: Change and variation in an urban vernacular. In P. Trudgill (Ed.), *Sociolinguistic patterns in British English*. London: Edward Arnold, 1978. Pp. 19–36.

Milroy, L. *Language and social networks*. Oxford: Blackwell, 1980.

Milroy, L. & Margrain, S. (1978) Vernacular language loyalty and social network. *Language in Society*, 1980, *9*, 43–71.

Milroy, L. & Milroy, J. Speech and context in an urban setting. *Belfast Working Papers in Language and Linguistics*, 1977, *2*, 1–85.

Morgan, P. A case of congenital word blindness, *British Medical Journal*, 7 November 1896, 1378.

Opie, I., & Opie, P. *The lore and language of schoolchildren*. London: Oxford University Press, 1959.

Quirk, R. *et al*. *A Grammar of contemporary English*. London: Longman, 1972.

Rosen, H. Linguistic diversity in London schools. In A. K. Pugh *et al*. (Eds.), *Language and language use*. London: Heinemann, 1980. Pp. 46–75.

Saifullah Khan, V. Provision by minorities for language maintenance. In *Bilingualism and British education: The dimensions of diversity*. London: Centre for Information on Language Teaching, 1976. Pp. 31–47.

Saifullah Khan, V. *Bilingualism and linguistic minorities in Britain*. London: The Runnymede Trust, 1978.

Saifullah Khan, V. The 'mother-tongue' of linguistic minorities in multicultural England. *Journal of Multilingual and Multicultural Development*, 1980, *1*, 71–88.

Sampson, G. Theory choice in a two-level science, *British Journal for the Philosophy of Science*, 1975, *26*, 303–318.

Saunders, C. *Census 1981—question on racial and ethnic origin*. London: The Runnymede Trust, 1978.

Smith, F. (Ed.) *Psycholinguistics and reading*. London: Holt, Rinehart & Winston, 1973.

Strong, B. M. H. *A history of English*. London: Methuen.

Stubbs, M. *Language and literacy: The sociolinguistics of reading and writing*. London: Routledge and Kegan Paul, 1980.

Stubbs, M. & Berry, M. The Duke of Wellington's gambit: Notes on the English verbal group. *Nottingham Linguistic Circular*, 1980, 9.

Thomson, D. *Gaelic in Scotland [Gaidhlig ann an Albainn]*. Edited by R. MacThomais, Glasgow: Gairm, 1976.

Trudgill, P. *Accent, dialect and the school*. London: Edward Arnold, 1975.

Vachek, J. *Written language: General problems and problems of English*. The Hague: Mouton, 1973.

Wiles, S. The multilingual classroom. In *Language development*, PE232. Milton Keynes: Open University Press, 1979.

Chapter **2**

An Analysis of Errors in
Written Communication

Martin Nystrand

INTRODUCTION

Until recently, the paths of writing and language research have rarely crossed. Many discussions of writing simply make no mention of language, and discussions of language commonly make scant mention of writing. Indeed, a number of seminal works in the history of linguistics (e.g., Bloomfield, 1933; Hockett, 1958; Sapir, 1921; Saussure, 1959) clearly exclude written language from the domain of language study altogether; and although rhetoric has historically examined the ways in which writers locate the available means of persuasion in any given case, the character of these means AS A PROBLEM IN ITS OWN RIGHT has not always been a focus of rhetoric.

Nonetheless, writers are users of language. Written texts are obviously not just so many blotches of ink: The marks are patterned and meaningful. They are patterned and meaningful in a special way too: Written texts clearly differ from other graphic representations such as pictures and paintings. For readers and writers, written texts are signs—carefully patterned inscriptions composed according to rules and governed by the writer's purpose. In an important sense, the writer is a grammarian—a written-text experimenter whose tacit inquiry qua writer has less to do with organizing the contents of expression and the aims of discourse than it does with systematizing the means of expression and synthesizing the resources of

WHAT WRITERS KNOW
The Language, Process,
and Structure of Written Discourse

the written language. The writer's problem is how to say something with pen and paper despite the fact that not one single stroke, word, or sentence corresponds naturally to what we call "thought." Written language is a very special resource for meanings, and its use and learning pose some very fundamental questions: How does the written language work? what unique resources does it offer its users? what do writers need to know (that beginners must learn) in order to draw on these resources? and how does written communication come about? These are a few questions involved in the study of written language and its use. The answers are neither trivial nor obvious. Indeed, the possibility of achieving communication and purpose by composing texts is a problem no less awesome and perplexing than any other aspect of language such as relations between thought and language, or the development of speech.

This chapter presents a conceptual framework for use in the study of written communication. The goal of this research—far from complete—is to describe how meaningful written communication comes about. My immediate purpose is to offer some speculations based on this research about what happens when written communication actually does take place.

THE USES OF ERROR IN PSYCHOLOGY AND LINGUISTICS

In his study of *The composing process and the teaching of writing: A study of an idea and its uses* (1977), Gundlach examines the documentary evidence for the composing process: the notes and scratched-over drafts that usually end up in the writer's wastebasket. Examining case histories of several nonfiction writers and two college students, he concludes that such analyses of "mistakes" and drafts-gone-astray provide "the least-studied, yet perhaps richest, kind of information about the process of composition."

This lack of error analysis in writing is indeed surprising and probably reflects how little historically writing has posed interesting questions and issues for linguists and psychologists. Aside from Luria's (1977–1978) little known experiment (discussed in this chapter), and Shaughnessy's (1977) study, little work has been done. This is especially surprising given the extensive use of error analysis in the investigation of other language processes, including speech production (e.g., Boomer & Laver, 1968; Fromkin, 1973; Garrett, 1975; Nooteboom, 1969) and reading (e.g., Goodman, 1965, 1967a, 1967b; Y. Goodman & C. Burke, 1969).

Error analyses have proved especially useful where the need for detailed theroetical explanations of psychological and linguistic phenomena has never been intuitively obvious. "A certain intellectual effort is required," Chomsky notes, "to see how such phenomena can pose serious problems. . . . One is inclined to take them for granted as necessary or somehow 'natural' [1972, p.24]" Generally, people seldom note the perplexity or intricacy of such faculties as perception, memory, speech, or general mental orientation until these faculties fail. Langer (1962) compares mental orientation in this respect to 'the pressure of the floor against our feet": it is "not normally in consciousness; but let it fail, and we are scarcely conscious of anything else [p.132]."

Many psychologists and linguists have offered penetrating conjectures about common phenomena through just such analyses. Freud (1901) first unlocked associative thought processes by scrutinizing various parapraxes, or "Freudian slips." Piaget (e.g., 1950, 1951, 1953, 1954) has charted general cognitive development by probing the explanations children give for wrong answers to logical puzzles. He has shown that these mistakes reflect the logic and structure of child thought, a logic which is qualitatively different from adult thought. Ervin-Tripp (1964) has showed that children's regularization of strong verbs (*goed, runned, sitted*) and plurals (*foots, mouses, tooths*) AFTER apparent mastery of the correct irregular forms depicts an important aspect of language acquisition. K. Goodman (1969) has characterized the reading process by showing that reader errors, which he calls "miscues," are not the result of haphazard guessing but rather efforts to make sense of the text in particular ways. Gardner (1974), in a towering account of "the shattered mind," sees the "fragmented world of the brain-damaged patient as a means of illuminating—precisely because of its distorted and fragmentary nature—the essential nature of human consciousness [p.45]." Goodman captures the general significance of error and failure analysis in psychology and linguistics when he notes, "One of the evidences that these processes are controlled is that [they] sometimes come out not quite the way we intended [them] to [1971, p. 459]."

Russian psychologist Luria (1978) conducted an ingenious investigation of children learning to write by just such a failure analysis. Luria and his associates created a situation where subjects COULD NOT SUCCEED, and then observed response to this predicament. The experimenters began by asking 3-, 4-, and 5-year-old children who could not yet write to remember long lists of sentences such as *Mice have long tails, There are 5 pencils on the table, There are many trees in the forest, There are many stars in the sky, I have 30 teeth.* When the children realized that there was too much information to remember, the experimenters provided pen and paper, and suggested subjects write things down. The bewildered children protested that they did not know how. The experimenters then pointed out that adults normally jot down what they need to remember, and encouraged the children to do the same. The results were a series of scribbles (see Figure 2.1). Subjects were then given recall quizzes and encouraged to use their notes as they wished. When quizzed about a particular squiggle ("What's that?"), one 5-year-old exclaimed, "That's how you write!"

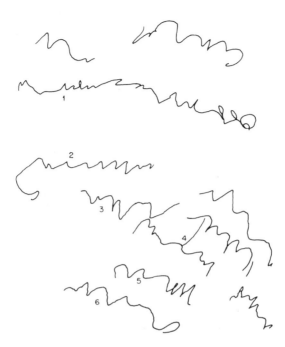

FIGURE 2.1. (1) There are five pencils on the table. (2) There are two plates. (3) There are many trees in the forest. (4) There is a column in the yard. (5) There is a large cupboard (written prematurely). (6) The little doll (written prematurely).

After many sessions a few children invented their own idiosyncratic scribbles that actually served to aid memory. Luria explains the significance of this development:

> This jump presupposes a little invention, whose psychological signifiance is interesting in that it alters the very psychological function of the sign by transforming the primary sign, which merely establishs ostensively the existence of a thing, into another kind of a sign that reveals a particular content. If this differentiation is accomplished successfully, it transforms a sign-stimulus into a sign-symbol, and a qualitative leap is thereby effected in the development of complex forms of cultural behavior [p.84].

From these case histories, Luria characterizes writing as a way of "organizing internal psychological operations"—a strategy "to make [performance of these operations] more efficient and productive." Learning to write requires insight that strokes of a pen are means to semantic ends, not just objects of curiosity.

Methodologically such demonstrations are significant because they demonstrate the usefulness of failure and error analysis in gaining knowledge of intangible mental processes. The demonstration of PATTERN OF ERROR

AND SYSTEMATIC DISCREPANCY offers important clues to the underlying structure of the behavior in question. Such investigations show how something works by observing it break down in particular ways, hence underscoring the structured, rule-governed character of behavior.

THE PROBLEM OF ERRORS IN WRITING: A PILOT STUDY

In 1975, the Trent Valley Centre of the Ontario Institute for Studies in Education began development of a battery of criterion-referenced tests of reading and writing for ages 6 through 15. Efforts to develop a viable test of writing floundered from the start. As Project members[1] sought to agree on the relative importance of various writing objectives, all concerned came to know firsthand what Remondino (1959) and Diederich and his associates (1961) concluded years ago: There is wide disagreement about the criteria of "good" writing. Both Remondino and Diederich attributed variations in ratings to evaluators' competing ideas of good writing, ideas that included quality of ideas, organization, style, spelling and mechanics, and expression. Though revealing in its own right, such vacillation among judgments entails a nightmare of erratic decimal places for the enterprising test developer who must be concerned about test reliability.

Any valid and useful assessment of writing must cope with enormous problems entailed by the absence of an abiding, lawful account of how writing works. For the test maker, it is an issue of construct validity in the absence of a construct, an issue that quickly raises questions of evidence: What shall the test maker be valid and reliable about? What's worth counting?

Although efforts to develop a viable criterion-referenced approach to writing assessment floundered from the very start, those of us involved in this project spent some time early on pursuing a novel use of the T-unit (any main clause with all of its modifying phrases: a standard unit used in measuring syntactic complexity). We speculated, for example, that if good adolescent writers were to write on the same topic for two distinctly different age groups (e.g., "The Meaning of Christmas," once for adults and once for 7-year-olds), one aspect of their ability might be measured by a suitable differential in mean T-unit length, in essence a measure of their awareness of their reader's needs. After deciding that such a columnist as Russell Baker might just win a Pulitzer Prize while proving us wrong, we gave up on this use of the T-unit. We were particularly unsuccessful in

---

[1]Twelve Ontario boards of education were involved: Leeds and Grenville, Frontenac, Lennox and Addington, Peterborough Separate, Hastings, Peel, Halton, Muskoka, Nippising, East Parry Sound, and Gray. Mr. Frank DiNoble of the Leeds and Grenville Board of Education kindly provided the student writing samples used in this study.

specifying appropriate differentials. We did not, however, abandon the notion that writing to a child constrains an adult writer in some ways that are different from writing to another adult.

For some time thereafter, we made little progress in writing assessment, though reading assessment seemed to move forward as we investigated the use of the cloze technique to assess comprehension. This procedure involves the systematic deletion of every n^{th} (usually every fifth) word from a minimum of 220–250 words of running text. Reader success in reconstructing these broken, or clozed, texts was first shown by Taylor (1953) to be a useful technique for measuring readability with any given group of readers. Cloze has also been used quite elegantly to measure comprehension where text difficulty has been established independently (e.g.,

TABLE 2.1.
Clozed Writing Sample

TOPIC: Does the Government Have the Right to
Impose Laws on Us for Our Own Protection?

Text	Word list
Yes, I _____	think
that the laws are _____ .	okay
The people that puts _____	out
the laws are doing it _____	for
us to help us, _____	not
to hurt us. The _____	seatbelt
law, since they made us _____	use
it my sister _____	said
that there isn't so _____	many
head injuries on U-2 _____	where
she is nursing. And the _____	laws
hasn't come out yet _____	about
death penalty but I _____	think
they should, because I _____	think
there won't be so _____	much
crime. I also think the _____	OPP's
could be harder on the _____	people
that steal, kill and _____ .	rapes
And the law for _____	going
over 60 on the _____	401
that is to _____	help
us to save _____ .	gas
But I am just _____	one
person with my _____	ideas
and it might be _____	different
then my friends, family and _____	maybe
you judges. I belive _____	in
all laws, some even _____	sounds
crazy but, what there _____	doing
is for us.	

(fold back here)

O'Reilly, Schuder, Kidder, Salter, & Hayford, 1977). Many studies (e.g., Bormuth, 1969; Hansen & Hesse, 1974; Rankin, 1974) have since corroborated the general usefulness of the cloze procedure though Kintsch and Vipond (1979) have noted that the statistical redundancy of a text, which is what the cloze measures, is not exactly comprehensibility. No doubt Kintsch and Vipond are correct in this assessment. Nonetheless, no one denies that redundancies of all kinds are essential to the comprehensibility of any text. Indeed, the **redundancies of argument repetition** are a critical text variable in Kintsch and Vipond's own proposed method for measuring readability. Whatever the cloze actually measures is not at issue in the present analysis, however, since its use here was strictly heuristic, a way of collecting data in an exploratory, first phase study.

TABLE 2.2
Adult Responses to Clozed Writing Sample

```
 1   Yes, I think
 2   that the laws are okay.  (2 good; right; 3 alright)
 3   The people that puts out    (3 down; 2 on; together; forth)
 4   the laws are doing it for   (3 to)
 5   us to help us, not
 6   to hurt us. The seatbelt
 7   law, since they made us use    (6 wear; okay; do)
 8   it my sister said          (4 says; knows; feels)
 9   that there isn't so many
10   head injuries on U-2 where     (because)
11   she is nursing. And the laws     (6 law; decision; government;
12   hasn't come out yet about     (against; on; 2 for; ---) police)
13   death penalty but I think
14   they should, because I think    (know)
15   there won't be so much         (many)
16   crime. I also think the OPP's    (police; 4 law; 3 laws; courts)
17   could be harder on the people    (criminals; kids)
18   that steal, kill and rapes.    (----; 6 rape; 2 rob; speed)
19   And the law for going    (3 driving; speed; 4 speeding)
20   over 60 on the 401       (6 highway; highways; -----)
21   that is to help    (2 make)
22   us to save gas.    (4 lives; ourselves; money)
23   But I am just one
24   person with my ideas      (10 opinions)
25   and it might be different    (that; wrong; alright; better)
26   than my friends, family and maybe  (teachers; others; also;
27   you judges. I belive in   (5 that)       police; ale; even)
28   all laws, some even sounds    (4 are; slightly; so; maybe; 2 is;
29   crazy but, what there doing                2 are; for)
30   is for us.
```

While considering the usefulness of cloze in reading assessment, we wondered about its possibilities for examining aspects of writing ability. Could we not use cloze to investigate writing ability PROVIDED RELEVANT READERS WERE IDENTIFIED EITHER BY OR FOR THE WRITER BEFORE WRITING? We reasoned that cloze scores of readers might bear on the success of the writer in making sense for intended readers. At no time did we assume that the higher the cloze score, the better the writing; we were mainly interested in looking at discrepancies between writers' words and readers' guesses. Hence we were far more interested in the low scores than the high.

Ten teachers from the Project probed the possibilities of this technique by filling in blanks of several clozed writing samples, all by eighth graders and all composed for a general adult audience. The writing samples were clozed and typed in an end-of-the-line format. The two forms shown in Tables 2.1 and 2.2 are typical. The first is a writing sample clozed; the second is the same sample in its entirety with discrepant reader guesses and their frequencies in parentheses.

WRITING MEANINGFULLY: CONSTRAINING THE READER

Our main effort was to describe and classify all discrepancies between writers' words and readers' guesses—not for the immediate purpose of explaining them and certainly not for the purpose of "assigning blame" to either writer (for poor writing) or reader (for poor comprehension)—but merely to note the ways in which written communication can break down. We conducted no controlled experiments in this initial probe; we sought instead to generate some interesting hypotheses, basing our speculations only on the working premise that communication requires writers to constrain their readers adequately by sharply delimiting the useful predictions readers are likely to make while reading. This single assumption suggested the following, initial taxonomy of constraints on written discourse production:

1. **Graphic constraints** govern matters of orthography, including strokes, letters, spelling, spacing, indentation, and layout. Adequate graphic constraints are the stuff of **legibility.** Misspellings (aside from homonym confusions, e.g., *your* for *you're*) are not often significant impediments to reader comprehension.

2. **Syntactic constraints** include factors that affect communication with respect to sentence structure. Homonym confusions, for example, are not just simple misspellings; *your* works differently syntactically than *you're* (*you're*, unlike *your*, can signal a verb phrase as in *You're going to make it;* see p. 67). Nor is the omission of certain marks of punctuation (e.g., the

comma in *By the time we finished our dinner was ready*) a simple graphic problem. Each of these examples will "misconstrain" readers specifically in terms of syntax. Such nonstandard usages as *He done it* or *between you and I*, by contrast, are not impediments to reader comprehension. Violations of prescribed usages rarely seem to affect reader comprehension very much.

3. **Semantic constraints** include all relevant assumptions and premises that the reader brings to the text about the writer's topic or argument. Sometimes referred to as **given information,** this knowledge serves in effect as backdrop for **new information** that the writer introduces. When writers misjudge what their readers know, communication will break down. [For further discussion, see Glatt, Chapter 4 this volume.] For example, technical writing that is clear for experts can easily be turgid jargon for general readers. For those who are not part of the readership of this study, the expression "graphic constraint" is jargon, a mystifying and obscure term for "legibility."

4. **Textual constraints** refer to certain aspects of written form and cohesion that are properties of the text itself—not individual sentences and not the context—and cannot be explained by reference either to word choice or syntax. Continuity of text is what Halliday and Hasan (1976) and others call **cohesion;** it owes specifically to those uses of reference, substitution, ellipsis, and conjunction that disambiguate or resolve presuppositions set up elsewhere in the text. The fact that ambiguity is actually quite rare in language use (especially compared to the situation suggested by au courant analyses of isolated sentences [Kintsch, 1974, p.11]) is testimony to what writers know about textual constraints, or the resources of the written language for **texture.**

5. **Contextual constraints** include relevant elements of a text's situation—such "extratextual" factors as format, genre, mode, type, and title as well as all aspects of the discourse not specific to the text per se. Some aspects of written communication cannot be explained by reference to the text at all. Sarcasm, irony, and understatement are good examples of the importance of contextual constraints.

We called discrepancies between writers' words and readers' guesses **misconstraints** rather than errors that might be attributed to either writer expression or reader comprehension, partly to avoid the suggestion that all such discrepancies are bad, but mainly to focus on the fundamental importance of interaction between writers and readers. Communication, we would note, has far less to do with a particular writer's expression or a particular reader's comprehension than it does with the presence or absence of interaction between the production skills of the one and the processing resources of the other. IN TERMS OF COMMUNICATION, writers and readers are not so much right or wrong in their expression and interpretations as they are IN OR OUT OF TUNE WITH EACH OTHER. A misconstraint is what happens when writers and readers are out of tune in this way—not a unit of text analysis per se but the result of mismatch between a particular writer's expression and a particular reader's comprehension.

Readers come to texts with certain expectations. They expect spaces between words; left-to-right sequences in multiple and progressive sequences from top to bottom of page; ideas related to each other in a coherent manner with interpretive shifts indicated appropriately by indentation, punctuation, and layout. The constraints noted previously distinguish certain salient resources of the written language available to writers for dealing with these expectations. When reader expectations and writer expression fail to match, the result is misconstraint and communication failure. Lucidity, on the other hand, is the result of fortuitous match, with the reader typically impressed with the cogency of the argument, the vividness of the description, and so on.

A CLASSIFICATION OF WRITER-READER INTERACTIONS

These preliminary investigations suggest an account of **writing ability** as **a sense of textual space on the part of the writer**—a tacit awareness on the part of the writer that a stage is being set and that, like the playwright, the composer probably will not be present when the audience attends. Writing ability in these terms may be thought of as **textual cognition.**

In many respects, the demands of textual cognition are analogous to those implicit in the photographer's task. If, as a photographer, I choose to show you the constellation Orion, for example, I fail by showing you the entire Milky Way. I also miss by showing you only two stars from the constellation itself. I succeed only when I frame the relevant stars, and I succeed precisely because I have attended to COM-POSITION, allowing by constraining you to form a meaningful image. I have shown you Orion, largely because you can see Orion.

We concluded this initial study by hypothesizing three possible kinds of writer-reader mismatch, or distortions of textual space:

1. **Simple misconstraint:** Reader is either misled or misinterprets altogether.
2. **Impaction:** Reader finds text abstruse, e.g., the tax code to the average taxpayer. Kintsch's (1974) **high propositional density texts** for the average reader are an example.
3. **Rarefaction:** Reader requires further elaboration, for example, the spouse who stumbles upon a cryptic, unsigned note (*It was lovely, darling—as usual. Love, J.*) on the closet floor. Kintsch's (1974) **texts that say too little about too many things,** compared to texts that say much about a few things, are an example.

The difference between impactions and rarefactions is quite subtle. They are best understood in comparison to each other. With rarefactions, the reader mainly needs more detail to be sure of the main idea; with impactions, the reader needs the main idea to cope with and organize all the details. BECAUSE THEY ARE CATEGORIES OF USE OR INTERACTION BETWEEN WRITER AND READER, THESE CLASSIFICATIONS CANNOT BE APPLIED CATEGORICALLY TO PARTICULAR TEXTS WITHOUT CONSIDERING THE CONTEXT OF USE. Hence, the tax code will undoubtedly be impacted and abstruse for the general taxpayer, though certain points may well be ambiguous to a tax attorney. By the same token, the note on the closet floor may be entirely abstruse and obscure to disinterested party (e.g., a carpenter hired to fix the closet door) but is intolerably ambiguous to the spouse, who already knows the main idea.

These three basic distortions of communication manifest themselves at five levels of discourse: the **graphic, syntactic, lexical, textual,** and **contextual.** For example, the legibility or typography of any text involves figure-ground relations, meaning what is left UNMARKED, as well as the spaces between words, strokes, and letters, is as important as those strokes made. The following examples of illegible scripts exhibit each of the three basic distortions:

I.A. **graphic misconstraint:** *now here* for "nowhere"
I.B. **graphic impaction:** *[scrawl]*
I.C. **graphic rarefaction:** N O   W   H E R E

In I.A., the inappropriate spacing renders the wrong word. In I.B., too much black and not enough white renders an opaque scrawl. And without more context, the strungout   N O   W   H E R E   renders an ambiguous word.

Although the traditional definition of the sentence as a unit expressing a complete thought is rough hewn to say the least, there is a sense of completeness or closure about the subject-predicate unit known intuitively to any fluent writer or reader. This aspect of textual space may also be distorted in the three basic ways:

II.A. **Syntactic misconstraint:** the presence of cues that generate syntactic predictions that cannot be confirmed on syntactic grounds alone. A confusion of homonyms (e.g., *your* and *you're; their there,* and *they're*) is one example: *your* signals a noun (e.g., *your **house***) or an adjective plus a noun (e.g., *your **lavish house***) to follow; whereas *you're* signals a verbal (e.g., *you're **going***), a noun phrase (e.g., *you're a **magician***), or an adjective (e.g., *you're **astonishing***) to follow.
II.B. **Syntactic impaction:** high syntactic density resulting from clustering or overembedding, and preventing readers from predicting. Consider: *In sum, we are dealing with a set of schemata whose dual nature stems from the fact that, whereas their structuring presupposes formal reasoning,*

they also derive from the most general characteristics of the structures from which the same formal thought arises [Inhelder & Piaget, 1958, p.106] for nonpsychologists.

II.C. **Syntactic rarefaction:** the lack of relevant syntactic unit(s) resulting in readers' inabilities to confrim predictions, as in *When I stopped pandering temporarily* with no further context.

Words have meaning in use and potential use. Words have meaning to the extent that readers and writers can combine and relate them. Lexical distortions of textual space are also possible:

III.A. **Lexical misconstraint:** the wrong word. Consider the following example from a student paper: *The law **against** drinking is for your own safety* (for; controlling; on). The writer is writing for an adult audience, yet assumes an audience of peers exclusively; and neglects or forgets that not everyone is prohibited by law from drinking. The intended readership has been precluded.

III.B. **Lexical impaction:** words that suggest a bewildering number of possible and potential combinations, to the extent that readers are unable to discern regularities and significant differences. Consider: *The cognitive schemata reflected by the grammar are functionally operative in many ways during the encoding process* for nonpsychologists.

III.C. **Lexical rarefaction:** words that are obscure in the sense that their nonsyntactic relations and potential relationships with other words are nebulous, resulting in readers' inabilities to confirm predictions. When Humpty Dumpty proclaims that his words mean "what he chooses them to mean—neither more nor less" and then proceeds to confuse Alice, he does so with several such amiguities and an utter contempt for the context of use: *"I dont't know what you mean by 'glory'"* Alice said. *Humpty Dumpty smiled contemptuously. "Of course you don't—till I tell you. I meant 'there's a nice knock-down-argument for you!" "But 'glory' doesn't mean 'a nice knock-down argument,"* Alice objected. *"When I use a word,"* Humpty Dumpty said, *in a rather scornful tone, "it means just what I choose it to mean—neither more nor less"* [Carroll, 1963, pp. 268–269].

Certain aspects of written form and coherence are properties of the text itself and cannot be explained by reference either to word choice or syntax. One way readers understand a given phrase or sentence is by way of its surrounding phrases and sentences. Thus *Biting sharks can be dangerous* loses its ambiguity when we read more text: *I wouldn't swim at that beach if I were you. We've lost three swimmers to the sharks this season. Biting sharks can be dangerous.* Or: *My swimming instructor used to tell me to keep my mouth shut more often when I swam. He would chuckle and say, "Biting sharks can be dangerous!"* Continuity of text is what Halliday and Hasan (1976) call **cohesion** (discussed before, see p. 65). Communication fails when cohesion of text is absent or weak:

IV.A. **Textual misconstraint:** communication failure due to elements of text beyond the sentence in question that generate aberrant predictions. Consider the following conclusion from a student paper on seatbelts: *I think that the **snowmobilers** will get used to these new laws, and people will see the laws the government put out are for our protection* (motorists; drivers). Up to this point, the writer has been discussing auto seatbelts, and fails to prepare the reader for "smowmobilers," which is anomalous in this context.

IV.B. **Textual impaction:** confusion due to elements of text that resolve reader predictions in more than one way so that readers ascertain neither a definite meaning nor the writer's intended sense. Automatic writing and children's monologs (see Piaget, 1926) are examples. So is the following from E. Sitwell's *Façade: When/Don/Pasquito arrived at the seaside/Where the donkey's head tide brayed, he/Saw the banditto Joe in a black cape/Whose slack shape waved like the sea—Thetis wrote a treatise noting wheat is silver like the/sea; the lovely cheat is sweet as foam; Erotis/ notices that she/Will/Steal/The/Wheat-King's luggage, like Babel/Before the League of Nations grew . . .* [from Sitwell, 1951].

IV.C. **Textual rarefaction:** ambiguity resulting when readers can find no resolution in surrounding text for presuppositions set up elsewhere in the text. Lack of pronoun-antecedent agreement is often an example: *It rained day and night for two weeks. The basement flooded and everything was under water. **It** spoilt all our calculations* [from Halliday & Hasan, 1976, pp. 52–53 q.v.]

Some aspects of written communication cannot be explained by reference to the text at all. Sarcasm, irony, and understatment are good examples of the importance of contextual information. Context refers to general elements of setting for the text proper, elements that strictly speaking, are not a part of the text. They include format, mode, and title.

Bransford and Johnson (1973) offer some empirical evidence regarding semantic aspects of the context of writing. They presented subjects with the following paragraph accompanied by no contextual information, with partial contextual information, and with appropriate contextual information:

If the balloons popped, the sound wouldn't be able to carry since everything would be too far away from the correct floor. A closed window would also prevent the sound from carrying, since most buildings tend to be well-insulated. Since the whole operation depends on a steady flow of electricity, a break in the middle of the wires would also cause problems. Of course, the fellow could shout, but the human voice is not loud enough to carry that far. An additional problem is that a string could break on the instrument. Then there could be no accompaniment to the message. It is clear that the best situation would involve less distance. Then there would be fewer problems. With face to face contact, the least number of things could go wrong [Bransford & Johnson, 1973, pp. 392–393].

Not surprisingly, Bransford and Johnson found a significant relationship between the comprehensibility of this passage and information in the context (in this case a cartoon), not the text itself.

Communication problems involving the context of writing include:

V.A. **Contextual misconstraint:** misleading context; general elements of the text's setting that generate aberrant predictions. A classic example is the reaction of naive readers to Swift's "A Modest Proposal." Readers often assume that, BECAUSE IT IS IN ESSAY FORM, the proposal is serious, and the contents of the essay are meant literally.

V.B. **Contextual impaction:** opaqueness due to too much implicit context and not enough explicit text. Abstract definitions for nonspecialists and mathematical equations for nonmathematicians are examples. Readers are easily confused by erudite definitions in any field of expertise that is obscure or new to them. The following may make sense to some phenomenologists, but it will baffle the general reader: *Epoché is the suspension of belief in the ontological characteristics of experienced objects* [from Schutz, 1970, p.318]. Most readers will require a lot less implicit context and a lot more explicit text to understand this definition.

V.C. **Contextual rarefaction:** ambiguity due to lack of necessary semantic cues beyond the text in question. Writing is incomprehensible when readers lack necessary contextual information. Examples are the identity of the mysterious "W.H." from Shakespeare's sonnets, as well as Egyptian hieroglyphics to Egyptologists before discovery of the Rosetta stone, in 1799.

All of these distortion types are summarized in the tyology of Table 2.3.

CONCLUDING COMMENTS

Prior to this pilot study, those of us involved in the Trent Valley Centre Project assumed that writing assessment involved examination of texts for strengths and weaknesses in the text. It did not concern us at first that we were acting simultaneously as readers and assessors, failing, in effect, to note that the meaning or worth of any text results as much from the act of reading as from the text that is read (Iser, 1978; Rothkopf, 1972). Finding this assumption inadequate and indefensible, we shifted ground and speculated that many of the salient features of written communication lie not in the text per se and not in the interaction of reader and text, but rather in the interaction between writer and reader by way of the text. Hence, we

TABLE 2.3

Typology of Textual Space Distortions

Distortion Type

Level of Analysis	A. SIMPLE MISCONSTRAINT	B. IMPACTION	C. RAREFACTION
I. GRAPHIC	I.A. *GRAPHIC MISCONSTRAINT* [handwritten] *for nowhere*	I.B. *GRAPHIC IMPACTION* [handwritten]	I.C. *GRAPHIC RAREFACTION* *n o w h e r e*
II. SYNTACTIC	II.A. *SYNTACTIC MISCONSTRAINT* *Your ___ going to get where your ___ with a seatbelt on (still)(going).*	II.B. *SYNTACTIC IMPACTION* *This is the preacher all shaven and shorn that married the man all tattered and torn that kissed . . . in the house that Jack built.*	II.C. *SYNTACTIC RAREFACTION* *when I stopped pandering temporarily*
III. LEXICAL	III.A. *LEXICAL MISCONSTRAINT* *[The law {on controlling}{for} drinking is for your own safety (against)] written to adults*	III.B. *LEXICAL IMPACTION* *DECK BOARD BOLT BOND CONTIGUITY TESTER INNOVATION* *[newspaper headline]*	III.C. *LEXICAL RAREFACTION* *[any key word whose meaning a reader must check to be sure of the meaning of the text]*
IV. TEXTUAL	IV.A. *TEXTUAL MISCONSTRAINT* Paragraph on seatbelts ends: *. . . I think that this new laws will get used to these new laws, and people will see the laws the government put out are for our protection (snow-mobilers).*	IV.B. *TEXTUAL IMPACTION* *When/Don/Pasquito arrived at the seaside/where the donkey's hide tide brayed, he/Saw the banditto Joe in a black cape/Whose slack shape waved like the sea . . . .*	IV.C. *TEXTUAL RAREFACTION* *When a pupil hands in a theme to the instructor, he is not always satisfied with it.*
V. CONTEXTUAL	V.A. *CONTEXTUAL MISCONSTRAINT* Swift's "A Modest Proposal" to naive readers	V.B. *CONTEXTUAL IMPACTION* *For most people: Epoché is the suspension of belief in the ontological characteristics of experienced objects* (Schutz, 1970, p. 318) with no further discussion	V.C. *CONTEXTUAL RAREFACTION* the mysterious *W. H.* of Shakespeare's sonnets

began to consider the text less as a focal object of analysis in its own right and more as a subsidiary element in a communicative, interactional process. As a consequence of this shift, our object of analysis became the process of interaction itself. This analysis yielded the classification scheme outlined in this chapter.

In the patterns that emerge from this classification, we may speculate on three levels of functional relations characterizing the written language: (*a*) the graphic relations of LEGIBILITY; (*b*) the syntactic and lexical relations of READABILITY; and (*c*) the textual and contextual relations of LUCIDITY. Clearly, writing works NOT in strokes, words, sentences, etc., but rather in relations set up among strokes, words, sentences, etc. Legibility, readability, and lucidity are less aspects of the text per se, and more the result of meaningful match or convergence between writer and reader by way of a text. As Halliday and Hasan (1976) note, "A text does not CONSIST OF sentences; it is REALIZED BY, or encoded in, sentences. If we understand it in this way, we shall not expect to find the same STRUCTURAL integration among the parts of a text as we find among the parts of a sentence or clause [p.2]. "Putting it another way," Saussure noted long ago, "*language is a form and not a substance.* This truth could not be overstressed, for all the mistakes in our terminology, all our incorrect ways of naming things that pertain to language, stem from the involuntary supposition that the linguistic phenomenon must have substance [1959,p. 122]".

The logic or structure of the written language seems missed, then, if the text itself is taken as the fundamental object of analysis or if text meaning is assessed apart from the context of its use. The fundamental object of written discourse analysis is not the text, but that system of rules that makes orthographic expression possible. The parameters of this system are wholly circumscribed by the arbitrary and conventional relations that obtain in the speech community of the written language. Rules governing orthographic text construction—writer expression—are broadly defined by what is acceptable to fluent, relevant readers.

When written communication fails, readers find the text misleading, turgid, or ambiguous. Aware of text rather than meaning, these readers are in effect excluded. By contrast, when written communication occurs, readers find the text legible, readable, and lucid—in short, "transparent": Unaware of text as text, they are "absorbed" into the world of its meaning. They dwell in the sphere of its meaning. Hence, nonreaders only SEE words which readers READ, that is, transform into meaning. This transformation of text points to a confluence of reader-writer consciousness—in effect underscoring their participation in a shared space. This space is not physical, but is nonetheless quite real as the possibility of exclusion clearly shows. It is semantic, textual space—phenomenal relations occasioned by writer expression and reader comprehension.

The systemic character of reader-writer discrepancies suggests the structure of this textual space. This structure is the sum total of functional relations which constitute and define the written language system. Writer expression is meaningful to the extent that it takes place against the background of these possibilities; reader comprehension is possible to the extent that the reader interprets the text in the context of these possibilities. In effect, this structure forms the necessary but unnoticed (ergo, "transparent") ground on which the figure of meaning is cut by writer and read by reader. Reading and writing both are participation in textual space. The analysis of reader-writer discrepancies presented here should be regarded as speculation about how textual space is organized and can be distorted, hence providing not only evidence of its reality, but also clues to its character.

REFERENCES

Bloomfield, L. *Language.* New York: Holt, 1933.

Boomer, D. S., & Laver, J. D. M. Slips of the tongue. *British Journal of Disorders of Communication,* 1968, *3,* 1–12.

Bormuth, J. Factor validity of cloze tests as measures of reading comprehension ability. *Reading Research Quarterly,* 1969, *4,* 358–365.

Bransford, J., & Johnson, M. Considerations of some problems of comprehension. In W. G. Chase (Ed.), *Visual information processing.* New York: Academic Press, 1973.

Carroll, L. *The annotated Alice.* Cleveland: World, 1963.

Chomsky, N. *Language and mind.* 2nd ed. New York: Harcourt Brace Jovanovich,1972.

Diederich, P., French, J., & Carlton, S. *Factors in judgements of writing ability. Educational testing service research bulletin no. 6.* Princeton: College Entrance Examination Board, 1961.

Ervin-Tripp, S. Imitation and structural change in children's language. In E. H. Lenneberg (Ed.), *New directions in the study of language.* Cambridge: MIT Press, 1964.

Frued, S. *The psychopathology of everyday life* Translated by Alan Tyson. New York:Norton, 1965.

Fromkin, V. (Ed.) *Speech errors as linguistic evidence.* The Hague: Mouton, 1973.

Gardner, H. *The shattered mind.* New York: Vintage, 1974.

Garrett, M. F. The analysis of sentence production. In G. H. Bower (Ed.), *The psychology of learning and motivation* (Vol. 9). New York: Academic Press, 1975. Pp. 133–177.

Goodman, K. S. Reading: A linguistic study of cues and miscues in reading. *Elementary English,* 1965, *42,* 639–643.

Goodman, K. S. *The psycholinguistic nature of the reading process.* Detroit: Wayne State University Press, 1967. (a)

Goodman, K. S. Reading: A psycholinguistic guessing game. *Journal of the Reading Specialist,* 1967, *4,* 126–135. (b)

Goodman, K. S. Analysis of oral reading miscues: Applied psycholinguistics. *Reading Research Quarterly,* 1969, *5,* 9–30.

Goodman, K.S. Decoding from code to what? *Journal of Reading,* 1971, *14,* 445–462.

Goodman, Y. M., & Burke, C. Do they read what they speak? *The Grade Teacher,* 1969, *86,* 144–150.

Gundlach, R. *The composing process and the teaching of writing: A study of an idea and its uses.* Unpublished Ph.D. dissertation. Evanston: Northwestern University, 1977.

Halliday, M. A. K., & Hasan, R. *Cohesion in English.* London: Longman, 1976.

Hansen, L., & Hesse, K. *A pilot reading literacy assessment of Madison Public School students: Final report.* Madison: The Madison, Wisconsin, Public Schools Department of Research and Development, 1974.

Hockett, C. F. *A course in modern linguistics.* New York: Macmillan, 1958.

Inhelder, B., & Piaget, J. *The growth of logical thinking from childhood to adolescence.* Translated by A. Parsons & S. Milgram. London: Routledge and Kegan Paul, 1958.

Iser, W. *The act of reading: A theory of aesthetic response.* Baltimore: Johns Hopkins University Press, 1978.

Kintsch, W. (Ed.). *The representation of meaning in memory.* Hillsdale, NJ: Lawrence Erlbaum, 1974.

Kintsch, W., & Vipond, D. Reading comprehension and readability in educational practice and psychological theory. In L. -G. Nillson (Ed.), *Perspectives in memory research.* Hillsdale, N.J.: Lawrence Erlbaum, 1979. Pp. 329-365.

Langer, S. *Philosophical sketches.* Baltimore: Johns Hopkins, 1962.

Luria, A. The development of writing in the child. *Soviet Psychology,* 1977-78, *16,* 65-114. From [*Problems of Marxist education*]. Moscow: Academy of Community Education, 1929.

Nooteboom, S. G. The tongue slips into patterns. In Nomen, *Leyden studies in linguistics and phonetics.* The Hague: Mouton, 1969. Pp. 114-132.

O'Reilly, R., Schuder, R., Kidder, S., Salter, R., & Hayford, P. *The validation and refinement of measures of literal comprehension in reading for use in policy research and classroom management.* Albany: State Education Department, Bureau of School and Cultural Research, 1977. ERIC document ED 133 363.

Piaget, J. *Psychology of intelligence.* Trans. by M. Piercy and D. E. Berlyne. London: Routledge & Kegan Paul, 1950.

Piaget, J. *Play, dreams, and imitation in childhood.* Trans. by C. Gattegno and F. M. Hodgson. London: Routledge & Kegan Paul, 1951.

Piaget, J. *The origin of intelligence in the child.* Trans. by Margaret Cook. London: Routledge & Kegan Paul, 1953.

Piaget, J. *The construction of reality in the child.* Translated by Margaret Cook. New York: Basic Books, 1954.

Rankin, E. The cloze procedure revisited. In P. L. Nacke (Ed.), *Interaction: Research and practice for college-adult reading.* Twenty-third yearbook of the National Reading Conference. Clemson S. C.: National Reading Conference, 1974.

Remondino, C. A fatorial analysis of the evaluation of scholastic compositions in the mother tongue. *British Journal of Educational Psychology,* 1959, *30,* 242-251.

Rothkopf, E. Z. Structural text features and the control of processes in learning from written materials. In J. B. Carroll & R. O. Freedle (Eds.), *Language comprehension and the acquisition of knowledge.* Washington D.C.: W. H. Winston, 1972.

Sapir, E. *Language: An introduction to the study of speech.* New York: Harcourt Brace, 1921.

Saussure, F. de. [*Course in general linguistics*]. Edited by C. Bally and A. Sechelaye in collaboration with A. Riedlinger. Translated by W. Baskin. New York: The Philosophical Library, 1959.

Schutz, A. *On phenomenology and social relations.* Chicago: The University of Chicago Press, 1970.

Shaughnessy, M. *Errors and expectations: A guide for the teacher of basic writing.* New York: Oxford, 1977.

Sitwell, E. *Façade.* London and New York: Oxford University Press, 1951.

Taylor, W. Cloze procedure: A new tool for measuring readability. *Journalism Quarterly,* 1953, *30,* 414-438.

Chapter 3

The Structure of Textual Space

Martin Nystrand

INTRODUCTION

If I board a train in Lisbon and overhear a conversation, I will not understand it. For me this talk in impenetrable. If I board a train in Chicago or London, however, I may well find myself absorbed in the conversation of others—even if I do not mean to listen. If the conversation intrigues me, only such radical action as change of seat or departure from the train can PREVENT my silent participation in this talk. I cannot understand talk in Lisbon even if I need to, whereas in Chicago I am an unwitting participant even if I mean not to be.

In Lisbon, speakers share a certain space from which I am effectively excluded. Though not material or physical, this space is quite real, as my exclusion from the conversation clearly shows. The space is textual; and to move around and get on in it, one clearly needs to know its rules and distinctive features.

Participation in textual space is characterized for the participants by a "transparency" of language. Chomsky is among those who note the "words we utter but scarcely ever hear [1972, p. 25]." In Chicago I am aware of meaning, not text; in Lisbon I am aware of text, not meaning: Words of a truly foreign tongue are either ambiguous or opaque— depending on how urgently I need to understand them.

Readers know the transparency of the written language. The fluent

WHAT WRITERS KNOW
The Language, Process,
and Structure of Written Discourse

reader "peers through" the printed page, finding only meaning. Hence readers will remember yesterday's news long after forgetting what the front page itself looked like. The nonreader will find the same text a cryptogram at best, so many blotches of ink at worst.

Writers have a peculiar (if any) awareness of the pen they use: They know it where it touches paper, not hand. Mainly writers pour themselves into their work, unaware of pen and paper altogether, concerned only about the sense they must make. Pen and paper are no more part of the writer's consciousness than the text of yesterday's newspaper is part of the reader's awareness, or the words of yesterday's train conversation are part of the listener's memory. Writers can make pen and paper vanish simply by writing.

How are these transformations possible? What is this textual space that language users create and share in their use? What are the unique features of this space? What knowledge does participation require and imply? What are the conditions of participation? And how does the participation of the writer differ from that of the reader and the speaker? What is the underlying structure of textual space?

INTERPRETATION AS THE CONSTRUCTION OF MEANING

Researchers and theorists increasingly agree that the reader is a critical factor in the meaning of any text. The graphic information of any text is insufficient for comprehension (Smith, 1971). Reading—even at the visual level—requires not just simple discrimination among letters; reading requires knowledge of which differences count in English orthography. Comprehension is never a case of the reader passively "absorbing the text's meaning," but rather the active business of bringing knowledge to the text. This knowledge is visual, lexical, syntactical, personal and cultural. Anderson (1978) provides substantial data to corroborate the contention that reader comprehension, and hence text meaning, depends on what knowledge of the world the reader brings to the text. This view should not be taken to mean that any text can mean anything (or that it can mean whatever the reader wants it to mean), but only that psychologically, the reading process requires "finding a schema which will account for [the text] [Rumelhart, 1976]."

Readability research and analysis of what makes certain texts harder than others have progressed precisely towards this view of the reading process, which has not always been obvious to reading researchers. Lorge (1959), Flesch (1949), Dale and Chall (1948), and Spache (1953) all associate reading difficulties with such text variables as sentence length and number of "hard" words. Taylor (1953) and Smith (1971), however, have shown that readability and comprehension are more adequately explained when reading theories account for such reader factors as general inference-making abilities, the reader's expectations for the author's sense, and the reader's knowledge of the world as it relates to the writer's purpose. Readability formulas that predict difficulty of text based on measures of syntax and vocabulary are still useful for predicting readabilities. Yet researchers increasingly agree that the cognitive aspects of readability and text meaning are more important both theoretically (Kintsch & Vipond, 1979; Rothkopf, 1972; Smith, 1971) and pedagogically (Smith, 1973, 1975a) than are the textual features identified by the readability formulas. As Miller and Kintsch (1980) note, "Readability is not a property of a text, to be measured by the right kind of formula"; more than anything, they conclude, "Readability is an interactive relationship between the properties of a text and the reader who is processing it" [p.348]".

Verbal ambiguity is often analyzed to highlight the role of the reader in constructing meaning given the graphic information of the text. Chomsky's (1957) ambiguous sentences are resolved when the reader chooses one deep structure rather than another, or when the reader elaborates context, that is, creates or imagines more text: *The bar was shut* is disambiguated by *The bar was shut because the barman was sick* [Wilks, 1972, p.16]. The role of the reader in text comprehension is analogous to the role of the viewer in figure perception as outlined by Gestalt psychology experiments involving ambiguous designs: Ambiguous figures are resolved according to the viewer's elaboration of the figure's context or ground (cf. Köhler, 1930; Coren & Girgus, 1979).

Clearly, if a given text or design remains materially the same and yet can have multiple meanings, the role of the interpreter (reader or viewer) in actively constructing a meaning is indisputable. This conclusion is supported by Smith's (1971) concept of nonvisual information in the reading process, Rumelhart's (1976) conclusions about the functioning of schemata in reader comprehension, and Greeno's (1976) empirical work on problem solving; it is further corroborated by the wealth of empirical and theoretical work on the construction processes of comprehension surveyed by Clark and Clark (1977, chap. 2). Meaning is not in a text, design, or sign of any kind in the way juice is "in an orange" or air is "in a tire." The character of language is not its propositional content, but rather the "*activity* by which something is made known [Rommetveit, 1974, p. 101]."

INTERPRETIVE ROLE, INTERPRETIVE ACT, AND SIGN

Interpretive acts such as reading, seeing, and hearing, are consequences of interpretive roles such as reader, viewer, and listener. Resolution of such ambiguous sentences as *Biting sharks can be dangerous* or of such ambiguous designs as Gestalt psychology's figures or vase—indeed comprehension of any sort—presupposes the interpreter's adoption of a particular stance toward the sign, a stance such as reader or viewer. This stance, or interpretive role, is fundamental to the interpretive act (reading, viewing), which is entailed by the role adopted.

The distinction here between interpretive role and interpretive act is typically unclear in analyses of ambiguity resolution. These discussions focus on the interpretive act, not the intepretive role. Hence *Biting sharks can be dangerous* is a matter of two readings; faces or vase is a matter of two viewings. The actual mode of interpretation and the particular role of the interpreter are never in question in these analyses.

The fundamental inportance of the interpretive role and its relation to the interpretive act is clear in yet another, different sort of ambiguity—the sort represented by the logo of the International Harvester Corporation.

Verbally we read the initials "I. H."; visually we recognize the image of a farm tractor. The designer of the logo has created an ambiguous sign that can be read as a message or viewed as an image. Like the famous examples of visual ambiguity from Gestalt psychology, interpretation of the logo is an either–or situation: Either one comprehends a message, or one perceives an image; message and image cannot be taken in simultaneously.

The verbal–visual ambiguity of the International Harvester logo differs, however, from the strictly visual ambiguity of figures such as Gestalt psychology's faces–vase. Faces or vase is in either case a matter of visual perception, which is to say, organization of distinctive features within a particular cognitive domain or mode. The ambiguity of the logo involves a fundamental alternation in interpretive role (viewer versus reader) and semiotic function (visual representation versus verbal reference).

Obviously, the logo design remains unchanged regardless of its interpretation. Furthermore, awareness of the ambiguity and possible dual interpretation is not inevitable: Viewers unable to read might see a tractor but will not read "I. H."; readers unfamiliar with tractors might read "I. H." (and even know what the letters stand for) but fail to see a tractor; and nonreaders unfamiliar with tractors could easily find the logo altogether so much undecipherable nonsense—an empty form. Obviously, what it "really means" will not be solved by appealing to the logo itself: The logo's ambiguity clearly shows that its meaning is not in its form. The meaning of any sign is never a property of the sign; rather, the sign bears semantic potential for those who know how to interpret it. I am very close to Rommetveit (1974) here when he warns against "the fallacy of assigning 'propositional content' to semantic potentialities [p. 80]." "What is made known," he writes, "is dependent upon what kind of meta-contract of communication has been tacitly and reciprocally endorsed. It can, accordingly, *not* be assessed by extrapolation from 'the text' *in vacuo* as, for example, some self-contained propositional content . . . [p. 58]."

Comprehension depends not on looking—not even looking hard. Comprehension depends on knowing what to look for. In short, the interpreter's participation, that is, an activity circumscribed by an interpretive role, is critical to finding meaning in any sign. Interpretation is an act constrained and informed by the particular role of the interpreter, a role such as reader, writer, viewer, or speaker. Plainly put, "what you see" (interpretive act) depends on "how you look" (interpretive role).

MEANING AS INTERPRETIVE PROMINENCE

If interpretation entails ordering events in a particular field of possibilities, meaning is the dominance or prominence which results from the ordering. The International Harvester logo acquires **image prominence,** for example, if we interpret it in a visual context: relevant elaborations include weeds, hay, barns, etc. The same design takes on **message prominence,** on the other hand, if we interpret it in a linguistic context: Relevant elaborations include other letters (INTERNATIONAL HARVESTER) collectively referring to the corporation.

The context of any interpretation is a system of functional relations, visual or linguistic in the case of the logo. Such relations are the ground upon which the figure of meaning is cut and hence interpretation made. Indeed the figure–ground relations of perception are the clearest and certainly the most familiar example of such interpretive prominence. There are many others. The language system (Saussure's *la langue*) is the interpretive context for language use (Saussure's *la parole*), which is why comprehension of a language is a prerequisite for accurate transcription. Sociologist Goffman's (1974) **frames** are the interpretive context for social events where, for example, identical remarks can be "cynical" in one setting, "genuine" in another. Cognitive scientists Schank and Abelson's (1977) **scripts** are the interpretive context for such standard episode sequences as ordering food in a restaurant and buying tickets for a concert (for the use of Schank and Abelson's work in writing research, see Black, Wilkes-Gibbs & Gibbs, page 325 this volume). Richards' (1942) **instances of artificiality,** such as rhythm, rhyme, metaphor, are the interpretive context for poems, "isolating the poetic experience from the accidents and irrelevancies of everyday existence [p. 110]." Historian of science Kuhn's

(1962) **paradigms** are the interpretive contexts for scientific events; and personality psychologist Kelly's (1955) **personal constructs** are the interpretive context for individual social experience. Individuals in these many interpretive roles understand the world as they do because their knowledge of it is couched in these interpretive frameworks.

In all cases, interpretation is a matter of locating events in a particular field of possibilities. Like figure–ground relations in perception, awareness of events is focal although awareness of the field itself is subsidiary (cf. Polanyi, 1958). The interpretive context is the NECESSARY BUT UNNOTICED ground upon which the figure of meaning is cut and known.

TWO MODES OF INTERPRETATION: EXPRESSION AND COMPREHENSION

Interpretation is most often associated with language reception—reading and listening. Language production, by contrast, is more often termed expression. There is a sense, however, in which all language use, both "passive" reception and "active" production, is interpretive activity. Like the painter who interprets a landscape or the musician who interprets a musical score, the speaker or writer interprets some idea or aspect of experience by speaking or writing about it. Rodgers (1966) sees paragraphing as just such an interpretive act:

> Paragraph structure is part and parcel of the structure of the discourse as a whole; a given [unit of discourse] becomes a paragraph not by virtue of its structure, but because the writer elects to indent, his indentation functioning, as does all punctuation, as a gloss upon the overall literary process underway at that point. . . . To compose is to create, to indent is to interpret [1966, p. 6].

It may seem strange to consider both language production and reception as analogous. They obviously differ in many fundamental ways, mainly in their respective constraints. Writers and speakers, for example, must express themselves within the constraints of their language; readers and listeners must deal with constraints of written and spoken texts. Nonetheless, as interpretive acts constrained by interpretive roles, expression and comprehension share a common cognitive base. The interpretation of expression involves giving shape to experience, putting it in order, making sense out of a particular concern or topic. The interpretation of comprehension involves bringing meaning to the world or someone else's interpretation of it (as in reading a written text). Always a sign is elaborated in a context of significant relations, a language system. The observation that listeners and readers are "passive" (they don't move much—not more than the eyes) must not obscure the fact that in each case the individual, far from passively accumulating information, brings meaning to the text. Discussions of the passivity of readers and listeners, compared to the activity of speakers and writers, reflect a superficial analysis of behavior and fail to note the underlying interpretive, cognitive aspects of each. In short, writing and reading, speaking and listening are not mirror processes of "encoding" and "decoding [Read, in press]": as with any cognitive activity—ranging from perception to mental operations, each is a way of acting on the world and experience in it. Van Dijk has elaborated in some detail the general cognitive basis that accounts for "macroprocessing" in both language production and comprehension (1977, chapter 5 *et passim*). (See, too, discussion of role of scripts in both comprehension and production: Black, Wilkes-Gibbs, and Gibbs [Chapter 12, this volume]). Expression and comprehension are each constructive acts which, in their unique ways, lend order to the "bloomin' buzzin' confusion" that William James once called the unmediated world. Expression and comprehension are the two basic modes of interpretation and define two distinct types of interpretive acts.

SPHERES OF MEANING AND SEMANTIC SPACE

Interpretation—whether expression or comprehension—is participation in a theatre of meanings where the significance of events comes clear against a background of possibilities. The interpretive act always defines some sphere of meaning or semantic space. Such spheres of meaning include the physical space of cartesian coordinates,[1] the visual space of painted canvases, the personal space of the individual in the world, the world of the theatre, the musical space of orchestral performance, and the textual spaces of spoken and written words. There are as many kinds of semantic space as there are systems of meaning and interpretive roles. Hence we may speak of

SPEAKERS who utter WORDS that LISTENERS render into MESSAGES
PAINTERS who arrange PIGMENTS that VIEWERS render into IMAGES
COMPOSERS who arrange NOTES that PERFORMERS render into MUSIC
WRITERS who compose TEXTS that READERS render into MESSAGES

In each case an interpreter renders meaning by dwelling in a particular sphere of meaning, transforming relevant particulars (words, pigments, notes, texts) into coherent wholes (messages, images, music, messages).

---

[1]As systems of reference, all notions of space are semantic—even the physical space of analytic geometry: three dimensional, cartesian space is after all an abstract construct used to locate physical objects and deal with their relationships. Space as such has no material existence whatever, even if the objects it specifies do. To the extent that we locate or relate events, concepts, and objects in a coherent framework, we are dealing with spatial relations, metaphorically the sphere of meaning in which particulars reside (or are placed).

TEXTUAL SPACE

The structure of any sphere of meaning is defined by its participants, that is, the community of interpreters. Examples include language, whose structure is determined by native speaker acceptability, and science, where there is "no standard higher than the assent of the relevant community [Kuhn, 1962, p.94]." The structure of any semantic space is

$$
\begin{array}{ccccccc}
\text{INTERPRETIVE} & & \text{INTERPRETIVE} & & & \text{INTERPRETIVE} & & \text{INTERPRETIVE} \\
\text{ROLE} & \rightarrow & \text{ACT/expression} & \rightarrow & \text{SIGN} \leftarrow & \text{ACT/comprehension} & \leftarrow & \text{ROLE}
\end{array}
$$

Textual space, for example, is the particular sphere of meaning involving readers and writers:

$$
\text{WRITER} \quad \rightarrow \quad \textit{expression} \quad \rightarrow \quad \text{TEXT} \quad \leftarrow \quad \textit{comprehension} \quad \leftarrow \quad \text{READER}
$$

Like all forms of expression, writing is a way of interpreting experience (Moffett, 1968; Nystrand, 1977; Young, Becker, & Pike, 1970). Like all spheres of meaning, the resulting textual space is phenomenal: A word in use looks different from the way it does to someone who meets it as a totally foreign word. Whether or not *psikhologiya* is more than bad spelling or random lettering depends on the reader's knowledge of romanized Russian. The familiar use of a word renders it transparent. Like the native speaker and the engaged listener, the fluent reader and the involved writer both participate in a sphere of meaning from which nonparticipants are excluded. Something quite striking happens when the material text comes to life in this way: A confluence of consciousness arises between conversants. This confluence is textual space, those phenomenal relations occasioned by writer expression and reader comprehension, and made manifest in the text.

A text is a unit of language in use (Beaugrande, 1980; Halliday & Hasan, 1976; Hartmann, 1963, 1964). As concrete manifestation of an interpretive role, a text is an interpretive or semantic unit. A text is a manifestation of the textual space whose parameters are defined by reader–writer interactions (see Nystrand, "An Analysis of Errors," Chapter 2 this volume).

The inaccessibility of this sphere of meaning to nonreaders underscores this semantic aspect. To speak of texts coming to life is to note that they are meaningful—not mere objects in the world as for nonreaders. They are intention-filled expressions of others in the world. To read is to dwell in textual space, to transcend the material text—seeing through this text to the expression of others (cf. Polanyi & Prosch, 1975).

In short, readers do not see words, they read them; writers do not feel their pens or copy words, they use their pens to write them. This phenomenal aspect of textual space is accomplished by rule-governed reader–writer transformations of particulars—particulars of text (distinctive features or cues) in the case of readers (Smith, 1971); particulars of skillful performance and strokes of pen in the case of writers (Bierwisch, 1972; Eden, 1961; Polanyi & Prosch, 1975).

To sum up, these three features—phenomenal transformation, transparency, and meaningfulness of written text—are the three distinguishing aspects of textual space shared by readers and writers. Fluent writers are no more aware of pen and paper than fluent readers are aware of the words they see. Their awareness of text is as unconscious as the unwitting participation of commuters in conversations overheard to and from work. For those who cannot read and write, however, this literate sphere of meaning that readers and writers share is as impenetrable as speech in a foreign land. Unlike beginning readers or nonreaders who are unable to "get into" the text, fluent readers are aware of the text's meaning, not the text itself. Similarly, fluent writers who have learned to transform pen and paper into means to semantic ends do not copy words, they write them.

This analysis is very different from the view that has been widely held in the English-speaking world (cf. Mathews, 1966) that writing is speech written down. This view is also very different from the long-standing disdain toward writing that Derrida (1976) notes among scholars such as Rousseau, Saussure, Jakobson, Halle, and Levi-Strauss, who see writing as "external," "arbitrary," "instrumental," "auxiliary," "parasitical," "static," "tyrannical," and "mechanistic"—a "pale shadow of the living word."

The analysis in this chapter is consistent, instead, with the contemporary linguistic view that writing is an alternative form of language to speech. For psycholinguist Smith, "the physical aspects of spoken and written language—the phonological and orthographic representations—are alternative surface structure forms of a common underlying language that do not map directly onto each other [1975b, p. 350]." For linguist Alarcos Llorach (1968), writing is a system of signs with a structure analogous to that of linguistic signs: differing mainly in *signans*, speech and writing share the same *signatum*—human experience in general (cited in de Ajuriaguerra and Auzias, 1975). Anthropologist Philips (1975) sees writing as one of many possible modes of communication—the "literate" mode.

CONCLUDING COMMENTS: WRITING VERSUS SPEECH

As a language system, writing differs from speech in several fundamental ways. These differences are due mainly to the context and character of the composing process. Unlike speech, writing is private, solitary activity, whose major purpose is to communicate with someone not immediately present. This process is comparatively laborious and tedious, and must be sustained without benefit of a conversant over a period of time. Writing requires a fine prehension of hand and a degree of motor control unlike anything involved in speech (de Ajuriaguerra & Auzias, 1975). By contrast, talk is a public activity involving continuous give and take between conversants who can ask questions, nod, and otherwise indicate their understanding (or lack of it) and sustain each other's expression. Written texts are indelible, durable, and transportable (Cohen, 1958), compared to spoken utterances, which are ephemeral.

Talk involves constant feedback from conversants; writing involves either delayed feedback or, often, no feedback. Unlike writing, the feedback involved in talk is continuous for everyone who is neither deaf nor aphasic from time of birth. Even in literate environments, written language does not so fully saturate the social environment as does the spoken language. For all these reasons, many have concluded that writing is harder to learn than talk: The feedback required to learn, plus the motor skills required to master the written language system, is necessarily less available to the learner. Rarely does a child learn to write before age 6 (de Ajuriaguerra & Auzias, 1975).

One gets the feeling, however, that all of these psychological and psycholinguistic factors are easily overcome by powerful social and cultural factors—namely, the importance of the world of written language as a central theatre of meanings in the individual child's life and social environment. That is, writing may after all be no harder to learn than any other language system if the learner has important reasons to learn it. On the other hand, the world of written textual space may forever remain foreign and impenetrable for other children who find no important reasons to venture into it. See Gundlach (Chapter 6, p. 129 of this volume) for further discussion of this point; see Britton's case study (Chapter 7, p. 149 of this volume) for the example of a child who entered quite readily into the world of written textual space before the age of 4.

REFERENCES

Ajuriaguerra, J. de, & Auzias, M. Preconditions for the development of writing in the child. In E. H. Lenneberg and E. Lenneberg (Eds.), *Foundations of language development: A multidisciplinary approach* (Vol. 2). New York: Academic Press, 1975, Pp. 311–328.

Alarcos Llorach, E. Les représentations graphique du langage. In *Le langage*. Paris: Éditions Gallimard, 1968.

Anderson, R. Schema-directed processes in language comprehension. In A. Lesgold *et al.* (Eds.), *Cognitive psychology and instruction*. New York: Plenum, 1978.

Beaugrande, R. de. *Text, discourse, and process: Toward a multidisciplinary science of texts.* Norwood, N.J.: Ablex, 1980.

Bierwisch, M. Schriststrunktur and Phonologie. *Probleme und Ergebnisse der Psychologie*, 1972, 43, 21–44.

Chomsky, N. *Syntactic structures.* The Hague: Mouton, 1957.

Chomsky, N. *Language and mind.* 2nd ed. New York: Harcourt Brace Jovanovich, 1972.

Clark, H., & Clark, E. *Psychology and language: An introduction to psycholinguistics.* New York: Harcourt Brace Jovanovich, 1977.

Cohen, M. *La grande invention de l'écriture et son évolution*. Paris: Imprimerie Nationale, 1958.

Coren, S., & Girgus, J. *Seeing is deceiving*. Hillsdale, N.J.: Lawrence Erlbaum, 1979.

Dale, E., & Chall, J. A formula for predicting readability: Instructions. *Educational Research Bulletin*, 1948, 27, 37–47.

Derrida, J. *Of grammatology*. Translated by G.C. Spivak. Baltimore: Johns Hopkins University Press, 1976.

Eden, M. On the formalization of handwriting. In R. Jakobson (Ed.), *Structure of language in its mathematical aspect*. Providence: American Mathematics Society, 1961.

Flesch, R. *The art of readable writing*. New York: Harper, 1949.

Goffman, E. *Frame analysis*. Cambridge: Harvard University Press, 1974.

Greeno, J. J. Cognitive objectives of instruction: Theory of knowledge for solving problems and answering questions. In D. Klahr (Ed.), *Cognition and instruction*. Hillsdale, N.J.: Lawrence Erlbaum, 1976.

Halliday, M. A. K., & Hasan, R. *Cohesion in English*. London: Longman, 1976.

Hartmann, P. *Theorie der Sprachwissenschaft*. Assen: van Gorcum, 1963.

Hartmann, P. Text, Texte, Klassen von Texten. *Bogawus*, 1964, 2, 15–25.

Kelly, G. A. *The psychology of personal constructs*. 2 vols. New York: Norton, 1955.

Kintsch, W., & Vipond, D. Reading comprehension and readability in educational practice and psychological theory. In L. Nilsson (Ed.), *Perspectives on memory research*. Hillsdale, N.J.: Lawrence Erlbaum, 1979.

Köhler, W. La perception humaine. *Journal de Psychologie Normale et Pathologique*, 1930, 27, 5–30.

Kuhn, T. S. *The structure of scientific revolutions*. Chicago: University of Chicago Press, 1962.

Lorge, R. *The Lorge formula for estimating difficulty of reading materials*. New York: Bureau of Publications, Teachers College, Columbia University, 1959.

Mathews, M. M. *Teaching to read: Historically considered*. Chicago: University of Chicago Press, 1966.

Miller, J., & Kintsch, W. Readability and recall of short prose passages: A theoretical analysis. *Journal of Experimental Psychology: Human Learning and Memory*, 1980, 6(4), 335–354.

Moffett, J. *Teaching the universe of discourse*. Boston: Houghton Mifflin, 1968.

Nystrand, M. *Language as a Way of Knowing*. Toronto: Ontario Institute for Studies in Education, 1977.

Philips, S. Literacy as a mode of communication on the Warm Spring Indian Reservation. In E. H. Lenneberg & E. Lenneberg (Eds.), *Foundations of language development: A multidisciplinary approach* (Vol. 2). New York: Academic Press, 1975. Pp. 367–382.

Polanyi, M. *Personal knowledge*. London: Routledge & Kegan Paul, 1958.

Polanyi, M., & Prosch, H. *Meaning*. Chicago: University of Chicago Press, 1975.

Read, C. Writing is not the inverse of reading for young children. In C. Frederiksen, M. Whiteman, & J. Dominic (Eds.), *Writing: The nature, development, and teaching of written communication*. Hillsdale, N.J.: Lawrence Erlbaum, in press.

Richards, I. A. *Principles of literary criticism*. New York: Harcourt Brace, 1942.

Rodgers, P. A discourse-centered rhetoric of the paragraph. *College Composition and Communication*, 1966, 17, 2–11.

Rommetveit, R. *On message structure*. New York: Wiley, 1974.

Rothkopf, E. Z. Structural test features and the control of processes in learning from written materials. In J. B. Carroll & R. O. Freedle (Eds.), *Language comprehension and the acquisition of knowledge*. Washington, D.C.: W. H. Winston, 1972.

Rumelhart, D. E. Understanding and summarizing brief stories. In D. LaBerge and S. J. Samuels (Eds.), *Basic processes in reading: Perception and comprehension*. Hillsdale, N.J.: Lawrence Erlbaum, 1976.

Schank, R. & Abelson, R. *Scripts, plans, goals, and understanding: An inquiry into human knowledge structures*. Hillsdale, N.J.: Lawrence Erlbaum, 1977.

Smith, F. *Understanding reading: A psycholinguistic analysis of reading and learning to read*. New York: Holt, Rinehart, and Winston, 1971.

Smith, F. (Ed.). *Psycholinguistics and reading*. New York: Holt, Rinehart, and Winston, 1973.

Smith, F. *Comprehension and learning: A conceptual framework for teachers*. New York: Holt, Rinehart, and Winston, 1975. (a)

Smith, F. The relation between spoken and written language. In E. H. Lenneberg & E. Lenneberg (Eds.), *Foundations of language development: A multidisciplinary approach* (Vol. 2). New York: Academic Press, 1975. Pp. 347–360. (b)

Spache, G. A new readability formula for primary-grade reading materials. *Elementary School Journal*, 1953, *53*, 410–413.

Taylor, W. Cloze procedure: A new tool for measuring readability. *Journalism Quarterly, 1953, 30*, 414–438.

van Dijk, T. *Text and context: Explorations in the semantics and pragmatics of discourse*. London: Longman, 1977.

Wilks, Y. *Grammar, meaning and the machine analysis of language*. London: Routledge & Kegan Paul, 1972.

Young, R., Becker, A., and Pike, K. *Rhetoric: Discovery and change*. New York: Harcourt, Brace and World, 1970.

Chapter **4**

Defining Thematic Progressions and Their Relationship To Reader Comprehension

Barbara S. Glatt

INTRODUCTION

Any given utterance typically communicates on several different levels at once. The most general level is the extent of world knowledge shared by conversants—relevant critical beliefs, assumptions, experiences, and so on, that neither party needs to explain but are nonetheless essential to their mutual understandings. Another, less general level is the context of the immediate moment—the shared perceptions of the environment or circumstance. Both of these contexts are situational, in effect essential things unsaid that give meaning to words actually said. In addition to situational context, communication obviously depends on the linguistic context, including previous text plus the manner in which any particular statement is made.

Fundamental to the balance between text and context at all these levels is a special agreement, namely the **given–new contract**—an implicit agreement between conversants pledging the speaker "(a) to use given information to refer to information she thinks the listener can uniquely identify from what he already knows and (b) to use new information to refer to information she believes to be true but is not already known to the listener [Clark & Clark, 1977, p. 92]."

Clearly, then, communication is more than just words stated. It depends on (*a*) words and ideas not actually uttered (but shared nonetheless); (*b*)

WHAT WRITERS KNOW
The Language, Process,
and Structure of Written Discourse

anything previously said (the immediate linguistic context) as well as the manner in which the words are stated; and, most fundamental of all, (c) the tacit agreement of conversants to abide by and operate according to the terms of the given–new contract. Hence, the following levels of context(uality): the extralinguistic, the linguistic, and the contractual.

The given–new contract encompasses these three levels of context. Much of the research on this agreement between conversants has focused on the contractual and extralinguistic contexts (cf. Clark & Clark, 1977). Haviland and Clark (1974) are among those who have studied the linguistic context for marking information and its relationship to language processing. They propose that when speaker and listener expectations match with respect to the identification of given and new information, communication occurs most expeditiously. They investigate many syntactic devices used in English for explicitly marking information types.

This chapter will examine yet another linguistic structure used for conveying given and new information: **thematic progression.** Thematic progression is the principle that old information ought to precede new information in sentences. It is an old prescriptive rule of English usage that will be (a) defined here according to the functional approach to language developed by the Prague Linguists (1953); and (b) related to the research on the given–new contract to assess its validity with respect to facilitating comprehension. Though this principle is not new, its relationship to the given–new contract has not been considered. Haviland and Clark (1974) studied the language of SPEAKERS and its effects on listeners; the use of thematic progressions in WRITING and its subsequent effects on reader comprehension will be the focus here.

In particular, this chapter seeks to: (a) relate the given–new research to thematic progressions; (b) consider if there is an interaction (as Haviland & Clark suggest) between processing time and various markings of given and new information via thematic progressions; and (c) examine the implications of this relationship for writing. It is hoped that a closer examination of how WRITERS can mark given and new information for reader identification may lead to a better understanding of the factors that contribute to the smooth exchange of written information.

GIVEN AND NEW

Given–New Contract

The research on the given–new contract has been mainly developed by Haviland and Clark (1974, 1977). They state the contract as an implicit agreement between two people whereby each identifies information that is known and unknown. The more accurately the speaker (writer) judges or evaluates the previous knowledge of his listener (audience), the more precisely he can express the terms of his contract with respect to given and new expectations.

When writer and reader expectations match, communication occurs more easily than in the case when there is a mismatch. The success of the given–new contract depends on this matching. For example, a writer might assume a certain idea to be already known by the reader and hence mark it as given information. If, in fact, this idea matches information already in the memory of the reader, a match occurs. Haviland and Clark (1974) used timed recognition and recall tasks to show that when there is a match between speaker and listener expectations—when given information is, in fact, represented in the memory structure of the listener—that successful communication takes less time, than when there is a mismatch, which results in longer processing time and may result in a communication breakdown altogether.

Linguistic Marking of Given and New Information

There are many English linguistic structures used for marking given and new information (cf. Halliday, 1967). Some of them include:

1. **Cleft constructions** mark new information at the beginning of the sentence by the introductory phrase *it is* , and place given information at the end. For example, *It was Frank's fear of snakes that Maria realized.*
2. **Pseudo-cleft constructions** use inversion and WH-words to mark given information at the beginning and new information at the end of the sentence. For example, *What Maria realized was that Frank fears snakes.*
3. **Passive voice** uses inverted sentence order to mark new information in the beginning and given information at the end. For example, *That Frank fears snakes was realized by Maria.*
4. **Anaphore** marks given information by repeated reference—a pronym that refers back to its antecedent. For example, *Maria realized that Frank fears snakes when she went to the farm with him.*

Given–New Strategy

Haviland and Clark (1974) distinguish the given–new contract from the **given–new strategy:** the contract refers to a theory of language organization; and the strategy represents a method for language comprehension. According to the strategy, the reader must identify and process the given and new information in sentences. Comprehension proceeds in a manner such that a reader searches memory for representations of the designated given information, and then integrates or adds on new information into the already existing 'given' memory representation.

Simply stated, the strategy proceeds as follows: Readers first identify the given information, next they match it to information already in memory, and then they integrate the new information into memory. The readers must be able to find or construct the appropriate referent in memory in order to integrate the new with the old. Any additional time in identifying the given information in the linguistic context, slows down the process. If the intended referent is clear, the remaining content of the sentence can be processed (more) easily. Unacceptability, ambiguity, awkwardness, and implicature (cf. Grice, 1967) are but a few of the dependent linguistic variables which can affect the speed and success of comprehending the information, and may, in fact, cause a breach in the reader's interpretation of the text according to the terms of the given–new contract.

Metaphorically, the information that the reader identifies as given is the address of the place' in memory—the node—where the information should be stored. For example, consider these two statements:

(1)   *Something is irritating Cara's skin.*
(2)   *It is those peanuts which are bothering her.*

If the writer is adhering to the given–new contract, the given information of the second sentence (x is bothering Cara) is the intended address or node where the message should go, and the new information (x = those peanuts) is the message itself. The reader must "divide the sentence into given and new information, search memory for a unique antecedent that matches the given information, and integrate the new information by replacing X by the appropriate index [peanuts] in the antecedent [Clark & Clark, 1977, p. 96]."

For the strategy to work efficiently, the intended given information must match information already available in the reader's memory, as a result of previous extralinguistic or linguistic cues. If the information has never been presented or has been presented too long ago (there are countless other miscommunication possibilities), then integration by the given–new strategy ought to become more difficult (Clark & Clark, 1977, p.96). Thus, the success of the strategy depends on whether the information that the writer assumes to be given is, in fact, already represented in the reader's memory; if it is, a match occurs.

Maintenance of the given–new contract, then, relies on the accuracy of assumptions made by the writer about the extent of the reader's previous knowledge of the subject matter. In particular, POOR JUDGMENTS AND/OR CONFUSED LINGUISTIC REPRESENTATIONS OF ANTECEDENTS result in a breach of the given–new contract and thus, a breakdown in communication between writer and reader. The writer assumes the burden of responsibility for the given–new contract; his accuracy of judgment regarding shared (and unshared) previous extralinguistic knowledge and, an appropriate representation via the linguistic context are important considerations. Shared knowledge can be explicitly represented syntactically by antecedence using any of the devices discussed earlier. If the referent cannot be determined by the reader, then judgments of givenness and newness are impaired.

Antecedence

Antecedence is at the heart of the given–new contract (Haviland & Clark, 1977, p. 4). This is true because the reader must be able to identify one, and only one unique antecedent (and that is the intended antecedent) in order for the rest of the text to be processed. It must be remembered that according to the strategy, the reader must first accurately identify the intended given information; the writer must mark this information by any linguistic device which conveys antecedence or given information. Then the rest of the text can be processed according to the terms of the given–new agreement. Sentences can, however, have more than one given referent and a complex internal given–new structure (cf. Haviland & Clark, 1977).

Haviland and Clark (1974) test the linguistic structures of anaphore, relative clauses, adverbials, and definite articles for explicitly marking information and their subsequent effects on reader comprehension. Regarding antecedence, Haviland and Clark distinguish two types: direct and indirect. The following, each using anaphoric constructions, are examples:

1. **Direct antecedence:** *I bought a canary at the pet shop. The canary sang beautifully.* In this sentence pair, anaphora consists of a repeated noun phrase (*canary*).
2. **Indirect antecedence:** *I bought a canary at the pet shop. The bird sang beautifully.* In this sentence pair, anaphora consists of a general category reference (*bird*) and a special case (*canary*), the latter in subordinate relationship to the former.

The direct antecedent represents an explicitly mentioned reference (repeated noun phrase), or given information; in indirect antecedence the reference is not repeated explicitly, as in 2. According to the terms of the given–new strategy, direct antecedents should facilitate the processing of target sentences better than indirect antecedents (Haviland & Clark, 1974, p. 514).

However, in effect, what Haviland and Clark set out to measure seems to be less a function of the given–new strategy per se, and more a product of repeated reference. Obviously, the repetition of the word *canary* denotes given information from the same class. Using *bird* and *canary* also represents repeated reference. However, the antecedent *bird* is in a superordinate relationship to the target referent, *canary*, in sentence pair 2. Canaries are a subset of the more general classification of birds.

Research on memory (e.g., Collins & Loftus, 1975; Quillian, 1968) has shown that concepts are generally stored in memory hierarchically; words or attributes associated with the same class of terms or concept are stored at the same general node—the highest applicable node. For example, the most general or uppermost level of a class of items appears at the top of the hierarchy and stems down to include more specific characteristics:

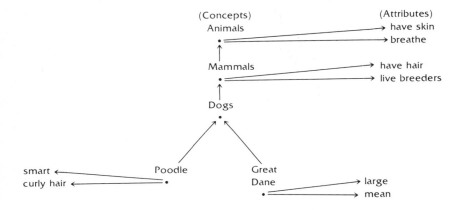

FIGURE 4.1. Concept pointers point UP to superordinate concepts and ACROSS to attribute notes.

Research on antecedence (e.g., Morles, 1977) has demonstrated that to travel anywhere within the hierarchy—from one node to another—INCREASES processing time as a function of hierarchical distance between concept nodes. Hypothetically, then, sentences that repeatedly activate the same referent or node, for example, *Great Dane*, should require less processing time, than those referents that are stored in memory at different concept levels, for example, activating simultaneously *Great Dane* and *dogs*.

The experimental evidence on anaphoric antecedence (mentioned earlier) by Haviland and Clark (1974) is an example of this measure of processing time with respect to hierarchical distance. Since *birds* and *canaries* are stored at two different concept nodes in the memory structure, processing time should increase as a function of hierarchical distance.

Whether this comparison between direct antecedence (repeated noun phrases) and indirect antecedence (semantically related noun phrases) also interacts with processing time as a function of the differing types of marking of given and new information as Haviland and Clark suggest, is questionable. Their research does not supply enough evidence to warrant this conclusion.

THE PRINCIPLE OF THEMATIC PROGRESSION

The principle of **thematic progression** (**TP**) states that given information ought to precede new information within sentences. This principle is not new and can be found in many rhetorics (e.g., Quintillian) and under various names including 'theme before rheme,' 'functional sentence perspective,' 'topic precedes comment,' 'end focus,' and others. The study of TP, as defined in this chapter, falls under the rubric of theme dynamics: descriptions of patterns of thematic cohesion within and between sentences. Theme dynamics is one of many approaches to text and intersentence grammars. "In other words, theme dynamics charts the patterns by which themes recur in a text and by which they run through a text, weaving their way from clause to clause and from sentence to sentence [Enkvist, 1973, 116]."

My purpose here is to consider some of these patterns: linear and run-through theme progressions, and interrupted linear and interrupted run-through progressions (to be defined later). The principle of TP incorporates four separate but highly related terms: theme, rheme, given, and new. Though many will agree that these terms are distinct, their precise definitions differ amongst researchers (cf. Enkvist, 1973; Firbas, 1964; Palkova & Palek, 1977).

Theme, Rheme, Given, and New

Theme is typically associated with the subject or what is being talked about. It is syntactically limited to initial surface structure subjects or noun phrases. The term **progression** refers to the referential relation of the thematic information within or between sentences. Consider:

(3) *Becky likes tropical fish.*
(4) *She visits the aquarium once a week.*

The thematic information of the first sentence (*Becky*) is coreferenced in the second sentence (*she*); in both, the thematic information remains in the initial sentence position. By contrast, consider:

(5) *Bud helped Sandra into the car.*
(6) *She has a severe physical handicap.*

The thematic information of the first sentence (*Bud*) differs from that of the second sentence (*She*); the thematic information of the second sentence is coreferenced to the rhematic information of the first sentence, and hence changes positionally from the first sentence to the second.

As theme refers to what is being talked about, **rheme** refers to what is being said about it. Generally, it is linguistically represented by the predicate.

Given information, on the other hand, theoretically refers to information that can be recovered (cf. Halliday, 1967) from the previous linguistic or extralinguistic context. However, the focus here is limited solely to linguistic resources available for marking this information (just as cohesive devices represent linguistic resources available for showing coherence (see Halliday & Hasan, 1976). In this way, anaphores and direct substitutes are syntactic devices used to coreference and therefore, by definition, convey given information: They enable one word or phrase to be replaced for another without changing the essential meaning of the sentence(s). The terms given and old are used interchangeably.

New information is information that technically is neither linguistically nor extralinguistically recoverable; it is the opposite of given information and will be similarly limited to linguistic context for this study. Thus, new information represents concepts that have not been explicitly mentioned in the previous context. Given or new information may be contained in the theme of a sentence—with the exception of the first sentence in a text wherein all thematic material would be considered new because it lacks linguistic contextual reference (again, note the particular framework set up here). Given or new information may appear in the rheme of the sentence.

Prague Linguists

English behaves in much the same way as Czech: word order marks chiefly the theme and rheme or surface subject and surface predicate in English. Case relations are marked by prepositions in English and by endings in Czech.

Definitions of theme, rheme, given, and new draw heavily from the work of the Prague Linguists. The study of the relation of theme within a sentence is historically rooted in the Prague Linguist's functional approach to spoken Czech. The concept of theme was one part of an approach to language known as **functional sentence perspective,** which describes the flow of information through sentences. The Prague Linguists noted that the syntax of a sentence communicated more information than simply the number and identification of noun and verb phrases. For example, the specific ordering of words serves to mark theme and rheme, convey given and new information and establish "communicative dynamism, or the extent to which a sentence element contributes to the development of the communication to which, as it were, it 'pushes' the communication forward [Firbas, 1966, p. 240]."

For the Prague Linguists, theme and rheme are determined solely by the linguistic context, not the extralinguistic context at all. Thus, theme and rheme are generally defined positionally with theme in the initial position and rheme in the noninitial position. (A possible and perhaps problematic exception is Firbas' claim on nonthematic subjects [cf. Firbas, 1966] where certain cases, such as verbs of appearance or existence on the scene, convey rhematic subjects: For example, *A girl came into the room: A girl =* rhematic subject).

These same parameters regarding theme and rheme will be adopted in this study: Both terms are distinct, both are dependent on linguistic context, and both are defined positionally in the sentence, such that theme is associated with initial sentence position and rheme with end position.

Theme Progressions

There are two principal types of thematic progression (Danes, 1974):

1. **Run-through progressions,** where the thematic information of sentence pairs is identical:

    (7) ab <u>The judge explained the contest rules.</u>
              (a)   (b)

    (8) ac <u>He was misunderstood by the contestants.</u>
              (a)   (c)

2. **Linear progressions,** where the thematic information of a sentence is the same as the rhematic information of the preceding sentence:

    (7) ab <u>The judge explained the contest rules.</u>
              (a)   (b)

    (9) bc <u>They were misunderstood by the contestants.</u>
              (b)   (c)

In both the case of run-through progressions and linear progressions, the THEMATIC information of the second sentence is given (coreferenced) information in the preceding sentence; GIVEN INFORMATION PRECEDES NEW in each case.

In contrast to these two thematic progressions are two other progressions:

3. **Interrupted run-through progressions,** where the rhematic information of one sentence is the same as the thematic information of the preceding sentence:

    (7) ab <u>The judge explained the contest rules.</u>
              (a)   (b)

    (10) ca <u>A participant misunderstood him.</u>
              (c)   (a)

4. **Interrupted linear progressions,** where the rhematic information of sentence pairs is identical:

    (7) ab <u>The judge explained the contest rules.</u>
              (a)   (b)

    (11) cb <u>A participant misunderstood them.</u>
              (c)   (b)

In both the case of interrupted run-through progressions and interrupted linear progressions, the RHEMATIC information of the second sentence is given (coreferenced) information in the previous sentence; NEW INFORMA-TION PRECEDES OLD.

Clearly, all four of these orderings are acceptable discourse patterns and can readily be found in texts, despite or in spite of the canonical rule of English usage that states that old should precede new, that is, the principle of thematic progression. However, it may be that certain sequences are easier to comprehend than others.

THEME PROGRESSIONS AND THE GIVEN–NEW CONTRACT AND STRATEGY

The theme–rheme conceptualization asserts that there is a preferred order or sequence of sentence elements, namely that theme ought to precede rheme. Though given and new, theme and rheme, and initial and noninitial sentence positions identify separate and distinct sentence components, they typically appear together in actual sentences. For example, in linear themes ab–bc and run-through theme progressions ab–ac, theme, given, and initial sentence position coincide, as does rheme, new, and end sentence position. By contrast, in interrupted linear progressions ab–cb, and interrupted run-through progressions ab–ca, theme, new, and initial sentence position coincide as does rheme, given, and end sentence position, thus resulting in a somewhat mixed message.

The Prague Linguists' studies on functional sentence perspective note that thematic information generally, though not necessarily, coincides with old information and that rhematic information generally coincides with new information. They note, too, that theme precedes rheme as the preferred order within sentences. The lowest degree of communicative dynamism tends to fall on the given information, whereas the highest degree is typically associated with the new information. Thus, their conclusions are in keeping with the principle of thematic progression which states that an overlap between given and theme in the initial sentence position and new and rheme in the end sentence position is the preferred pattern for effective communication. This supports the time-honored maxim of English usage that old information should precede new, and strongly suggests that this rule has definite linguistic implications that, in turn, will improve written communication (language understanding for readers).

One would suspect that when theme, given, and initial sentence position, and rheme, new, and noninitial sentence position coincide—as in thematic progressions ab–ac and ab–bc—that these overlappings have a combined effect of redundantly marking information as given or new; and that by the terms of the given–new contract, this should aid the reader's identification of them. Consequently, one would expect, in constructions where the three elements coincide respectively, that these sentences are more direct with regard to given–new identification and hence less confusing and more readable than when theme represents new information and/or rheme represents old information as in the progressions ab–ca and ab–cb.

To review: according to the given–new strategy, the reader must identify given information in the sentence, locate the appropriate memory structure, and integrate the new information. When sentences adhere to the principle of thematic progression, theme and old information coincide, as do rheme and new information. This dual reinforcement, as well as the appropriate markings of given and new information by initial and noninitial sentence positions strongly aids the reader in the task of identifying the intended given information in the linguistic text. This identification is crucial to the given–new strategy.

One would furthermore expect thematic progression ab–bc to be a preferred pattern because antecedent information is directly and immediately available in the preceding sentence. This recency effect stands in sharp contrast to the confusion caused by interrupted linear progression ab–cb, where new precedes old (cb), and given information is contained in the rhematic noninitial position of the second sentence. According to the given–new strategy, these additional steps in identifying and locating the appropriate antecedent information will increase processing time.

These predictions follow from research on memory representation indicating that information presented according to the preferred pair (ab–ac or ab–bc) continually reactivates the same memory area (or node) by the repeated reference of given information. Each time a node is activated, it presumably strengthens the link or pathway, thereby decreasing the number of reinstatement searches (Kintsch, 1974) and facilitating subsequent storage or integration of the new information with the old (Collins & Loftus, 1975).

The prediction that thematic progressions ab–ac and ab–bc will be easier to comprehend than other progressions (ab–ca and ab–cb) also follows from research on the discourse pointer (cf. Carpenter & Just, 1977), described as a symbol in the reader's mind that "indicates the current topic of discourse [p. 217]." Placement of the pointer is dependent, in part, on syntactic cues, which set the discourse pointer at a particular place in memory, thereby activating that concept. The established pointer, that is, activated concept node, in turn, plays a major role in the organization and integration of subsequent information related to the topic at hand.

Consequently, the syntactic marking of given information through either repeated reference and/or thematic ordering should set the discourse pointer and indicate how the remaining information and sentences relate to one another. Carpenter and Just (1977) have found that when the information marked as given corresponds to the contents of the discourse pointer, comprehension is facilitated. Consider these sentence pairs again:

(7) ab *The judge explained the contest rules.*
(8) ac *He was misunderstood by the contestants.*

Here the discourse pointer is initially set according to the first noun phrase of the first sentence, *the judge.* Since the anaphore *He* marks the additional context as referring to previously encountered text, or given information, the discourse pointer does not move. The additional text is directed to the same place or address in memory as the first sentence, since the topic of discourse remains the same. Thus, since the given information is explicitly marked, the discourse pointer can be set more easily and in this case, remains stationary.

Once additional text is processed, the discourse pointer may be reset or may remain in the same place, depending on the relationship between the initial sentence and the remaining text. Carpenter and Just assume that there are many possible factors that control the movement of the discourse pointer; these include anaphores, connectives, and repetition (1977, p. 226).

Clearly, research on memory, the given–new contract and strategy, and the relationship of linguistic marking devices to comprehension predicts that the thematic progressions ab–ac and ab–bc will be easier to understand, and hence take less time to process than their counterparts— progressions ab–ca and ab–cb.

EXPLORATORY STUDY

An exploratory study was undertaken to determine if, in fact, thematic progressions ab–ac and ab–bc are easier to comprehend than other types of progressions, such as ab–ca and ab–cb. Multiple choice recognition tests served as the measure of comprehension.

Subjects

The randomly selected sample consisted of 20 college freshmen students. All were enrolled in an introductory composition course at the University of Illinois at Chicago Circle.

Test Construction

A pool of sentences was created consisting of 11 stimulus sentences. For each stimulus sentence, four targets were created. For example:

STIMULUS: *The surprise play was forgotten by the team.*   (ab)
TARGETS: *It could have saved the game last night.*   (ac)
       They could have saved the game last night.   (bc)
       The game could have been saved by it.   (ca)
       The game could have been saved by them.   (cb)

Thus, a total of 44 (11 × 4) sentences were developed.

Targets represented each of the progressions discussed earlier; actives and passives were counterbalanced. Each stimulus sentence was assigned one target, yielding four sentence pairs—each one containing the same stimulus sentence. The number of words, syntax, and meanings for all targets (within each four sentence pair) remained relatively equal given the word order shifting. References in the sentence pairs were unambiguous, no proper names were used so as to avoid unnecessary bias, and hierarchical distance was controlled: The antecedent information was always in a subordinate relationship to its pronym.

Test booklets consisted of 11 isolated sentence pairs; each one was on a separate page. A test of recognition corresponded to the booklets. Four different test booklets and forms were used. This was done because it was suspected that there might be some kind of interaction between the manner in which the progressions were ordered and reader comprehension. For example, if the booklet and corresponding test were to consist of only linear theme progression sentence pairs, it was not clear whether the reader's response might be a measure of recognition or rote memory (with subjects able to figure out the monotonous patterning of each pair) or both. Nor was it clear how mixing the different sentence progressions in the booklet and test might interact with reader comprehension. For example, if one is presented with the progressions ab–ac followed by ab–cb and then ab–ca—is that sequence equal (with respect to language processing demands) to a booklet and test ordered ab–ac, ab–bc, ab–ca?

Thus, four forms of booklets and tests were constructed to examine this issue. Three of the forms equally distributed the number of linear (ab–bc), run-through (ab–ac), and interrupted run-through progressions (ab–ca). Each of the three forms represented a different random ordering of these progressions. (The interrupted linear progression was left out.)

By contrast, the fourth form of the booklet and test consisted solely of interrupted linear progressions (ab–cb), except for one interrupted run-through progression (ab–ca), which appeared near the end.

Procedures

Each subject was given a numbered test booklet consisting of 11 different sentence pairs; these were followed by a distractor task. They were informed that this experiment was designed to test their memory. When the

subjects finished reading the test booklet, it was exchanged for its correspondingly numbered multiple-choice test. Tests contained the original
stimulus sentence in the same order as the booklet, followed by four possible target sentences. Each subject was instructed to circle the target he
remembered reading in the test booklet.

Data Analysis

Data were examined only for trends because the sample size in this
exploratory study was so small ($N = 20$). A description of the data on the
effects of progression types and comprehension follows:

Progression		Number correct/total	Proportion	Test form
Run-through	ab	37/50	.74	Equally
	ac			distributed
Linear	ab	48/60	.80	Equally
	bc			distributed
Interrupted	ab	36/55	.65	Equally
run-through	ca			distributed
Interrupted	ab	47/55	.85	Unequally
linear	cb			distributed

These proportions suggest the trend that linear and run-through progressions (ab–bc and ab–ac) where given, theme and initial sentence position coincide, are easier to recognize, and hence understand, than interrupted run-through progressions (ab–ca).

The results of the individual scores for each test form are summarized in
the following:

Sample	Test Form	Individual Mean Score	Variance
$N = 5$	1 (equally distributed)	4.6	6.5
$N = 5$	2 (equally distributed)	6.2	4.1
$N = 5$	3 (equally distributed)	4.4	3.7
$N = 5$	4 (unequally distributed)	7.8	7.3

Statistical tests for differences among test forms would be misleading because of the low statistical power of tests based on small sample sizes ($N =$
5). Nonetheless, one may note the trend of higher scores for the test form
4, which incorporated primarily one type of progression, ab–cb, which
might suggest that subjects recognized the repeated patterning of the sentence pairs in test form 4. However, the small sample size and high variance score obtained (7.3) make it difficult to draw a definite conclusion.
Similarly, those forms that randomly ordered approximately equal numbers of progressions, gave rise to relatively equal scores, suggesting the

lack of interaction between ordering sentence progression pairs and reader comprehension.

Discussion

The exploratory study indicated that progressions may have varying effects on reader comprehension. Thematic progressions where given precedes new is the preferred order of sentence elements. In order to further confirm or disconfirm this hypothesis, additional data utilizing larger samples, more sentence pairs, and timed tests of recognition are needed.

Further research might also assess the interactive effect (if any) between the ordering of the items themselves, such as using different test forms with respect to the sequencing of items, as previously discussed. In addition, timed recall data may add further insights and more specific information about progression types and their effects on reader processing.

Other questions that need to also be addressed include: Does the thematic progression ab–ac take less time to process than ab–bc—or conversely, is ab–ca easier to comprehend than ab–cb; is there a discernible differential effect? What might account for any difference? Is there any dependence on the particular surrounding context—is one progression preferable for some linguistic contexts and not others? Is a difference in processing time due to a more explicit marking of given and new information? Is the difference in processing progressions a result of the recency effect on memory storage and retrieval? Is the difference dependent on each individual's memory structure? These and many other questions remain unanswered.

CONCLUDING REMARKS: SOME IMPLICATIONS FOR WRITING

As mentioned earlier, communication is dependent on a certain "degree of agreement" between conversants. This contract applies to writers and their readers, as well as speakers and their listeners. Like the speaker, the writer must assess such audience characteristics as extent of shared previous knowledge about the subject matter. The more sensitive a writer is to his audience and to the resources of the written language for expression, the more effective the communication will be. What the writer assumes to be given and new information for the reader, as well as an awareness of linguistic conventions for expressing these characteristics, contributes to the smooth exchange of ideas.

One of the things a writer considers, whether consciously or not, are certain expectations regarding the audience's familiarity or previous knowledge about the topic of discourse. Based on these judgments, the writer determines how much background and detailed information to include in his text. Furthermore, the writer also makes judgments as to HOW to present this information.

To sum up, thematic progressions define an important way in which writers present information. These progressions set up linguistic patterns in the text that, in turn, relate sentences to each other. The patterns also build on reader expectations. When their use reinforces the markings of given and new information, the resulting communication can be most effective; one way the writer helps ensure that information will be appropriately tagged or identified by the reader is by placing given information in the thematic position, and new information in the rhematic portion of the sentence. These orderings conform to an intuitive sense that given and new is marked according to their position in the sentence. These sequences also conform to the principle that what is being talked about is given information and should appear first, and that what is being said about it is new information and should appear last—in effect, "pushing" forward the development of the communication. Placing given information before new is in keeping with a canonical rule of English usage that states that old information OUGHT to precede new information in sentences. This progression of theme is also supported by the research of the Prague Linguists on the functional sentence perspective of language.

All of the research reported here seems to indicate that simple linear and/or run-through thematic progressions are easier to process than their counterparts, interrupted linear or interrupted run-through progressions. In other words, one would predict that information ordered according to ab–ac and ab–bc (where the first letter in each pair represents the theme and initial sentence position, and the second letter represents rheme and noninitial sentence position, and repeated letters represent given information) will be easier to comprehend than the same information ordered according to ab–ca or ab–cb.

In thematic progressions, the marking of theme, given, and initial sentence position coexist as does the marking of rheme, new, and noninitial sentence position. These parallel conditions further ensure successful communication according to the research on the given–new contract. Antecedence is clearly marked to aid in the discrimination of intended given and new information and therefore encourage writer and reader identification of these information types to match.

If matches between writer and reader expectations regarding given and new information, as communicated linguistically by thematic progressions, do make a difference with respect to facilitating comprehension, then that canonical rule of English usage that states that old information ought to precede new information in sentences, should take on a more definitive meaning for writers.

REFERENCES

Bormuth, J. R. The anaphora; its surface manifestations. Unpublished manuscript, n.d.

Carpenter, P. A., & Just, M. A. Integrative processes in comprehension. In D. LaBerge & S. J.

Samuel (Eds.), *Basic processes in reading: Perception and comprehension.* Hillsdale, N.J.: Lawrence Erlbaum, 1977.

Clark, H. H. Inferences in Comprehension. In D. LaBerge & S. J. Samuels (Eds.), *Basic processes in reading: Perception and comprehension.* Hillsdale, N.J.: Lawrence Erlbaum, 1977.

Clark, H. H., & Haviland, S. E. Comprehension and the given–new contract. In R. O. Freedle (Ed.), *Discourse production and comprehension.* Norwood, N.J.: Ablex, 1977.

Clark, H. H., & Clark, E. V. *Psychology and language.* New York: Harcourt Brace Jovanovich, 1977.

Collins, A. M., & Loftus, E. F. A spreading activation theory of semantic processing. *Psychological Review,* 1975, *82,* 407–428.

Dahl, W. What is new information? In N. Enkvist & V. Kohonen (Eds.), *Reports on text linguistics: Symposium on the interaction of parameters affecting word order.* Turko: Abo Akademi, 1976.

Danes, F. *Papers on functional sentence perspective.* The Hague: Mouton, 1974.

Enkvist, N. *Linguistic stylistics.* The Hague: Mouton, 1973.

Enkvist, N. Notes on valency, semantic scope, and thematic perspective as parameters of adverbial placement in English. In N. Enkvist & V. Kohonen (Eds.), *Reports on text linguistics: Symposium on the interaction of parameters affecting word order.* Turko: Abo Akademi, 1976.

Firbas, J. On defining theme in functional sentence analysis. *Travaux linguistiques de Prague,* 1964, *1,* 267–280.

Firbas, J. Non-thematic subjects in contemporary English. *Travaux linguistiques de Prague,* 1966, *3,* 239–256.

Firbas, J. On the thematic and non-thematic section of the sentence. In H. Ringborn (Ed.), *Style and text.* Stockholm: Skriptor, 1975.

Grice, H. P. William James Lectures, Harvard University, 1967. Published in part as "Logic and Conversation." In P. Cole & J. L. Morgan (Eds.), *Syntax and semantics, Vol. 3: Speech acts.* New York: Seminar Press, 1975. Pp. 41–58.

Halliday, M. A. K. Notes on transitivity and theme in English: II. *Journal of Linguistics,* 1967, *3,* 199–244.

Halliday, M. A. K., & Hasan, R. *Cohesion in English.* London: Longman, 1976.

Haviland, S. & Clark, H. H. What's new? Acquiring new information as a process in comprehension. *Journal of Verbal Learning and Verbal Behavior,* 1974, *13,* 512–521.

Kintsch, W. *Representation of meaning in memory.* Hillsdale, N.J.: Lawrence Erlbaum, 1974.

Morles, A. *Hierarchical distance and comprehension of the anaphora.* Unpublished doctoral dissertation, University of Chicago, 1977.

Palkova, A. & Palek, B. Functional sentence perspective and textlinguistics. In W. U. Dressler (Ed.), *Current trends in textlinguistics* (Vol. 2 of Research in text theory). Berlin: DeGruyter, 1977.

Quillian, M. R. Semantic memory. In M. L. Minsky (Ed.), *Semantic information processing.* Cambridge: M.I.T. Press, 1968.

Richek, M. A. *Reading comprehension of selected paraphrase alternation: Pronominal forms.* Unpublished doctoral dissertation, University of Chicago, 1974.

Context as Vehicle: Implicatures in Writing

Marilyn M. Cooper

INTRODUCTION

Writing theory often concerns itself primarily with what writers know about themselves and their intentions and what they know about their readers' needs and wants. But writers also take into account what they know about the world they find themselves in and what they know about the activity of writing. What writers know about the world is more or less what everyone knows: facts, empirical laws, and various culture-bound conventions—laws, social codes, religious rites, and so forth. What writers know about writing is more specialized knowledge: written works themselves and linguistic and genre conventions. How do writers use this variety of information in forming their works, and how do they relate this larger context to the immediate problem of communicating with their readers? Using H. Paul Grice's theory of implicatures, I will explain the various ways in which writers draw on and exploit context to communicate their intentions.

READERS AND WRITERS

First, I must make explicit something about the context of my writing. I assume that writing is a communicative act. To some, this is a truism, but it

WHAT WRITERS KNOW
The Language, Process,
and Structure of Written Discourse

entails two beliefs less widely acceded to: that writers and readers operate on the basis of the same knowledge, and that the meaning of texts, as with all other communications, depends heavily on contexts. The only chance writers have of communicating their meanings is by assuming that potential readers have largely the same knowledge of those facts about the world relevant to their meanings as they themselves do, and that readers will, when faced with a text (an object that is always multiply ambiguous), use the same interpretive strategies that the writers would. Writing and interpreting are mirror-image processes, as Stanley Fish explains:

> what utterers do is give hearers and readers the opportunity to make meanings (and texts) by inviting them to put into execution a set of strategies. It is presumed that the invitation will be recognized, and that presumption rests on a projection on the part of a speaker or author of the moves *he* would make if confronted by the sounds or marks he is uttering or setting down [1976, p. 485].

This depiction is intuitively satisfying, especially when we consider how writers, in revising, read over their texts to test the meanings produced by the interpretive strategies they assume their readers will use. There are, of course, breakdowns in communication, most of which arise from a mismatch between writers' and readers' knowledge. Nevertheless, writers always act from the belief that communication is possible.

CONTEXTS IN WRITING

Because in writing the means of communication—the text—is more concrete and long lasting than in speaking, writing is usually considered to be a much less situated communicative act than is speaking. Teachers often point out to beginning writers that many contextual determinants of meaning available in speaking situations are lacking in writing—intonation, gestures, facial expressions, and location in time and space. As Mina Shaughnessy has explained, basic writers know this lesson only too well:

> For the BW student, academic writing is a trap, not a way of saying something to someone. The spoken language, looping back and forth between speakers, offering chances for groping and backing up and even hiding, leaving room for the language of hands and faces, of pitch and pauses, is generous and inviting. Next to this rich orchestration, writing is but a line that moves haltingly across the page, exposing as it goes all that the writer doesn't know, then passing into the hands of a stranger who reads it with a lawyer's eyes, searching for flaws [1977, p. 7].

But no one denies that student writing takes place in a context, and one thing these writers need to learn is how to deal with it. The power imbalance between students and teacher is aggravated by their not knowing how to code gestures and intonation in linguistic forms or how to successfully hedge, equivocate, and predict the response of their reader.

Chapter **5**

James Britton terms this type of writing transactional, writing that "is intended to fit into, to articulate with, the ongoing activities of participants [1970, pp. 174–175]." Transactional writing is the focus of most composition courses and programs, but it is only one type. Britton terms the other type of public writing poetic writing, and it is with this type that acontextuality is most strongly insisted on. Britton says that poetic writing, rather than articulating with the activities of participants, interrupts them "by presenting an object to be contemplated in itself and for itself. . . . A reader is asked to respond to a particular verbal construct which remains quite distinct from any other verbal construct anybody else might offer. A response in kind is not therefore inherent in the situation [1970, p. 174]." Jay Schleusener concisely summarizes the position of many literary theorists:

> works of literature differ from ordinary speech because they are not tied to an immediate social context. . . . Authors and readers . . . can hardly be said to meet anywhere at all. Their only common ground is the text, and they share nothing but the words that pass between them. Meanings that might be clear enough in the social context of ordinary speech tend toward ambiguity in this circumstantial void where author and reader must do without a common world of reference and make the best of a language that cannot rely on the casual support of facts [1980, pp. 669–670].

Texts are admittedly easier to decontextualize than are utterances: writers' names are more easily separated from their texts than speakers' presences are from their utterances, and because texts are, in a sense, physical objects, they are more permanent and portable, and thus more likely to turn up in alien contexts. But this is as true of nonliterary as literary texts. Nor is this any argument that writers or readers ever treat texts as acontextual.

Few teachers of literature would agree that literary language does not "rely on the casual support of facts." To take just two examples, I. A. Richards laments his students' "surprising unfamiliarity with the elements of the Christian religion [1929, p. 42]." And Martha Banta, discussing the cause of her literature students' "will to ignorance," notes:

> Over and over, against the grain of all my experiences, out of my unending hope and innocence, I keep asking, if only because a novel or poem or essay is waiting for its built-in references to be cleared up before we can go any further: "What is meant by 'He has met his Waterloo?'" and "Who was Cupid's mother?" and "Why did Lazarus stink?" and "Who did Jacob wrestle with and why?" and "Why did Leda get mixed up with a swan?" and "Who was Thor and why was Thoreau interested in him?" and "Who *was* Dwight David Eisenhower?" I ask; I rarely receive [1980, p. 111].

When Richards asked his students to respond to and comment on unidentified poems, the students continually attempted to make sense of the poems by providing the missing contexts. They guessed at the authorship: "a spinster devoted to good works, and sentimentally inclined, or perhaps

Wordsworth [Richards, 1929, p. 23]." They guessed at the literary period: "Reminded of the pitched-up movement or strong artificial accent
of post-Elizabethans. But this is without their complexity of thought . . . . a
deliberate loading of rhythm—influence of the didactic pretentions. Wordsworth? Spurious. Mid-Victorian poetic drama? [Richards, 1929, p. 23]."
They compared the poems with other poems they knew: "'Tho' world
of wanwood leafmeal lie'—gloriously melancholy (worthy of Keats' 'La
Belle Dame sans Merci') [Richards, 1929, p. 81]." They drew on what
they knew of poetic method: "This is clearly an experiment in sound and
in striving after effect the sense suffers considerably [Richards, 1929, p.
86]." They guessed at the author's pragmatic intentions by projecting the
purpose the poem fulfilled for them: "An atmosphere of peace, and deep
reverence, which transports the reader into another world, more pure and
white than this [Richards, 1929, p. 95]." To interpret the actions of the
people in the poems, they drew on their beliefs about how people should
act: "The parent or whoever it is advising Margaret is a bitter, hard individual who seems to be trying to take away all the hope and happiness of
the child. I don't think that any really kind person would feel so little
sympathy for a child's trivial sorrow, and make her unhappy by telling her
the worse is yet to come [Richards, 1929, p. 83]." And they guessed at the
intentions of the writers by projecting their own attitudes toward subjects
of the poems: "if we are meant to take the situation in profound meditation
closing in self-absorbing remorse, then the whole thing is clearly vicious
and preposterous. The idea of an eternity spent in turning up the files of
other people's sins or crouching to cry *peccavi* for our own is either amusing
or disgusting or both [Richards, 1929, p. 169]."

Meanings carried by the conventional rules of language are exceedingly
impoverished. Clearly, reading and writing require the reader and writer
to hypothesize a whole communicative situation, just as in conversing
face-to-face we assume many things about the situation we are in. The
encounter between writer and reader is in one sense less immediate than
the encounter between speaker and hearer: Writers and readers are not
(usually) physically in each other's presence and cannot respond directly to
each other. But actual presence makes little difference in the communicative process. Readers typically have a strong sense of the writer's immediate presence, and skilled writers develop the same sense of their
readers' presence. Interaction does occur. As readers, have you never
asked of a writer, "What are you referring to here?" and searched back
through the text or in your knowledge of context for a clue? As writers,
have you never asked, "What must I tell my readers next?" as you thought
about how they would understand what you were writing? Schleusener
concludes:

We come to know the author in much the same way that we come to know anyone else:
not by historical research or by hypothetical deduction but on our own authority and

through our own experience. To the extent that we succeed in developing a useful notion of his character, our assessment is legitimized by our understanding of the conventions he has used and by our familiarity with the relevant notions of agency and action. We could do little more to legitimize our acquaintance with persons we meet face to face [1980, p. 679].

I have insisted on the similarities between communicating in writing and communicating in speaking because the widespread tendency to dwell on the differences between the two obscures the fact that the fundamental communicative process remains the same. Readers and hearers use both their knowledge of linguistic and other conventions and their knowledge of the relevant aspects of context to assign meanings to texts and to utterances, and writers and speakers count on their ability to do this. The differences between writing and speaking are differences in the conventions that are employed, not differences in the means of employing them.

Beginning writers, it is often observed, use the same situational devices in writing that they use in talking with their friends. One of my colleagues received an essay that began, "This is the place I work at that's suppose to be a gas station." The meaning of his utterance depends on a context in which he and the person he's addressing are standing in front of the gas station: The deictic *this* refers to an object present in the addressee's world; the definite article *the* marks the place as known to the addressee, as it would be if he or she were standing near the place referred to. The intended sarcastic tone depends on intonation—a stress on *suppose*. But the writer and his reader are not in the context his meaning depends on, which imperils the success of his communication. *This* and *the place* may refer perfectly successfully in conversation, but in writing reference depends on definite descriptions and proper names that create the objects referred to in the readers' minds. The emphasis on *suppose* will convey sarcasm in conversation, but in writing that emphasis must somehow be marked typographically (typically by italics or underlining) or be specified lexically. I could suggest that the student rewrite his sentence as follows: *The gas station where I work is a sadly deficient token of its type.* (Of course, I wouldn't.) In suggesting these changes to him, am I simply telling him to reduce his dependence on context and increase his dependence on convention? No. But I am telling him the two contexts are different and different conventions are needed to communicate his intentions. Note that the reference of *I* remains, strictly speaking, ambiguous; *I* will be identified with whichever name is written at the top of the page or whoever hands the text to the teacher. *This* and a stress on *suppose* are just as conventional as the definite description of the gas station and the lexical meaning of *sadly deficient*. Furthermore, note that the revised sentence, if spoken by a person standing in front of the gas station where he works, is just as vulnerable to misinterpretation as the spoken version is when it's handed to a teacher as an essay. Both versions use conventions adapted to the demands of the contexts in which they are to be received. In fact, given the actual context of the student's writing, he would not be best advised to write as explicitly as I have in my first revision of his text. The student knew that his reader knew that he had been assigned to write about a familiar place he had some attitude toward, and he knew that his reader knew that most of his students had part-time jobs. I would better advise him to write simply, *The place where I work is* **supposed** *to be a gas station*—which preserves his "voice" while removing the undesirable marks of illiteracy (*at,* and misspelling of *supposed*).

How much readers rely on context in interpreting texts can be demonstrated by one further example. The other day, I picked up my copy of the October 6 issue of *The New Yorker* and turned to "The Talk of the Town." On reading the first sentence—"In 1969, when 'The Selling of the President,' by Joe McGinniss, was published, showing that Richard Nixon had used Madison Avenue advertising techniques to the full in his recent election campaign, the book was regarded as an exposé [p. 47]"—I said to myself, with this year's campaigns you wouldn't need an exposé. As I read on, my meaning prediction was verified: The argument of the piece was that in current political campaigns "the techniques by which public opinion is manipulated are proudly displayed to the world [p. 47]." How did I (and several other readers I asked about this article) so quickly grasp the writer's intended meaning? The answer is obvious: As a longtime reader of *The New Yorker* I am well acquainted with that eye-glassed gentleman who regularly discourses on current events in these pages. I know what subjects are likely to interest him, and what attitude he is likely to take toward them. I know that the first piece in this section is often a serious political commentary. I know that, if the first sentence of such a piece refers to a long past event, that event most likely provides a context relevant to the subject the writer intends to discuss. I know this piece was written fairly recently and that it will relate to something that has just happened or is still happening. I know that we are once again (as I read) in the middle of a presidential campaign: I have seen the candidates' television advertisements and read their aides' explanations of how engaging in debates would affect their candidates' images. In short, what I know about the writer's interests and attitudes, about the conventions of *The New Yorker,* and about the political situation at the time and place of the publication of this text allows me to correctly infer a meaning from relatively few linguistic cues. I certainly did not read each word in the first sentence, either, and I probably needed only five words to cue the meaning: *advertising techniques, election campaign, exposé.* That the writer of this piece used more than these five words to convey his meaning does not mean that he does not rely on his readers' having this knowledge, for no matter how much he writes he knows that any change in readers' knowledge will affect their interpretation of his meaning.

Most texts come richly provided with contexts. The student's paper was produced at a particular time (1970s) at a particular place (Minneapolis) in a particular course (composition) at a particular school (University of Minnesota) in a particular society (which includes the concepts of "working" and "gas station") in response to a particular teacher's particular assignment with particular intentions on the student's part (to fulfill the teacher's assignment, to pass composition, and possibly to explore his own feelings about the place where he works)—all of which is known by both reader and writer. Similarly, *The New Yorker* arrived in my mailbox in Los Angeles on about October 6 (the date on its cover); its format (paper cover, staple binding, ads interspersed with articles) and weekly appearance marked it as a known type of cultural artifact (weekly magazine) designed to sell products by offering information and diversion; the subtitle of the section ("Notes and Comments") and the subjects addressed in the section marked that as a known journalistic genre (editorial column) in which writers express opinions on current happenings—and all this is known to both the writer and the readers of *The New Yorker*. Very rarely do we encounter texts stripped of all this information. Richards in his experiment noted that "the precise conditions of this test are not duplicated in our everyday commerce with literature [1929, p. 5]," and he not surprisingly discovered that under these conditions readers have exceeding difficulty in *"making out the plain sense* of poetry [1929, p. 12]."

GRICE'S THEORY OF IMPLICATURES

Communicating meanings depends on knowledge: interpretations are inferences based on beliefs and conventions.[1] As Richard Young and his colleagues explain in their composition textbook, "there can be no interaction between writer and reader, and no change in their thinking, unless they hold certain things in common, such as shared experiences, shared knowledge, shared beliefs, values, and attitudes, shared language [1970, p. 172]." The mix of knowledge called up by any communication varies. In the gas station example, readers use linguistic conventions and nonconventional beliefs such as that discourse is normally oriented to the speaker and that gas stations are places of business. In the *New Yorker* example, readers use linguistic conventions and genre conventions and nonconventional beliefs about the writer's personality and the current political situation. But many communicative acts are even more dependent on context than are these two. In his lectures on "Logic and Conversation,"[2] Grice describes communicative acts in which what is meant departs radically

---

[1]Cf. Martin Steinmann, Jr., chapter 11, in this volume.
[2]Three of the lectures have been published separately; see Grice, 1969, 1975, 1978.

from the conventional meaning of the words that were used. He elaborates a set of nonconventional beliefs about how conversants interact that help us to perform and to understand these "indirect" communicative acts that he calls **implicatures**.[3] Implicatures are common in everyday conversations, as Grice reveals. But they are also common in writing, and what he says about conversation applies equally well to all communication.

Grice argues that CONVERSATION IS A COOPERATIVE ENDEAVOR, that what enables conversation to proceed is an underlying assumption that we as conversants have purposes for conversing and that we recognize that these purposes are more likely to be fulfilled if we cooperate.[4] These purposes can vary greatly, they can be mixed, and they might not be shared by all participants in the conversation. We nevertheless assume, unless there are indications to the contrary, that we have a shared purpose for conversing, and our actions reflect this assumption. Grice states the assumption as an imperative and calls it the **Cooperative Principle** (CP): "Make your conversational contribution such as is required, at the stage at which it occurs, by the accepted purpose or direction of the talk exchange in which you are engaged [1975, p. 45]." From the CP he derives a series of "maxims":

QUANTITY
1. Make your contribution as informative as is required (for the current purposes of the exchange).
2. Do not make your contribution more informative than is required.

QUALITY
1. Do not say what you believe to be false.
2. Do not say that for which you lack adequate evidence.

RELATION
Be relevant.

MANNER
1. Avoid obscurity of expression.
2. Avoid ambiguity.
3. Be brief (avoid unnecessary prolixity).
4. Be orderly.

Although these maxims are also stated as imperatives, they do not rule conversation in any sense. We rarely violate the maxims casually, for no reason, but we do violate them intentionally for a variety of reasons. The most interesting reason for violating a maxim is to thereby say something indirectly; Grice calls this strategy an implicature. Other reasons for violating maxims are: (*a*) to mislead, in which case the violation will be hidden from hearers; (*b*) to "opt out" of a conversation in which we do not want to

---

[3]For a more complete discussion of the status and applicability of Grice's maxims, see my *Implicatures in dramatic conversations*.
[4]Cf. Young, Becker, and Pike: "The writer's goal is to engage in some sort of cooperative activity with the reader [1970, p. 171]."

participate; and (c) to avoid violating another maxim. And we may unintentionally, through ineptitude, negligence, or absent-mindedness, violate a maxim.

Speakers who wish to implicate something violate maxims in a characteristic way: They violate them in a way that draws their hearers' attention to the violation; they blatantly violate them; Grice says they "flout" the maxims. Hearers who assume that the speakers are being cooperative are forced to look for a reason for the violation in what they know of the speaker's knowledge or beliefs, and what they infer about this reason is what the speaker has implicated. Implicatures can also arise when no maxims are clearly violated,[5] as in Grice's initial example:

> SITUATION: A and B are talking about a mutual friend C who is working in a bank. A asks how C is getting on in his job, and B replies:
> SAID: Oh, quite well, I think; he likes his colleagues and he hasn't been to prison yet.
> REASONING: B in saying "he hasn't been to prison yet" has apparently failed to fulfill the maxim of relation. There is no reason to assume B is not fulfilling the CP. B must think that:
> IMPLICATED: C is potentially dishonest [See Grice, 1975, pp. 43, 50].

In this way speakers can convey meaning beyond that carried by the conventional meaning of what they say. Grice offers a formal definition of the notion of conversational implicature:

> A man who, by (in, when) saying (or making as if to say) that p, has implicated that q, provided that (1) he is to be presumed to be observing the conversational maxims, or at least the cooperative principle; (2) the supposition that he is aware that, or thinks that, q is required in order to make his saying or making as if to say p (or doing so in those terms) consistent with this presumption; and (3) the speaker thinks (and would expect the hearer to think that the speaker thinks) that it is within the competence of the hearer to work out, or grasp intuitively, that the supposition mentioned in (2) is required [1975, pp. 49–50].

Grice emphasizes that implicatures must be intentional; speakers must know they are violating a conversational maxim and must intend their hearers to know that too and know that they are observing the CP, for the communication of meaning depends on this knowledge. What is implicated is thus determined by speakers' intentions, even though in some instances, when there are several possible suppositions that could be consistent with the presumption that speakers are being cooperative, what is implicated may be indeterminate from the hearers' point of view.

Grice formulated his maxims with representatives in mind, but clearly all types of speech acts can be used to implicate. In order to emphasize the generality of the maxims and to rid them of their misleading imperative

---

[5]Michael Hancher (1978) explains that an implicature that involves no maxim violation "simply *invokes a maxim* as a ground of interpretation."

form, I have proposed the following restatement of the CP and maxims. A "no" answer to a question marks a maxim violation.

> CP: Is the conversational act such as is required at the stage at which it occurs by the accepted purpose or direction of the talk exchange in which we are engaged?

QUANTITY
1. Is the act sufficient?
2. Is the act not more than sufficient?

QUALITY
1. Does the act accord with the speaker's beliefs and feelings?
2. Is there an adequate reason for the act?

RELATION
Is the act relevant?

MANNER
1 Is the act perspicuous?
2. Is the act unambiguous?
3. Is the act brief?
4. Is the act organized?
5. Is the act consistent?

Quantity 1: Is the act sufficient? If the act is an assertion, speakers provide the required amount of information; if the act is a question, speakers make sure that the hearer knows what information has been requested; if the act is a promise, speakers say enough to make clear to hearers what they are undertaking an obligation to do; if the act is a congratulation, speakers make sure hearers know for what they are being congratulated. Grice's professor writing a recommendation in which he fails to comment on the applicant's skill at philosophy violates this maxim. So does Alice when she asks directions of the Cheshire Cat: "Would you tell me, please, which way I ought to go from here?" The cat reasonably responds that he cannot answer the question as phrased: "That depends a good deal on where you want to get to."[6]

Quantity 2: Is the act not more than sufficient? Speakers avoid asserting what need not be asserted, asking for information their hearers would have volunteered anyway, making promises to do things they would have done anyway, and so forth. Grice feels this maxim may be disputable, in that overinformativeness is "merely a waste of time" and that it overlaps the maxim of relation. But overinformativeness can be uncooperative if it deliberately impedes the exchange of information. In a paper on "Conversa-

---

[6]Carroll, 1976, pp. 71–72. My thanks to Michael Hancher for this example.

tion as Paranoia," one reason for violating this maxim is explained as "The principle of maximizing talking, or the fillibuster principle": "Always try to talk as much as possible, in order to keep other people from saying what they want to say [Aelgh, 1978, p. 75]." Furthermore, this maxim can be flouted to produce implicatures. For example, X and Y are rigging a sailboat, and X, an experienced sailor, has made a series of absent-minded errors, dropping cotter pins overboard, attaching the mainsail to the jib halyard, and cleating the main sheet before raising the sail. Finally they are ready to put out, and Y says to X, "If you want to turn the boat, shove on the tiller," flouting the second quantity maxim and implicating that X has not demonstrated much skill at this activity so far. An act that is too informative because the information is not needed violates this maxim; an act that is too informative because the information is not relevant violates the maxim of relation. Grice's example, "A wants to know whether p, and B volunteers not only the information that p, but information to the effect that it is certain that p, and that the evidence for its being the case that p is so-and-so and such-and-such [1975, p. 52]," is indeed an example of the violation of the second maxim of quantity; the excess information is relevant but was not in question to begin with.

Quality 1: Does the act accord with the speaker's beliefs and feelings? This maxim is equivalent to Searle's sincerity condition. Speakers believe their assertions, want answers to their questions, intend to do things they promise to do, are pleased about the events they congratulate others for, and so forth. Rhetorical questions violate this maxim, for the questioner does not want an answer, whether the answer is known to him or not. In the opening scene of Pinter's *The Collection*, Harry asks the voice on the phone, "Do you know it's four o'clock in the morning?"[7] Harry does not really know the answer to his question, but it is clear he does not want an answer either. By flouting this maxim he implicates his annoyance at the early morning phone call. Ironic utterances also characteristically flout this maxim.

Quality 2: Is there an adequate reason for the act? Speakers assert things they have reason to believe are true; they ask questions to which they do not know the answers and believe their hearers can answer; they promise to do things they can do and their hearers want them to do; they congratulate people for real accomplishments. Exam questions violate this maxim; examiners know the answers to the questions they ask (usually) but still want the questions answered.

Relation: Is the act relevant? When Grice proposed this maxim, he observed that "its formulation conceals a number of problems that exercise me a good deal: questions about what different kinds and focuses of relevance there may be, how these shift in the course of a talk exchange, how to allow for the fact that subjects of conversation are legitimately changed,

[7]Pinter, 1961, p. 43. My thanks to Ralph Chapman (1978) for this example.

and so on [1975, p. 46]." He repeated his concern in his fifth lecture: "Also needed: . . . a more precise specification of when relevance is expected [Grice, 1967]." Ruth Kempson notes that the maxim "is normally construed as the relation between utterance and event, or between utterance and utterance [1975, p. 195]," and she suggests an additional relation maxim: "Make the form of your utterance relevant to its content [1975, p. 196]." Grice had already suggested much the same thing in his third lecture, where he notes that in explaining the meaning of stress it might be useful to "introduce a slight extension to the maxim enjoining relevance, making it apply not only to what is said, but to features of the means used for saying what is said [1978, p. 122]." Kent Bach and Robert Harnish suggest a sequencing sub-maxim of the relation maxim to the effect that the force of the utterance be appropriate to the stage of the talk exchange: "questions are to be answered, requests and commitments acknowledged, greetings reciprocated, constatives concurred with (or dissented from, or elaborated upon), and so on [1979, p. 63]."

Conversants' judgments about the relevance of a conversational act can be based either on the content or on the form of the act. Changing the subject of a conversation, I think, always violates the maxim of relation; conversants attempt to figure out the reason for the violation and may or may not allow the subject change. The violation may be the result of a clash with the first maxim of quantity—speakers may have nothing more to say on this subject. Or the violation may signal that speakers are opting out, not wanting to talk about the subject further. Grice's example of the faux pas at the tea party (1975, p. 54) is an example of a change of subject that results in an implicature.

And using an inappropriate illocutionary force indicating device (a device that conventionally marks the illocutionary force of an utterance)[8] is a common way of violating this maxim to produce an implicature. For example, a child arrives home two hours after school has let out and greets his father, "Hi, Dad." His father sternly replies, "Where have you been?" His utterance does not violate the quantity and quality maxims for questions: His son knows what information is being requested; it is not obvious that the boy would, unprompted, provide the information; and the father doesn't know where the boy has been and wants to know. Nor is the content of the utterance irrelevant to the situation: The boy has been absent from home for quite a while, and people who are close usually have an interest in each other's activities. But the interrogative form of the utterance violates the sequencing submaxim; greetings should be reciprocated. By flouting the relation maxim, the father here implicates he is angry about not knowing where the boy has been for the last two hours, and his utterance, marked as a question, has the force of both a question and a reproof.

[8]See Searle, 1969, p. 30.

Manner: Manner maxims might seem to overlap some of the other maxims. Acts that are obscure, ambiguous, and/or disorganized might also be insufficient or irrelevant; acts that are inconsistent might also belie the speaker's beliefs and/or feelings. Grice takes some care to distinguish the manner maxims (1975, pp. 54-56), and in all cases manner maxims apply after it has been determined that the other maxims are holding; they apply to the way in which the act has been realized. An act may be sufficient for the purposes of the conversation yet still be obscure, ambiguous, or disorganized; conversants then ask themselves why the act is embodied in this form. Prolix acts are judged to be such if they add more words but no more information. And inconsistent acts may accord with the speaker's beliefs and/or feelings at the time of the utterance, although they conflict with beliefs and/or feelings evidenced earlier in the conversation.

INTERACTIONS BETWEEN MAXIMS AND OTHER BELIEFS AND CONVENTIONS

Although I argue that Grice's maxims are universal—that they are used by all conversing (and, indeed, all cooperating) persons—the standards for compliance with the maxims may vary from society to society. Elinor Keenan notes that in Malagasy society conversants are much more secretive than in Western societies, and, in our judgment, they might be seen to be continually violating the first quantity maxim (1977, p. 258). But the maxims provide axes for interpretation, not rigid standards against which conversational contributions are to be measured. Within societies, judgments about whether maxims have been violated will be relatively uniform.

More interesting is the way in which the maxims interact with other beliefs and conventions in the interpretive process. Communicators are always performing mediating acts in their minds, adjudicating between the demands of various beliefs and conventions. Beliefs about speakers' and writers' intentions, as I mentioned earlier (p. 112), cause maxim violations to be interpreted in different ways: Those who hide their violations (and are caught) are taken to be liars and disbelieved; those who violate maxims so as to obstruct communication are taken to have reasons for their uncooperativeness; those who do not know they have violated a maxim are taken to be psychologically or mentally deficient in some way; and maxim violations that come about as a result of desires not to violate other maxims or other conventional standards or nonconventional principles[9] are simply not regarded as significant. Only when speakers and writers intentionally, overtly, and cooperatively violate maxims do implicatures occur, and speakers and writers are taken to be communicating something indirectly.

When a maxim suggests that in a particular communicative situation a particular act is required, another belief or convention, more important in the situation, may cause a speaker or writer to violate the maxim. To the extent that the hearer or reader knows that the other belief or convention is the cause of the violation and believes that it is indeed more important, the maxim violation will not be marked. Speakers and writers are commonly faced with clashes between maxims and a wide variety of other beliefs and conventions. Beliefs about politeness (explored in detail in Brown and Levinson, 1978) often clash with the quality maxims, causing "white lies." Such violations, explains Sissela Bok, "deceive no one, except possibly those unfamiliar with the language [1979, p. 61]." Conventions of court-ship also supercede quality maxims; in Sonnet 130 Shakespeare satirizes lovers who obviously cannot believe what they say: "My mistress' eyes are nothing like the sun."

Conventions of written genres clash with maxims too. Newspaper re-ports, structured for readers who may read only the first paragraph or two, repeat information, thus violating the first quantity maxim. An article in the *Los Angles Times* headlined "No deal has been made to free hostages, Muskie says" repeats this information in the first sentence—"Secretary of State Edmund S. Muskie on Saturday repeated Administration denials that a secret deal has been worked out to free the 52 Americans in Iran"—and again in the sixth paragraph—"'There is no deal,' he said." In articles like *Time* magazine's regular "Essay," writers surveying a broad perspective are not held strictly accountable to quality maxims. How can Lance Morrow know what he seems to know in the opening paragraph of his essay on revenge? "Americans found themselves thinking about it a little more than usual last week as they watched Iranians displaying charred American bodies in front of the Tehran embassy [Morrow, 1980]." This convention is a kind of synecdoche; the writer's reactions to an event are allowed to stand for the reactions of a whole group of people. In the next paragraph, the writer follows a more common linguistic convention and again violates the quality maxims: "Such scenes open a little trap door at the base of the brain. From that ancient root cellar they summon up dark, flapping fantasies of revenge [Morrow, 1980]."[10]

Thus, maxim violations may be rendered insignificant when the maxims conflict with other beliefs and with conventions. The opposite is true in the case of implicatures. Maxim violations (and maxim invocations) exist only by virtue of other beliefs and conventions. What is required in any com-

[9]Grice calls a situation in which a maxim is violated to avoid violating another maxim a clash (1975, p. 49). Here I extend the notion of a clash to include situations in which maxims clash with any other belief or convention.

[10]As Grice points out, metaphors "characteristically involve categorical falsity [1975, p. 53]"; he says that they convey meaning by flouting the first quality maxim. I would argue that the maxim violation simply marks the presence of a metaphor (and not all metaphors violate the quality maxim); it does not define the nature of metaphor.

municative situation can be ascertained by reviewing the other beliefs and conventions that the people involved in the situation hold. In Grice's example (1)[11] of the bank employee (see p. 113), A knows that B has failed to fulfill the maxim of relation because he knows, among other things, that the information B volunteers about C's situation is meant to explain, or give cause for, B's judgment that C is doing "quite well" in his job. Thus A knows that the statement *he hasn't been to prison yet* is meant to be related to the statement that C is doing quite well (and in writing the relation is marked by the use of the semicolon), though, on the face of it, the two statements do not seem to be related. B in his remark raises the question of how the two statements can be related, thus invoking the relation maxim and implicating that C is potentially dishonest.

Other beliefs and conventions not only define maxim violations and evocations, they also serve as the basis on which we work out what's been implicated. Look again at Grice's bank employee example. We decide that B believes C is potentially dishonest on the basis of things we believe about the world, specifically things we believe about prisons and banks. A variety of scholars have recently proposed that our knowledge of the world can best be represented as frames, structures of associated facts.[12] Teun van Dijk defines **frames** as "knowledge representations about the 'world' which enable us to perform such basic cognitive acts as perception, action, and language comprehension [1977, p. 19]." And, of course, language production. Grice's example depends on two frames to convey the implicature: the "bank" frame, which includes the notion that bank employees are faced with temptations to be dishonest, and the "prison" frame, which includes the notion that people are sent to prison for illegal acts, one of which is dishonesty. (See also Black, Wilkes-Gibbs, and Gibbs' discussion of SCRIPTS, PLANS, GOALS, and THEMES, Chap. 12 this volume.)

IMPLICATURES IN WRITING

In communicating their meanings, speakers and writers always depend on context much more than they do on the linguistic shape of their utterances or texts. Implicatures are simply the most radical cases, in which speakers and writers draw on and exploit mutual knowledge of beliefs and conventions in order to communicate meanings that are in no way encoded in linguistic forms or that contradict the conventional meanings of the linguistic forms used. To demonstrate the variety of knowledge of context

[11]Bold face numbers key the examples to Table 5.1 (p. 120), where all implicatures are outlined schematically for ease of comparison.

[12]Frame theorists assume that the knowledge contained in frames is conventional in the sense that such knowledge relies on perceptions of the world rather than on objective fact. This sense of *convention* is much broader than that assumed by many language theorists and defined by David Lewis (1969).

TABLE 5.1

Written Implicatures

Linguistic form	Facilitating beliefs and/or conventions	Maxim violated	Interpretive beliefs and/or conventions	Implicated
1. Oh, quite well, I think; he likes his colleagues and he hasn't been to prison yet.	"Judgment" frame Punctuation convention (;)	Relation	"Bank" frame "Prison" frame	C is potentially dishonest.
2. We think they qualify at least for something like the New Egalitarianism.	"Wage level" frame "Inheritance" frame	Quality 1	"U.S. principles" frame	These proposals are unfair and bad.
3. We will probably find shores that have been ravaged by man.	"Human powers" frame	Quality 2	"Environmental action" frame	Too many people value the acquisition of resources over the protection of the environment.
4. Will the Governor charge $60 an hour? (etc.)	"Governor" frame	Relation	"Psychiatrist" frame	Psychiatrists might make bad governors.
5. Mr. X's command of English is excellent, and his attendance at tutorials has been regular.	"Recommendation" frame "Philosophy" frame	Quantity 1	"Criticism" frame	Mr. X is no good at philosophy.
6. A woman was murdered . . . the real killer was never found.	Text coherence convention	Relation	"Murder" frame "Marriage" frame	Her husband was suspected of her murder; the butcher knife was the murder weapon.
7. That, too, is nature.	Text coherence convention	Quantity 1	"Predation" frame	This series presents an idealized view of nature.

#	Example	Feature	Maxim	Frame	Implicature
8.	My copy has margin notes: Pages 1, 11, 16, 37.	Text coherence convention	Quantity 1	"Reading for erotic stimulation" frame	This book is best considered a piece of eroticism.
				"Reviewing" frame	Foster is still of some use.
9.	I'll protect you.	Narrative convention (abstract)	Relation	"Game" frame	This book offers sinful delights.
				"Family" frame	This series is pleasant but misleading.
10.	Since [the erotic passages] are the reason thou mayst covet it....	Archaic forms	Quality 1	"Bible" frame	
11.	Well, sir, it sure would pleasure a feller...	Dialect forms	Quality 1	"Backwoods" frame	
12.	Be as *complete* and *specific* in your answers as possible: I am not a mind reader.	Punctuation convention (:)	Relation	"Communication" frame	Implicit answers will not count.
				"Examination" frame	You are not my intended audience.
13.	This was a tool whose only purpose was to make holes in human beings. (etc.)	Past tense form	Quantity 2	"Time" frame	
14.	We at Boise Cascade haven't been able to . . . yet.	Negation	Quantity 2	"Corporate image" frame	Boise Cascade is a good corporation.
15.	Nobody does it better.	Deixis (pronoun reference)	Manner 1	"Product" frame	No one produces better cigarettes than Winston.
				"Worker" frame	Winston smokers are good workers.
				"Sexual relations" frame	Winston smokers are good lovers.

writers can exploit in implicating meanings, I will, in the rest of this discussion, examine an array of examples of implicatures in writing.

The contextual knowledge writers draw on most heavily is the beliefs they share with their readers about the world they inhabit. In some implicatures, frame knowledge both defines the maxim violation and serves as the basis for interpreting what was meant. An editorial in the *Los Angeles Times* entitled "Laying Golden Eggs" (2) commented on two economic proposals made by Ronald Reagan: one to abolish the minimum wage "without favoritism. . . . for adults and teenagers alike" and another to abolish the inheritance tax "without partiality. . . . no inheritance tax for either the rich or the poor." The writer remarked: "He did not seem to think that they warranted a grandiose label like the New Deal or the Reagan Doctrine, but we think he was too modest. We think they qualify at least for something like the New Egalitarianism ["Laying Golden Eggs", 1980]." Despite the approving tone of these remarks, readers know that the writer is not applauding Reagan's new policy direction. The writer is being ironic: By flouting the first maxim of quality that you believe what you say, he implicates that Reagan's proposals are unfair and thus are bad proposals.[13] Two frames reveal the insincerity of the egalitarian label: the "wage level" frame, which includes the fact that teenagers are paid less than adults, and the "inheritance" frame, which includes the fact that the poor inherit much less than the rich. The writer cannot believe that such unfair policies are laudable, and by referring to the "U.S. principles" frame, which stipulates, among other things, that government policies ensure equal opportunity for all, readers infer that the writer thinks the proposals are bad.

A letter to the editor of the *Times* in response to an article about sea otters (3) similarly depends on a value frame to convey its meaning. The writer fails to fulfill the second quality maxim, for she has no way to know her prediction will come true. She says, "we would be delighted to find a sea otter population, the sign of a healthy marine environment, south of Point Conception in 15 years, but instead we will probably find shores that have been ravaged by man—stripped of their resources and smeared with oil [Fulton, 1980]." We know that people's powers do not include seeing into the future (a fact in the "human powers" frame), but by referring to the "environmental action" frame the writer evokes we can infer a proposition that she does have reason to believe is true: Too many people value the acquisition of resources over the protection of the environment.[14]

One tactic writers often use to implicate is the evocation of two apparently unrelated frames. Roger Rosenblatt in writing about the psychiatrist who was running for Governor of Washington State (4) asks: "Will the Governor charge $60 an hour? Will his hours last 45 minutes? Will his staff

---

[13]For a more complete discussion of irony and the quality maxim see Robert L. Brown, Jr. (1980).

[14]For a parallel example in spoken discourse, see Grice, 1975, pp. 53-54.

know each other's last names? More urgent: Where will he be in August? [1980]." Rosenblatt invokes the maxim of relation: These questions have no apparent referents within the "governor" frame. But the "psychiatrist" frame contains the propositions questioned as part of the knowledge we have of psychiatrist's terms of employment. By thus juxtaposing the frames, Rosenblatt allows readers to conclude that the psychiatrist might be tempted to retain his old terms of employment in his new job, and that such a course of action might not be in the public's best interest. Grice's example of the professor who, in writing a letter of recommendation, violates the first quantity maxim by not commenting on the applicant's skill at philosophy (5) is also facilitated by a frame that explains what information is necessary: Letters of recommendation are characterized by their containing information bearing on the subject of the letter's qualifications for the position in question.

Invoking the relation maxim as a way of implicating meanings is facilitated by A FUNDAMENTAL CONVENTION OF WRITTEN DISCOURSE: THE PRESUMPTION THAT ALL PROPOSITIONS IN A SINGLE TEXT ARE SOMEHOW RELATED. **Coherence** is largely an inference writers allow readers to make, as van Dijk explains: "Linear coherence . . . depends on interpolated propositions that remain implicit in the expressed discourse and are inferred from the other propositions of the discourse with the help of lexical meaning postulates and frame information [1977, p. 18]." Here's an example (**6**) of a text that invokes the maxim of relation in that its individual propositions do not seem to cohere:

> *A woman was murdered in this room last year. The police suspected her husband. The butcher knife turned up in the garden two months after her death. But the real killer was never found.*

Propositions that remain implicit in this text are that the woman's husband was suspected of her murder and that the murder was done with a butcher knife. Readers, because of the **text coherence convention,** assume the sentences are meant to be related and use the "murder" frame evoked in the first sentence to assign roles to the husband and the butcher knife and reasons for the action of the police.[15] (The "marriage" frame also helps explain why the police suspected the husband.) The implicit propositions are what the writer has implicated.

Written texts that do not state their central point often implicate it. The convention of text coherence not only demands that all propositions in a text be related but also demands that there be some proposition to which

[15]Case grammars, like those proposed by Charles Fillmore and by Wallace Chafe, are a kind of frame analysis of linguistic semantics; they seek to explain how certain beliefs about the world are encoded in language. If these relations are considered to be part of the conventions of the language, the implicatures here are examples of what Grice calls conventional implicatures, implicatures determined by "the conventional meanings of the words used [Grice, 1975, p. 44]."

all other propositions in the text can be related. If such a proposition is not stated in the text, the writer fails to fulfill the first maxim of quantity. Reviewers often implicate their judgment of the work they are reviewing via this route. Robert MacKenzie began a review of the television show "The Life and Times of Grizzly Adams" (7) by posing the question, "What's in Grizzly Adams' stew?" He noted that "this may be one television series that could be accused of unnecessary nonviolence" and reflected on how the meat for that stew must be procured: "when we're not looking, Grizzly Adams konks one of his little furry friends with an ax." He concluded: "That, too, is nature [MacKenzie, 1977]." By failing to fulfill the quantity maxim and by evoking the "predation" frame, MacKenzie implicates that this series presents an idealized view of nature.

In reviewing Gay Talese's *Thy Neighbor's Wife*, Harvey Mindess also fails to fulfill the first maxim of quantity and implicates his opinion of the value of the book (8): that it serves best as a piece of eroticism. He quotes a particularly vivid description of an orgy scene and says, "my copy has margin notes: Pages 1, 11, 17, 37 [Mindess, 1980, p. 10]." He repeats this ploy three more times in the review, each time listing page numbers. Those remarks cannot be directly related to anything Mindess says in the review about his opinion of the book, though he does comment that the book, "like an overrated call girl . . . fails to live up to her hype [1980, p. 1]," and that the writing is on the level of *Esquire* and *Playboy*: "topical, clever, flashy, and crass [1980, p. 10]." But the listing of pages evokes a frame that might be called "reading for erotic stimulation," and Mindess exploits this piece of shared knowledge to implicate what the primary value of the book is.

A narrative convention similarly helps story writers implicate the point or "message" of their stories. William Labov remarks that in oral narratives he has elicited, "it is not uncommon for narrators to begin with one or two clauses summarizing the whole story [1972, p. 363]." He calls this part of the narrative the abstract, that part which encapsulates the point of the narrative. In written narratives, the title often serves the function of abstract, and the propositions in the story are supposed to be related to such a title. Thus writers often invoke the relation maxim in order to implicate how the story embodies the title. John Updike's story "Still of Some Use" is a good example (9). He tells us about the activities of a modern extended family—a divorced man, his exwife, their two almost grown sons, his exwife's new lover, and a girlfriend of the older son—in ridding an attic of old, unwanted items. In the conclusion, the man responds to the younger son's request that he come with him to the dump; the boy says it's a scary place. "'O.K.,' Foster said, greatly lightened. 'I'll protect you' [Updike, 1980, p. 54]." How do readers understand what Updike has implicated here? They assume Foster's statement is somehow related to the title of the story, though not in a straightforward fashion; Updike apparently fails to fulfill the maxim of relation. But he evokes two frames from which readers can infer the relation: Throughout the story, Foster has identified with the "forgotten, broken games" they found in the attic—of no use to his exwife and of little use to his sons, who are striving for independence. The "game" frame and the "family" frame both specify roles for players, and together the frames enable the reader to conclude that Foster is trapped in a game and role that no longer allows him to feel useful: exhusband and out-grown father. But the final incident reestablishes him in one role that fathers assume: He can still protect his younger son; he can still be of some use.[16]

A particularly interesting type of implicature in writing comes about through writers using archaic forms or dialect forms. Such forms connote a speaker of a certain time or place or role, and when the writer is not that kind of speaker, he or she fails to fulfill the first quality maxim and may implicate something. Mindess, in the review of *Thy Neighbor's Wife* discussed previously, picks up on the biblical forms *thou, thee,* and *thy* to implicate the sinfulness of the delights the book offers (**10**): "Since the erotic passages are the reason thou mayst covet it, I'll tell thee where to find them. . . . I will insert the page numbers from time to time and thou canst use thy imagination [1980, p. 10]." MacKenzie in his review of "Grizzly Adams," also discussed previously, uses a backwoods dialect to implicate that the series, though pleasant, is misleading (**11**): "Well, sir, it sure would pleasure a feller to settle back and enjoy this easygoing, outdoorsy NBC series, if it wasn't for this question that keeps on a-naggin' me [1977]."

Other aspects of linguistic form may also draw attention to maxim violations. Punctuation marks signal meaning relationships and thus specify that certain clauses should be related. The colon, for example, "indicates that the next clause to come will clarify, expand, or illustrate the idea just mentioned [Glorfeld, Lauerman, & Stageberg, 1977, p. 31]." When the clause following the colon does not seem to be related to the clause preceding the colon, the writer may evoke the maxim of relation. Here's an example (**12**) from some examination instructions: "Be as *complete* and *specific* in your answers as possible: I am not a mind reader." By referring to the "communication" frame (a part of which I am attempting to explicate in this chapter) and to the "examination" frame, readers understand that the writer has implicated that she will not grant credit to implicit propositions in answers to the questions on the exam.

Throughout his novel *Breakfast of Champions,* Kurt Vonnegut uses the past tense to signal an invocation of the second quantity maxim that you not supply more information than is needed (**13**). I'll cite just three examples: above a drawing of a revolver, he writes, "This was a tool whose only

[16]Mary Louise Pratt (1977) explains implicatures in "the literary speech situation" in a significantly different way. I discuss her approach in my *Implicatures in Dramatic Conversations.*

purpose was to make holes in human beings [Vonnegut, 1973, p. 49]'';
above a representation of Einstein's formula, he writes, ''I wrote again on
my tabletop, scrawled the symbols for the interrelationship between matter
and energy as it was understood in my day [Vonnegut, 1973, p. 241]''; and
under a drawing of a handshake, he writes, ''This was a symbol of friendship between men [Vonnegut, 1973, p. 276].'' Readers in 1973, when this
book was published, need to have none of these things explained. But if
they hypothesize a time frame in which Vonnegut's statements are
cooperative and do fulfill the second quantity maxim, they can work out
what he is implicating: that when the present time is past time, these
things will need to be explained to readers, and thus that the intended
readers for this book are not the readers who are currently reading it—a
rather unsettling message.

The use of negation may mark a failure to fulfill the second quantity
maxim, because usually to say that something did not happen is to say
something more than is required. Labov takes note of the use of negation
in narration: ''What reason would the narrator have for telling us that
something did not happen, since he is in the business of telling us what did
happen? . . . The use of negatives in accounts of past events . . . expresses
the defeat of an expectation that something would happen [1972, pp. 380–
381].'' A current ad for Boise Cascade Corporation (**14**) implicates its message in this way. They ask, ''Can you find the glue in this tree?'' then add,
''We at Boise Cascade haven't been able to . . . yet.'' The glue they're looking for, they explain, is lignin, which could replace the oil-based glues now
used to stick plywood together. Why would Boise Cascade want to tell us
they have not lived up to their expectations of themselves? We have only to
refer to the ''corporate image'' frame to discover what they are implicating:
Corporations that aspire to better our lives through research are good
corporations.

Advertisers are particularly apt to use implicatures to convey their meanings, since one of the benefits of such indirect communication is that
speakers or writers cannot be held accountable for what they implicate in the
same way they are held accountable for the conventional meaning of
their utterances or texts. My final example of an implicature in writing
(**15**) is found in a current series of ads for Winston cigarettes, which
proclaim, ''Nobody does it better.'' Because the referent for the pronoun *it*
is not supplied, the statement fails to fulfill the manner maxim that enjoins
perspicuity. The advertisers evoke at least three frames on the basis of
which an implicature can be worked out. The ''product'' frame allows the
inference that no one produces better cigarettes. The ''worker'' frame
evoked by the photographs of hard-hatted men allows the inference that
Winston smokers are good workers. And the ''sexual relations'' frame,
evoked by the allusion to the popular song from which the line comes,
allows the inference that Winston smokers are good lovers. The last two
inferences are less clearly cases of implicature in that it is doubtful that the

advertisers intend readers to make the inferences consciously; the strategy does not have the quality of openness that marks most implicatures.

Certainly writers need much skill and much knowledge of all aspects of the context of their writing to convey their meanings in this indirect way. Many inexperienced writers are misunderstood because their attempted implicatures rely on contextual knowledge that readers do not possess. For example, in a letter to the editor about the language problem in Southern California, David Arthur attempts to ask a rhetorical question: "Is it unrealistic for me to assume a businessman and his employees should be able to communicate in English to their customers? [1980]." Rhetorical questions fail to fulfill the first quality maxim. The writer is not looking for an answer to the question; rather, he is implicating that the answer to his question is obvious—all residents of Southern California should be able to communicate in English. But this implicature depends on his readers sharing his opinion that bilingualism is detrimental to a society. Readers like me who do not share this belief may read his question as a real question, answer it in the affirmative, and infer that the writer is a provincial bigot. All teachers of composition are familiar with students who try and fail to be ironic or sarcastic in their writing. They are not yet acquainted with the formal written markers of such intentions, nor with the genre conventions that can signal such intentions, nor are they proficient in ascertaining and exploiting their readers' beliefs. This is the goal of all the exercises in editing, imitating models, and analyzing audiences. For when writers have mastered these special skills, they can then use them to communicate as flexibly, subtly, and economically as they do in speaking. Implicatures represent an especially effective communicative strategy, and because they depend so heavily on mastery of the conventions of writing, as well as on beliefs about the world, and on knowledge of audience's beliefs, they are among the last strategies writers acquire.

REFERENCES

Aelgh, H. Conversation as paranoia. In T. Ernst & E. Smith (Eds.), *Lingua pranca*. Bloomington: Indiana University Linguistics Club (mimeograph), 1978.

Arthur, D. Letter to the editor. *Los Angeles Times*, 25 Oct. 1980, Sec. 2, p. 5.

Bach, K., & Harnish, R. M. *Linguistic communication and speech acts*. Cambridge: M.I.T. Press, 1979.

Banta, M. Anxiety of influence in the classroom, or, the will to ignorance. *College English*, 1980, 42, 109–120.

Bok, S. *Lying: Moral choice in public and private life*. New York: Vintage, 1979.

Britton, J. *Language and learning*. Harmondsworth, England: Penguin Books, 1970.

Brown, P., & Levinson, S. Universals in language usage: Politeness phenomena. In E. N. Goody (Ed.), *Questions and politeness: Strategies in social interaction*. Cambridge, England: Cambridge University Press, 1978, pp. 56–289.

Brown, R. L., Jr. The pragmatics of verbal irony. In R. Fasold & R. Shuy (Eds.), *Language use and the uses of language*. Washington, D.C.: Georgetown University Press, 1980.

Carroll, L. *The complete works*. New York: Vintage, 1976.

Chapman, R. Power and politeness: The logic of conversations in Pinter's *The collection*. Unpublished manuscript, University of Minnesota, 1978.

Cooper, M. M. *Implicatures in dramatic conversations*. Unpublished Ph.D. dissertation, University of Minnesota, 1980.

Dijk, T. A. van. Semantic macro-structures and knowledge frames in discourse comprehension. In M. A. Just & P. A. Carpenter (Eds.), *Cognitive processes in comprehension*. Hillsdale, N.J.: Lawrence Erlbaum, 1977, pp. 3–32.

Fish, S. E. Interpreting the *Variorum*. *Critical Inquiry*, 1976, *2*, 465–485.

Fulton, C. Letter to the editor. *Los Angeles Times*, 29 May 1980, Sec. 2, p. 6.

Glorfeld, L. E., Lauerman, D. A., & Stageberg, N. C. *A concise guide for writers*. 4th ed. New York: Holt, Rinehart and Winston, 1977.

Grice, H. P. *Logic and conversation*. William James Lectures, Harvard, 1967.

Grice, H. P. Utterer's meaning and intention. *Philosophical Review*, 1969, *68*, 147–177.

Grice, H. P. Logic and conversation. In P. Cole & J. L. Morgan (Eds.), *Syntax and semantics* (Vol. 3): *Speech acts*. New York: Academic Press, 1975, pp. 41–58.

Grice, H. P. Further notes on logic and conversation. In P. Cole (Ed.), *Syntax and semantics* (Vol. 9): *Pragmatics*. New York: Academic Press, 1978, pp. 113–127.

Hancher, M. Grice's 'implicature' and literary interpretation: Background and preface. Forum. MMLA Convention. 4 Nov. 1978, Minneapolis.

Johnston, O. No deal has been made to free hostages, Muskie says. *Los Angeles Times*, 2 Nov. 1980, Sec. 1, pp. 1, 12.

Keenan, E. The universality of conversational implicatures. In R. Fasold & R. Shuy (Eds.), *Studies in language variation: Semantics, syntax, phonology, pragmatics, social situations, ethnographic approaches*. Washington, D.C.: Georgetown University Press, 1977.

Kempson, R. *Presupposition and the delimitation of semantics*. Cambridge, England: Cambridge University Press, 1975.

Labov, W. The transformation of experience in narrative syntax. In *Language in the inner city: Studies in the Black English vernacular*. Philadelphia: University of Pennsylvania Press, 1972. Pp. 354–396.

Laying golden eggs. *Los Angeles Times*, 11 Feb. 1980, Sec. 2, p. 6.

Lewis, D. K. *Convention: A philosophical analysis*. Cambridge: Harvard University Press, 1969.

MacKenzie, R. Review of "The life and times of Grizzly Adams." *TV Guide*, 28 May 1977, p. 34.

Mindess, H. In terms of love and letting go, Talese treads a delicate terrain. *Los Angeles Times Book Review*, 27 Apr. 1980, Pp. 1, 10.

Morrow, L. The temptations of revenge. *Time*, 12 May 1980, p. 84.

Pinter, H. *Three plays*. New York: Grove, 1961.

Pratt, M. L. *Towards a speech act theory of literary discourse*. Bloomington: Indiana University Press, 1977.

Richards, I. A. *Practical criticism*. New York: Harcourt Brace Jovanovich, 1929.

Rosenblatt, R. The people's analyst. *Time*, 29 Sept. 1980, p. 92.

Schleusener, J. Convention and the context of reading. *Critical Inquiry*, 1980, *6*, 669–680.

Searle, J. *Speech acts: An essay in the philosophy of language*. Cambridge, England: Cambridge University Press, 1969.

Shaughnessy, M. *Errors and expectations: A guide for the teacher of basic writing*. New York: Oxford University Press, 1977.

Updike, J. Still of some use. *The New Yorker*, 6 Oct. 1980, 52–54.

Vonnegut, K. *Breakfast of champions*. New York: Dell, 1973.

Young, R., Becker, A., & Pike, K. *Rhetoric: Discovery and change*. New York: Harcourt Brace Jovanovich, 1970.

Chapter 6

Children as Writers: The Beginnings of Learning to Write

Robert A. Gundlach

THE OFIS IN THE ADICK

At my hose I have a ofis upstars in my adick, writes Michael, who is 7 years old and in first grade, *and its are printing ofis that we print newspapers at.* Approaching the bottom line of his sheet of paper, Michael decides to suspend his text and draw a picture, centered on the bottom line, of a boy sitting at a desk. It is a head-on view, drawn in red, blue, yellow, and black crayons.

Michael switches back to his pencil and resumes his text on a new sheet: *and we prent sports and we prent news and we even tipe som. The end.* In the space that remains at the bottom of the second page, Michael draws a larger side view of the boy (same black hair, same red shirt, same blue pants) sitting at a desk, which is now equipped with a typewriter. To the left of this scene is a rectangle containing words—a sign posted on the office wall. It reads: *ofis/BOSCHRIS/PRINTERMICHAEL/SECRETERE/CARRIE.*

Until quite recently, compositions like Michael's held little interest for researchers studying children's language development. Studies of children's language acquisition have concentrated on how children acquire spoken language during the preschool years (see de Villiers & de Villiers, 1978) and research on literacy has been dominated by studies of how children learn to read (see Graves, 1978).

Now, however, interest in children as writers has begun to increase.

WHAT WRITERS KNOW
The Language, Process,
and Structure of Written Discourse

Probably the major cause of this new attention to children's writing has been the widespread publicity about a "writing crisis" in American education—in December, 1975, for example, *Newsweek* ran a cover story purporting to explain "Why Johnny Can't Write." With the publicity has come a new emphasis on writing instruction in American schools and colleges, and new allocations of research funds in government agencies and foundations. Some of the recent trends in research on children's language, however, have also led to an interest in children as writers, and furthermore have influenced some of the studies that have come in the wake of the "crisis." Charles Read (1975), seeking to learn more about the way children categorize speech sounds in the course of their phonological development, studied the "invented spellings" produced by several pre-school children who, each on his own, had fashioned a makeshift writing system out of the name–sounds of the letters in the alphabet and thus had begun to write before they had learned to read. In addition to contributing insights into children's phonological development, Read's studies demonstrated that at least some children apply the powerful strategies that help them acquire spoken language to their early learning of written language, and demonstrated as well that learning to read does not necessarily precede learning to write—as Chomsky (1971) has put it, some children "write now" and "read later."

In reading research, there has been an emphasis recently on studies of the process of reading comprehension, and particularly on studies of the cognitive representations of text structure that readers use to comprehend the texts they read (e.g. Stein & Glenn, 1979). This interest in the cognitive operations of comprehending texts has broadened in the last few years to an interest in "discourse processing" (e.g. Freedle, 1979), and recently research has been undertaken to learn about the cognitive processes children undergo when they write. Complementing inquiry of this sort is recent research by Graves (1979), Calkins (1980), and Sowers (1979), which adapts and builds on Emig's (1971) pioneering studies of children's composing behavior and children's attitudes toward the writing process.

Reading researchers have also become interested recently in the nature of the written language that children encounter before they are able to read, and in the ways children use these "encounters with print" to develop fundamental concepts of both reading and writing (see Anderson, Teale, & Estrada, 1980; Harste, Burke, & Woodward, forthcoming). Heath (1980) has studied the social foundations of the child's early concepts of reading and writing and has presented ethnographic research that demonstrates the cultural variations in children's early experiences with written language.

In light of this recent work, even a single example of children's writing such as Michael's account of his newspaper printing enterprise suggests much about children as writers. Michael's misspellings—ofis for *office,* adick for *attic,* tipe for *type*—offer interesting bits of evidence that children use their various linguistic resources to construct spellings of words they can speak and wish to write (see Beers & Henderson, 1977; Bissex, 1980; Read, 1975). Further, we note that the misspellings of beginning writers can be viewed in the same way we view errors of noun and verb inflection ("foots" for *feet,* "goed" for *went*) in young children's speech, as evidence of learning-in-progress rather than merely as deviations from convention (see Gundlach, 1981).

Michael's repetition of *and* to connect independent clauses (*and we prent sports and we prent news and we even tipe som*) puts him in the company of many young writers who write sentences that teachers call "run-ons" and that some educators believe children should be trained to combine into more fully embedded syntactic structures (see Mellon, 1969; O'Hare, 1973). Yet we also notice that Michael's account begins with relatively complex syntax (*At my hose I have a ofis upstars in my adick and its are printing ofis that we print newspapers at*) and that the function of this part of the text is to present background information establishing a context for the generalized events Michael proceeds to narrate. Recent studies of children's concepts of narrative structure (Applebee, 1978; Stein & Glenn, 1979) suggest that along with learning a grammar of sentence structure, children also learn a "grammar" or a "schema" for the structure of stories: hence we must recognize that at the same time children are learning to write increasingly complex sentences, they are also learning to construct increasingly complex stories, explanations, and arguments.

Reflecting on the structures of Michael's text, we are led to questions about the process by which Michael produced his composition. We wonder, for example, whether Michael had a clear idea from the start of how he wanted to organize his account, or whether he decided what he wanted to say as he went along. Are the narrative clauses he strings together the result of a conscious decision about how he wanted his story to sound and what information he planned to include, or is his repetition of this pattern the result of a series of momentary decisions to say more, to keep going, to "make it last"? (Keenan, 1977). Studies by Graves (1974) lead us to consider the relationship between Michael's drawings and his writing. Are the drawings simply embellishments, illustrations for a self-contained text, or did the activity of drawing play a crucial role in Michael's composing process, contributing to the meaning-making activity of writing by enabling Michael to create a fuller frame of reference for the experience he wanted to represent? Was Michael able to sustain the composing process by alternating between writing and drawing, or did he add pictures simply because his teachers and parents expect pictures with children's writing, or even just because he enjoys illustrating his written compositions?

If we impose a rough general analysis on our considerations of Michael's piece to this point, we can see that in learning to write, children learn

forms of written language and they learn writing **processes.** A third basic dimension of learning to write is learning **uses** of written language. Recent work by educational anthropologists (see Florio, 1978; Heath, 1980, forthcoming) leads us to consider the situations in which children write, both at school and at home. Michael's account was written at school, first thing in the morning, as a part of a daily routine in which he and his classmates write about recent experiences and read their writing aloud to their peers. Thus writing in this instance functions as an extension of the time-honored school use of spoken language for "show and tell." The experience that Michael has chose to write about—publishing a newspaper at home with his brother and sister—suggests that Michael may write in different situations and for other purposes at home, when he plays with his siblings. Florio (1978) and Applebee (1980) demonstrate convincingly the importance of understanding the situations in which children write at school. The subject Michael has written about makes clear, however, that to understand the full range of children's uses for writing, we must consider the writing children do outside of school as well (see Bissex, 1980; Gundlach, forthcoming).

LEARNING TO TALK, LEARNING TO WRITE

Although Michael's composition offers intriguing hints about children as writers, it does not represent an extraordinary accomplishment for a 7-year old child, as anyone who has observed children writing often and for their own purposes can attest. Donald Graves has observed that children who are given opportunities to write—or who make opportunities for themselves—"make some of the most rapid and delightful [writing] growth of their entire lives [1979, p. 2]." The most promising prospect of the new interest in children's writing as a part of the study of children's language development is that research is likely to proceed from the assumption that learning to write involves more than being taught; thus we may move beyond considering only the short-term effects of various teaching programs on groups of children and can begin to identify the range of potential influences on the individual child's development of writing abilities.

Yet we must confront the fact that although some children apparently teach themselves to write before they start school (see Britton, Chapter 7 of this volume), many children do not write much or at all before they receive instruction, and even then, many children do not flourish as writers. We can assume, in studying children's language development, that virtually all children will mature as speakers. We cannot make the same assumption about children as writers.

It seems plausible to attribute this difference to the greater cognitive and neuromuscular demands that the process of writing makes on children; however, Higgens' "developmental comparison of oral and written communication" led him to conclude that "oral–written differences cannot be explained in terms of greater difficulty in written production [1978, p. 143]" and Graves' studies of first-grade children indicate that "we underestimate what children can do in the writing process [1979, p. 2]."

I believe that if we are to understand why some children develop as writers and why others do not, we must turn our attention to the comparatively more difficult time children have in discovering significant uses for written language. Anyone who gives a moment's thought to the matter will have no trouble imagining why a young child might want to speak. So central to the human enterprise is speaking that most scholars who have studied the question believe that babies are, in one sense or another, "born to talk [Weeks, 1979]." In contrast, as Connie and Harold Rosen have put it, "It is easy to think of many reasons why a young child should not want to write and difficult to think of reasons why he should [Rosen & Rosen, 1973, p. 85]."

BUILDING BRIDGES TO WRITING

Much has been written (and no doubt spoken) about the contrasting uses to which adults in literate societies put speech and writing (for recent examples, see Hirsch, 1977; Olson, 1977; Stubbs, 1980). Such discussions usually point out that the use of spoken language is "dependent in every case upon nonlinguistic and paralinguistic cues," whereas written language is an "autonomous system for representing meaning [Olson, 1977, p. 275]" and is thus normally used to communicate across distance and through time, or to record information that a reader (sometimes a particular reader, sometimes an unspecified reader, and sometimes the writer himself) might or might not consult later. When discussions of this sort turn to the question of how children learn to use written language, the suggestion is usually made that, as Michael Stubbs has put it, "young children often have difficulty in understanding the purposes of written language, since many of these purposes are completely beyond their needs and experiences [1980, p. 99]." Following this line of analysis (and although there are alternatives—see Heath, forthcoming—I have found that this view prevails among both researchers and educators), we are left a bit awed by children who teach themselves to write and uncertain about what to make of—or do for—children who do not.

Frequently, as a concession to the child's inability to adopt adult-like uses for writing, beginning writing instruction in schools emphasizes manipulating written language as a code rather than accomplishing purposes through writing, in the hope that by the time the child matures to the point of taking on authentic uses for writing, he will have already become "fluent" and will have mastered the tools—conventions of punctuation and spelling, stylistic principles of sentence structure, and the "logic" of paragraphs. Exercises are evaluated rather than read, with the result that some children come to regard the written language they must produce in school as "but a line that moves haltingly across the page, exposing as it goes all that the writer doesn't know, then passing into the hands of a stranger who reads it with a lawyer's eyes, searching for flaws [Shaughnessy, 1977, p. 7]." Other children do, of course, learn fuller and more potent uses for writing, presumably, from the perspective of this analysis, by a little-understood process of socialization that initiates them into the community of readers and writers.

To understand more about how children learn uses for writing, we may be best served in the long run by investigating particular uses separately, recognizing that with the single term "writing" we refer to many different kinds of activity. It would be helpful, however, if we were able not only to identify the general problem that children face as they begin to write, but also to identify children's strategies for solving that problem. To accomplish this, we need an approach that accounts more fully for the developmental context of children's early writing than does the broad social analysis I have sketched above. Such an approach can be fashioned, I think, from Vygotsky's remark that "make-believe play, drawing, and writing can be viewed as different moments in an essentially unified process of written language development [1978, p. 116]," and Bruner's observation, meant to explain how infants develop the "pure point" as a communicative gesture, that "new forms of communication emerge initially to fulfill old functions, then bring in new functions with them [1978, p. 7]." From the perspective suggested by these two notions, we can ask whether in their early experiments with the new medium of written language, young children first use writing to serve and perhaps to extend functions already served for them by certain kinds of speech, by drawing, by various forms of play. We can ask whether this is the basic strategy that some children discover as they build bridges from "not writing" to writing. And we can ask whether this is the strategy that children who find no reason to write fail to discover—or discard, having to contend instead with instructional programs that deem all but a few uses of writing uninteresting, irrelevant, or even unacceptable. We shall want to hold these questions in mind as we consider the early steps in children's written language development.

FIRST STEPS IN LEARNING TO WRITE

Not much is known with any certainty about children's initial steps in learning to write, or even about whether there are common first steps or many possible starting points. We do have, however, a number of interesting speculations to consider. Howard Gardner, reflecting on his own experience of "becoming a dictator"—learning to compose writing aloud, into a dictating machine, instead of by hand or with a typewriter—comments in passing that "the development of writing skill . . . begins in the drawings of childhood and has, in its initial stages, little if any connection with speech [1980a, p. 15]."

At the level of common sense, Gardner's remark seems odd, indeed wrong. Writing is, after all, a way of speaking, even if the tools of writing are similar to the tools of drawing. Vygotsky's (1978) recently translated paper, "The Prehistory of Writing," offers a way out of this quandary. Vygotsky saw as the "first precursor of future writing" the "meaningless and undifferentiated squiggles and lines" that children 3- and 4-years old drew, and later referred to, when a researcher asked them to "write" a list of phrases so that they might use their notations to help them recall the list later (p. 115; see also Luria, 1978). Explaining how these scribblings might be regarded as the precursors of written language, Vygotsky commented:

> It is easy to see that the written signs are entirely first order symbols at this point, directly denoting objects or actions, and the child has yet to reach second order symbolism, which involves written signs for the spoken symbols of words. For this the child must make a basic discovery—namely that one can draw not only things, but also speech [p. 115].

In this view, learning to read and learning to write are both aspects of the single general process of written language development, and the process begins when the child starts to differentiate between graphic signs—pictures, in the broadest sense—and graphic symbols that can be understood as meaningful in the same way that speech is meaningful. This process of differentiation is essentially the process of learning the forms of written language and their relation to the forms of spoken language.

Just as children learning to talk learn the underlying principles that govern the system of spoken language, making hypotheses and revising them as they make new conceptual connections, children also seem to develop general hypotheses about the principles that govern the system of written language. The little empirical evidence we have of this process suggests that it is gradual rather than sudden. Reporting on her studies of "children's viewpoints" of the relationship between spoken and written language, Ferreiro (1980) argues persuasively that "children go a long and complicated way before discovering that the writing surrounding them is alphabetic in nature," and she points out that many children explore the possibilities of the "syllabic hypothesis"—that a spoken syllable is represented by a single graphic symbol—before they revise their conception of written language to encompass the orthographic principles of alphabetic writing (p. 24; see also Ferreiro, 1978).

Scollon and Scollon (1979) and Heath (1980) demonstrate that for many children, the discovery that written language can be transformed into speech and speech into written language is not at all accidental. Parents in many cultural groups engage their children in "school-oriented book-reading [Health, 1980]," beginning with the picture-labeling games that parents play with their infants (see Ninio & Bruner, 1978) and continuing in the ritual of telling and reading bedtime stories. Through participating in these activities, some children develop a "literate orientation" well before they begin school and before they are able to read or write very much on their own. It seems likely that experiences such as these, along with the experience of observing parents and older children as they write, provide the impetus for some children to conduct their own experiments with writing. We do not know what percentage of preschool children write, or the precise ages when those who do write begin; if, however, the children studied by Read (1975), Bissex (1980), and Gundlach (forthcoming) represent a larger population, it is reasonable to suppose that many children experiment with writing before anyone begins to teach them composition as we know the subject in school.

It is not too simple to say that children begin to write because they want to—because they have come to value written language from their interactions with their parents, siblings, and other members of their immediate communities. But once children begin to write, what uses do they discover for the activity? Gardner and Wolf note that during the preschool period from 2 to 5 years of age, a child learns to use symbols of several kinds—he "becomes able in this period to use various vehicles—both those devised by himself and those donated by culture—to capture aspects of his experience, to make reference, and to communicate messages to others with increasing clarity [1979, p. vii]." Thus it may be that in the early stages of written language development, while the child continues to differentiate between the forms of drawing and the forms of writing and continues to establish correspondences between writing and speech, he also extends the functions of several symbol systems—of speaking, drawing, and play—into the new activity of writing. He begins to write because he has come to value written language, and he uses written language for the purposes already important to him when he talks, when he draws, and when he plays.

SOME EXAMPLES OF CHILDREN USING WRITING

Writing and Drawing

Many observers have noted that when young children write, they often draw pictures as part of the same activity. Studying the composing processes of second-grade children, Graves (1974) found that some 7-year olds seemed to use the activity of drawing as a "rehearsal" for writing, whereas other researchers have suggested that for beginning writers, writing and drawing sometimes function as a single "mixed medium" (Harste, Burke, & Woodward, forthcoming; Gundlach, forthcoming). In his recent study of children's drawings, Gardner (1980b) notes that in some cases in which children combine drawing and writing, the representational role of writing is secondary early in the child's written language development and becomes increasingly dominant as the child becomes a more fluent writer. To demonstrate his point, Gardner reports the case of a child whose drawings were collected by Gertrude Hildreth at Columbia Teacher's College in the 1930s. Hildreth's subject was apparently "obsessed with trains, [and] drew many hundred such vehicles over a ten year period [p. 155]." Gardner continues:

> If one looks at the role of writing in these drawings, one can observe a subtle yet ultimately decisive transition in the depiction of the trains: in the preschool years, letters and words are used merely as decorations upon the trains; but in the years of middle childhood it is the vehicles and tracks that are merely decorative, for the major thrust of the narrative is now carried by verbal means [p. 155].

It seems plausible to suggest that this particular child built a bridge for himself from the activity of drawing to the activity of writing. He initially used written language to support the functions already served by drawing and then, once he became more adept at handling the forms of written language, in his later combinations of drawing and writing he more fully exploited the narrative potential of language. There is no reason to suppose that this link provided the only bridge to the child's explorations of the possible uses of writing; rather, it seems likely that children make connections of several kinds between various symbol-using activities and the activity of writing.

Bissex (1980) suggests that her son Paul used writing as an extension of both speech and drawing in the developmentally significant process of organizing and naming the parts of his world. She says of Paul:

> As a five year old he was still absorbed in naming, in knowing his world by naming its parts; through his signs and labels and captions he extends this process in writing. In the next year or two, as his reasoning developed and his need to know and control the world around him became expressed through categorizing, this process was reflected in his charts and other organizational writing [p. 101].

In my own observation of children writing (see Gundlach, 1981; Gundlach, Litowitz, & Moses, 1979), I have seen many examples of children combining writing and drawing to label and organize. One particularly clear example can be seen in the writing activity of a first-grade boy at home on the evening of his seventh birthday. He had just received as a birthday gift a "rainbow pad"—a thick pad of 3" × 5" sheets in light shades of several different colors. Of the several compositions that he made on sheets of the new pad that evening, one is dominated by drawings, with four carefully drawn automobiles organized symmetrically in the four quadrants of the sheet. The only writing on this sheet is a heading: *raceing cars*. A short time after making these drawings, the 7 year-old went to work on a new sheet, and this time he relied exclusively on written language. At the top of the sheet he wrote, *thig's with weel's*, and beneath this heading he wrote five words, each underscored and each on a separate line: *Train's/ Truck's/car's/wagon's/modersicle's*.

Telling Stories

As Britton (1970; Chapter 7, this volume) and Applebee (1978) have pointed out, some children use written language to extend the storytelling function of speech—particularly the sort of speech that their families use for bedtime stories (see Heath, 1980). It is important to recognize that in this case children do not simply use written language to serve the purpose served by written language in books they have read, but rather build a bridge to writing from the speech that is used by adults and children when they read books aloud to one another and when they tell stories not recorded in writing. Often these early written stories embody fantasies significant in the child's emotional life—such are the "uses of enchantment" (Bettelheim, 1976; see also Pitcher & Prelinger, 1963). One 6-year old girl, for example, used a free period in her first-grade class to write a compact fantasy of encountering a beautiful butterfly and taking it home with her:

> *One day I saw a buteefl*
> *butr fli and I sid I wil*
> *bring hr hom with me and*
> *thne hee wil lik me far avr.*

Applebee, Britton, Bettelheim, Pitcher and Prelinger, and many others have demonstrated that for many children, the motivation for telling and listening to stories is very strong. Indeed, perhaps Reynolds Price, a novelist, has not overstated the case in claiming that "a need to tell and hear stories is essential to the species *Homo sapiens*—second in necessity apparently after nourishment and before love and shelter [Price, 1979, p. 3]." No doubt children use their experience of hearing stories and of reading stories together with adults as a principal resource in writing stories of their own. Children also, however, construct narrative fragments in their play activity, ranging from play with puppets and dolls to dramatic role-playing with companions and siblings (see Garvey, 1977). Some of the

stories young children write suggest that this sort of narrative construction in play also extends into the early writing of stories. Thus the impulse to tell stories is strong, and the resources the child brings to the activity of writing stories may be drawn both from spoken storytelling and dramatic play. Let us consider, as an example, the following story written by a 6-year old girl. In this story the young writer plays out a dramatic family scene—the arrival of a new baby.

THE NEW BABY

Once upon a time there was a little girl. She was a only child. She was six. her name was Deian. She was gratefull for a baby. She waned to play with someone. who can I play with asked Deian. Her father said oh" There is the door bell. Oh"! your sister.

This beginning writer has clearly drawn on her reading experience—stories she has read herself and the stories she has heard read aloud—for storytelling conventions (a title, the opening—"once upon a time") and for elements of narrative structure (background explanations, the formulation of a problem—*she waned to play with someone*). Indeed, as the story begins to unfold, the author seems very consciously to be constructing her tale. At the end of the story, however, events seem to overrun the narrator's craft: The doorbell rings, the father speaks, and the new sibling arrives on the scene. The narrator's voice gives way to the voices of characters, and the final part of the story seems not so much a consciously shaped narrative as an improvised puppet show, or even a transcript of the language of a child playing at a dollhouse.

A similar pattern is evident in "The Big Fight," a narrative written by a 7-year old girl:

THE BIG FIGHT

Once upon a time there was two little girls. They always fighted. One morning they had a new swing set in thire yard. But they had a parbom. One of the swings were broken. And they both wonted to swing. And thats where the fight started. I want it! its mine! its mine! I saw it first. The end.

Children write many kinds of stories and draw on a number of sources for the material they write about and the structures they use. In early instances such as "The New Baby" and "The Big Fight," young writers seem to combine features of spoken storytelling, dramatic play, and written storytelling and to combine the functions of those activities as well. As children increase their control over the conventions of writing stories, their written texts may seem more completely governed by principles for constructing written narratives. It may be, however, that children's uses for writing stories—their reasons for composing narratives—continue to grow not only out of reading experience and spoken storytelling, but also out of play activity. When I asked some children in an elementary school to answer the question, "What makes you want to write," one 10-year old girl wrote:

> Ideas I get from books, trips, or just playing with my friends. For instance last year my sisters and I were playing on a swing set in our backyard. We were pretending we were kids whose parents were dead, and we were on a boat in the middle of the ocean. Another time we pretended we were kids running away from an orphanage run by a mean man named Seth Brown. I haven't written a story about either of those times but I plan to.

Writing and Play

Along with using written discourse as an arena for manipulating and playing out remembered or make-believe situations, children also extend the functions of play into the activity of writing by experimenting with voices and perspectives in the roles they adopt as writers. Sometimes writing of this sort is initiated by the child—among the most common examples are the newspapers that many children write and draw at home (see Bissex, 1980). On other occasions, teachers ask children to adopt roles in their school writing assignments. One third-grade teacher, for example, asked her students to write diary entries from the point of view of children crossing the Atlantic on the Mayflower back in the seventeenth century. The 8-year old author of the following diary entry placed her narrator in a dangerous situation—a storm at sea—and exploited the graphic properties of written language by carefully simulating print written in an unsteady hand to emphasize the severity of the storm. It is interesting to note that the child's decision to introduce the make-believe storm into the school writing situation led her to comment on (indeed, to defend) the adult-like use of written language to create a record that will outlive the creator.

> Today is November 25, 1620. Friday afternoon. There is a storm going on. That's why my handwriting is not very good. You might think I am crazy because I might die but I want to write this diary so I can pass it on to my child and my child can pass it on to her child. On the top floor of the Mayflower the big mask fell down and I got very very scared. And also a big box fell overboard and I got a big bump on my head. I hope the storm ends soon.

It may be that some children first experiment with adult-like uses of writing by trying out different voices and roles—by experimenting, in the terms used by Gregory and Carroll in their analysis of "language varieties and social contexts" (1978), with "fields of discourse" (purposive roles) and "functional tenor" (the speaker or writer's particular purpose in a specific situation). Catherine Garvey's discussion of "enactment" in children's play—a "technique for communicating make believe play"—is suggestive for our speculations about how children extend the functions of play into their early writing activity. Garvey illustrates the child's technique of enacting roles by considering the example of a child who takes on the role of an infant while playmates assume the roles of mother and father. The child enacts the role of the baby "by speaking as a baby speaks, saying and doing the things a baby would do, and expressing baby-like needs, desires, and attitudes [1977, p. 88]." In a similar way, beginning writers sometimes seem to "enact" the roles of the writers of materials they have read. Although in this sense children draw on their reading experience for models, this playlike enactment of the writer's role is not always merely copying or even close imitation. Rather, as Garvey says of enactment in make-believe play, "The actual behavior in enactments has been filtered through the child's understanding of his world. . . . [and] represents information gained by the child as he learns more and more about the nature of the social world and about himself as a part of it [1977 p. 88]."

As an example of a child's enactment of the role of a writer with authority in a particular field of discourse whose purpose is to explain his special knowledge to his readers, let us consider a passage of expository writing composed by a 7-year old girl in the latter part of her first-grade year. She and one of her classmates initiated this project themselves, telling their teacher that they wanted to make a book about "humans and animals—their class had recently been talking, reading, and watching films on aspects of that large subject, and the girls wanted to make a book about what they were learning. Each girl wrote her own section and their teacher helped them combine the sections into a single volume when they were finished. In the following passage (the opening sentences of one girl's section), the rhetorical question (and answer), the making of categories and distinctions, even the chatty, tour-guiding style, all may be seen as elements of the child's enactment of the role of the writer of expository prose for children. In trying on the writer's voice, the child is also trying out the writer's uses for written language.

> *A hummen body is a anemll. An anemll is not a hummen like you. You are a special hummen anemll. You are diffrant! Do you know? Well I dont think you do. Well I can exsplane the hummen body. Oh I haveant tolled you all about the anemll! Well Ill tell you about the gray squirrel. When the mother squirrel finds new pussy willow buds to eat she knows that spring in coming!*

Writing Letters and Notes

Assuming a new role, or expanding one's current social role to encompass new options and new responsibilities, may be the child's motive for beginning to write letters and notes both at home and at school. In one school I have visited, for example, a kindergarten child must bring a note from a parent if the child is to go home with a friend after school instead of going to his own home. As the kindergarten group arrived one April morning, a 5-year old boy handed his teacher a note he had written himself:

> IAMGOIGTOMIK
> S AFTTERSCHOOL
> AND WONT BE BAKTOL
> 5 O KLOOK
> APIRIL24HT

After checking a few matters of interpretation with the writer, the kindergarten teacher was able to recognize that the note read: *I am going to Mike's after school and won't be back til five o'clock.* The child's mother had initialed the note, making clear that the child was not trying to deceive (unlike the child of the apocryphal story who, when his teacher called on the telephone to report misbehavior, answered, "This is my mother, what do you want?"). Rather, the kindergarten child wanted to take control of the transaction himself, and had been encouraged by his mother—it turns out that she had helped him when he asked for the spelling of "school." The child wanted to take on the role of the person of authority, the person who writes permission notes. In the narrow sense, the child used writing on this occasion to inform his teacher of a change in routine, and like other beginning writers, his selection of information did not match completely with the information suitable for the purpose (his teacher did not need to know that he would be staying at Mike's until five o'clock). In the fuller sense, however, the child used writing to enact a social role; his purpose was not only to inform, but also to assume new authority for regulating his own affairs.

This is not to say that children do not write notes for direct communicative purposes; many children do. Higgens suggests that in situations calling for "practical interpersonal communication," children write—and write successfully, within the limits of their control over the conventions of written language—"for the same motive as children speak—for effective interpersonal interaction [1978, p. 148]." Indeed, writing for this purpose can come very early in the child's experiments with written language. For example, Bissex reports that her 5-year old son, failing in his attempts to interrupt her as she read, handed her this note: RUDF. She had no trouble understanding that the note said, "Are you deaf?" She offers the interesting interpretation that her son had resorted to writing in an effort to "break through print with print," and adds: "Of course, I put my book down [1980, p. 3]."

In some of their notes, children attempt to make contact with readers with whom they are unable to communicate by talking. A 7-year old boy, for example, wrote the following message on an envelope that he left under his pillow for the tooth fairy:

(*Don't take my*)
(*touth I'v had*)
(*it since*)
(*I was ten days old*)

The boy's family had a tradition of trading teeth for money, and he was eager to cash in on a tooth he had recently lost. Yet he wanted to save the tooth, too, having heard the family lore that the tooth had been with him almost from the start of his life.

Another young boy, an avid reader of *Peanuts* cartoon books whose older brother had teased him by telling him that the Great Pumpkin, a mythic character in that series, did not really exist, wrote the following note (not mournfully but gleefully—he figured he would put his brother in hot water with the Great Pumpkin by revealing the scandalous rumor):

Dear Great Pumpkin
How are you? Dave
siad the Great Pumpkin
is nothing.

Some of the notes children write clearly represent the child's use of writing as a substitute for speech, or as an alternative when speech fails for one reason or another. We should recognize, however, that many families have as one means of keeping their daily routines organized a system of domestic correspondence, in which parents leave notes for children and children are expected to leave notes for parents. In this context, writing is an established way of speaking in the immediate community of a single family, and the child participates just as he fills other family roles. Often the child writes notes when he leaves the home, explaining where he is and when he expects to return. Sometimes these messages are simply informative. A 7-year old boy, for example, left this note on the kitchen counter:

Mom Im at Bills house. I am playing
there. I will be back later. David.

But children have a keen sense of the communicative requirements of familiar social situations, and hence their notes are sometimes more elaborate and aim to persuade as well as to inform. One 8-year-old boy, for example, who had been told to stay home after school until his mother returned from work, left a note explaining that he had gone to a nearby park to play baseball *because no one was home and they neded me* (see Gundlach, Litowitz, & Moses, 1979).

The domestic correspondence in some families extends the functions of regulatory speech, with adults writing reminders and instructions for their children and for one another. In one family I know, Tim's mother (Tim is 9

years old) occasionally leaves him notes on the table beside his bed reminding him what to do—and what not to do—when he wakes up in the
morning. Using his mother's notes as models of both a form and a function
of writing, Tim sometimes writes notes for himself. During a period when
he needed to remember to place a patch over one of his eyes each morning,
he wrote this note before going to sleep and placed it in a conspicuous
place on his bedside table (Mark is Tim's younger brother):

Tim do these things please.
In the morning:
Patch eye. Wash glasses.
Brush teeth. Get away from Mark.
get dressed. (practis clarenet).
make bed.

It is possible that this note represents an early stage in Tim's development
of the use of writing to help him remember plans or chores or even stray
thoughts—an early stage in learning to make and use lists. Indeed, it may
be that for some children, learning to write for oneself in this way runs a
course parallel to the development of "inner speech"—talking to
oneself—as Vygotsky (1962) describes it. That is, it may be that for some
children the private use of written language to make lists has its origins in
social interaction, and that in the transition stage between social and private uses of language of this sort the child's written "utterances" are more
elaborated, more "socialized" (*Tim do these things please*) than they will
eventually become when they are compressed to lists that omit contextual
information unnecessary for the purpose at hand.

If this is in fact the way that some children develop the use of writing to
help themselves remember, surely other children, drawing on different
models, take different routes to the same destination. Indeed, that is the
point: Children develop uses for writing by extending the functions of
familiar symbol-using activities to the new activity that written language
makes possible, and certainly the familiar activities from which children
build bridges to writing vary greatly across cultural communities and even
among families within a particular cultural community.

CONCLUSION

I recently told a colleague who teaches English to college students that I
was working on a paper about how children learn to write. He looked
surprised. "But they don't, do they? Isn't that the problem?"

If there is a problem, or even a crisis, part of the solution is for us who
teach or conduct research to pay more attention than we have to children
as writers. Many children do learn to write, or at least make a strong start

of it. As I have said, children apparently begin to write because they want to, because they come to value written language. They discover significant uses for writing by building bridges from the familiar activities of speaking, drawing, and playing to the new activities that writing makes possible. Children write to name and organize parts of their worlds, to capture and savor their experiences, to tell stories, to try out voices and roles, to fulfill family and school responsibilities, to communicate messages to readers near and far, and to make lists that will help them remember what they have to do.

Whether we are working with children who have made a strong start on learning to write or children who have not yet begun, our challenge as educators is to help all children develop their command over the forms of written language, help them increase their control over writing processes, and, perhaps most important, help them develop their use of writing as "an extension of the functional potential of language [Halliday, 1978, p. 57]." To accomplish these goals, we who teach must become intelligent readers of children's written language. We must learn to hear the coherent voices that often speak in fragmented and uncontrolled written forms; we must learn to recognize the merging of several functions in individual compositions; and we must learn to detect evidence of learning-in-progress in the errors and immaturities in children's written texts. We must also become intelligent observers of children as they write; we must learn to intervene when coaching will be helpful and instructive, and learn to stay out of the way at other times, allowing children to control their own writing projects. We must learn to look for rapid progress, and we must learn to be patient.

Finally, and crucially, we must learn how to create writing opportunities for children that make sense to them and that do not trivialize the uses of written language. We must let children write and we must help them discover purposes that writing can serve for them.

If the publicity about a writing crisis in American education is a signal of a new commitment to helping all children develop writing abilities, then educators have much work to do. The proper role for the new research in writing, it seems to me, is to help educators get on with this important work.

REFERENCES

Anderson, A. B., Teale, W. B., & Estrada, E. Low income children's preschool literacy experiences: Some naturalistic observations. *The Quarterly Newsletter of the Laboratory of Comparative Human Cognition*, 1980, 2 59–65.

Applebee, A. N. *The child's concept of story: Ages two to seventeen.* Chicago: University of Chicago Press, 1978.

Applebee, A. N. *A study of writing in the secondary school*. Final Report to the National Institute of Education, NIE-G-79-0174. September, 1980.

Beers, J. W., & Henderson, E. H. A study of developing orthographic concepts among first graders. *Research in the Teaching of English*, 1977, *11*, 133–148.

Bettelheim, B. *The uses of enchantment: The meaning and importance of fairy tales*. New York: Alfred A. Knopf, 1976.

Bissex, G. L. *GYNS AT WORK: A child learns to write and read*. Cambridge: Harvard University Press, 1980.

Britton, J. N. *Language and learning*. London: Penguin, 1970.

Bruner, J. Learning how to do things with words. In J. Bruner & A. Garton (Eds.), *Human growth and development: Wolfson College lectures 1976*. Oxford: Claredon Press, 1978.

Calkins, L. M. Children learn the writer's craft. *Language Arts*, 1980, *57*, 567–573.

Chomsky, C. Write now, read later, *Childhood Education*, 1971, *47*, 296–299.

de Villiers, J., & de Villiers, P. *Language acquisition*. Cambridge: Harvard University Press, 1978.

Emig, J. *The composing processes of twelfth graders*. Urbana: National Council of Teachers of English, 1971.

Ferreiro, E. What is written in a written sentence? A developmental answer. *Journal of Education*, 1978, *160*, 25–39.

Ferreiro, E. The relationship between oral and written language: The children's viewpoints. Paper presented at the meeting of the International Reading Association, St. Louis, Mo., May, 1980.

Florio, S. The problem of dead letters: Social perspectives on the teaching of writing. Research Series No. 34. East Lansing: Michigan State University, 1978.

Freedle, R. O. (Ed.) *New directions in discourse processing II*. Norwood, N.J.: Ablex, 1979.

Gardner, H. On becoming a dictator. *Psychology Today*, 1980, *14*, 14–19. (a)

Gardner, H. *Artful scribbles: The significance of children's drawings*. New York: Basic Books, 1980. (b)

Gardner, H., & Wolf, D. The dimensions of early symbol use. *New directions for child development: Early symbolization*, 1979, *3*.

Garvey, C. *Play*. Cambridge: Harvard University Press, 1977.

Graves, D. H. *Children's writing: Research directions and hypotheses based upon an examination of the writing processes of seven year old children*. Ann Arbor: University Microfilms, 1974, No. 7408375.

Graves, D. H. *Balance the basics: Let them write*. New York: Ford Foundation, 1978.

Graves, D. H. The growth and development of first grade writers. Paper presented at the meeting of the Canadian Council of Teachers of English, Ottawa, Canada, May, 1979.

Gregory, M., & Carroll, S. *Language and situation: Language varieties and their social contexts*. London: Routledge and Kegan Paul, 1978.

Gundlach, R. A. When children write: Notes for parents and teachers on children's written language development. Mimeographed paper distributed to the parents of children in the Winnetka Public Schools, Winnetka, Illinois, 1977.

Gundlach, R. A. On the nature and development of children's writing. In C. Frederiksen, M. Whiteman, & J. Dominic (Eds.), *Writing: The nature, development, and teaching of written communication*. Hillsdale, N.J.: Lawrence Erlbaum, 1981.

Gundlach, R. A. *How children learn to write: Perspectives on children's writing for educators and parents*. Washington, D.C.: National Institute of Education, forthcoming.

Gundlach, R. A., Litowitz, B.E., & Moses, R. A. The ontogenesis of the writer's sense of audience: Rhetorical theory and children's written discourse, In R. Brown & M. Steinmann, Jr. (Eds.), *Rhetoric 78*. Minneapolis: University of Minnesota Center for Advanced Studies in Language, Style, and Literary Theory, 1979.

Halliday, M. A. K. *Language as social semiotic*. Baltimore: University Park Press, 1978.

Harste, J., Burke, C., and Woodward, V. Children's language and the world: Initial encounters with print. In J. Langer & M. Smith-Burke (Eds.), *Bridging the gap: Reader meets author.* Newark, Del.: International Reading Association, forthcoming.

Heath, S.B. What no bedtime story means: Narrative skills at home and school. Paper prepared for the Terman Conference, Stanford University, November, 1980.

Heath, S. B. Protean shapes: Ever-shifting oral and literate traditions. In D. Tannen (Ed.), *Written and spoken language.* Norwood, N.J.: Ablex, forthcoming.

Higgens, E. T. Written communication as functional literacy: A developmental comparison of oral and written communication. In R. Beach & P. D. Pearson (Eds.), *Perspectives on literacy.* Minneapolis: University of Minnesota College of Education, 1978.

Hirsch, E. D. *The philosophy of composition.* Chicago: University of Chicago Press, 1977.

Keenan, E. O. Making it last: Repetition in children's discourse. In S. Ervin-Tripp & C. Mitchell-Kernan (Eds.), *Child discourse.* New York: Academic Press, 1977.

Luria, A. R. The development of writing in the child. In M. Cole (Ed.), *Selected writings of A. R. Luria.* White Plains, N.Y.: M. E. Sharpe, 1978.

Mellon, J. C. *Transformational sentence-combining: A method for enhancing the development of syntactic fluency in English composition.* Urbana: National Council of Teachers of English, 1969.

Ninio, A., & Bruner, J. The achievement and antecedents of labelling. *Journal of Child Language,* 1978, 5, 1–15.

O'Hare, F. *Sentence combining: Improving student writing without formal teaching.* Urbana: National Council of Teachers of English, 1973.

Olson, D. R. From utterance to text: The bias of language in speech and writing. *Harvard Educational Review,* 1977, 47, 257–281.

Pitcher, E., & Prelinger, E. *Children tell stories.* New York: International Universities Press, 1963.

Price, R. *A palpable god.* New York: Atheneum, 1978.

Read, C. *Children's categorization of speech sounds in English.* Urbana: National Council of Teachers of English, 1975.

Rosen, C., & Rosen, H. *The language of primary school children.* Harmondsworth, England: Penguin Education, 1973.

Scollon, R., & Scollon, S. The literate two year old: The fictionalization of self. *Working Papers in Sociolinguistics.* Austin, Texas: Southwest Regional Laboratory, 1979.

Shaughnessy, M. *Errors and expectations.* New York: Oxford University Press, 1977.

Sowers, S. A six year old's writing process: The first half of first grade. *Language Arts,* 1979, 56, 829–835.

Stein, N. L., & Glenn, C. G. An analysis of stroy comprehension in elementary school children, In R. Freedle (Ed.), *New directions in discourse processing II.* Norwood, N.J.: Ablex. 1979.

Stubbs, M. *Language and literacy: The sociolinguistics of reading and writing.* London: Routledge and Kegan Paul, 1980.

Vygotsky, L. S. *Thought and language,* Edited and translated by E. Hanfman and G. Vakar. Cambridge: M.I.T. Press, 1962.

Vygotsky, L. S. *Mind in society: The development of higher psychological processes.* Edited by M. Cole, V. John-Steiner, S. Scribner, & E. Souberman. Cambridge: Harvard University Press, 1978.

Weeks, T. *Born to talk.* Rowley, Mass.: Newbury House, 1979.

Chapter 7

Spectator Role and the Beginnings of Writing

James Britton

Only by understanding the entire history of sign development in the child and the place of writing in it can we approach a correct solution of the psychology of writing.—L. S. Vygotsky, 1978, p.106

IN SEARCH OF A THEORY

Literary and Nonliterary Discourse

Works of literature constitute a form of discourse: We have theories of GENRE to distinguish among works of literature, but no satisfactory theory to account for what is common to all such works and in what general ways they differ from nonliterary discourse. The 1958 interdisciplinary symposium on "Style in Language" at Indiana University attempted to make such a distinction, but the only consensus that seemed to emerge was the low-level generalization that literary discourse is "noncasual discourse." Moreover, in summing up that symposium, George Miller remarked, "I gradually learned to understand a little of what the linguist has on his mind when he begins to talk; his verbal behavior during these past days has not puzzled me quite the way it once would have. But the critics have some mystic entity called a "poem" or "literature," whose existence I must take on faith and whose defining properties still confuse me. (The fact that they cannot agree amongst themselves on what a poem is adds to the mystery.) [Sebeok, 1960, p.387]."

Since a great deal of (mostly unpublished) writing by nonprofessionals, by children in school and students in college, takes on forms that are clearly related to literary forms, it seems appropriate that any study of the psychology of writing should attempt to deal with this problem; and that the theory adumbrated should seek both to relate the artlike writings to literary works of art, and to distinguish between them.

One of the most important contributors to the Indiana symposium was Roman Jakobson who put forward his model of the 'constitutive factors' in a speech situation:

$$
\begin{array}{lll}
& \text{Context} & \\
& \text{Message} & \\
\text{Addressor} & \text{Contact} & \text{Addressee} \\
& \text{Code} &
\end{array}
$$

and the functions assignable to an utterance or part utterance in accordance with the factor on which it focuses:

$$
\begin{array}{lll}
& \text{Referential} & \\
\text{Emotive (or} & \text{Poetic} & \text{Conative} \\
\text{Expressive)} & \text{Phatic} & \\
& \text{Metalingual} &
\end{array}
$$

He made it clear that a verbal message was very unlikely to be fulfilling one function only, but that in taking account of the various functions liable to be copresent we might expect to find them hierarchically ordered, one function being **dominant.** "The verbal structure," he added, "depends primarily on the dominant function [Sebeok, 1960, p.353]."

I want to accept as starting point his view that the poetic function (in the broad sense of 'poetic,' equivalent to the verbal arts) may be defined as a "focus on the message for its own sake," and to agree in principle that the poetic function may be either dominant or merely accessory. But Jakobson goes on to say:

> Any attempt to reduce the sphere of poetic function to poetry or to confine poetry to poetic function would be a delusive oversimplification. Poetic function is not the sole function of verbal art but only its dominant, determining function, whereas in all other verbal activities it acts as a subsidiary, accessory constituent [Sebeok, 1960, p.356].

Any linguistic choice made on the sole grounds that "it sounds better that way" would seem to exemplify Jakobson's conception of the poetic function in an accessory role. Yet it seems to me that the urgent necessity is to characterize the structure and status of verbal messages in which the poetic function is dominant, that is, to find ways of distinguishing poetic from nonpoetic discourse. Jakobson's model itself might even suggest a dichotomy of this kind, a dominant focus on the message itself for its own sake being in contrast with a message dominantly focused on something beyond or outside itself.

Susanne Langer (1953) recognizes such a dichotomy when she comments on the switch required when readers or listeners turn their attention from nonliterary to literary discourse. An "illusion of life," she says,

> is the primary illusion of all poetic art. It is at least tentatively established by the very first sentence, which has to switch the reader's or hearer's attitude from conversational interest to literary interest, i.e., from actuality to fiction. We make this shift with great ease, and much more often than we realize, even in the midst of conversation; one has only to say "You know about the two Scotchmen, who..." to make everybody in earshot suspend the actual conversation and attend to "the" two Scots and "their" absurdities. Jokes are a special literary form to which people will attend on the spur of the moment [1953 p.213].

And, speaking of Blake's poem *Tyger*, she comments, "The vision of such a tiger is a virtual experience, built up from the first line of the poem to the last. But nothing can be built up unless the very first words of the poem EFFECT THE BREAK WITH THE READER'S ACTUAL ENVIRONMENT [p.214, emphasis added]."

In *The Reader, the Text, the Poem*, Louise Rosenblatt (1978) makes a broad distinction between two types of reading process, **efferent** and **aesthetic.** In efferent reading the reader's concern is with what he takes away from the reading (hence "efferent" from *effero* [I carry away]). In aesthetic reading, in contrast, "the reader's primary concern is with what happens DURING the actual reading event.... The reader's attention is centered directly on what he is living through during his relationship with that particular text [1978, pp 24–25]." She is careful to point out that this is no hard and fast division but rather a continuum between two poles. Thus, "given the assumption that the text offers a potentially meaningful set of linguistic symbols, the reader is faced with the adoption of either a predominantly efferent or a predominantly aesthetic stance [1978, p.78]." We shall return to this matter of the relation between a reader's and a writer's options.

Support for a general distinction between literary and nonliterary discourse comes also from a linguist's work in stylistics. Widdowson (1975) claims that what is crucial to the character of literature is that "the language of a literary work should be fashioned into patterns over and above those required by the actual language system [1975, p.47]." I shall return to consider this claim in a later section.

Spectator and Participant Roles

As we have noted, many of the features we find in poetic discourse (the language of literature) we find also widely distributed in many other forms of discourse. A mere study of the distribution of such features will not, I believe, add up to an adequate description of the verbal structure of a message in which the poetic function is dominant. We have no difficulty in practice in recognizing the difference between a novel with a political purpose and a piece of political rhetoric or persuasive discourse. What are the factors that shape the literary work as a whole?

The theory I want to pursue is one that I first put forward many years ago (Britton, 1963), in what seems to me now a crude form. My purpose then was to find common ground between much of the writing children do in school and the literature they read. I was concerned that, unlike the arts of painting and music, literature, as far as schools and universities were concerned, was not something that students DO, but always something that other people HAVE DONE. To bridge this gap, I looked for what seemed to be the informal spoken counterparts of written literature—not the anecdote as such, I decided (Langer's tale of the two Scotsmen)—but the kind of gossip about events that most of us take part in daily. To quote from that account, "The distinction that matters . . . is not whether the events recounted are true or fictional, but whether we recount them (or listen to them) as spectators or participants: and whenever we play the role of spectator of human affairs I suggest we are in the position of literature [Britton, 1963, p.37]." The roles of spectator and participant were differentiated in this way:

> When we talk about our own affairs, clearly we can do so either as participant or as spectator. If I describe what has happened to me in order to get my hearer to do something for me, or even to change his opinion about me, then I remain a participant in my own affairs and invite him to become one. If, on the other hand, I merely want to interest him, so that he savours with me the joys and sorrows and surprises of my past experiences and appreciates with me the intricate patterns of events, then not only do I invite him to be a spectator, but I am myself a spectator of my own experience. . . . I don't think it is far-fetched to think of myself talking not about my own past, but about my future, and, again, doing so in either of the two roles. As participant I should be planning, and asking my listener to participate by helping or advising or just 'giving me the necessary permission'. As spectator I should be day-dreaming, and inviting my listener to share in that kind of pleasure [Britton, 1963, p.39].

To complete the account, I then made reference to taking up the role of spectator of imagined experiences in fantasy or fiction.

Three years later I prepared an advance paper for discussion at the Anglo-American Seminar at Dartmouth, a paper on "Response to Literature" (Britton, 1968), and as a brief postscript to that document, I referred to the "unorthodox view of literature" that characterized it as a written form of language in the role of spectator and so related it to the spoken form, gossip about events. The paper was discussed by a study group under the chairmanship of the British psychologist, D. W. Harding. It was not until the first meeting of the study group was over that he asked me whether I knew his own papers putting forward a similar view; and that evening, in Dartmouth College Library, I read for the first time "The Role of the Onlooker" (Harding, 1937) and "Psychological Processes in the Reading of Fiction" (Harding, 1962). There I found a fully and carefully argued case for distinguishing the role of an onlooker from that of a participant in events and for relating gossip to literature as activities in the former role.

The final report of that study group was prepared by Harding and included this comment:

> Though central attention should be given to literature in the ordinary sense, it is impossible to separate response to literature sharply from response to other stories, films, or television plays, or from children's own personal writing or spoken narrative. In all of these the student contemplates represented events in the role of a spectator, not for the sake of active intervention. But since his response includes in some degree accepting or rejecting the values and emotional attitudes which the narration implicitly offers, it will influence, perhaps greatly influence, his future appraisals of behavior and feeling [Harding, 1968, p. 11].

D. W. Harding

In the two articles I have referred to, Harding explored the relationship between three processes that seemed to him to have much in common: (*a*) watching events without taking part in them; (*b*) exchanging gossip— informal recounting or description of events; and (*c*) reading (or writing) fiction. An understanding of the first of these, that of being literally in the role of spectator, is essential to an understanding of his view of the other two. An onlooker, he says, (*a*) ATTENDS (and this will range from "a passing glance" to a "fascinated absorption") and (*b*) EVALUATES (within a range from "an attitude of faint liking or disliking, hardly above indifference" to one of "strong, perhaps intensely emotional" response). What we attend to, he suggests, reflects our interests (if we take interest to mean "an enduring disposition to respond, in whatever way, to some class of objects or events"); how we evaluate reflects our sentiments, if we take a sentiment to be "an enduring disposition to evaluate some object or class of objects in a particular way [Harding, 1972, p.134]."

A major aspect of a spectator's response to the events he witnesses will be a concern for the people involved and an interest in the way they react, but there is likely to be present also an interest in and evaluation of the pattern events take, with a sense that what is happening here might one day happen to him. Both aspects are, in a broad sense, learning experiences: As spectators we not only reflect our interests and sentiments but also modify and extend them. "In ways of this kind," Harding writes,

> the events at which we are "mere onlookers" come to have, cumulatively, a deep and extensive influence on our systems of value. They may in certain ways be even more formative than events in which we take part. Detached and distanced evaluation is

sometimes sharper for avoiding the blurrings and bufferings that participant action brings, and the spectator often sees the event in a broader context than the participant can tolerate. To obliterate the effects on a man of the occasions on which he was only an onlooker would be profoundly to change his outlook and values [1962, p.136].

To be one of a number of spectators is to take part in a mutual challenging and sanctioning of each other's evaluations. "Everything we look on at is tacitly and unintentionally treated as an object lesson by our fellow spectators; speech and gesture, smiles, nudges, clicks, tuts and glances are constantly at work to sanction or correct the feelings we have as spectators [Harding, 1937, p.253]."

This aspect of a spectator's experience is sharply emphasized when we turn to the second of the three processes I have listed, that of deliberately taking up the role of spectator of represented or recounted experiences, as for example when we go home in the evening and chat about the day's events. We HAVE BEEN participants but are so no longer; taking up the role of spectator, we invite our listener to do the same. Harding goes so far as to imply that this familiar habit is something we indulge in for the purpose of testing out our modes of evaluating; having, in fact, our value systems sanctioned or modified by others whose values, in general, we reckon to share. We do not recount everything that happens to us: What we select constitutes a first level of evaluation. But it is as we recount the events in a manner designed to arouse in our listeners attitudes towards them that chime with our own that we more specifically invite corroboration of our ways of evaluating. On this basis, I think it is no distortion of Harding's account to suggest that as participants we APPLY our value systems, but as spectators we GENERATE AND REFINE the system itself. In applying our value systems we shall inevitably be constrained by self-interest, by concern for the outcome of the event we are participating in; as spectators we are freed of that constraint.

Harding goes on to suggest that what takes place informally in chat about events is in essence similar to what is achieved by a work of fiction or drama. "True or fictional, all these forms of narrative invite us to be onlookers joining in the evaluation of some possibility of experience [1962, p.138]."

The London Writing Research Project

At the time of the Dartmouth Seminar my colleagues and I at the University of London Institute of Education were beginning to plan the Schools Council Project on the written language of 11- to 18-year-olds. Our first and major task was to devise modes of analysis of children's writings by means of which the development of writing abilities might be documented. We envisaged a multidimensional analysis and worked on what seemed to us two of the essential dimensions. The first resulted in a set of categories we called "sense of audience" (Who is the writing for?) and the second in a set of function categories (What is the writing for?). These are fully described in *The Development of Writing Abilities, 11–18* (Britton, Burgess, Martin, McLeod, & Rosen, 1975) and for my present purpose I need only indicate how the spectator–participant distinction was taken up and developed as the basis of the function category set.

To relate gossip to literature is not only to show a similarity in that they are both utterances in the spectator role, but also to indicate a difference. The formal and informal ends of the spectrum have very different potentials. One of the important ways in which we frame an evaluation and communicate it is by giving a particular shape to the events in narrating them; at the formal end of the scale all the resources of literary art, all the linguistic and conceptual forms that a literary artist molds into a unity, are at the service of that shaping and sharing.

Clearly, an account given of an experience in a letter to an intimate friend might also be placed at the informal end of the scale, in contrast perhaps to the same event narrated by the same writer as part of a short story or a published autobiography. (Dr. Johnson wrote a letter from the Hebrides to a friend in which he said, "When we were taken upstairs, a dirty fellow bounced out of the bed on which one of us was to lie"; this appears in his *Journal* as "Out of one of the couches on which we were to repose there started up at our entrance a man black as a Cyclops from the forge"—more of a parody of the point I am making than an illustration, I think!)

The informality of a chat or a personal letter is certainly in part a reflection of a relaxed relationship between the communicating parties—closeness rather than distance, warmth rather than coldness. Perhaps influenced also by Moffett's model of kinds of discourse in which he sees the **I–you** rhetorical relationship and the **I–it** referential relationship as intimately connected (Moffett, 1968, p.33), we came to identify the informal end of this continuum with expressive language as Sapir (1961, p.10) has defined it; further, to see that the "unshaped," loosely structured end of the spectator role continuum merged into the informal pole of language in the role of participant. This gave us three major categories of function: transactional, expressive, and poetic. **Transactional** is the form of discourse that most fully meets the demands of a participant in events (using language to get things done, to carry out a verbal transaction). **Expressive** is the form of discourse in which the distinction between participant and spectator is a shadowy one. And **poetic** discourse is the form that most fully meets the demands associated with the role of spectator—demands that are met, we suggested, by MAKING something with language rather than DOING something with it.

Though our principal source for the term "expressive" was Edward Sapir, we found it was one widely used by other linguists. Jakobson labeled the function arising from a focus on the addressor either "emotive" or "expressive" and saw it as offering "a direct expression of the speakers attitude towards what he is speaking about [Sebeok, 1960, p.354]"; a point that Dell Hymes later glossed: "A sender cannot help but express attitudes towards each of the other factors in a speech event, his audience, the style of the message, the code he is using, the channel he is using, his topic, the scene of the communication [1908, p.106]." Labov (1966, p.13) characterizes the expressive function as "the role of language as self-identification," and it is this aspect that Gusdorf elaborates: "The relation to others is only meaningful insofar as it reveals that personal identity within the person who is himself speaking. To communicate, man *expresses* himself, i.e. he actualizes himself, he creates from his own substance [1965, p.69]." Thus the expressive function in our model is not simply the informal end of two scales, the neutral point between participant and spectator role language, but has its own positive function to perform—a function that profits from the indeterminacy between carrying out a verbal transaction and constructing a verbal object to be shared. The positive function of expressive speech is, in simple terms, to make the most of being with somebody, that is, to enjoy their company, to make their presence fruitful—a process that can profit from exploring with them both the inner and outer aspects of experience.

But in expressive writing the presence, the "togetherness" is simulated: The writer invokes the presence of the reader as he writes; the reader invokes the presence of the writer as he reads. Thus a working definition of expressive writing would be "writing that assumes an interest in the writer as well as in what he has to say about the world." We might add that it would be foolish to underestimate the importance of expressive speech or writing as means of influencing people and events. Advertisers and propagandists are only too ready to exploit its effectiveness.

Our description of expressive writing thus distinguished it from a verbal transaction on the one hand and a verbal object on the other. The verbal transaction and the verbal object are communicative rather than expressive, being in both cases language in the public domain; yet they communicate in very different ways. Expressive and referential strands, as Sapir explains, intermingle in all discourse, but the degree to which the former predominates is criterial in distinguishing expressive from transactional discourse. The change from expression to communication on the poetic side is brought about by an increasing degree of organization—organization into a single complex verbal symbol.

H. G. Widdowson

It is this last distinction that is illuminated by the work in stylistics of Widdowson (1975). He cites from literature examples of nongrammatical expressions that are nevertheless interpretable, finds such expressions in nonliterary texts, but concludes that they occur randomly in nonliterary writing, "whereas in literature they figure as part of a pattern which characterizes the literary work as a separate and self-contained whole [p.36]." Interpretation of these expressions that violate the grammatical code relies on viewing them in the light of the context; and he goes on to show that this is also true of most metaphorical expressions (which again occur randomly in ordinary discourse but as part of a total pattern in a work of literature). Context, however, in ordinary language will include aspects of the social situation in which the utterance takes place and re-marks that have gone before; whereas in literature context consists of the verbal fabric alone. Widdowson identifies patterns of three kinds to be found in literary works: phonological (metre and verse form are obvious examples), syntactical (parallel structures, for example, can invest an item with meaning which is, so to speak, by halo effect from other items in the series), and patterns formed by semantic links between individual lexical items. "At the heart of literary discourse," he concludes, "is the struggle to devise patterns of language which will bestow upon the linguistic items concerned just those values which convey the individual writer's personal vision [1975, p.42]."

He goes on to suggest that the effect of the patterning over and above the patterns of the language code is "to create acts of communication which are self-contained units, independent of a social context and expressive of a reality other than that which is sanctioned by convention. In other words, I want to suggest that although literature need not be deviant as text it must of its nature be deviant as discourse [1975, p.47]." This he achieves princi-pally by pointing out that normal discourse features a sender of a message who is at the same time the addressor, and a receiver of a message who is also the addressee, whereas in literary discourse the author, as sender, is distinguished from the addressor, and the reader, as receiver, from the addressee. Striking examples of this disjunction illustrate his point ("I am the enemy you killed, my friend" from Owen; "With how sad steps, O moon" from Sidney), but he goes on to indicate that this modified relation-ship holds in general for works of literature. An addressor thus fuses meanings associated with a grammatical first person with those associated with a third, an addressee those of the second and third persons. This account of a systematic modification of the grammatical code he completes by showing how third person and first person are fused when in fiction a narrator describes the experiences of a third person sometimes in terms of what might have been observed, sometimes in terms of inner events that only the experiencer could know. On these grounds he concludes: "It would appear then that in literary discourse we do not have a sender addressing a message directly to a receiver, as is normally the case. Instead we have a communication situation within a communication situation and a message whose meaning is self-contained and not dependent on who sends it and who receives it [p.50]."

In defending this view against likely objections, he makes two interesting points that are relevant to my theme. In many literary works, particularly perhaps in lyric poems, it is evident that the "I" of the work is the writer himself. In arguing that "it is not the writer as message sender, the craftsman, the 'maker' that the 'I' refers to but to the inner self that the writer is objectifying, and the very act of objectifying involves detaching this self and observing it as if it were a third person entity [1975, p. 53]," Widdowson sketches out, somewhat loosely, three forms of discourse in terms of the role of the "I": (a) In diaries and personal letters there is no distinction between sender and addressor: The writer may reveal his inner thoughts and feelings, and in doing so he takes responsibility—his readers may assume that he is "telling the truth." (b) In all other forms of nonliterary language, the writer, as sender and addressor, adopts a recognized social role and what he says and how he says it are determined by that role: "he is not at liberty to express his own individual sentiments at will. . . . [H]is addressee will be concerned with what he has to say in his role and not with his private and individual thoughts [p.52]."; (c) literary discourse, where the sender and addressor are disjoined, is concerned with the private thoughts and feelings of the writer, but in "bringing them out of hiding" he objectifies them and may explore them through the creation of personae, so that "we cannot assume that when a literary writer uses the first person he is describing his own experiences or making a confession." The literary writer, in fact, aware of the convention that distinguishes sender from addressor, is "relieved from any social responsibility for what he says in the first person [p.53]." (Love letters, he notes, count as evidence in a court of law, love poems don't!)

This analysis provides an interesting gloss on the three major function categories in our model: expressive, transactional, and poetic.

The second objection Widdowson anticipates relates to the familiar problem of "the novel with a message." Our claim that a literary work was a verbal object and not a verbal transaction was objected to on just these grounds, and we argued in reply that a poetic work achieved its effect indirectly, via the poetic construct taken as a whole. Widdowson's claim that a literary work is a self-contained unit independent of a social context risks the same kind of objection: His answer is

that it may indeed be the purpose of a writer to stir the social conscience but he does not do so by addressing himself directly to those whose consciences he wishes to stir. He expresses a certain reality, a personal vision, and the reader, as an *observer* of this reality, might then feel constrained to act in a certain way. But he is not directed to act by the writer (1975, p.53).

Widdowson then develops a point that will be familiar to readers of Jakobson (1971, e.g., p.704); he explores the way paradigmatic relationships invade the area of syntagmatic relationships in poetic discourse, and illustrates this at the level of phonemes and the grammatical level of words and phrases. Phonological distinctions that by the normal language code exist as a range from which **selection** is made (the story for example is about a cat and not about a hat, a bat or a mat) invade the syntagmatic relationship, the process of **combination** in a literary work, as for example when a poet chooses "bright" in preference to "shining" because that word fits into the sound pattern, including perhaps both rhythm and rhyme, of his poem. More germane to his principal argument is Widdowson's example of a series of verbal groups any one of which might have served to complete a sentence in a T. S. Eliot poem. Widdowson then shows how Eliot in fact does not SELECT, but COMBINES: "Words strain, Crack and sometimes break..." etc. This strategy, Widdowson notes, reflects the writer's struggle to resolve ambiguities and allows him to invite the reader to take part in that process. By such means works of literature communicate "an individual awareness of a reality other than that which is given general social sanction but nevertheless related to it [1971, p.70]."

Contextualization

One of the important ways in which we may characterize the difference between transactional and poetic discourse is by reference to the way a reader grasps the message. If what a writer does when he draws from all he knows and selectively sets down what he wants to communicate is described as 'decontextualization', then the complementary process on the part of a reader is to 'contextualize', interpreting the writer's meaning by building it into his existing knowledge and experience. We have suggested (Britton *et al.*, 1975, pp. 85–86) that in reading a piece of transactional discourse we contextualize the material in piecemeal fashion; passing over what is familiar, rejecting what is incomprehensible to us or perceived as inconsistent with our own thinking, accepting in piecemeal fashion what seems to us interesting, building our own connections between these fragments and our existing knowledge (which is open to modification, of course, in the process). With poetic discourse, on the other hand (and much of what Widdowson has said will support this difference), we apply our own knowledge and experience to the reconstruction of the writer's verbal object, and until we have done this, until we have the sense of a completed whole, a single unique symbol, we are in no position to reexamine our own thoughts and feelings in the light of the author's work. This we have called **global contextualization.** I think our response to a novel with a message may sometimes be a deliberate reexamination of the kind this suggests, but I have come to believe that in most cases global contextualization is a process that goes on over time and one we may not even be conscious of. We are constantly learning from our own first-hand experiences and mostly, because of the wide-ranging and diffuse nature of the process, without being aware that we are doing so. I am inclined to think that our response to a work of literature is like that.

We do of course contextualize in piecemeal fashion while reading works of literature: We pick up clues as to what life is like in places we have never visited, what it was like at times before we were born. But this is quite subsidiary, for most of us, to the main effects of literature; and it has its risks, since the verbal object, as Widdowson shows, deals with a reality "other than that which is given social sanction." There may be pygmies in the Australian rain forests the novelist describes, but that is no guarantee that they exist in fact. Nevertheless, for historians or sociologists, say, to study literature for the information they can glean is of course a legitimate option; they will be employing a process of piecemeal contextualization where what the author offered was a work to be contextualized globally. Louise Rosenblatt (1978), as we have mentioned, has paid close attention to this matter of the reader's options and raised some important issues. In defining a literary work of art as "what happens when a reader and a text come together [p.12]," she is I think loading the dice in the reader's favor, but the weight has for so long been on the author's side that this is understandable. There are of course anomalies, as when a text produced by an author as propaganda survives when its injunctions are no longer appropriate, and survives as a piece of literature; or when an informative text (Gibbons *Decline and Fall* is the stock example) survives when much of its information has been superseded and even discredited, to be read now not as information but for the unique and individual qualities typical of a work of literature.

There are anomalies, but without wishing in any way to infringe on the reader's freedom to choose, I do suggest that in the vast majority of cases the general conventions chosen by the writer—whether to produce expressive, transactional, or poetic discourse—are in fact the conventions by which the reader chooses to interpret.

YOUNG FLUENT WRITERS

L. S. Vygotsky

I have known a number of children who by the age of 5 or 6 had taught themselves to write. In each case it was stories that they wrote, and usually the stories were made up into little books, with pictures as well as writing. I take it as some evidence of the extraordinary ability human beings have of succeeding in doing what they want to do. One of these young children, under the age of 4, began by producing a little book with "pretend writing" in it—and surely, just as we pretend to BE someone we want to be, so we pretend to DO something we want to do. Some 20 months later the scribbled lines had given place to a decipherable story. Evidence of this kind is too often ignored, and it takes a Vygotsky, speaking across the decades since his death, to observe that the attempt to teach writing as a motor skill is mistaken (Vygotsky, 1978, p.117); that psychology has conceived of it as a motor skill and "paid remarkably little attention to the question of written language as such, that is, a particular system of symbols and signs whose mastery heralds a critical turning-point in the entire cultural development of the child [p.106]." It was his view that make-believe play, drawing and writing should be seen as "different moments in an essentially unified process of development of written language [p.116]." And this he contrasted with what he found in schools: "Instead of being founded on the needs of children as they naturally develop and on their own activity, writing is given to them from without, from the teacher's hands [p.105]."

I suggest that the 4-year-old I have referred to made what Vygotsky calls "a basic discovery—namely that one can draw not only things but also speech [1978, p.115]." Since pictorial representation is first-order symbolism and writing is second-order symbolism (designating words that are in turn signs for things and relationships), Vygotsky saw this discovery as a key point in the development of writing in a child; yet he recognized there was little understanding of how the shift takes place, since the necessary research had not been done (p.115). We are not much wiser today, though the labors of Donald Graves and others [see, for example, Gundlach, Chapter 6, of this volume] gives us good reason to hope.

Outline for a Case Study

My records of the development of Clare, the 4-year-old whose pretend writing I have referred to, may illustrate some of the points Vygotsky has made in his account of "the developmental history of written language."

(1) Her conversational speech was quite well developed by the time she was 2 years old. Much of her talk was playful (seeing me at the washbasin, *What have you got off, Daddy?*—at 2:3) and she used made-up forms freely (*I'm spoonfuling it in, I'm see-if-ing it will go through, smuttered in your eyes*—for uncombed hair—all at 2:7). Her curiosity about language was in evidence early (*When it's one girl you say "girl" and when it's two three four girls you say "girl s." Why when it's two three four childs you say "child ren"?*—at 2:10; *Fairy girl with curly hair," that makes a rhyme, doesn't it?*—at 2:11; on hearing something described as 'delicious,' *Is delicious nicer than lovely?*—at 3:1).

(2) Extended make-believe play, involving her toy animals in family roles, was established by the time she was 3. Storytelling developed from it, the animals becoming the audience. The toy animals (she was given dolls from time to time but they were never adopted into the family) seem to have sustained a key role. They were the *dramatis personae* of her make-believe play, the subject of the stories she told, of her drawings, and later of the stories

she wrote. Vygotsky's point that in make-believe play the plaything is free to take on a meaning that does not rely on perceptual resemblance is amusingly illustrated by the fact that when Clare enacted a queen's wedding, the least suitable of the animals—a scraggy, loose-knit dog—was chosen for the role of queen!

(3) Her earliest recognizable drawings came just before she was 2 and though they are clearly attempts at human figures, the talk that always accompanied the drawing was often in anthropomorphic terms (*the mummy bird, the daddy bird*). A picture drawn in colored chalks at 3:5 shows a large figure of a girl on the left-hand side and a house on the right. Her commentary as she drew explained: *The girl is carrying a yellow handbag and she has a brown furry dog on a lead. Her feet are walking along. . . . I have put a car outside the house. I am putting blue sky, now I am putting in the sunshine.* (Here the diagonal blue strokes that had indicated the sky were interspersed with yellow ones.) *She's got a tricycle with blue wheels and a chain. Mrs. Jones across the road has yellow and brown on her windows. I shall put yellow and red on mine.*

It is an important part of Vygotsky's thesis that a young child's drawing is "graphic speech," dependent on verbal speech: The child draws, that is to say, from the memory of what he knows rather than from what he presently observes; and that what he knows has been processed in speech and is further processed in the speech that accompanies the drawing. The space in Clare's picture is well filled, but not in terms of topographical representation: The girl and the house are upright; the car is drawn vertically standing on its head; the dog vertically sitting on its tail; and the tricycle has its frame, wheels and chain spread out, looking more like an assembly kit.

(4) What circumstances could be supposed to facilitate the process that Vygotsky calls the move from drawing objects to drawing speech? Imitating the general pattern of writing behavior, Clare at the age of 3:6 produced parallel horizontal lines of cursive scribble, saying that she was *doing grown-up's kind of writing*. At 3:11 she produced the little story book I have described with similar lines of scribble but interspersed with words she could actually write (*mummy, and, the*) and with a drawing on the cover. The stories she wrote from 5:6 onward were in cursive script with headings in capitals. She was by this time reading a good deal, mainly the little animal stories by Beatrix Potter and Alison Uttley.

Turning from the general pattern to the detail, Clare at the age of 3 played very often with a set of inch-high letters made of plastic in various colors. Among more random, playful uses, she learned to make her name in these letters and she was interested in what each letter was called. (One effect of this play was evident: When first she attempted to write words, an "E," for example, was an "E" for her whether it faced right or left or up or down.) One of her activities represented a link between letter recognition and writing behavior in general: At 3:5, in imitation of picture alphabets she knew, she was drawing a series of objects and writing the initial letter of each beside the drawing. Most of them she knew, but she came to one she did not: "rhubarb." When I told her, she said, *R—that's easy—just a girl's head and two up-and-downs!*

(5) The final stage in Vygotsky's "developmental history" is that by which the written language ceases to be second-order symbolism, mediated by speech, and becomes first-order symbolism. I can offer no evidence of this from the records of Clare, and indeed I seriously doubt whether that transition is ever entirely appropriate to the written language we have been concerned with, that of stories.

(6) I think the most important conclusion to be drawn from the case of Clare and other children who have taught themselves to write by writing stories is a point that is central to Vygotsky's argument, that of the effect of INTENTION on a child's performance. It would appear that the spoken language effectively meets young children's needs in general, and we must surmise that it is only as they come to value the written language as a vehicle for stories that they are likely to form an intention to write. Much of Clare's behavior indicated that she had done so. Slobin and Welsh (1973) have effectively demonstrated that mastery of the spoken language cannot be adequately assessed without account of "the intention to say so-and-so"—a lesson that as teachers or researchers we have been slow to learn.

Writing and Reading

Clare continued to read and write stories for many years. Animal fantasies predominated until the age of 7, pony stories and adventure stories (often featuring an animal) followed until, from the ages of 12 to 14 she gave herself up almost entirely to reading women's magazine stories and writing herself at great length in that vein. Here, to represent successive stages, are some opening lines:

At 6:   *I am a little Teddy Bear. I've got a pony called Snow and I live in a little house with a thatched roof.*
At 8½: *Mrs Hedgehog had just had three babies. Two of them were like ordinary hedgehog babies, covered with soft prickles. But the third had none.*
It was a dead calm as the Sand Martin and crew glided out of the small harbour at Plymouth. Phillip and Jean were the eldest. They were twins of fourteen.
At 11:   *Fiona Mackenzie lay in bed in her small attic bedroom. She turned sleepily over, but the morning sun streaming in at her small window dazzled her, and she turned back.* (A story about horses in the Highlands.)
At 12:   *Derek looked into her face, and his green eyes burning fiercely with the white hot light of intense love gazed into the liquid depth of her melting, dark brown ones.*
At 14:   *The dance was in full swing, and Giselle was the acknowledged belle of it. More radiant, more sparkling than ever before, she floated blissfully in the arms of James Wainforth.*

Her comments on her reading and writing were sometimes illuminating. At 3:8 she described the Cinderella story as *A bit sad book about two ugly sisters and a girl they were ugly to.* At 8:7 she was asked what sort of things she liked reading. *Well,* she said, *there's* Treasure Island—*that's a bloody one for when I'm feeling boyish. And* Little Men, *that's a sort of half-way one.* "And don't you ever feel girlish?" she was asked. *Yes. When I'm tired and then I read* The Smallest Dormouse. At 10:2 she wrote a story about children finding a treasure: *It's like Enid Blyton's story mostly,* she said, *except longer words.* A few months later she was struggling to get through Mrs. Craik's *John Halifax, Gentleman,* but gave up with the comment, *It's a bit Lorna Doonish, a lot of cissy boys in it. It's so sort of **genteel**—I can't stand it!*

That her writing was influenced by her reading shows up dramatically (though from a limited aspect) in the following figures relating to mean T-unit length and subordination at four age-points. The figures for a passage from a women's magazine story she had read are shown in parentheses.

Age:	6	9	13	(Magazine)	17
Number of words taken:	331	332	340	(330)	322
Mean T-Unit length:	4.1	8.0	6.9	(6.7)	11.5
Number of subordinate clauses:	7	17	6	(9)	19

Spectator Role and the Beginnings of Writing

In the light of current school practices, it is as important as ever today to stress Vygotsky's view that learning to read and learning to write must be seen as inseparable aspects of one process, that of mastering written language. We have come to recognize the way this process is grounded in speech but have not yet acknowledged the essential contribution of other forms of symbolic behavior, gesture, make-believe play, pictorial representation. In my account of Clare's development, I have added one other activity, that of manipulative play with the substance of written language. Bruner (1975) has pointed out that such play contributes to learning because it is a 'meta-process,' one that focuses on the nature itself of the activity. (Children learn to walk for the purpose of getting where they want to be; PLAY with walking—early forms of dancing—involves a concern with the nature of the walking process, an exploration of its manifold possibilities.)

It remains for me to point out that make-believe play (embracing the social environment children construct with their playthings), storytelling, listening to stories, pictorial representation and the talk that complements it, story reading and story writing—these are all activities in the role of spectator. As I have suggested, I believe it is this characteristic that develops a need for the written language in young children and the intention to master it. In such activities children are sorting themselves out, progressively distinguishing what is from what seems, strengthening their hold on reality by a consideration of alternatives. Clare, for example, at the age of 8:6, writes what at first sight appears to be a variant of the kind of animal fable she was familiar with from earlier reading of Beatrix Potter:

HEDGEHOG

Mrs Hedgehog had just had three babies. Two of them were like ordinary hedgehog babies, covered with soft prickles.

But the third had none. He was like a hedgehog in any other way. He ate like a hedgehog and he lived like a hedgehog and he rolled up in a ball like a hedgehog, and he went to sleep in the winter like a hedgehog. But he had no prickles like a hedgehog.

When he was a year old a fairy came to him and said, "Go to China and get three hairs from the Emperor Ching Chang's seventh guinea-pig. Throw the hairs in the fire, and then put it out with six bucketfuls of water. Put some of the ash on your head, and leave it for the night. In the morning you will be covered with prickles." Then she faded away.

[The story tells how he carried out these instructions, and concludes:]

He went to sleep beside the stream. In the morning he woke up feeling rather strange. He looked at his back. It was covered in prickles. He spent four days in China, then he went home in the boat. His family were very surprised to see him!

For those who knew Clare, it was not difficult to recognize here an account of her own struggle to establish herself in the family in competition with a more confident and more relaxed younger sister. *His family were very surprised to see him!* Without knowing the writer, one might guess that a similar self-exploration was taking place, unconsciously, in the 6-year-old girl who wrote:

There was a child of a witch who was ugly. He had pointed ears thin legs and was born in a cave. he flew in the air holding on nothing just playing games.

When he saw ordinary girls and boys he hit them with his broomstick. A cat came along. he arched his back at the girls and boys and made them run away. When they had gone far away the cat meeowed softly at the witch child. the cat loved the child. the child loved the cat the cat was the onlee thing the child loved in the world.

It has often been pointed out that in one sense a tiny infant is lord of his universe, and that growing from infancy into childhood involves discovering one's own unimportance. But the world created in the stories children write is a world they control and this may be a source of deep satisfaction. As one of the children recorded by Donald Graves remarked, she liked writing stories because "you are the mother of the story."

Whether to read or to write, a story makes fewer demands than a piece of transactional writing since one essential element of the latter process is missing in the former. The reader of an informative or persuasive piece must construct himself the writer's meaning and inwardly debate it (an essential part of the piecemeal contextualization process); the reader of a story accepts, so to speak, an invitation to enter a world and see what happens to him there. The writer of a transactional piece must attempt to anticipate and make provision for the reader's inner debate; the writer of a story constructs a situation to his own satisfaction, though thereafter he may be willing, even eager, to share it.

Expressive Writing

Edward Sapir observed that "ordinary speech is directly expressive [1961, p.10]." Because expressive writing, though it differs in substantial ways from speech, is the form of written discourse closest to speech, the London Writing Research team suggested that it provided a "natural" starting point for beginning writers, assisting them at a time when they have rich language resources recruited through speech, but few if any internalized forms of the written language. Progress from this point consists, we believe, in shuttling between those spoken resources and an increasing store of forms internalized from reading and being read to. (It may prove that vocal reading, whether their own or somebody else's, is in the early stages a more effective route to that internalization.)

We might describe this early form as an all-purpose expressive. As the writer employs it to perform different tasks, fulfill different purposes, and increasingly succeeds in meeting the different demands, his all-purpose expressive will evolve: He will acquire by dissociation a variety of modes. Expressive writing is thus a matrix from which will develop transactional and poetic writing, as well as the more mature forms of the expressive.

What the Young Writer Needs to Know

My argument has been that Vygotsky's account offers an explanation of the phenomenon I have noted, that of Clare and the other children who mastered written language by producing storybooks at an early age. Let me now go on to ask, "What does a writer acquiring mastery in this way need to know?"

First and foremost he must know from experience the SATISFACTION that can come from a story—perhaps first a story told to him, but then certainly a story read to him. Sartre (1967, p. 31) has commented on the difference: Accustomed to having his mother tell him stories, he describes his experience when first she reads to him: *The tale itself was in its Sunday best: the woodcutter, the woodcutter's wife and their daughter, the fairy, all those little people, our fellow-creatures, had acquired majesty; their rags were magnificently described, words left their mark on objects, transforming actions into rituals and events into ceremonies.*

Then he must know something of the structure of a story, a learning process that Applebee (1978) has very helpfully described in developmental terms for stories told by children between the ages of 2 and 5 (but with implications for later stages). He sees two principles at work, one of **centering,** a concern for the unity of a story, and one of **chaining,** a concern for sequence; and in terms of these two principles he outlines a series of plot structures that parallel the stages of concept development described by Vygotsky (1962). It should be noted, at the same time, that recall of events in narrative form is something that all children achieve a year or more before they are ready to tackle the written language.

Some forms of story writing will only be possible if the writer is familiar with the conventional associations that govern our expectations in listening to stories—the role expected of a wolf, a lion, a fox, a witch, a prince, and so on (Applebee, 1978, chap. 3). Such built-in associations are, of course, a resource that a young writer may in his own stories exploit, improvise on, invert, or ignore.

Knowledge of the linguistic conventions of stories—the *Once upon a time* and *happily ever after* conventions—are often familiar to children before they can read or write, as are more general features of the language of written stories. (I saw a story dictated by a 3-year-old which contained the sentence, *The king went sadly home for he had nowhere else to go*—a use of *for* which is certainly not a spoken form.)

But production of these and all other written forms relies, of course, on a knowledge of the written code itself, the formation of letters, words, sentences. How this is picked up from alphabet books and cornflake packets, picture books, TV advertisements, and street signs remains something of a mystery, though two governing conditions seem likely: a context of manipulative play and picture-making, and the association of this learning with the purpose of producing written stories. I am sure we underestimate the extent of such learning when a powerful interest is in focus. In my recent experience of reading stories to a 3-year-old, I have been amazed at her ability to fill the words into gaps I leave when the story I am reading is one she cannot have heard very often. Michael Polanyi's account of the relation of subsidiary to focal awareness certainly helps us to see this learning process as feasible (Polanyi, 1958, chap. 4).

Finally, the writer must know from experience the SOUND of a written text read aloud. How else can he come to hear an inner voice dictating to him the story he wants to produce? An apprenticeship of listening to others will enable him later to be aware of the rhythms of the written language in the course of his own silent reading.

A Final Speculation

I believe the successful writer learns all these things implicitly; that is to say, in Polanyi's terms, by maintaining a focal awareness of the desired performance that acts as a determining tendency guiding and controlling his subsidiary awareness of the means he employs. I believe, further, that any attempt to introduce explicit learning would be likely to hinder rather than help at this early stage. When we are dealing with poetic writing, there is much that could not in any case be made explicit: We simply do not know by what organizing principles experience is projected into a work of art.

It is this problem that Susanne Langer has been investigating over many years. Her distinction between discursive and presentational symbolism— between a message encoded in a symbol system and a message embodied in a single unique complex symbol; her recognition of the key role of the arts as offering an ordering of experience alternative to the cognitive, logical ordering achieved by discursive symbolism—these are foundation stones in our theory of language functions.

From her exploration of the laws governing a work of art she makes one very interesting suggestion: that in all works of art there is a building-up and resolution of tensions and that the intricate pattern of these movements, this rhythm, somehow reflects the "shape of every living act [Langer, 1967, chap.7]."

To speculate on her speculations: We give and find shape in the very act of perception, we give and find further shape as we talk, write or otherwise represent our experiences. I say "give and find" because clearly there is order and pattern in the natural world irrespective of our perceiving and representing. At the biological level man shares that order, but at the level of behavior he appears to lose it: The pattern of his actions is more random than that of the instinctual behavior of animals. In learning to control his environment he has gained a freedom of choice in action that he may use constructively and harmoniously or to produce disharmony, shapeless-ness, chaos. When, however, he shapes his experience into a verbal object, an art form, in order to communicate it and to realize it more fully himself, he is seeking to recapture a natural order that his daily actions have for-feited. Understanding so little of the complexities of these processes, we can do no more than entertain that idea as a fascinating speculation.

REFERENCES

Applebee, A. N. *The child's concept of story.* Chicago: University of Chicago Press, 1978.

Britton, J. N. Literature. In J. N. Britton (Ed.), *The arts and current tendencies in education.* London: Evans, 1963. Pp. 34–61.

Britton, J. N. Response to literature. In J. R. Squire (Ed.), *Response to literature.* Champaign, Ill.: National Council of Teachers of English, 1968. Pp. 3–10.

Britton, J. N., Burgess, T., Martin, M., McLeod, A., and Rosen, H. *The development of writing abilities, 11–18.* London: Macmillan, 1975.

Bruner, J. S. The ontogenesis of speech acts. *Journal of Child Language,* 1975, *2,* 1–19.

Gusdorf, G. *Speaking.* Evanston: Northwestern University Press, 1965.

Harding, D. W. The role of the onlooker. *Scrutiny*, 1937, *6*, 247–258.

Harding, D. W. Psychological processes in the reading of fiction. *British Journal of Aesthetics*, 1962, *2*, 133–147.

Harding, D. W. Response to literature: The report of the study group. In J. R. Squire (Ed.), *Response to literature*. Champaign, Ill.: National Council of Teachers of English, 1968. Pp 11–27.

Hymes, D. The ethnography of speaking. In J. A. Fishman (Ed.), *Readings in the sociology of language*. The Hague: Mouton, 1968.

Jakobson, R. *Selected writings* (Vol. 2). *Word and language*. The Hague: Mouton, 1971.

Labov, W. *The social stratification of English in New York City*. Washington, D.C.: Center for Applied Linguistics, 1966.

Langer, S. K. *Feeling and form*. London: Routledge and Kegan Paul, 1953.

Langer, S. K. *Mind: An essay on human feeling*. Baltimore: Johns Hopkins Press, 1967.

Moffett, J. *Teaching the universe of discourse*. Boston: Houghton Mifflin, 1968.

Polanyi, M. *Personal knowledge*. London: Routledge and Kegan Paul, 1958.

Rosenblatt, L. *The reader, the text, the poem*. Carbondale, Ill.: Southern Illinois University Press, 1978.

Sapir, E. *Culture, language and personality*. Berkeley: University of California Press, 1961.

Sartre, J. P. *Words*, Harmondsworth: Penguin Books, 1967.

Sebeok, T. *Style in language*. Cambridge: M.I.T. Press, 1960.

Slobin, D. I., & Welsh, C. A. Elicited imitation as a research tool in developmental psycholinguistics. In C. A. Ferguson & D. I. Slobin (Eds.), *Studies of child language development*. New York: Holt, Rinehart and Winston, 1973.

Vygotsky, L. S. *Mind in society*. Cambridge: Harvard University Press, 1978.

Widdowson, H. G. *Stylistics and the teaching of literature*. London: Longman, 1975.

PART II

THE PROCESSES AND STRUCTURE OF WRITTEN DISCOURSE

Chapter **8**

The Role of Production
Factors in Writing Ability

Marlene Scardamalia
Carl Bereiter
Hillel Goelman

INTRODUCTION

Most cognitive research on writing, including the bulk of our own, focuses on what Sternberg (1980), in his componential theory of intelligence,
calls **metacomponents.** These are components of performance having to do
with goals, plans, strategies, task-related knowledge, and the like. The
very title of this volume, *What Writers Know,* reflects this emphasis; for, if it
were to be translated into psychological jargon, the title might well be
rendered as *Metacomponents of the Composing Process.*

It is easy to see why these components should receive the main attention
of people trying to understand composition. Writing, as we experience it,
consists largely of the interplay of these metacomponents, and it is this
interplay which is captured through thinking-aloud protocols (e.g., Hayes
& Flower, 1980) and through clinical–experimental interactions (e.g.,
Scardamalia & Bereiter, in press).

There is a whole other range of mental activity involved in writing,
however, that is but little accessible to consciousness and that has been
little investigated. It involves what Sternberg calls **performance components.** (In the context of language production, we shall refer to these as
production factors.) Performance components, according to Sternberg, are
processes used in the actual carrying out of decisions arrived at through
action of the metacomponents. Among these processes are recognizing,

WHAT WRITERS KNOW
The Language, Process,
and Structure of Written Discourse

relating, evaluating, and, of course, overt responding, as in directing the motor activities of handwriting. When we listen to people thinking aloud as they write, we find indications that these processes are occurring, but we do not witness the process.

Here is a typical bit of thinking aloud during composition (drawn from Emig, 1971):

> Now the problem is how to start. I could say that I walked into the living room one evening after work and there it was sitting in the middle of the living room. Or else, I could say something like, it's going to sound like a third grade introduction, but something about, "Can you imagine our surprise when we received a three foot by three foot cardboard packing thing in the mail?" That's not too good a start . . . [p.131].

The writer poses a problem and then immediately produces a possible solution. The idea for a beginning of the composition seems to come out of nowhere; the protocol gives us no clue to the process of memory search and construction by which the idea was produced. The writer then proposes an alternative idea for a beginning. This suggests that some evaluation has taken place, which has found the first idea wanting, but again there is no indication of an evaluation process going on. The second idea, however, appears to have been classified and evaluated even before it was expressed.

Clearly much of the interesting work of composition goes on in between the points that are mentioned in thinking-aloud protocols. It consists of mental acts of short duration—comparisons, memory searches, inferences, etc.—of which only the major outcomes rise to consciousness. Yet it would seem that much of the success or failure of writing must depend on these processes. At the conscious level, success might depend on thinking of the right idea. But whether or not one thinks of the right idea and thinks of it at the right time might depend on a variety of undetected production factors—on the speed at which memory is searched, on the length of time information is held in short-term memory and the speed with which it is placed in more permanent storage, on the number and nature of competing demands for attention and on the efficiency with which one can program the switching of attention among competing demands, and a host of other factors of this sort.

A theory that explains the composing process will need to encompass both metacomponents and performance components—both properties of the writer's knowledge and properties of the writer's psychological system that constrain the use of that knowledge. This is particularly true if we want a theory that accounts for what happens in learning to write—as compared to a theory that only accounts for performance as it is observed in discrete time frames. If one considers only metacomponents, then it is not clear why novice writers cannot be turned into experts simply by tutoring them in the knowledge expert writers have. To some extent, of course, this can be done, and it should become increasingly feasible as we develop a better understanding of the procedural knowledge that guides expert performance. But still there are limits on what young writers are ready to learn, and these limits would appear to have much to do with production factors. Children's ability to incorporate new principles and procedures into their composing processes must surely depend in part on what they are able to hold in mind while writing, and this will depend on such underlying factors as how much they can retain in short-term memory for how long, how many things are competing for attention while they write, and how efficiently they can distribute attention to these demands.

Our goal in this chapter is a relatively modest one, stopping short of any attempt to formulate a model that embraces both metacomponents and production factors in an integrated picture of the composing process. We believe the research base is far too weak for that. A strong research base is needed as soon as one tries to venture theoretically beyond conscious levels of the composing process because inferences are necessarily based on very indirect evidence, and one no longer has one's own tacit knowledge of the composing process to use as a tempering influence on speculation.

Our aim in this chapter is to develop and test a few preliminary ideas about ways in which the conditions of text production may influence cognitive processes in composition. Manipulating conditions of text production while keeping the writing task the same is one obvious way of investigating production factors, because in keeping the task the same one presumably holds constant the effect of a wide range of metacomponents (those having to do with rhetorical and world knowledge) and thus may with greater confidence attribute observed effects on writing to the action of production factors. As we shall see, however, the separation of effects is never clean. Consequently, in order to make progress in the interpretation of findings, it is necessary from the outset to rely on psychological intuitions that run in advance of the experimental findings, and which the experimental findings serve mainly to strengthen or weaken.

Let us, accordingly, begin with an intuitive consideration of the act of writing so as to get an idea of the range of production factors that might be relevant to it. To start with a concrete example, consider a normal third-grade class engaged in a writing assignment. Almost all the children will write very slowly and many with obvious labor, some more drawing than writing the letters. There is likely to be audible sounding of words or at any rate lip movement as the children write (Simon, 1973). Even without direct evidence it seems reasonable to infer two things: (*a*) that handwriting is taking up considerable attention, which accordingly must be taken away from other aspects of the writing task such as content planning (Graves, 1978); and (*b*) that the slow rate of production must create problems of remembering—not only problems in remembering immediately forthcoming words but also problems in remembering higher-level plans and intentions.

In more mature writers, of course, handwriting is fluent and automatic enough that production problems associated with it should be greatly reduced. But writing remains a complex activity in which many different processes must compete for limited attentional capacity and it remains slow enough that writers will frequently be heard to complain that they cannot keep up with their thoughts. It seems reasonable to suppose, therefore, that how well a person writes will continue to depend not only on what conceptual and procedural knowledge the person has available but also on how successfully the operations involved in using it are coordinated.

Research on speech production has revealed the elaborate orchestration of mental functions that must go on in this apparently effortless activity. (See for instance the two chapters devoted to this topic in Clark and Clark, 1977.) While part of the cognitive system is concerned with articulation and coordinating speech with gestures and eye contact, another part is occupied with planning ahead. These processes use some of the same resources, however, so that finely organized time sharing is required, and even at that the system is frequently overtaxed, with the result that speech is filled with errors and unplanned pauses (Butterworth & Goldman-Eisler, 1979).

Written language production differs from conversational speech production in several ways that should make production factors less problematic: Writing is less time-constrained and there is not the immediate social situation that requires monitoring. (Butterworth and Goldman-Eisler, 1979, note, for instance, that during planning phases of speech production the speaker is vulnerable to interruption and will therefore often break eye contact with listeners so as to keep the floor.) The absence of incoming social stimuli may also, however, create serious problems.

A key factor in fluent language production seems to be temporal organization of subprocesses. By this we mean the fine-grain (small fractions of a second) distribution of time among various levels of planning so that language production both proceeds steadily and maintains purposefulness and high-level organization. By the time children begin learning to write, they already speak fluently and coherently enough that it seems the major temporal organization of language production processes must already have been achieved. This organization has developed through conversational experience, however. It would be reasonable to expect, therefore, that the programming of performance components would be keyed to conversational events. There is substantial evidence that metacomponents of the composing process still bear the stamp of conversational circumstances in young writers (Bereiter & Scardamalia, 1981). It therefore seems worth investigating the possibility that some of the difficulty children have in writing production has a more profound basis than the slow and demanding qualities of handwriting, that it reflects breakdown in the organization of subprocesses when language production must go on in the absence of signals from the conversational milieu.

To get a concrete sense of what such a breakdown of organization could be like, readers who are touch-typists might try the following experiment. Put your fingers on a table top and try to go through the motions of typing a simple sentence such as, "When in Rome, do as the Romans do." In informal tests, we find that proficient typists are at least slowed down and are sometimes immobilized by this task. Evidently then, typists are dependent on reactions of the keyboard for organization of the typing process. In this instance we have a kind of behavior that would seem to proceed entirely from the inside out, and yet we find that for some people at least its organization depends on response of the passive instrument to which it is directed. In conversation, we deal with reciprocal action rather than passive response, and so we may expect that the organization of processes will depend even more on feedback, as it does in such other reciprocal activities as tennis and dancing. (See Schmidt, 1975, on the interaction of feedback with internal programming in skilled performance.)

This intuitive analysis of the act of writing depicts it as a complex, internally regulated process characterized by slow and attention-demanding output. The analysis has suggested three production difficulties that we shall explore further in this paper: (a) short-term memory loss, to which slow rate of production could be a contributing cause; (b) interference from mechanical demands of the written medium that compete for mental resources with the higher-level demands of content planning and the like; and (c) general discoordination of language production resulting from the lack of external signals.

In the following section we shall review the small amount of available evidence bearing on these three possibilities. Then we shall report in detail an experiment that examines all three at once. In a final discussion we shall press toward a more integrated view of production factors and their relation to metacomponents in writing.

RESEARCH ON PRODUCTION FACTORS IN WRITING

Writers on speech production often remark on its extraordinary neglect by researchers, compared to speech comprehension. As regards written language, the disparity is even greater. The only sustained program of research on production factors in writing has been that of John Gould (summarized in Gould, 1980); and Gould's work, though ranging widely in the production factors considered, has been limited to capable adults composing business letters. Another significant entry in the sparse literature on production factors in writing has been the work of Matsuhashi on pauses and other behaviors that may be observed through microanalysis of videorecordings of writers at work. We shall not deal with that work here, however, since it is the subject of Chapter 10 in this volume. Instead we shall focus on our own research with school-age children, relating it to Gould's work, which it parallels in many ways, and more broadly to research on speech production, in so far as generalizations may be drawn from it to writing.

Short-Term Memory Loss Due to Slow Writing Rate

The most obvious place to look for an effect of production factors on written composition is at the interface between the mental process of language generation and the physical process of transcription. Models of language production generally place at this interface a buffer, a short-term memory store, that holds language already composed while it awaits translation into physical speaking or writing responses (e.g., Fodor, Bever, & Garrett, 1974). Such temporary storage is a necessity, even if we imagine the slowest of planners. Even someone who planned only a single word ahead would need to hold that word in mind long enough to write it. But no one could produce coherent language without planning farther ahead than that, and so somehow the products of planning must be held in mind while transcription goes on.

In writing, because of its slowness, the products of planning must often be held in mind for some seconds, an appreciable period of time by short-term memory standards. This raises the possibility that "forgetting what one was going to say" may be a more significant factor in writing than in speaking. Some relevant data on memory loss in writing come from a study by Bereiter, Fine, and Gartshore (1978).

This was an exploratory study, using a very simple methodology. Subjects wrote, in the presence of an experimenter, on any subject of their choice. At irregular intervals the experimenter would halt the writing process by suddenly placing a screen over the writing paper. Subjects were then to report any words they had already formed in their minds, but they were urged not to make up any new material. After each forecast, the screen was removed and subjects resumed writing where they had left off. After a paragraph was completed, the subjects were asked to repeat from memory, as exactly as they could, the paragraph they had just written. The forecasting part of the experiment was explained to subjects in advance, but they were not forewarned of the recall task. The study was conducted on 14 children in fourth grade and 14 in sixth grade (mean ages approximately 10 and 12 years).

The experimental procedure made it possible to compare at certain points in each composition (*a*) what subjects reportedly intended to write;

(*b*) what they actually did write; and (*c*) what they remembered having written.

The number of words per forecast—that is, the number of words children supposedly already had formed in their minds in advance of the last word they had written—averaged five to six. There was great variability, however, the forecast tending to run to the end of a clause regardless of the number of words that took. (Compare Fodor, Bever, and Garrett, 1974, on the clause as the basic unit of planning in speech production.) When we count only words spoken before the first pause of a second or longer, however, the mean is two words less, and the forecasts no longer regularly run to the ends of clauses. The rationale for this stricter count is that pauses of a second or longer are typically assumed to be planning pauses (Matsuhashi, Chapter 10 this volume), and therefore suggest that the child has started fabricating new material rather than reporting language already held in short-term storage.

Regardless of which criterion is used, however, the outstanding finding is that what children say they will write they by and large do write. The average number of discrepancies between forecasts and actual writing was .5 per forecast. Thus, for about half of the forecasts children subsequently wrote exactly the words they had claimed to have in mind. Furthermore, of the discrepancies, 78% were stylistic variations that carried the same meaning in writing as in the forecast. (More about these variations presently.)

In 17% of the discrepancies, however, significant words uttered in the forecast failed to appear in writing. In about half of these cases the result was a syntactic anomaly—for instance, the forecasted phrase *on the way to school* was written *on the to school*. Lapses of this kind clearly indicate language getting lost somewhere between its storage in an output buffer and its translation into handwriting movements. But, just as clearly, these lapses cannot be described as "forgetting what one was going to say." For one thing, the lapses were almost invariably repaired on recall: in the case of *on the to school*, for example, the author not only intended to write *on the way* but claimed later to have written it.

Lapses of this kind are common in first-draft writing by experienced writers (Hotopf, 1980). They probably represent a lack of monitoring of the written output, the result of devoting conscious attention entirely to planning ahead, while leaving the process of transcription to run "on automatic." If this is what children are doing as well, then it is a sign that temporal organization of the writing process is already well advanced for them, making it possible for them to carry on planning and transcribing operations in parallel.

Such a speculation gains interest when related to the developmental observations of Simon (1973). Simon observed that primary-grade children tended to dictate to themselves, mouthing each letter or syllable as they wrote it. This activity would bespeak a heavy investment of conscious attention in the process of transcription, making it unlikely that any planning ahead could occur while the child was transcribing. This simultaneous mouthing of the words was observed to give way after the first couple of years, however, to the practice of mouthing a string of words and then writing them. This latter practice would clear the way for planning while transcribing.

Simon's findings were replicated and extended somewhat by a study conducted in our laboratory by Gartshore. Mouthing of individual letters and words during transcription was found to be common in children in second and third grades but to virtually disappear by fourth grade. On the other hand, mouthing of language during pauses in writing was almost nonexistent in second and third grades but was shown by half the children in fourth grade. Moreover, at fourth grade the rated quality of compositions was positively correlated with the frequency of subvocalization during pauses. This correlation lends further support to the notion that parallel planning and transcribing processes come into play around fourth grade and that they significantly enhance composing ability.

The existence of such parallel or overlapping processes means that we cannot look for a simple connection between production rate and short-term memory or other performance components. A variety of mental activities may be going on while the writer's pencil is in motion. Some of these may interfere with retention of language in the buffer and its translation into writing, others may have no such effect, and still others might provide rehearsal of buffer contents, thus reducing the effects of delay in transcription. It remains, however, a question of some interest whether, on the whole and for whatever reasons, loss of information from short-term storage may be a significant factor in written language production. There is evidence from the forecasting study that it is, at least for elementary school children.

Seventeen percent of the discrepancies between forecasts and actual written text involved some information loss whereas only 5% involved some information gain (usually in the form of an inserted word not present in the forecast). When lapses of the kind mentioned previously, resulting in linguistic anomalies, are eliminated, there are still twice as many information losses as information gains. The typical result of these losses was reduced richness of detail. For instance, a reference to *the purple martians* appeared in writing simply as *the martians*. The data would suggest that in perhaps 1 out of 10 sentence constituents written by elementary school children there is some loss of content due to short-term memory loss. This would be an upper-bound estimate, since it does not take account of the possibility that some deletions may be intentional—that the child might have decided against representing the Martians as *purple,* for instance. The results thus suggest that short-term memory loss is at most an appreciable, but not a predominant, factor influencing the content of children's writing.

But does this short-term memory loss have anything to do with slow rate of production? The forecasting study has no evidence to offer on this question. Between the forecast and the appearance of the written language, not only did time elapse but also the child had to contend with whatever difficulties might have arisen in transcription—spelling problems, for instance. And so memory losses could as well be attributed to interference from other attention demands as to the lapse of time between input to the buffer and output. Isolation of the effects of rate would require an experimental situation in which production rate varied while mechanical demands of the output medium remained constant. In an experiment to be reported later, we tried to isolate rate in this way.

The evidence considered in this section serves mainly to remind us that even in fairly young children the process of writing is organized with sufficient complexity that single production factors can only be understood in relation to the process as a whole. Studies of speech production suggest that output rate presents different kinds of problems at different stages in discourse production. At an early stage of expressing a unit of discourse, when time is needed for assembling content and language, speakers may find that the output rate forced on them by the press of conversation is too fast for their needs (Clark & Clark, 1977). Once the unit has been mentally constructed, however, speakers will tend to speed up output so as to "clear the decks" for construction of the next unit—that is, free up short-term memory capacity for use in storing the products of advance planning. The kinds of memory loss that might occur would seem to differ, depending on what stage the speaker was in, and might be caused by excessive output speed in one case and excessive slowness in the other. In writing, where there is usually no social press to maintain a high rate of output, slow rate of output might be beneficial or at least harmless during the extensive constructive phases of composition and be detrimental only during those periods when clearing the decks is called for. If this is true, then an understanding of the relation between production rate and short-term memory loss will depend both on more sophisticated methodology than is currently available and on more fine-grained models of the composing process.

Interference from Mechanical Requirements of Written Language

Although ideas about production factors tend to be esoteric, there is one such idea that seems already to be firmly established in conventional wisdom. This is the idea that having to attend to low-level considerations such as spelling and punctuation interferes with attention to higher-level concerns of composition. Some teachers operate on this idea by urging their students to pay no attention to correctness, at least until after a first draft has been produced. Others take the approach of stressing early mastery of these mechanical aspects of writing so that they need no longer demand much attention. The policies are different, but the underlying psychological premise is the same, that the writer has a limited amount of attention to allocate and that whatever is taken up with the mechanical[1] demands of written language must be taken away from something else.

This premise cannot be accepted in so simple a form, however. We must ask what gets interfered with and when. Although language production is often a rapid process, the development of an utterance through stages of intention to choice of syntactic frame to construction of constituents to overt output covers a time span that is not trivial in the time scale of cognitive operations. What gets interfered with when a writer is caught up by a spelling problem is the other cognitive activity going on at that moment. If the meaning of the sentence being written has already been fully constructed in the writer's mind, then ipso facto attention to a spelling problem cannot interfere with construction of THAT unit of meaning— although it could interfere with construction of some other unit of meaning if the writer was thinking about it at the time. Thus we must consider possible interference in relation to the temporal unfolding of the composing process, which, as we have already noted, is greatly complicated by the existence of parallel or overlapping mental activities. We must furthermore take account of the possibilities of time sharing. In an unhurried activity such as writing, it seems likely that a writer with a well-developed executive system for sharing time among different activities could tolerate all sorts of additional attentional burdens without reducing the total amount of attention devoted to any single one of them. Additional burdens would simply call for filling in spare time slots or extending total time (cf. Spelke, Hirst, & Neisser, 1976).

In the forecasting study (Bereiter et al., 1979), discussed in the preceding section, we have indicated that the small amounts of information loss observed between forecasts and actual writing might reflect interference from the attentional demands of mechanics. This would not show interference with higher-level composing processes, however, simply interference with short-term storage of language already composed. Consequently we would expect this type of interference to have only minor effects on the composing process. We also noted evidence of a different kind of interference resulting in syntactic anomalies. But this phenomenon

---

[1]By mechanics of writing we do not mean merely handwriting or other means of transcription. Mechanics also includes spelling, capitalization, punctuation (for the most part), hyphenation, indentation, etc. In short, mechanics comprises all those parts of the writing task that are avoided when one dictates.

seemed attributable to HIGH-LEVEL processes interfering with LOW-LEVEL ones—the very opposite of the phenomenon we are concerned with here.

We have not yet, however, considered the 78% of discrepancies found in that study between forecasts and actual writing that did not involve meaning changes or errors but simply stylistic variations. The nature of these discrepancies might offer a clue as to the kinds of language processing going on very late in the production process and, hence, the kinds of language processing that would be susceptible to interference from mechanical demands of writing that also apply to that late stage.

We have not been able to discover any significant regularities in the nature of these stylistic variations, but there was a tendency for the written versions to differ from the forecasted versions in the direction of greater formality, suggesting that at a late stage in production children may have been editing their language according to understood requirements of the written medium. The failure to find a consistent tendency in this direction might reflect inconsistencies in children's knowledge of written English conventions.

Whatever the nature of these stylistic variations, their frequency has interesting implications for theories of written language production. It adds support to suggestions that what is stored in the output buffer waiting to be translated into script is not fully formed language, but rather some more general kinds of syntactic and semantic choices, with more detailed choices remaining to be made "at the point of utterance," as Britton (1978) puts it. Krashen (1977) has proposed a model that accords with our observations that "shaping at the point of utterance" seems to take the form of shaping in the direction of written English. According to Krashen's Monitor model, language is generated according to an unconscious rule system acquired through natural language experience. Conscious, "learned" rules have no generative capability. Instead, they have their effect through a Monitor, which applies to language after it is generated but before it is uttered and edits it according to the learned rules. What we might therefore be observing in the discrepancies between forecasts and actual written text is the difference between relatively unmonitored spoken language as spontaneously generated and language as it has been altered by action of the Monitor. Indeed, our instructions to subjects to tell us only the language they already had in their minds and not to make up any new language might have had the effect of getting them to bypass the Monitor, much like the psychoanalyst's instructions to free associate.

Krashen's Monitor model is interesting when applied to writing (it has mainly been applied to second language learning). Writing appears as an activity in which the Monitor plays an unusually large role, compared to most oral language activities—an essential role, in that so many writing conventions must be applied consciously at first, but a role that could be severely constraining on children's generative capabilities.

Unfortunately, Krashen's model has not been elaborated or tested sufficiently to show whether it can serve as a viable model of language production. What kind of mechanism would enable the Monitor to edit language even though it could not generate it? Such a mechanism is certainly conceivable, in as much as there is computer software that can perform fairly sophisticated monitoring functions even though it cannot generate a sentence from scratch (Frase, 1980). But it is not obvious how the editing and generating functions could be so sharply divided within a human information processing system.

Whether or not there is a distinct, late in the process phase, at which more recently learned operators apply, the notion of gradual refinements from global to specific features is common to most views of language production (Clark & Clark, 1977; Luria, 1976; Vygotsky, 1962). Thus, in keeping with the ideas underlying Krashen's Monitor model, we may suppose that much of a writer's knowledge about written language style and about conventions of punctuation, spelling, capitalization, and the like will be applied at a very late stage in language production.

On the basis of these theoretical considerations, it seems that we must reject the commonplace idea that attention to how written language is to be spelled or punctuated will interfere with its content. If concerns about mechanics only enter after the original intention has already been shaped into propositions, then it is too late for them to interfere with the construction of meaning. The meaning of the sentence in question will already have been constructed.

There remain, however, three ways in which attention to low-level aspects of writing could interfere with the higher-level metacomponents.

1. It could lead to forgetting high-level decisions already made. In the preceding section we considred only forgetting of material that was already at an advanced stage of shaping into utterance. We did not consider and have no direct evidence bearing on the possibility of forgetting less-developed intentions and meanings—for instance, concentrating on details of expression and in the process forgetting what purpose a sentence was intended to serve. We have introspective reason to believe that this occurs, having paused to consult a dictionary and finding, on return to writing, that although we could recall the rest of the interrupted sentence, we had forgotten what it was supposed to be leading up to. As we shall consider further toward the end of this chapter, this effect will depend on how intentions are represented in the writer's memory. We shall also consider the possibility that having to reconstruct intentions periodically may be an aid rather than a hindrance to planful writing.

2. Concern with mechanics could interfere with high-level planning of the NEXT unit of discourse. This could happen if people are simultaneously expressing one unit and planning another, and we have already noted

indications that even children as young as 10 years old do this. The result of this kind of interference would be that whereas individual sentences would be well expressed, overall coherence and the complexity of content integration would suffer. Thus evidence on the low level of content integration in children's writing (Scardamalia, 1981) could be taken to suggest interference of this sort.

3. Finally, attention to problems of mechanics could interfere with considerations of intentionality AT THE POINT OF UTTERANCE.

This last possibility has interesting implications, but it is one for which systematic evidence is entirely lacking. Bracewell (personal communication) has observed that skilled writers make, as they go along, small changes in wording that seem to an observer to have no point to them. One word or phrase is replaced by another that has no discernible semantic or stylistic claim to preference. Leaving aside the possibility that the writer has more refined sensibilities than the observer, we may speculate that the writer makes such changes in order to make the expression more closely fit his or her intentions. Having no independent knowledge of those intentions, the observer cannot judge one expression to be more valid than the other, although the astute writer can. But, considering that the writer has already written one thing and then changed it to another, it seems that this very precise fitting of expression to intention goes on into the very latest stage of written language production. Consequently, if this stage is being occupied with concerns about spelling, capitalization, or even penmanship, there will be little opportunity for this fine fitting to occur.

Although effects on text due to the production factors just discussed might be variable, they should account for some variance in global impressionistic judgments of text quality. The most obvious way to isolate variance due to the mechanical demands of writing is to compare oral and written text production. The control is imperfect, because speaking and writing also differ in other characteristics, for instance, rate; however, the comparison may at least provide suggestive findings. Note that comparing oral and written text production is not the same as comparing writing with speaking in the normal sense. It is comparing two ways of producing what is eventually to become a written text. (Blass and Siegman, 1975, provide an interesting example of the opposite kind of study, one that compares oral and written modes of conversational interaction.) In the oral mode of production—that is, in dictation—the author generates language but need not be concerned at the time with such low-level requirements of writing as spelling, penmanship or typing, punctuation, and capitalization. Although speech production has its own requirements, we assume that speech articulation is highly learned and automatized (as might not be the case if, for instance, one were speaking in a foreign language).

Gould (1980) has done extensive comparisons of writing and dictating, using adults who were either novices or experts at the latter. One of his initial hypotheses was similar to the ones being considered here—that dictating might produce superior compositions because of less interference and forgetting. In a long series of experiments, however, quality differences have failed to appear. But with capable adults producing business correspondence it could be that the low-level parts of writing production are so well learned that there is no interference to be removed. Although dictating was found to be somewhat faster than writing (20–65%), it was not enough faster that time alone could have much effect on memory.

With children, however, interference and/or speed factors might be considerably more important. A study by Scardamalia and Bereiter (1979) investigaged these factors in children (grades four and six) and furthermore introduced an experimental procedure for separating the effects of mechanical interference from the effects of rate. This was done by introducing a third production mode, in addition to writing and normal dictation. In this third mode, called **slow dictation,** the children dictated to an experimenter who transcribed according to each child's previously determined writing rate. Thus it was possible to isolate the effects of mechanical interference by comparing writing with slow dictation, since they were equivalent in speed; it was correspondingly possible to isolate the effects of speed by comparing slow dictation with normal dictation, since these were alike in their mechanical demands but differed substantially in speed (normal dictation being in fact about five times faster than slow dictation and writing).

Results suggested that mechanical demands and rate were additive in their effects on quantity of production. Children produced 86% more words in slow dictation than in writing and 163% more in normal dictation than in writing. With respect to quality, however, the differences were small. There was a tendency, significant at the .06 level, for ratings on quality of presentation to differ in the order writing (lowest), normal dictation, slow dictation (highest). Results suggested, therefore, that freeing children from concerns about written language mechanics improved the quality of their writing, but that a more rapid rate of production was not an aid to quality.

This study indicated that the low-level requirements of writing do make a difference to children. Take away those requirements and children produce considerably more and do it a great deal faster. The quality ratings, however, indicated that mechanical demands of writing had only a weak effect if any on higher-level components of the writing process. As in Gould's studies with adults, the most striking result of this study with children was the similarity of products from different modes of production.

Hidi and Hildyard (1980) have compared oral and written composition in two genres, opinion essay and narrative, using children in grades three and five. Their results are generally compatible with those obtained by us comparing writing with normal dictation: Subjects produced significantly more in the oral mode, but quality did not differ. Hidi and Hildyard assessed quality both on the basis of cohesion at the sentence-to-sentence level and on the basis of being well formed at the level of text structure.

Discoordination Resulting from Lack of External Signals

In our discussion so far we have presupposed a model of the composing process that consists of a number of subprocesses governed by an executive system (or monitor, as it is called in the Hayes and Flower [1980] model). The production difficulties that we have considered so far all have to do with one subprocess impinging on another—with motor output delays impinging on retention of language in short-term storage, with attention to mechanics interfering with planning, etc. In every case we have had to allow that the effect of these production factors will depend on how the system as a whole functions—on how well it can share time among competing attentional demands, for instance. In other words, the way in which one subprocess impinges on another will depend on the executive system, which regulates or orchestrates the subprocesses.

We turn now to a different and potentially much more significant class of production factors. These are ones that impinge on the executive system itself, influencing how reliably it functions and what capacity it has to cope with demands such as we have considered previously. The most fundamental of these factors is one that we shall not deal with at this point, although it serves as background to much of our analysis. This is the limitation imposed on executive functioning by the capacity of working memory, the same limitation that affects subprocesses. As Brown and Campione (1980) put it, "The executive competes for workspace with the subroutines it controls." It is probably this factor more than any other that limits the novice's ability to profit from being taught the strategies of the expert. Because the novice's subprocesses are not fully mastered and therefore require large amounts of attention, the novice has little spare capacity to be used for implementing more sophisticated executive procedures.

This is a general problem, however, affecting the acquisition of executive procedures in all areas of intellectual functioning (Case, 1980; Scardamalia & Bereiter, 1980). In this section we want to focus on a factor specific to executive functioning in writing. The factor has been referred to in the introduction as discoordination of language production resulting from the lack of external signals. We assume that the child develops an executive system to control everyday speech production and that, in learning to write, the child does not construct a whole new executive system but instead tries to adapt the existing one to the new requirements. But the existing system is an interactive one, designed to respond to signals from the external environment, specifically signals from conversational partners. Without such inputs, it has trouble functioning, much as we have noted that typists have trouble functioning without a keyboard to provide cues for programming their motor output.

In order to understand the child's predicament from the standpoint of production factors, we must rather ruthlessly abstract elements from the social situation. For conversation is a very complex social activity that impinges on the individual's language production system in a number of ways. In so far as conversation provides meanings to which the individual responds, it is implicated in the metacomponents of language production. Meanings (broadly conceived, so as to include those of both linguistic and paralinguistic origin) are of course the main elements of conversation; and no doubt the main strand in the story of how children acquire literacy is the story of how they learn to produce meaningful discourse without the dialectical exchange of meanings that occurs in conversation (Bereiter & Scardamalia, 1981; Olson, 1977). But there is more to conversation than meaning, and it is this remainder that we need to examine if we are to understand the workings of the executive system in writing rather than understanding only the content it works on.

In the present discussion and in the experiment reported thereafter, we focus on what is perhaps the most elemental feature of conversation from the standpoint of executive system functioning. This is **production signaling**—that is, signaling that simply activates the executive system to produce another unit of language. In conversation, we assume, the executive system is attuned to such signals; it normally responds to them when they are presented and does not respond without such signals, since to do otherwise is to violate conversational etiquette. In composition, however, there is usually no partner nor anything else in the environment to provide production signals. Therefore, in order to produce continuous discourse, the language production system must somehow provide its own means of sustaining production.

More dramatically than anything else, children's writing is characterized by low quantity. In the "slow dictation" study cited previously (Scardamalia & Bereiter, 1979), the average written opinion essay was only 18 words long. In the Hidi and Hildyard (1980) study the comparable length was 32 words. Although compositions are longer when dictated, the quantity is still low enough to support the conjecture that children's compositions are equivalent to single conversational turns (Bereiter & Scardamalia, 1981). It is as if children take a turn as they would in conversation, wait for a response, and, receiving none, stop—again, just as they might do in conversation. There are circumstances in which children will go on to produce longer compositions. The best documented is that of writing a story (Hidi & Hildyard, 1980; Britton, chapter 7 this volume). But this does not violate the generalization, since storytelling is a special case in conversation as well, characterized by taking extended turns (Sacks, 1976).

How do children acquire the ability to sustain language production without external signals? One answer is that perhaps they never do—entirely. The problem of keeping going seems to be a recurrent one, even for many accomplished writers, and it is often amazing what trivial stimuli will suffice to get a stuck writer unstuck—something as slight as the question, "Well, what is it you're trying to say?"

People do learn to produce longer compositions, however, and a reasonable conjecture in the light of current discourse processing theory is that they do so by learning more extended schemata or scripts for discourse production. With such schemata—for instance, a schema that tells you what kinds of elements to include in an opinion essay and that guides you in selecting and ordering these elements—the writer will keep producing under the guidance of high-level knowledge about what to do next. But how are these discourse schemata acquired? Partly through reading and listening, no doubt. But in order for the schemata to become functional in language production, it seems that they would also have to develop through use, that is, through constructive activity.

Therein, we suspect, is the point at which production factors impinge on the development of high-level executive strategies. The child who is writing 18-word opinion essays is not getting much practice in using an opinion essay schema. Thus we have the makings of a double bind, where in order for the child to learn how to produce more, the child must already produce more.

In the experiment to be reported in the next section we introduced a simple form of production signaling as an experimental variable. Although the signaling was done by social means, through words spoken by the experimenter, the intent was NOT to duplicate the social situation of conversation but rather to abstract from conversation this sole element of production signaling without the meaning elements that normally accompany it. When we undertook the experiment we had few expectations other than that external production cueing would increase the quantity of text produced. It did that, but it also had such a variety of other striking effects as to make us believe that the production factors most urgently in need of further study are those that impinge directly on functioning of the executive system.

AN EXPERIMENT INVESTIGATING PRODUCTION MODE AND PRODUCTION SIGNALING

In the preceding sections we have considered three production factors that might have a significant effect on the ability of people, especially children, to realize their intentions in writing. Some evidence was found of short-term memory loss in writing, but it was not possible to tell whether this was due to the slow rate of children's writing or to interference from the mechanics of writing. This second factor, interference from the mechanical requirements of written language, was found to have a significant effect on quantity of text produced, both in children and adults, but far more so in children. There was little indication that this factor had any influence on the quality of writing at any age, although the possibility remains that interference from mechanical requirements might have a long-term effect on writing development through its effect on the allocation of attention at critical points in the writing act. For the third factor, discoordination resulting from lack of signals, it is possible to build a strong circumstantial case that this factor is a major impediment to children's writing and interferes with their developing adequate executive structures to direct the composing process. However, direct evidence is lacking.

In addition to the shortcomings just noted, there are two other shortcomings that characterize research to date. Production factors have generally been studied in isolation, so that little is known of their interaction, and their effects have generally been measured only in global ways. Thus, for instance, although we have evidence that written and dictated compositions do not differ much in overall judged quality, we do not know if they differ in the stylistic and structural means by which quality is achieved. The study to be reported here is a step toward remedying these two shortcomings and also toward remedying the lack of any direct evidence bearing on the third production factor noted previously.

The present study used an elaborated and refined version of the procedure previously described for the Scardamalia and Bereiter (1979) study comparing writing, normal dictation, and slow dictation. Like its predecessor, the study was run on children in grades four and six, 24 of each. Each child produced three compositions, one using each of the three production modes, and each on a different one of the following opinion essay topics:

Is it better to be an only child or to have brothers and sisters?
Should children be allowed to choose what subjects they study in school?
Should boys and girls play sports together?

The assignment of topics to conditions was counterbalanced so that each topic–condition pairing occurred with equal frequency. Order of condition was counterbalanced, with the limitation that subjects always composed in the writing mode before they composed in the slow dictation mode. The reason for having all subjects compose in the writing mode first was that their writing rate was used to determine the rate at which the experimenter transcribed in the slow dictation condition.[2]

---

[2]This was done by dividing total time by total words in the written composition. In slow dictation the experimenter then paced himself so as to average the same number of seconds per word in total elapsed time. Thus what was controlled was composing rate, which included

All sessions were conducted with children individually. In the writing session the children were asked simply to write as much as they could on the given topic. In normal dictation the instructions were similar except that the children were told to speak their composition into a tape recorder and were told that "some people at OISE" would type the composition from the tape. Slow dictation may best be understood from the instructions given to the children, which were as follows:

> *Remember what we did before? Well, today we're going to do something a little different. I'm going to give you another question to talk about, and you are to say as much as you can about it, just like before. Only this time you don't have to write it. You just say what you think, and I will write it for you. But, when I write, I will write at the same speed you did when you wrote the other day. The stop-watch is here in front of me so I know that I am writing at the same speed you did. It is not to time you, but to time me. Now, here is an example of how you wrote the other day. You wrote the words——. Now, I'm going to write those words at the same speed you did, so you watch how fast I write (demonstrate example). There, that's how fast I'll be writing when you tell me what to write. We'll need a bit of practice before you get the new topic, so you talk about the topic (specify) that you wrote about the other day, and I'll write what you say. Don't try to say exactly what you wrote from memory, just tell me what you think about the topic.*

Several differences in procedure from the original Scardamalia and Bereiter (1979) experiment were introduced in order to overcome the unusually low quantity of text produced by children in the first experiment. Whereas in the first study children produced all three compositions in one session, in the present study they produced them in separate sessions spaced a day apart. Furthermore, in the present study children in all conditions were instructed to write or say as much as they could on the assigned topic, whereas no such urging was given in the earlier study. These efforts were apparently successful, since children produced about three times as many words in each condition as comparable children did in the first experiment.

Other changes in procedure reflected an increased sensitivity to the possible importance of subtle social inputs to the composing process. In the two dictation conditions, as in the writing condition, the experimenter sat beside subjects while they were dictating and avoided eye contact with them, whereas in the earlier experiment (and we suspect in other experi-

---

both pauses and transcribing time, rather than transcribing rate alone. Composing rate was, with few exceptions, so close to transcription rate that transcribers could not adjust speed of transcription precisely enough to differentiate between the two rates. Data was analyzed separately for the few children whose rates were different enough that transcribers could have in fact adjusted their speeds to accommodate the differences, but such reanalyses had no significant effects on results. Adequacy of the experimental procedure was judged by comparing logarithms of time per word. The mean rates for writing and slow dictation were almost identical and the correlation between the two, calculated over all subjects, was about .75.

ments comparing speaking with writing) no such controls were imposed and the experimenter may well have responded to the speaker through expressions and nods, thus unintentionally introducing conversational elements into the experimental conditions.

The major distinction of the present experiment, however, was the addition of a further experimental intervention. At the point when the child had apparently finished his or her composition, the experimenter introduced the first of three contentless "production signals" intended to encourage the child to continue speaking or writing:

SIGNAL 1: *You're doing fine. Now I know this is a bit tough, but can you say (write) some more about this?*

After each of the next two cessations of production yet another signal was offered:

SIGNAL 2: *That's fine. This is hard to do, but now can you say (write) even more?* If children asked if they could say the same thing again, the experimenter responded, *Try to say even more than you've already said.*

SIGNAL 3: *Do you think you could say (write) 10 more sentences about this?* If the child responded negatively, the experimenter said, *What about 5 more?* If the response was still negative, the experimenter said, *Then try just two more sentences.*

The experimenter tried to give the cues in an encouraging and not belittling manner.

The purpose of introducing these production signals was to get some more direct information than has previously been available on the extent to which children's language production depends on external data inputs. Most normal kinds of conversational response include both content-relevant and contentless elements. The response, *Is that so?*, for instance, not only provides the speaker with a signal to continue speaking but it also calls on the speaker to provide warrant or confirmation for an assertion just made. If inputs of this kind are found to aid language production, there is no way to determine whether they have their effect at the level of production factors or at the level of metacomponents. It is impossible, that is, to separate the extent to which such inputs directly help the language production system to keep going from the extent to which they provide information useful in planning the next utterance.

We wanted to provide inputs of a kind to which children would already be used to responding and that would seem natural to them in the situation. We did not, therefore, want to resort to lights that would flash on to signal "write more" or anything of that sort. But on the other hand we wanted, for purposes of comparability across conditions, inputs that could be standardized and that would not carry any suggestions as to content. Of particular interest was the extent to which production cueing might serve to eliminate some of the previously observed differences between oral and written modes of composition.

RESULTS

In the analyses that follow, each composition is treated as providing three different text bases:

1. The standard portion. This is the portion of text produced before administration of the first production signal. It is called the standard portion because it constitutes what under normal test conditions would have been the complete composition.
2. The signaled portion. This is the additional portion of text produced in response to the prescribed series of production signals.
3. The extended composition. This is the combined standard portion and signaled portion, treated as a single text.

The first results to be reported will be those that permit comparison to the findings of other research—namely, results in terms of numbers of words produced and global quality ratings. Table 8.1 summarizes these results for the standard portion and for the extended composition. Results for the standard portion of text provide results similar in profile to those obtained in the earlier study (Scardamalia & Bereiter, 1980). Even though in the present study children produced far more words in every condition than in the previous study, the relative differences are the same: Children produce most in normal dictation, least in writing, and an intermediate amount with slow dictation, suggesting again an additivity of the effects of production rate and of the oral-versus-written difference. When production signaling is added, however, normal dictation retains its large quan-

TABLE 8.1
Mean Word Counts and Quality Ratings for Compositions Produced in Three Modes

	Number of words				Quality Rating			
	Standard portion		Extended composition		Standard portion		Extended composition	
Production mode	Grade 4	Grade 6	Grade 4	Grade 6	Grade 4	Grade 6	Grade 4	Grade 6
Writing	57	90	112	194	2.45	2.97	2.78	3.10
Normal Dictation	97	143	167	336	2.54	3.19	2.52	2.73
Slow Dictation	72	108	119	193	2.54	3.06	2.43	2.84

Note: N = 23 in each grade.

titative advantage but the difference between writing and slow dictation largely disappears. Overall, however, the effect of production signaling is quite pronounced. In both the writing and the normal dictation conditions it resulted in a doubling of the total quantity of words produced.

The quality ratings are ratings on a five-point scale of quality of presentation, taking into account clarity and cohesion. Ratings are the average of two independent ratings. The standard portions of compositions were rated in separate batches from the extended compositions, so that the part compositions were never compared directly to the wholes. It should be kept in mind, however, that the standard portions are whole compositions in the ordinary sense, even though they subsequently form parts of larger compositions. Quality ratings of the standard portions do not show any significant differences between production modes, although there is a significant grade difference ($F(1, 44) = 11.42$, $p = .002$). The tendency, however, is similar to that in the earlier study in showing the written compositions to be rated lowest. Ratings of the total compositions show a distinctly different profile, and this time the difference between production modes is statistically different ($F (2, 88) = 4.32$, $p = .016$). In both grades now the written compositons are rated highest. When the standard portions are compared to the extended compositions, it is seen that for written compositions the material added after signaling raises the judged quality whereas for the dictated compositions the added material lowers total quality.

Apparently production signaling has a more positive effect on writing than it does on normal or slow dictation. Before speculating on the possible causes of this effect, we need to look more closely at its nature. What do children do differently in the writing condition from what they do in the dictating conditions? In the next section of results we look for clues to this through analysis of the compositions.

Coherence Analysis

At the level of observable behavior, the preceding results could be interpreted as showing that in writing children stop too soon, whereas this is not true when they dictate. Thus, when children are prompted to continue producing, their written compositions improve whereas their dictated ones decline—possibly because in dictation they have already said all they have to say and therefore start repeating themselves or going off topic. In the analyses that follow, these latter conjectures are tested. More generally, the analyses are concerned with what determines when children normally end a composition and what happens when they continue generating text beyond that point.

Clearly, such analyses must deal with content and structure. The analyses to be reported here progressed through three stages: first, a parsing of the texts into functional units and a classification of these according to their text grammar functions; second, an analysis of the distribution of these functional units without regard to their structural relationships; and, third, an analysis of sequences of these functional units in terms of coherence. Although the methods employed have numerous roots in other work on text analysis, they are sufficiently novel and sufficiently critical to the conclusions that follow that the methods will be explained in some detail.

Parsing and Classification of Text Units

The parsing scheme for opinion essays generally follows Toulmin's analysis of arguments as consisting of premises and warrant for premises (cf. Kneupper, 1978). Table 8.2 shows the scheme as it was applied in this study. The main categories are premises enunciating one side or other of an issue, reasons providing warrant for these premises, and conclusions. A particular text element is classified as either an initial statement of one of these or as an elaboration on it. The scheme obviously does not capture all the complexities of argument structure. For instance, elaborations on elaborations are here simply treated as further elaborations on an initial statement, and there is no way of representing arguments embedded within arguments. The lack of such refinements may be justified for present purposes on grounds (a) that the analyses to be performed would not be likely to benefit from more elaborate parsing and (b) that rater reliability was found to decline sharply when the level of analysis was finer than the one used here.

Texts were segmented into minimal parsable units—that is, into the smallest units that could constitute separate entries into the matrix illus-

TABLE 8.2
Schema For Classifying Opinion Essay Text Function Units

	Original position					Contrasting position				
	Initial statement	Elaborations				Initial statement	Elaborations			
		1	2	3	—		1	2	3	—
Premise										
Warrant										
Reason 1										
Reason 2										
Reason 3										
⋮										
Conclusion										
Nonfunctional units										

trated in Table 8.2. For instance, if the first sentence of a text read *Children should not eat junk food because it is bad for their health, Children should not eat junk food* would be treated as a unit, since it can be classified as the initial statement of a premise. Accordingly, a number 1 would be so entered in the matrix. *Because it is bad for their health* would be treated as the second unit and entered in the matrix as the initial statement of reason 1, since it provides a warrant for the premise stated in the first unit. Potentially parsable idea units that, however, did not appear to play any role as premises relevant to the topic, as warrant, or as conclusion, were entered in the "nonfunctional" category. The nonfunctional category included material that was tangential to the argument being presented or that repeated, with no discernible rhetorical purpose, statements already made. The nonfunctional category did NOT include units that might be judged nonfunctional on quality grounds—unconvincing reasons, for instance. Units clearly intended to serve a function in the argument were classified according to that function regardless of how well or poorly they served it. Hence the parsing of texts was as much as possible descriptive, not evaluative.

Distribution of Text Function Units.

The frequencies with which major categories of text units were used are presented in Table 8.3, which shows in each case the frequency of units in text produced before the first production signal (the standard portion) and the frequency in text produced after signaling began. Two main findings emerge from these data:

TABLE 8.3
Frequency of Test Function Units before and after Production Signaling ($N = 46$)

	Production Mode					
	Writing		Normal dictation		Slow dictation	
	Before Signaling	After Signaling	Before Signaling	After Signaling	Before Signaling	After Signaling
Total units	4.70	4.15	7.04	6.77	6.00	3.27
Reasons	1.81	.77	2.36	1.04	2.09	.50
Elaborations	1.43	1.75	2.13	2.43	1.52	1.18
Nonfunctional Units	.31	1.20	1.13	2.75	.90	1.27
Reasons per unit	.37	.19	.37	.20	.34	.14
Elaborations Per unit	.24	.42	.26	.35	.21	.42
Nonfunctional Units per unit	.06	.25	.10	.30	.12	.31

1. In normal dictation children produce more of every kind of text unit than they do in either slow dictation or writing. This is true both before and after production signaling. These results parallel the results for number of words produced. These differences between production modes vanish, however, when the PROPORTION of text units falling into the various categories is considered. Analyses of variance showed a significant production mode effect ($p < .05$) for all three categories of elements, reasons, elaborations, and nonfunctional units; but when the ratios of each of these to total number of units were analyzed, no significant production mode differences were found.

2. These ratios did, however, differ significantly between the standard and signaled portions. Reasons per unit, elaborations per unit, and nonfunctional units per unit all differed at beyond the .001 level of significance between portions. Reasons were twice as frequent in the standard portion, elaborations and nonfunctional units were twice as frequent in the signaled portion. In the standard portions, reasons are the most frequently used text unit, accounting for 36% of all units. After production signals are introduced, elaborations become the most frequently used unit, accounting for 59% of the total. Nonfunctional units, which constitute only 10% of units before signaling account for more than a fourth of the units produced afterward.

These findings give us an idea of how children respond to calls for further text production after they have reached the normal end of composing. They add more material mainly by elaborating on points made previously. The distribution analyses do not, however, give us any clue as to why the judged quality of written compositions is increased by these additions while that of dictated compositions is diminished. Such clues might have appeared in analyses of variance as an interaction between production mode and signaling condition, but no significant interactions of this kind were obtained. Consequently, in the next section we look not to the frequency of text function units but to their interrelationships for clues to quality changes.

Coherence Evaluation

Following Widdowson (1978), we here treat **coherence** as the tying together of meanings in text and distinguish it from **cohesion** (Halliday & Hasan, 1976), which refers to linguistic means by which coherence is displayed in surface structure. Several investigators have used cohesion as an index of development in children's ability to compose text (Bamberg, 1980; Bracewell, Fine, & Ezergaile, 1980). An underlying expectation, of course, is that where there is cohesion there is also coherence, but this is not necessarily true, and in children's efforts to present reasoned arguments exceptions are not uncommon.

Consider the following sentences, which open a fourth-grader's composition:

> *I think they should because sports are for girls and boys and there is no difference between girls and boys. The girls might not be good in sports, so that's why the boys don't like the girls to play.*

There are ample cohesive links between the two sentences, but the concatenation of ideas is incoherent. The second sentence seems to be an elaboration on the reason offered in the first sentence but in fact it is not, and it even contradicts the first sentence. Subsequent text might, of course, provide a linking idea that would restore coherence, although in the actual case it did not. The point is, however, that it is the network of ideas and not the use of cohesive devices that determines coherence. Cohesion provides help in discovering the network if one exists.

Furthermore, especially with unsophisticated writers, coherence can exist even with marked failures of cohesion. The fragment of text quoted previously affords an illustration of this as well. *I think they should because . . .* shows two faults in cohesion, the unreferenced pronoun *they* and the ellipsis, *should . . .* , without previous occurrence of the omitted verb. Nevertheless the meaning is clear. The reader does not, as is the case with real incoherence, have to guess at communicative intent.

The present analysis is built around the idea of a **coherent string.** A coherent string is a sequence of text function units that contains no non-functional units and no incoherent orderings of units. Coherence is inherently relative—relative to the amount of speculation that the reader is prepared to apply to the text. Almost any two propositions can be rendered coherent by the addition of unstated ideas. In the text fragment we have been considering, for instance, it is possible to achieve a coherent reading of the two sentences by assuming that what the writer means by *no difference* between girls and boys is "no difference in basic needs and dispositions." But nowhere in the text does the writer suggest that this is what is meant.

The standard for coherence set in the present study was fairly conservative. There had to be some definite warrant within the text for coherence-creating inferences. Thus, in the example cited, the second sentence was scored as a break in the coherent string, because there was no warrant anywhere in the text for inferences that would establish a logical connection between it and the preceding sentence.

A coherent ordering of units was one that followed the main pattern of premise followed by reasons, with elaborations incorporated in either of the following ways: (*a*) in series immediately following the initial statements to which they are related (for instance: premise, elaboration on premise, reason 1, elaborations of reason 1, reason 2, elaborations on reason 2; or (*b*) in parallel with the initial statements on which they elaborated (for instance: reason 1, reason 2, reason 3, elaboration on reason 1, elaboration on reason 2, elaboration on reason 3). Any departure from these patterns was treated as a break in the coherent string. For instance, the sequence—premise, reason 1, reason 2, elaboration on reason 1, reason 3—was scored as having a break in coherence after reason 2.

Arguments on an opposing side could be introduced provided they consisted of at least a premise and a reason. Introducing an opposing premise with no support or a contrary reason with no explicit premise were both scored as incoherent. Any nonfunctional unit constituted a break in coherence. This follows almost by definition, since to be scored as nonfunctional a text unit had to have no discernible function in developing the argument.

Two dependent variables were analyzed: (a) the length of the longest coherent string in each composition, as measured by number of text units it contained; and (b) the location of the end of the first coherent string—whether before, at, or after the point at which the writer ended the standard portion of the composition. Length of longest string was regarded as a general index of coherence that would have special relevance to the study of production factors, since it would be sensitive to various kinds of interference and breakdowns in processing. The "end of first string" variable was of particular interest for what it might show about the effects of production signaling: Would such signaling to produce more disrupt coherence or would it lead to extending coherent strings or would coherence already have been broken before signaling began?

Results for these two variables are presented in Tables 8.4 and 8.5. An analysis of variance on length of longest string showed that the only significant effect was an interaction between grade and production mode (F (2, 88) = 3.79, $p < .05$). As Table 8.4 indicates, fourth-grade children produced their longest strings in normal dictation, whereas sixth-grade children produced theirs in writing. Slow dictation yielded the shortest strings in both grades. The crossover between grades is sufficiently pronounced that by grade six children were actually showing weaker performance in normal dictation than the fourth-grade children. This suggests that developmental changes in language production are going on that not only improve writing but that make speaking a less satisfactory means of generating extended coherent text.

TABLE 8.4
Mean Length of Longest Coherent String of Text Elements

Grade	N	Production mode		
		Writing	Normal dictation	Slow dictation
4	23	4.13	5.22	3.78
6	23	6.26	4.61	4.52

TABLE 8.5
Mean Continuity Index[a]

| | | | Production mode | |
Grade	N	Writing	Normal dictation	Slow dictation
4	23	.26	−.17	−.17
6	23	.17	−.39	−.35

[a]Continuity index = +1 if the initial coherent string ended after production signaling began; 0 if it ended at the point signaling began; and −1 if it ended before signaling began.

The second dependent variable was quantified as a **continuity index** by assigning a score of +1 to initial coherent strings that extended past the onset of production signaling, 0 to coherent strings that ended precisely at the onset of signaling, and −1 to coherent strings that ended before that point. Mean continuity indices, shown in Table 8.5, indicate that children at both grades four and six tend to continue the first coherent string beyond the onset of production signaling when they are writing but that when they are dictating the coherent string tends to have been broken before they get to that point, that is before they get to the normal ending points of their compositions. In an analysis of variance on the continuity index, a significant effect for production mode was the only one to emerge (F (2, 88) = 4.63, $p < .025$). This finding is the first to offer a clue as to what lay behind the increase in rated quality of written compositions after production signaling compared to the decrease in rated quality of dictated compositions. Evidently signaling to produce more led children in writing to extend coherent strings whereas in the dictated compositions the initial coherent string was usually already ended.

DISCUSSION

In this section we shall briefly reassess, in light of the experiment just reported, earlier speculations about the role of production factors in writing. Following that we shall offer some more general ideas about how a theory of the writing process might incorporate both production factors and metacomponents.

Short-Term Memory Loss Due to Slow Rate of Production

From previous research, the only evidence pointing to short-term memory loss was the Bereiter et al. (1979) study showing information loss between forecasted and written text. However, as noted previously, such loss might be accounted for by interference from the mechanical demands of writing. In the present study the slow dictation condition was introduced to permit separation of effects due to speed of production and those due to interference from low-level demands of writing. Inquiry into effects of speed alone are best addressed through comparison of normal and slow dictation, since in this comparison mechanical demands of the medium are held constant.

Results show that speed of production has a substantial positive effect on quantity produced. Furthermore, differences in quantity are not reduced by urging children to continue beyond their normal stopping point. The additional text added in response to production cueing, in fact, increases the disparity in quantity between normal and slow dictation modes.

Turning to questions of quality, we see that speed of production, and the increased quantity that goes along with it, do not lead to texts of higher rated quality. In both the present study and in Scardamalia and Bereiter (1979), differences in quality ratings due to dictation speed were small and inconsistent. In analyses of coherence, fast and slow dictation emerged as similar; wherever differences appeared they were between writing and dictation, not between the two speeds of dictation.

Consistent now over two experiments we have the factor of production speed favoring quantity but showing no corresponding advantage when it comes to quality. These results do not support the hypothesis that loss from short-term memory is aggravated by the slow rate of output in writing. The present research does not, of course, address this hypothesis directly, but then neither does any previous research. If the slower output condition had led to substantially greater loss of intended content, we should have expected this to be reflected in lower quality ratings. If slower output had led to forgetting of high-level intentions and plans, we should have expected this to be reflected in lower scores on coherence variables or in a greater relative frequency of nonfunctional text units. None of this was found either.

The possibility remains that effects of output rate on memory loss occurred but were too slight to be detected by the variables assessed. It is also possible that they occurred but were offset by other variables that favored slow dictation. Clearly output rate has an effect on language production, but in the absence of positive evidence we are left with little ground for supposing that this effect can be accounted for by loss of material from short-term storage. What might account for the effect is a question we shall take up further in a later section.

Interference from the Mechanical Demands of Writing

This factor was assessed fairly directly in the present study, in the comparison between writing and slow dictation, where production rate was held constant and where the mechanical demands of writing (handwriting, spelling, etc.) were eliminated in the dictation mode. The results here do not lend themselves to a simple interference interpretation. There does seem to be interference, over and above that produced by a slow output rate, which prevents children from producing as much text when they are writing as when they are dictating slowly. However, differences that did exist in quantity of output between writing and slow dictation were eliminated by production signaling. (Recall that such signaling did NOT serve to eliminate differences between normal and slow dictation.)

Findings for quality mirrored those for quantity: Quality of texts produced before signaling favored the slow dictation mode, as it did in a previous study (Scardamalia & Bereiter, 1979). The difference, though not statistically significant in either study, was in the same direction in both grades in both studies. Thus, having held up through four replications, the difference in favor of slow dictation appears to be reliable. But when production cueing was added, the difference was reversed. This suggests that quality of the written compositions was limited by their low quantity. It therefore appears that children are not producing discourse of inferior quality when they are writing, they are simply producing less of it. Accordingly, when they can manage to get the quantity of their output up to what it is in the slow dictation condition, the disadvantage due to the written medium disappears. The present study indicates, in fact, that writing is the superior medium for producing coherent and well-expressed compositions.

Overall, interference due to mechanical demands of writing appears to be a factor, but it seems to affect quantity of text produced, not quality of written products, as might be expected. Thus its effect would seem to be on the child's ability to sustain production and to carry on planning. This is a matter we shall take up in greater detail later.

Discoordination Resulting from Lack of External Signals

Results of the present study suggest that this is a very potent factor influencing text production in school-age children. The administration of contentless production signals, after children had ostensibly written or dictated all they could, led to their going on to produce about as much additional text as they had produced up to the point signaling began. Although the resulting extensions of text contained an increased proportion of nonfunctional text units, including repetitions, more than 70% of the material added was functional, consisting mainly of elaborations and additional support for opinions.

Production signaling was found to interact with other production factors. It enhanced the judged quality of writing in comparison to dictating.

A possible basis for this interaction was found in the analysis of coherence. After signaling, children in the writing condition tended to continue a structurally coherent string of text units, whereas in dictation they did not. We shall consider in the next section what this might mean in terms of cognitive processes.

Production Factors as They Relate to Planning

In this final section we shall try to present an organized set of ideas that make provisional sense of the research reported and cited in this chapter. The key idea in this discussion is that the production factors we have been examining affect performance through their influence on mental representation of text.

In order to construct coherent extended discourse, the writer or speaker must build progressively on the text already produced. In writing, this is true in the concrete sense that the writer keeps adding lines to the lines already written. But in oral composition there is no concrete text to build on, and even in writing people are able to construct coherent text without being able to see what they have written (Gould, 1980). From a psychological standpoint what counts in composition is the mental representation of text (Scardamalia & Bereiter, in press). The physical text, when there is one, is important only in so far as it influences the mental representation.

The following postulates serve as the basis for the subsequent interpretation of experimental results:

1. THERE IS NOT ONE SINGLE MENTAL REPRESENTATION OF A TEXT. IN-STEAD, THERE ARE A NUMBER OF POSSIBLE REPRESENTATIONS CORRESPOND-ING TO THE DIFFERENT KINDS OF TEXT PROCESSING THAT A WRITER MAY EN-GAGE IN. The key idea here is that the text is not represented in memory as a single more-or-less accurate copy of the actual text. Rather, we assume that when writers are engaged in high-level planning they draw on a representation that consists of goals, central ideas, structural decisions, and the like. When they are dealing with problems of DEVELOPMENT (see Beaugrande, this volume), they may draw on this same high-level representation, but in addition on a more detailed representation of gist units (cf. Kintsch & van Dijk, 1978). When they are working at the level of generating actual language, they will need a representation that contains at least a substantial amount of verbatim record in order for them to keep exophoric reference under control and to avoid unpleasant lexical repetitions.

2. IN GENERAL, THESE REPRESENTATIONS ARE NOT AUTOMATICALLY FORMED AND STORED, READY FOR IMMEDIATE RECALL. INSTEAD, THEY HAVE TO BE CONSTRUCTED OR RECONSTRUCTED EVERY TIME THEY ARE NEEDED. We assume in this discussion a multilevel interacting model of composing,

such as that presented by Beaugrande in this volume, with different mental representations corresponding (though not necessarily in a one-to-one fashion) to the different parallel stages of processing. One view of mental representations might accordingly be that they are simply the continuously up-dated traces of mental activity at the different levels. We reject this hypothesis because it implies either very chaotic and overly detailed representations or else a great deal of mental effort continually going into revising and consolidating representations at every level. It seems more plausible to adopt a constructive view of memory (e.g., Minsky, 1980). According to this view, there would be no fixed types of mental representations. Instead, representations are constructed for purposes of the moment, using retrieved information of quite variable kinds. A given set of conditions could give rise to various representations of the same general type and a given representation could have been constructed from more than one body of retrieved information.

3. CONSTRUCTIVE MENTAL EFFORT IS REQUIRED IN GOING FROM LOWER TO HIGHER LEVELS OF TEXT REPRESENTATION. THE LOWER THE LEVEL OF REPRESENTATION THAT A WRITER IS PRESENTLY ATTENDING TO, THE GREATER THE AMOUNT OF CONSTRUCTIVE ACTIVITY REQUIRED TO REACH A GIVEN HIGHER LEVEL. *High* and *low* here refer to levels of inclusiveness; no preferential distinction is implied. Since one meaning subsumes a variety of possible expressions, meaning representation is at a higher level than lexical representation; one word may subsume a number of possible spellings, etc. This postulate says that if you are currently dealing with a very low level representation of your text—worrying about a doubtful spelling, for instance— and you need to switch to a high level, such as a representation of the overall plan for a text segment, this will require more mental work than if you had already been working witl: a higher level of representation—say a representation at the level of gist units. The rationale for this postulate is simply that when one is constructing a representation at a neighboring level, much of the relevant information will already be activated. In jumping from a very low to a high level of representation, on the other hand, one is more likely to start cold with the question, *Now, where was I?*

4. MENTAL REPRESENTATIONS OF TEXT MAY VARY FROM VAGUE AND FRAGMENTARY TO SHARPLY DELINEATED AND DETAILED. Completeness of the representation will depend on a number of factors including (*a*) the level of sophistication of the writer, especially as sophistication entails having a repertoire of general plans or genre schemes (Bereiter, 1980) to structure text representations; (*b*) how frequently the writer has previously reconstructed this representation, assuming that representations will get increasingly rich as they are repeatedly reconstructed; and (*c*) the needs of the moment. A minimal representation may suffice if all the writer wants to do is test whether some new idea fits the plan; a much fuller representation may be needed if the writer lacks an idea for what to write next and must

deliberately generate one appropriate to an overall plan. The fullness with which content is represented will vary considerably depending on whether one is sketching ideas for a naive audience or working on a presentation that must withstand expert scrutiny.

Armed with these postulates, let us now interpret what went on in the experimental comparison of writing, normal dictation, and slow dictation. In normal dictation, as best we can judge from protocols of children composing aloud, attention is mainly concentrated on representations involving gist units and syntactic plans (Scardamalia, Bereiter, Woodruff, Burtis, & Turkish, 1981; Tetroe, Bereiter, & Scardamalia, 1981). We assume that children edit their spoken language but little, so that there is not much attention to the verbatim level, and in dictation there is of course no graphical representation. Since children are mostly switching between neighboring levels of representation (gists and syntactic plans), very little reconstructive activity has to go into representation. Such references as need to be made to the top-level representation require only minimal development of that representation, one that is easily reconstructed as needed. The result is easy, rapid composition, with the maximum opportunity for one gist unit to suggest another one, producing an abundance of topically relevant content.

Slow dictation would be similar to normal dictation, except that the frequent pausing to wait for the scribe to catch up should lead to more constructive activity at the verbatim and syntactic plan levels—rehearsing previously planned language or revising and adding to the language within constraints of the syntactic plan. This should result in more carefully planned language than normal dictation, but at the expense of greater difficulty in returning to constructive activity at the gist level. Thus the amount of content generated should be less than in normal dictation.

With writing we add the further element of attention to the graphical level of representation. When attention is focused at this level, memory for meaning and structure tends to get lost. Among children with very undeveloped writing skills, meaning and structure may stay lost, with the result that writing is fragmentary and often incomprehensible. But most children of the ages we have studied (10 years and older) seem able to maintain at least some degree of coherence. In order to do this, while also devoting attention to problems at the graphical level, it would seem that they must engage in a considerable amount of reconstructive activity of the "Now where was I?" variety. This continually having to reconstruct gists and plans is a serious enough impediment to fluent production that it results in shorter compositions than are produced orally, either by slow or normal dictation, but it pays a dividend. Ordinarily, it seems, this dividend remains unrealized for children, but in our experiment it was brought to realization through production signaling.

Production signaling, it will be recalled, was introduced only after children claimed to have dictated or written all they could. At that point, the child's top-level mental representation should be that of a completed text. An opinion has been stated and reasons in support of it have been presented. In being urged to go on, the child is in effect being urged to treat this representation no longer as the representation of a whole text but rather as the representation of a text segment forming the first part of a larger whole. What is being forced on children is something we assume they do not normally face, although it is similar to what more mature writers face continually in all but very brief compositions. The children are faced with a major text juncture, one that requires a focus on levels of representation above the gist unit.

This is where the extra mental work done by children in the writing condition pays off. The work of repeatedly reconstructing gist units and higher-level text representations should, as we indicated in the fourth postulate, lead to more sharply delineated and detailed mental representations of text. Thus, when faced with a major text juncture, children in the writing condition can more readily reconstruct representations that are sufficiently complete that they can build on them or use them as guides for generating coherently related new material. By contrast, in oral composition children have had to do little reconstructive activity at the gist unit and higher levels, because their attention has been occupied most of the time with gist units. Consequently, they have less often had to face the "Where was I?" problem. When unexpectedly faced with a major text juncture, they are less able to construct a text representation suitable for planning a coherent continuation. This is because their top-level representations, though sufficient for testing the adequacy of gist units thought of spontaneously, are too vague to serve a useful generative function.

What happens, we suspect, is something like this. Suppose the child has been composing an essay on the evils of junk food and claims such food causes pimples and tooth decay. Now, under the instigation of production cueing, the child tries to extend the essay, and so tries to recall what has been said so far. A vague gist unit representation might capture only the topics—pimples and tooth decay. With only this much information to go on, the child might digress about pimples or tooth decay or might generate an additional topic of the same class. The result would be something more or less connected with the previous text, but something that might not rate very high in coherence or be judged to raise the overall quality of the text. This, then, is what we conjecture tended to go on in the two dictation conditions.

In writing, however, the child, having already had to reconstruct the gist units, might be able at the text juncture to reconstruct a more complete representation. The gist might be something like this: *I said junk food was bad because it causes pimples and I said it was bad because it causes tooth decay.*

With this more complete representation, the child is in less danger of generating an incoherent or irrelevant continuation and is in a better position to invent a reasonable continuation—to add a parallel reason or an appropriate elaboration. This is because the representation includes not only items of content but also information as to the purpose and organization of the content.[3]

These interpretations of the experimental results are, of course, speculative and involve a number of premises that need independent confirmation. One of the current focuses of the Writing Research Group in Toronto is on mental representation of text, but the research is at too early a stage for us to say what it might reveal about the tenability of the interpretations advanced here.

From the standpoint of understanding the composing process as a whole, the present view has much to recommend it over a view that treats production factors merely as variables that must somehow be taken into account in computing the relationships between metacomponents and performance. Instead of viewing composing as a process in which mental products are created, held in buffers awaiting use, and occasionally lost through decay or interference, we view it as a process in which mental representations are continually being reconstituted. This gives the three production factors that we considered at the beginning of this chapter a different import. The important production factor is not memory loss but rather reconstructive activity that influences the writer's ability to plan at all levels of composition from the lowest levels of mechanics to the highest levels of rhetorical intent. We no longer view attention to mechanics as interfering with higher-level processes. Rather, it creates the need for a greater amount of reconstructive activity at higher levels of text representation, and this can have benefits as well as disadvantages as far as the production of extended discourse is concerned—benefits in terms of coherence, disadvantages in terms of richness of content.

Another factor, discoordination of executive functioning due to lack of external signals, takes on even greater potential significance in the current view. Composition begins to appear very much like the job of the proverbial one-armed paperhanger. Mental effort at a number of levels is continu-

---

[3]In interpreting the changes that take place after production signaling, we must not neglect the possible role that availability of the written text may have had in boosting performance in the writing condition. We did not collect data on rereadings and so we cannot judge the extent to which children in the writing condition may have used their actual texts as an aid in reconstructing a high-level plan at the onset of production signaling. Our impression, based on one-to-one work with scores of children, is that they almost never consult text for this purpose. Observations by Gould (1980) on adult writers support this impression. Hayes-Roth and Walker (1979) found, furthermore, that students were better able to synthesize information drawn from memory than information available in text.

ously required, and there is not some neat high-level plan sitting there and quietly directing activities. The demands for skillful internally regulated coordination of activities are so severe that we find it remarkable children as young as 10 years are able to function in composition as well as they do. It has to be recognized, however, that most children still have a long way to go before their composing behavior shows the versatile "juggling of constraints" revealed in the protocols of mature writers (Flower & Hayes, 1980). Furthermore, the initial strategies that children devise for coping with this complex task may stand in the way of their acquiring self-regulations adapted to higher-level goals of writing (Bereiter & Scardamalia, 1980; Scardamalia & Bereiter, 1980). The present study, with its investigation of one elementary kind of signaling, has barely touched the large topic of control processes in composition.

In concluding, we should like to mention one practical suggestion that emerges from the research reported here. Our analysis suggests that in school-age children oral and written composition differ in the extent to which they bring various kinds of mental representations of text into play. Oral composition fosters the mental representation of gist units and syntactic plans, whereas writing fosters the active reconstruction of higher level representations in order to achieve coherence. Both are important, and so it would seem that both ought to have a place in school language arts curricula. Writing already does, of course, but oral composition does not. We are referring here specifically to oral composition, not to oral activities such as discussion and conversation, which have educational values of their own and which are common at least in some schools. Oral composition is, like written composition, the sustained and solitary production of a self-contained text. Extemporaneous speaking (planned but not scripted) would qualify, as would dictating texts, one child to another, and producing audiotaped compositions for listening. Such oral composition as does exist in schools seems to be reserved for children who are not yet literate enough to produce written compositions (except where extemporaneous speaking reappears as a specialty in college speech courses). It seems likely that it would be beneficial in fostering fluency of content generation and spontaneity of expression throughout the school years.

ACKNOWLEDGMENTS

This chapter is based on research that was supported by grants from the Alfred P. Sloan Foundation and the Ontario Institute for Studies in Education. The authors wish especially to thank Larry Turkish for his many contributions to execution and analysis of the "slow dictation" studies. We are also grateful for contributions of Sondra Gartshore and Jud Burtis to the research and of Carol Broome to bibliography and manuscript preparation. Valuable comments on a draft of this chapter were generously provided by Robert de Beaugrande and Elizabeth Goldstein.

REFERENCES

Bamberg, B. *Cohesive relations in written discourse at three age levels.* Paper presented at the annual meeting of the American Educational Research Association, Boston, 1980.

Bereiter, C. Development in writing. In L. W. Gregg & E. R. Steinberg (Eds.), *Cognitive processes in writing.* Hillsdale, N.J.: Lawrence Erlbaum, 1980.

Bereiter, C., Fine, J., & Gartshore, S. *An exploratory study of micro-planning in writing.* Paper presented at the annual meeting of the American Educational Research Association, San Francisco, 1979.

Bereiter, C., & Scardamalia, M. *Cognitive coping strategies and the problem of "inert knowledge."* Paper presented at the NIE-LRDC Conference on Thinking and Learning Skills, Pittsburgh, October, 1980.

Bereiter, C., & Scardamalia, M. From conversation to composition: The role of instruction in a developmental process. In R. Glaser (Ed.), *Advances in instructional psychology* (Vol. 2). Hillsdale, N.J.: Lawrence Erlbaum, 1981.

Blass, T., and Siegman, A. W. A psycholinguistic comparison of speech, dictation and writing. *Language and Speech,* 1975, *18*, 20–34.

Bracewell, R. J., Fine, J., & Ezergaile, L. *Cohesion as a guide to writing processes.* Paper presented at the annual meeting of the American Educational Research Association, Boston, 1980.

Britton, J. The composing processes and the functions of writing. In C. R. Cooper & L. Odell (Eds.), *Research on composing: Points of departure.* Urbana, Ill.: National Council of Teachers of English, 1978.

Brown, A. L., & Campione, J. C. *Inducing flexible thinking: The problem of access.* Champaign, Ill.: Center for the Study of Reading, University of Illinois at Urbana-Champaign, January, 1980. (Technical Report No. 156)

Butterworth, B., & Goldman-Eisler, F. Recent studies on cognitive rhythm. In A. W. Siegman & S. Feldstein (Eds.), *Of speech and time: Temporal speech patterns in interpersonal contexts.* Hillsdale, N.J.: Lawrence Erlbaum Associates, 1979.

Case, R. *A developmentally based approach to the problem of instructional design.* Paper presented at the NIE-LRDC Conference on Thinking and Learning Skills, Pittsburgh, October, 1980.

Clark, H. H., & Clark, E. V. *Psychology of language.* New York: Harcourt Brace Jovanovich, 1977.

Emig, J. *The composing processes of twelfth graders.* Champaign, Ill.: National Council of Teachers of English, 1971. (Research Report No. 13)

Flower, L., & Hayes, J. R. The dynamics of composing: Making plans and juggling constraints. In L. W. Gregg & E. R. Steinberg (Eds.), *Cognitive processes in writing.* Hillsdale, N.J.: Lawrence Erlbaum, 1980.

Fodor, J. A., Bever, T. G., & Garrett, M. F. *The psychology of language: An introduction to psycholinguistics and generative grammar.* New York: McGraw-Hill, 1974.

Frase, L. T. *Writer's workbench: Computer supports for components of the writing process.* Paper presented at the annual meeting of the American Educational Research Association, Boston, 1980.

Gould, J. D. Experiments on composing letters: Some facts, some myths, and some observations. In L. W. Gregg & E. R. Steinberg (Eds.), *Cognitive processes in writing.* Hillsdale, N.J.: Lawrence Erlbaum, 1980.

Graves, D. H. Research update: Handwriting is for writing. *Language Arts,* 1978, *55,* 393–399.

Halliday, M. A. K., & Hasan, K. *Cohesion in English.* London: Longman, 1976.

Hayes, J. R., & Flower, L. Identifying the organization of writing processes. In L. W. Gregg & E. R. Steinberg (Eds.), *Cognitive processes in writing.* Hillsdale, N.J.: Lawrence Erlbaum, 1980.

Hayes-Roth, B., & Walker, C. Configural effects in human memory: The superiority of memory over external information sources as a basis of inference verification. *Cognitive Science,* 1979, *3,* 119–140.

Hidi, S., & Hildyard, A. *The comparison of oral and written productions of two discourse types.* Paper presented at the annual meeting of the American Educational Research Association, Boston, 1980.

Hotopf, N. Slips of the pen. In U. Frith (Ed.), *Cognitive processes in spelling.* New York: Academic Press, 1980.

Kintsch, W., & van Dijk, T. A. Toward a model of text comprehension and production. *Psychological Review,* 1978, *85*(5), 363–394.

Kneupper, C. W. Teaching argument: An introduction to the Toulmin model. *College Composition and Communication,* 1978, *29,* 237–241.

Krashen, S. D. The Monitor Model for adult second language performance. In M. Burt, H. Dulay & M. Finocchiaro (Eds.), *Viewpoint on English as a second language.* New York: Regents, 1977.

Luria, A. R. A neuropsychological analysis of speech communication. In J. Prucha (Ed.), *Soviet studies in language and language behavior.* Amsterdam: North-Holland, 1976.

Minsky, M. K-lines: A theory of memory. *Cognitive Science,* 1980, *4,* 117–133.

Olson, D. R. From utterance to text: The bias of language in speech and writing. *Harvard Educational Review,* 1977, *47*(3), 257–281.

Sacks, H. On getting the floor. *Pragmatics Microfiche,* (April, D11-E5) 1976, *1,* 7–8.

Scardamalia, M. How children cope with the cognitive demands of writing. In C. H. Frederiksen, M. F. Whiteman, and J. F. Dominic (Eds.), *Writing: The nature, development and teaching of written communication.* Hillsdale, N.J.: Lawrence Erlbaum, 1981.

Scardamalia, M., & Bereiter, C. *The effects of writing rate on children's composition.* Paper presented at the annual meeting of the American Educational Research Association, San Francisco, 1979.

Scardamalia, M., & Bereiter, C. *Fostering the development of self-regulation in children's knowledge processing.* Paper presented at the NIE-LRDC Conference on Thinking and Learning Skills, Pittsburgh, October, 1980.

Scardamalia, M., & Bereiter, C. The development of evaluative, diagnostic, and remedial capabilities in children's composing. In M. Martlew (Ed.), *The psychology of written language: A development approach.* London: Wiley, in press.

Scardamalia, M., Bereiter, C., Woodruff, E., Burtis, J., and Turkish, L. *The effects of modeling and cueing on high-level planning.* Paper presented at the annual meeting of the American Educational Research Association, Los Angeles, 1981.

Schmidt, R. A. A schema theory of motor skill learning. *Psychological Review,* 1975, *82,* 225–260.

Simon, J. *La langue écrite de l'enfant.* Paris: Presses Universitaires de France, 1973.

Spelke, E., Hirst, W., & Neisser, U. Skills of divided attention. *Cognition,* 1976, *4,* 215–230.

Sternberg, R. J. Sketch of a componential subtheory of human intelligence. *Behavioral and Brain Sciences,* 1980, *3,* 573–614.

Tetroe, J., Bereiter, C., & Scardamalia, M. *How to make a dent in the writing process.* Paper presented at the annual meeting of the American Educational Research Association, Los Angeles, 1981.

Vygotsky, L. S. [*Thought and language*]. Edited and translated by E. Haufmann and G. Vakar. Cambridge: M.I.T. Press, 1962.

Widdowson, H. G. *Teaching language as communication.* Oxford: Oxford University Press, 1978.

Chapter 9

Psychology and Composition: Past, Present, and Future

Robert de Beaugrande

HISTORICAL BACKGROUND

A Discouraging Record

The evolution of psychological theories in the domain of language development has been sporadic and disappointing in the past. A decade ago, James Deese (1971, p. 157) remarked: "The endless labors of an army of philosophers, linguists, psychologists, educators, teachers, and plain eccentrics have produced a mountain of literature on the psychology of language learning. There is distressingly little in that literature that should be of interest to the teacher of English. In the main, it is a dreadful and largely empty literature." In general, scholars of language psychology showed small concern for methodologies of language instruction (cf. Kintsch & Vipond, 1979, p. 329). It might well seem unduly optimistic to revive hopes in such an enterprise now. Yet the failure of past efforts need be no indictment of all possible efforts. Instead, we should strive to uncover the reasons for that failure in the nature of old-style theories.

An important relationship in the structure of scientific disciplines is that of **antecedence.** A general science of cognition and communication should be antecedent to a science of language: The latter should in turn be antecedent to the disciplines that deal with reading and writing skills; and so on. Due to historical conditions, however, scientific **fragmentation** has been the usual state of affairs in America. Psychologists believed that behavior could be explained with no regard to the human mind. Linguists asserted that language must be studied independently of everything else: language use, communicative settings, memory capacity, writing, and so forth. Consequently, the relationship of antecedence was obscured in favor of that of **extrapolation:** The more or less direct transfer of a theory or finding from its original context to a wholly different domain. The justification for this tactic, and the actual correspondence between the two domains, were often left unexplored; the extrapolated theory was apparently deemed to cover all possible objections with its scientific prestige.

The production of discourse was generally not studied in its own right—a deficit recently noted in psychology (Osgood & Bock, 1977, p. 89), psycholinguistics (Fodor, Bever, & Garrett, 1974, p. 434), and artificial intelligence (Goldman, 1975, p. 289). Hence, only vague theories were occasionally derived via doubtful extrapolations from the prevailing notions. I shall review the general history of these extrapolations in regard to the two dominant outlooks in language psychology: **physicalism** and **mentalism.**

Although these outlooks are upheld by few proponents today (at least in the most orthodox form), it is essential to understand their strengths and weaknesses in order to design more successful theories and models. Each one held some tenets that, in my view, deserve to be retained in future explorations. The downfall of these outlooks lay rather in their energetic, embittered polemics against each other, such that confrontation triumphed over compromise. The general public has thus imagined that we are facing a forced choice between the two. The physicalist school of behaviorism was totally predominant from the 1920s through the 1950s; the mentalist school of abstract grammar ruled during the 1960s and 1970s. The discrediting of mentalism now seems to be taken as a pretext for a simple reversion to physicalism: electric shocks in psychotherapy, rote drills in language classes, and so forth. Meanwhile, the surviving mentalists withdraw steadily further into abstruse idealizations whose unrelatedness to human activity is openly proclaimed with bizarre elan. I for one can only regard these trends with consternation: a symptom of helplessness and hopelessness at best, and a blatant disregard for the needs of the learning child at worst.

Physicalism

In the tradition of positivism (with its ancestors like John Locke), the concepts of the physical sciences are the only legitimate, credible basis for any theory.[1] "Behaviorist" psychology since Watson (1924) reflected pre-

[1]The chief document for this outlook is the *Encyclopedia of Unified Sciences,* concerning which Piaget (1976, p. 112) remarks: "we cannot help but be struck by the insistence of the school's

cisely this ambition. The human being figured as a organism whose "responses" to direct "stimuli" in the environment were governed by a strict "law of effect" (cf. Keller & Schoenfeld, 1950). Hence, the scientist need merely observe these openly manifest phenomena and seek to formulate the applicable "laws." Extravagant claims were advanced (and often believed) for the "objectivity" of direct observation and statistical measurement. To control the behavior of an organism, the experimenter needed merely to "reinforce" a desirable activity with some tangible, obvious reward, and to discourage undesirable ones. Hence, the animal's behavior was gradually "shaped" by strategic adminstration of food for rewarding and electric shocks for punishing. Learning was measured when the organism increased the RATE at which it "emitted" some bit of behavior (Skinner, 1950).

It seems to be a general rule in science that the more simple-minded scientific theories become in their QUALITATIVE aspect, the more elaborate is the use of QUANTITATIVE techniques. Since behaviorism was the most simplistic account of human activities imaginable, the methods of statistical evaluation took on an intimidating complexity that silenced all opposition from the general public. In exchange, large segments of the human situation were entirely eclipsed: symbolic generalization, planning, goal-generating, analogy-formation, deduction, and many more. Even when these limitations were later relaxed, the emphasis always fell on statistical measurement for adjudicating highly simplified theories.

The core of behaviorism arose in the animal-training laboratory with organisms (like rats and pigeons) whose reasoning powers are not overwhelming. The fatal turn was the extrapolation from this straightforward, tightly controlled setting over to the complex behavior of human beings in the real world. Theories of language were an egregious case in point. In the view of Bloomfield (1933), a human being is "stimulated" by an environmental event and "responds" with an utterance: this response "stimulates" another human to "respond" with a reply, and communication is in full swing (like a tennis game). Mowrer (1954) viewed the sentence as a conditioning device, where the subject is the conditioned stimulus and the predicate the unconditioned one—in traditional terms, the subject is the given point of departure and the predicate says something new. Though more insightful than Bloomfield's extrapolation, Mowrer's adds to the traditional account nothing that is precisely comparable to animal conditioning.

Skinner (1957) hoped to explain utterances as "verbal operants" of sev-

---

logicians, linguists, and psychologists" "who repeat in emulation of each other that the mentalist concepts of thought, etc., no longer correspond to anything whatsoever, that all is language, and that access to logical truth is assured by no more than a healthy exercise of language."

eral types. A "mand" is "a verbal operant in which the response is reinforced by a characteristic consequence and is therefore under the functional
control of relevant conditions of deprivation or aversive stimulation"; for
example, "the mand *pass the salt*[2] specifies an action (*pass*) and an ultimate
reinforcement (*salt*) [1957, pp. 35f.]." A "tact" is a verbal operant in which a
response of given form is evoked (or at least strengthened) by a particular
object or event or property of an object or event," such as *How do you do?* or
Thank you (1957, pp. 81f.). These two types are stressed because they most
obviously illustrate the relations between stimulus, response, and reinforcement. In exchange, Skinner is quite vague about more complex communicative occurrences, for example, those he calls "textual behavior"
(1957, pp. 65–69). The internal structuring of utterances is largely left to
"autoclitics," that is, reponses in "behavior which is based upon or depends upon other verbal behavior": for example, "informing the listener of
the kind of verbal operant it accompanies"; "describing the state of
strength of a response"; "indicating the emotional or motivational condition of the speaker"; and so forth (1957, pp. 315f.). Via a further "extension," grammar and syntax are viewed as "autoclitic processes," apparently since they serve to signal "relations" among the essential "responses" (e. g., nouns and verbs) (1957, pp. 331–343). The sketch of these
processes is highly fragmentary and evasive.

The dangers of such an extrapolation from animal conditioning are not
hard to envisage. Chomsky (1959, p. 54) observes: "if we take [Skinner's]
terms in their literal meaning, the description covers almost no aspect of
verbal behavior, and if we take them metaphorically, the description offers
no improvement over various traditional formulations." For example, the
notion of "reinforcement" is unequivocal in the laboratory setting: The rat
does something obvious and gets a food pellet or an electric shock. Lacking
any comparable mechanism in human activities, Skinner (1957, pp. 438ff.)
must aver that people are "automatically reinforcing themselves" in such
ways as "thinking," "verbal fantasy," "rationalization," or whatever.
Chomsky (1959, pp. 37f.) concludes: "we see that a person can be reinforced though he emits no response at all, and that the reinforcing
'stimulus' need not impinge upon the 'reinforced person' or need not even
exist (it is sufficient that it be imagined or hoped for)." In this manner, the
originally clear meaning of "reinforcement" has become entirely
metaphoric.

From the standpoint of language education, it is ominous that Skinner
(1957, p. 311) wants to "convert the speaker into an interested bystander"
whose "contribution" as an "inner agent" is insignificant compared to
environmental controls. That contribution is described as "deliberate composition" in contrast to uttering "memorized sentences emitted as purely

[2]I italicize linguistic samples, preserving original spelling and punctuation.

intraverbal sequences," "reproduced as echoic or textual behavior," or "blended" from "a few key responses with stock patterns [1957, p. 346]." Composition is broken down into: "(1) its essential operants, (2) the intra-verbals possibly arising from these operants in the course of emission (often composing thematic groups of responses), and (3) the autoclitic framework [1957, p. 349]." Here also, the "essential operants" are the message units eliciting or signalling responses, and everything else does little more than organize and link the essentials. Writing is touched on only marginally as a medium substituting space for the time dimension of speaking (1957, pp. 353f.).

The composition instructor is presumably "interested in evoking verbal behavior"; Skinner (1957, pp. 253f.) offers us "all" of the "available techniques." His illustration is getting someone to say *pencil*. We could "mand the response by saying to the subject 'Please say *pencil*.'" We could "make sure that no pencil or writing instrument is available, then hand our subject a pad of paper appropriate to pencil sketching, and offer him a handsome reward for a recognizable picture of a cat." We could "provide echoic stimuli (a phonograph in the background occasionally says *pencil*) and textual stimuli (signs on the wall read *pencil*)," or "produce inter-verbal responses: the phonograph occasionally says *pen and*——and there are other signs reading *pen and*——." Finally, we can "put a very large or unusual pencil in an unusual place clearly in sight—say, half-submerged in a large aquarium or floating freely in the air near the ceiling."

Now suppose that our composition instructor hopes for more elaborate utterances—maybe even those of a Shakespeare? Imagine the assemblage of props and confused personnel need to elicit (*Romeo and Juliet*, I, ii):

(1) *It is written that the shoemaker should meddle with his yard and the tailor with his last, the fisher with his pencil and the painter with his nets.*

Still more awesome would be the pageantry and carnage for (*King John*, III, i, 236–238):

(2) *Heaven knows they [our hands] were besmeared and overstain'd*
    With slaughter's pencil, where revenge did paint
    The fearful difference of incensed kings.

The implications here are obvious. The heavy machinery of behavioral conditioning is so inefficient that we could hardly hope to elicit a written theme during a single human lifetime. To claim that a large part of any text is due to the history of the speaker (the "schedule of reinforcement") is partly trivial, because of course language patterns must be learned within the community; and partly over-general, since quite different language aspects are all thrown together under the same categories, e. g. as "autoclitics." Thus, the different ways of saying the same thing in some situation cannot be distinguished from each other, as long as they evoke the same response in the audience's behavior. The important role of STYLE thereby goes unnoticed.

To appreciate the consequences of these shortcomings, we can examine Robert Zoellner's (1969) proposal for a "behavioral pedagogy of composition." He advocates a direct application of orthodox "operant conditioning" to the classroom setting: The instructor waits for the student to emit a desirable "bit of behavior" and then "reinforces" the latter immediately and frequently. "The reinforcement results in learning if the initial bit of behavior that was reinforced now begins to occur at a rate or frequency higher than the base-line rate of the naive animal [1969, p. 275]." Accordingly, the objective of training is to increase the FLUENCY of writers by tapping their previously conditioned fluency of speaking. The students first utter what they want to express and then instantly write it down on large pads or blackboards. Conversely, the instructor must not "tell a student to *think*" lest there ensue "an immediate drop in the density and variety of external behavior [1969, p. 298]"—for the behaviorist, a sure sign that learning has failed. Indeed Zoellner's examples (1969, pp. 270ff.) suggest that good writing is recognized as the fluent, rapid placement of words on paper; critics readily note that many good writers are not fluent in this superficial way (e. g., Boyle, 1969, pp. 694f.). In this regard, speaking and writing are not genuinely comparable (see pages 240–259 in this chapter).

Zoellner praises the use of electric shocks to treat stutterers, because "the behavioral therapist" is "able to direct his full attention to events which are observable, measurable, and manipulable. At no point is he forced to deal with invisible and abstractive psychic entities [1969, p. 290]." It emerges that Zoellner himself has no model of language production whatsoever, not even Skinner's simplistic verbal-operant model. No reference is made to the "autoclitic processes" of grammar which, one would think, ought to be a legitimate concern of the composition teacher; nor to the means whereby utterances react to or affect the environment. Moreover, Zoellner seems unaware of the other behaviorist language models besides Skinner's (e. g., Lounsbury, 1965; Osgood, 1964; Pike: 1967; see below). The extensive literature on word associations (e. g., Deese, 1962, 1965; Ervin, 1961) and on word learning (e. g., Underwood & Schultz, 1960) goes entirely unnoticed. Zoellner's references focus instead on rat training and psychotherapy, domains whose relevance for writing seems the most opaque.   In consequence, Zoellner (1969, p. 299) "must assume that the student has already thought the rhetorical problem out, and that it is only necessary to get him to *say* what he already *knows*." Put in behaviorist terms: The entire process of selecting and organizing content is viewed as part of the "naive repertory of the animal," and need only be appropriately "reinforced." Empirical evidence (some of which we examine later) indicates, however, how both speakers and writers have not settled "the rhetorical problem," not even in the very moment of text production: They may have selected a general goal and a main idea, but the RHETORICAL problem—the problem of decision and selection—often requires experimentation and revision. The outcome is then nothing like the "sustained, articulated, rapid-fire segement of sound-stream... which communicates... effectively and quickly" as envisioned by Zoellner (1969, p. 273). The outcome is rather a provisional pattern of contingencies whose mutual demands upon each other have not been fully respected. Zoellner's term "schizokinesis" (after Gantt, 1953) for the lack of coordination within or among systems (1969, pp. 303f.) labels as quasi-pathological the perfectly natural outcome of the complexity and asymmetry of communicative subsystems (cf. discussion on pp. 235–240 this chapter).

With no model of communicative processes, Zoellner's approach offers no STANDARDS for distinguishing between utterances of different quality, and thus for deciding what "bits of behavior" deserve to be "reinforced." In one openly behavioristic composition experiment (Shutt, 1969), reinforcement was given by each student's "editing partner" for activities such as attending regularly, talking in class, giving reports, and summarizing a reading selection; and for certain features of each written paper: spelling, punctuation, "effective opener," "effective closing," "subject matter," "organization," and "diction" (Shutt, 1969, p. 664). None of these features besides spelling is self-evident and protected from disputes. A behaviorist might measure the "effectiveness" of "openers" and "closings" by observing audience behavior during the early or final moments of presenting a paper, though it is doubtful whether audience response would be visible. But "subject matter," "organization," and "diction" represent domains in which operant conditioning is fatally weak, precisely because environmental effects can exert themselves only indirectly.

Shutt's solution is quite reminiscent of Zoellner's, though she began her experiments before his paper appeared. In effect, she implied that the essential features of writing were already part of the students' naive repertory when she said: "inductively, the students developed their own criteria for determining effective opening sentences [Shutt, 1969, p. 664]." No information is given on the other features, but the procedure was presumably the same.[3] Similar objections must be voiced again: that the students in most classes have not "thought" these "rhetorical problems out" and may fail to do so at all if left alone. Teachers can use their own judgment about standards of quality, but the students are still left in the dark and remain dependent on outside approval—indeed, behaviorism foresees no means whereby students could generalize from teacher comments toward important underlying strategies of cognition in writing.

In all fairness, we must bear in mind that behaviorists also realized the

---

[3] I could not verify this sketch, since Ms. Shutt is now deceased.

narrowness of Skinner's orthodox approach. Osgood introduced the concept of "mediation" between the simulus and the response: "the mediating reaction to the sign is not the same as the reaction to the significate, but rather consists of those most readily conditionable, least effortful, and least interfering components of the total original reaction": he can thereby "break the behavior sequence . . . into two independently variable parts, decoding habits and encoding habits [Osgood, 1964, p. 740]." In this fashion, both the stages within production or comprehension of utterances and the correspondences between the two activities can be elaborately differentiated. An incoming utterance is first registered as a pattern of sensory signals, then integrated, and finally assigned a representation (a meaning). To produce an utterance in reply, the speaker works in the other direction: an "intention" to be "meaningful" is relayed to the "skills" of "integration" and from there to the "execution" of "projection" procedures (1964, p. 741). The guiding control upon operations is the strength of relative **probabilities:** the "combination and patterning" within various "hierarchies" of options determine "the momentary probabilities of dependent alternatives": the "momentarily most probable" is then selected (1964, p. 741).

Three components are proposed to account for the meaning of sentences. The speaker's vocabulary is drawn from a vast "word-form pool" that contains the simple forms without their meanings. These forms are passed to the "semantic key sort" which assigns the most probable meanings—meaning being viewed as "a bundle of simultaneous semantic features" (minimal units like "animate versus inanimate"). In a sentence, these meaning-bundles are integrated by a "cognitive mixer" that obtains an overall "response" by establishing "congruity."[4] Thus, to create or understand an "assertion," the mind performs a "semantic fusion" on associated items (e.g., on *Tom* and *thief* in *Tom is a thief*), and a "semantic dissolution" on any dissociated items (e.g., in *Tom is not a thief*) (1964, p. 748).

Unlike Skinner's "kiddie-car model" (to borrow Osgood's designation), this model has the major advantage of trying to come to terms with word meanings beyond simple conditioning. In his 1964 paper (p. 741), Osgood still hopes to get by without considering "cognition," "purpose," and "volition"—he stretches the notion of probability to cover all such factors. Thus, the organism believes that it intends or wants to do something, and that it knows how; but for the psychologist, these factors merely strengthen the probability that the organism will do it. Each decision or selection on a higher level like "intention" is a "stimulus" for some "response" on a lower level like "execution." (It seems plausible that these

---

[4]On the principle of "congruity," cf. Osgood and Tannenbaum (1955).

level interactions must exist; but we might do better to term them **preferences** and **contingencies** rather than "stimulus–response chains.")

Lounsbury (1965) undertakes to formulate a general speech model in terms of "transition probabilities" operating within "habit–family hierarchies." He contends that all selections are made under the constraints of "reshuffled probabilities" in a steady progression, so that every utterance shows a rising probability curve toward its end. Pauses should mark points of greatest uncertainty, where the probabilities of the succeeding occurrence are the lowest. Experiments have demonstrated, however, that the probability curves of utterances need not rise in any such linear fashion (Tannenbaum, Williams, & Hillier, 1965). For example, predictability varies according to whether a particular point is located within or between major constituents (Johnson, 1966)—a fact which Osgood (1964, p. 743) construes as evidence "that simultaneous and sequential hierarchies combine in the understanding and creating of sentences." Moreover, I have myself suggested that a major technique in upholding audience participation is to introduce IMPROBABLE elements at strategic points, that is, elements whose motivation can only be reconstructed after an initial moment of surprise (Beaugrande, 1979a, 1980).

Unlike Skinner, who continues to deny the justification for any cognitive processing notions (e. g., association, abstraction, mind, will, thought, intention, and knowledge) (Skinner, 1978), Osgood has modified his position. He has more recently postulated a "non-linguistic cognitive system" that "is shared" both by "perceptual signs" and by "linguistic signs" (Osgood, 1971, pp. 498ff.). He conducted and reported a straightforward experiment in which sentences were produced to describe observed states of affairs, such as *An orange ring is on the table*. The correlations between the states of affairs and the observers' descriptions were regular enough to lend credence to Osgood's long-standing view that language is simply one aspect of general behavior. Of course, people can describe situations they have never experienced; but such a task could be achieved by creating new constellations of learned "semantic features," that is, of "bipolar reaction systems" that "can only be in one state at any time [1971, p. 524]." This process might be akin to the "cognitive mixing" depicted in the 1964 paper.

These further modifications render more palatable Osgood's unaltered contention that the cognitive processes of language are essentially geared toward "representational mediation" of "overt behaviors" because all "symbolic processes" originate in "perceptuo–motor behaviors"; thus, "significates... (referents or things signified) are simply those patterns of stimulation [that] regularly and reliably produce distinctive patterns of behavior [1971, pp. 522f.]." However, the notion of "mediation" is potentially so powerful as to burst the very foundations of stimulus–response theory and thereby to obviate the theoretical framework Osgood wishes to preserve.[5] We already saw how Skinner's extrapolations from animal conditioning effectively destroyed any substantive validity his notions might have originally possessed. By the same token, we might as well adopt the cognitive processing models along the lines proposed in pp. 000–000 and leave the stimulus–response vocabulary alone.

Whereas Osgood worked steadily from behavior toward a theory of language, Pike (1967) progressed from structuralist linguistics (which, since Bloomfield [1933] had a behaviorist orientation) toward a "unified theory of the structure of human behavior." Pike's evidence was gathered not in the laboratory, but in field work with languages about which nothing was known. This research situation immediately reveals "the interdependence of language and non-language behavior" because, lacking dictionaries, interpreters, etc., the investigator can only "correlate particular sequences of sounds" with "the particular environment in which they are uttered and with the particular non-language activity which is then going on [1967, p. 29]." However, the notion of "stimulus–response" is not the core of Pike's "unified theory." The theoretical groundwork is instead drawn from slot-and-filler analysis enriched with an unconventional physicalist perspective. The major procedure is the discovery of units within encompassing sequences and contexts. The "tagmeme" is a "structural position plus its manifesting class [1967, p. 288]" that is, a slot plus the set of items that can fill the slot.

This basic set-up was interpreted in light of three notions borrowed directly from physics: "particle," "wave," and "field" (Pike, 1959). The particle perspective stresses static, discrete units; the wave perspective stresses the dynamic continuum of evolution; and the field perspective addresses the multi-dimensional, systemic context (cf. the example of *Pike's house* in Young, Becker, & Pike, 1970, pp. 122ff.). In conventional linguistics of the time, only the particle view was well developed. The other two were pressingly needed in order to expand research into large complexes of human behavior, such as the 'football game' or the 'family breakfast' in Pike (1967, pp. 98ff., 122ff.).

Unfortunately, the slot-and-filler framework is not elaborate enough to support Pike's monumental undertaking. He insists that "the objective study of objective responses, whether in the form of verbal activity or nonverbal activity, is the source of [the analyst's] determination of the presence and nature of meaning and purpose. In utilizing meaning and purpose it is not necessary to have direct access to mental events." The "objective data" of "a particular response regularly following the utterance

---

[5]Fodor (1965) argued that mediation theory is reducible to orthodox single-stage learning theory, but in fact, there is an essential difference in operational power (cf. Osgood, 1966, for a reply).

of a language pattern" is claimed to be "sufficient" (1967, p. 156). Researchers who are genuinely determined to accept this restriction upon evidence will need a much more elaborate model than slot-and-filler if the "objective data" is to be truly revealing or significant. They will have to explain the mechanisms, many of them hierarchical or simultaneous rather than sequential, that decide what "slots" are there to be "filled" and why. The number of cases where an occurrence is due entirely to "conditioning" of a linguistic environment (cf. Pike, 1967, pp. 164ff.; 204ff.) is small compared to that of cases where language users perform "mental events" of decision and selection in pursuit of complex goals which may remain invisible.

My critical outline of behaviorist language theories is not intended to suggest that they should be discarded wholesale. On the contrary, some behaviorist tenets remain, in my view, significant and convincing, for example:

1. A theory of human language should be an integral part of a general theory of human behavior (Skinner, 1957; Osgood, 1964; Pike, 1967). We must be concerned with "a broader field," namely "the behavior of a most complex creature in contact with a world of endless variety [Skinner, 1957, p. 456]."

2. "What needs to be explained is the total speech episode," that is, "all relevant events in the behavior of both speaker and listener in their proper temporal order" [Skinner, 1957, p. 36]." It is clear that in this "total event," language behavior and non-language behavior are fused [Pike, 1967, p. 26]."

3. "Verbal behavior is characteristically dynamic, regardless of size or complexity": it follows that the utterance "is a lively unit, in contrast with the sign or symbol of the logician or the word or sentence of the linguist [Skinner, 1957, pp. 345, 312]."

4. "The listener" is "an essential part of the situation in which verbal behavior is observed"; "the change which is thus brought about in the behavior of the listener is appropriately called 'instruction' [Skinner, 1957, pp. 172, 362]."

5. Language education should start from "the actual here-and-now behavior of a given student or a given classroom of students [Zoellner, 1971, pp. 232ff.]."

6. Learning should take place via successive approximations moving steadily toward the desired final skill (Sidman, 1962).

What must be rejected is the energetic, strident insistence of behaviorism that it is useless to appeal to all notions regarding the internal organizational and processual faculties of the human being (e. g., in Skinner, 1978). That line of argument forces upon us constant omissions, simplifications, reductions, and denials that impede the exploration of such human capacities as motivation, planning, creativity, imagination, abstraction, deduction, analogy, and many more.

Mentalism

The impact of such assaults on behaviorism as Chomsky's (1959) review of Skinner would have doubtless been slight if there had not been an alternative approach at hand with its own legions of articulate advocates. As Kuhn (1970) stresses, no theory is even abandoned unless a successor is already provided. In the history of ideas, mentalism had come to the fore in a variety of guises, for example, Cartesian rationalism, Kantian idealism, Freudian psychoanalysis, Gestalt theory, and so forth. Broadly speaking, mentalism would be a designation of any approach where explanation of a phenomenon is sought in human intuitions, mental processes, tacit knowledge, or organization of the mind as such. Yet the mentalism that soon came to dominate linguistics and psycholinguistics in the 1960s was very selective about its ancestry. An essential Cartesian framework (cf. Chomsky, 1966a) was blended with the essentially syntactic logic envisioned by Rudolf Carnap—a figure in logical positivism that one might expect to find more on the physicalist side. However, Carnap's axiomatic logic offered a foundation sufficiently abstracted away from experience and external behavior that no conflicts arose.

Unlike those of behaviorism, the extrapolations of mentalism were reasonably obvious because of the resemblances between artificial languages of logic and natural languages of human communication. Human languages were thus defined as a set of **basic axioms** ("kernels") produced by **formation rules** ("phrase-structure rules"), plus all **strings** ("sentences") which could be created by applying **derivation rules** ("transformational rules") to the axioms (Chomsky, 1957). As we can see, all emphasis falls upon syntax; later on, semantics was added as an after-the-fact "interpretation" performed on syntatically "generated" strings (cf. Chomksy, 1972a, Jackendoff, 1972). Thus, the notion of "well-formedness" or "grammaticalness" displaced empirical evidence as the chief method of proving or disproving theories. A grammar was "correct" if it could assign "structural discriptions" to all the well-formed sentences of the language, and to no ill-formed ones. All rules had to be **categorical** (applying correctly regardless of context) rather than merely **probabilistic** (applying with a certain likelihood in particular contexts).

Though apparently straightforward, these extrapolations entailed a crucial "working hypothesis": that "the formal devices of language should be studied independently of their use [reported in Chomsky, 1972a, p. 198]." This hypothesis pervaded language study with an ominous, unsettling dualism. Chomsky acknowledged "using the term 'grammar' with a systematic ambiguity (to refer, first, to the native speaker's internally represented 'theory of language' and, second, to the linguist's account of this) [1965, p. 25]." The same ambiguity between human capacities or knowledge and a formalized abstraction can be uncovered in all major notions of Chomskyan mentalism, giving rise to endless ambivalences, misunderstandings, and spurious claims. Above all, linguists felt apparently freed from the responsibility of providing empirical demonstrations for their hypotheses.

This difficulty was already present in Chomsky's (1959) Skinner review. On the one hand, he claimed that "the construction of a grammar which enumerates sentences in such a way that a meaningful structural description can be determined for each sentence does not in itself provide an account of this actual behavior"; on the other hand, he presents the "grammar" as offering "a statement of the integrative processes and generalized patterns imposed upon the specific acts that constitute an utterance," and the "rules of the grammar" as "the selective mechanisms involved in the production of a particular utterance [1959, p. 56]." The apex of equivocation was perhaps attained by Jackendoff (1972, p. 386), who (no doubt sardonically) answered the question, "if we open up a human being, what do we find?" with these words:

> We find a four-chambered heart, a spine, some intestines, and a transformational grammar with two or more syntactic levels.

Despite such statements, criticisms of transformational grammar as unrealistic are always answered with the argument that we are only dealing with an abstraction or idealization not intended as a human model. This line of argument seems to me disingenuous on two grounds, even if we overlook the kind of passages I cited previously. First, the terminology of the "standard theory" deliberately suggests human processing: "generate," "competence," "speaker–hearer," "language acquisition device," "assertion," "utterance," and so forth. The special definitions offered for these terms are not helpful as long as their everyday, commonsense meanings are continually being utilized wherever the linguistic undertaking of such a grammar is being defended. If a clear, unambiguous terminology were established, we would have to say things such as *the grammar assigns a structural description to this string* rather than *the speaker generates this utterance;* or *the grammar assigns a semantic interpretation to this sentence* rather than *the hearer understands this utterance;* or *the linguist constructs the grammar X* rather than *the child acquires the natural language X;* and so on. The latter usage in each pair is just as metaphorical as Skinner's usage so unsparingly castigated by Chomsky (1959).[6]

---

[6]While admitting that his "terminology" has occasioned "a continuing misunderstanding," Chomsky [1965, p. 9] can see no reason for a revision." He may have realized how essential the misunderstanding was for the appeal of his theory.

224 Robert de Beaugrande

This reservation brings us to my second point. Chomsky (1965, p. 27) argues that the "internal" justification of a grammar as "its relation to a linguistic theory that constitutes an explanatory hypothesis about the form of language as such" is far more important ("deeper") than the "external" justification of a grammar as "corresponding to linguistic fact." The former justification offers "explanatory adequacy," and the latter only "descriptive adequacy," because the internal viewpoint selects one grammar from all of those which "correctly describe its object." I cannot conceive of any sensible definition of "correctness" in linguistics except: "being an accurate account of what people do with language." And in that view, the priorities are exactly reversed here: given a set of internally consistent grammars— Bierwisch (1966, p. 130) suggests that for any language, an INFINITE set may be constructed—we should rather select as "explanatory" the one closest to "linguistic fact."

Now, the central "fact" that transformational grammar purported to "explain" is the relationship between the simple declarative active (or intransitive) sentence and other sentence formats such as the passive, the relative clause, and the modifier. But the relationship of the active sentence, say, to its corresponding passive is in fact NOT SYNTACTIC in nature at all, except in the most trivial sense possible: that both formats contain the same basic set of categories like "noun phrase," "verb phrase," and so forth. The relationship is rather based upon the potential of alternative syntactic formats for casting or recasting the expression of one event or state of affairs in several ways, according to the speaker's COMMUNICATIVE INTENTION. Therefore, to write abstract rules that convert actives to passives, ignoring communicative intentions as mere "performance," is a pointless academic exercise that (even if eventually successful on "internal" grounds) certainly "explains" no significant "linguistic facts." We obtain at most a very fragmentary **theory of paraphrase** (Beaugrande, 1980, p. 37). How such a theory can claim to be the central question of language science remains an impenetrable mystery.

No doubt the fatal flaw in this mentalist approach lies in the determined rejection of the behaviorist antithesis. Hence, the "description of speech habits" and the discovery of "patterns" in "observed speech" are claimed to "preclude the development of a theory," even one of "actual performance" (Chomsky, 1965, p. 15). "Reliable operational criteria for the deeper and more important notions of linguistics," it is asserted, will NEVER "be forthcoming [Chomsky, 1965, p. 19]." The "sharpening of the data by more objective tests" is dismissed as "a matter of small importance," unlikely to bring any "gain in insight and understanding"; the professional linguist's own personal "intuitions" as a "native speaker" are asserted to be "an enormous mass of unquestionable data [Chomsky, 1965, p. 20]"—a contention contradicting the most fundamental principles of behaviorist research.

In this ambient, it is not surprising if Chomsky's supporters assert: "A study of competence abstracts away from the whole question of . . . how language is processed in real time, why speakers say what they say, how language is used in various social groups, how it is used in communication, etc. [Dresher & Hornstein, 1976, p. 328]." It is also not surprising if Chomsky's critics ask what transformational grammar offers the human sciences and reach answers like this: "The cult of personality, a priori dogma, esprit de corps, notation (but also notational flimflam), history without history, language without speakers, speakers without societies, societies without environments, in sum linguistics without language [Maher, cited in Anttila, 1974, p. 26]."

Deese (1971, p. 162) mildly remarks that transformational grammar "has not yet resulted in either comprehensive or particularly insightful studies in language learning as it is faced in the classroom." If taken seriously enough, this brand of mentalism engenders two possible strategies. First, since every child is already equipped with an "innate language acquisition device" that abstracts a "correct grammar" from the often degenerate input of everyday speech (cf. Chomsky, 1965, section 1.8), and since "perform-ance," being "the actual use of language in concrete situations," "obviously could not directly reflect competence [Chomsky, 1965, p. 4]," language education might as well be abolished as useless. However, this strategy is unappealing to the English teacher whose classroom is for some reason not filled with "ideal speaker–hearers who know their language perfectly" and are exempt from "memory limitations, distractions, shifts of attention and interest, and errors [Chomsky, 1965, p. 3]."

The second strategy would be to devise training methods that support and encourage the development of a "correct" mental grammar by rehears-ing phrase structures and transformations. This angle was taken by pro-ponents of "sentence combining," a technique for transforming basic sentences (like "kernels") into complex ones, for example, by forming modifiers and relative clauses. Bateman and Zidonis (1964, pp. 2ff.) main-tained that "generative grammar . . . is in essence a representation of the psychological processes of producing sentences"; it follows that "pupils must be taught a system that accounts for well-formed sentences before they can be expected to produce more of such sentences themselves."[7] Their project involved showing that direct instruction in transformational grammar can increase the "language complexity" of high-school writers while reducing their grammatical errors. Their results were positive and have been frequently replicated.

In a more cautiously formulated study, Mellon (1969 [1967])[8] probed the growth of "syntactic fluency in English composition," "using a transfor-

---

[7]As Mellon (1969, p. 9) observes, the quantifier "more" "seems to turn the statement into a self-contradiction": How could the pupils have produced any if they "must be taught a system" beforehand?

[8]I refer to the 1969 rather that the 1967 version because the epilogue is of interest here.

mational grammar written for the occasion by the experimenter [1969, p. 39]." Noting how "the range of sentence types in free student writing increases . . . as the student matures," he "stipulatively defined" the notion of "maturity of sentence structure . . . in a strictly statistical sense, in terms of the range of sentence types observed in representative samples of a student's writing [1969, pp. 15f.]." However, he takes pains to stress that "the process which grammars describe is speaker-hearer neutral, . . . differing from that which might be formulated in a description of production [1969, p. 13]."

Despite these reservations and through no fault of his own, Mellon is overtaken by the "systematic ambiguity" which, as we saw, is irrevocably built into Chomskyan mentalism. In assuming the claim that "transformational grammars describe the process of sentence formation" to be "correct [1969, p. 13]," Mellon cannot help participating in the well-known metaphorical extrapolations so commonplace in linguistic discussions. The impression that arises is documented in Richard Braddock's editorial introduction (Mellon, 1969, p. v, emphasis added): "John C. Mellon asked whether seventh graders would produce, on the average, more structurally elaborated sentences, HENCE, MORE MATURE ONES, if they were given practice in combining kernel sentences into single statements." Christensen (1968) pointed out that the sentence complexity in question is no adequate measure of "a mature style." Mellon (1969, pp. 79f.) replied that the only measure in question is that of "mature syntactic fluency." But even this more restricted notion seems to be a metaphorical extrapolation as long as the correspondence between sentence transformations and actual human writing processes is left wholly unexplored.

Even the detailed classroom practices encounter these difficulties. The use of syntactic placeholders, though common in abstract grammar, yields palpably implausible sample sentences like these (Mellon, 1969, pp. 95–99):

(3) *Something will very likely hinder something.*
(4) *Something meant something.*

No doubt the students were warned that such sentences were mere stepping stones, not serious examples; but the distinctions involved in a grammar that explains human language without reference to what humans do in communication are surely beyond the average seventh-grader, having evaded the linguist and the general public so often over the years. Moreover, the facile assumption that transformations leave meaning unchanged (Katz & Postal, 1964) is belied by some of Mellon's illustrations:

(5) a. *[The] building rising high into the sky towered above [the] tenements . . .*
     b. *The building was rising into the sky.*

In (5)b. only, the strange implication arises that the building has been freed from its foundations and is floating aloft like a balloon. Instances like these strengthen the impression articulated by Moffett (1968) that sentence-combining is an unnatural activity.

Under fire from such critics, Mellon's 1969 epilogue avers that "sentence combining practice... [has] nothing to do with the teaching of writing"; "syntactic fluency... [is] an aspect of language production (in this case writing) over which one does not and can not (except on occasion and by artifice) exercise conscious control [1969, p. 81]." This disclaimer is surely too extreme. In fact, sentence combining has become a familiar part of many composition courses, proving its value for diverse uses. Moreover, the editing and revising of written papers often entail "exercising conscious control" over syntactic choices, though the same is much less true for spontaneous speech. However, these considerations demand that we start from "the here-and-now behavior of a student [cf. p. 14]." A case in point is the vague use of *this* at sentence beginnings in basic writing: The best revision is often done by sentence-combining. Here are some actual passages from my students with their revisions:

(6) a. *They must know what they're doing at all times. This can be quite a problem.*
     b. *Knowing what they're doing at all times can be quite a problem.*
(7) a. *They must learn to develop that gift. And this is where the effort is needed.*
     b. *Developing that gift is where the effort is needed.*

The placeholder *this* is not stipulated by transformational grammar (which of course prefers *something,* as we saw), but it is a frequent weakness in student usage.

The usefulness of sentence-combining is therefore reasonably clear. But the original mentalist approach must be supplemented in important ways. For one thing, "Chomsky's generative grammar, even in its full-blown transformational form, says nothing whatsoever about decision making" (Osgood, 1964, p. 742). This lack is due to Chomsky's (1965, p. 11) determination to disregard "acceptability" as far less "important" than "grammaticalness," the latter notion having no "operational criterion"; thus, he rates these sentences "high on the scale of grammaticalness":

(8) *I called the man who wrote the book that you told me about up.*
(9) *The man who [sic] the boy who [sic] the students recognized pointed out is a friend of mine.*

To preclude such syntactic snarls, our students will need decision-making procedures that take account of context and intention (cf. my sketch in Beaugrande, 1979b; 1980a, pp. 207ff.). Obviously, such a demand can never be met by a theory in which the "grammatical sentence" is presupposed as the central notion, and the only "processes" are syntactic conversions.

Like his antagonist Skinner, Chomsky has remained inflexible on these issues over the years. The "standard theory," in which "semantic interpretation" was done only on "deep structure," has been "extended" to one in which "surface structure" is also "interpreted" (Chomsky, 1972a). More recently, a "surface structure" annotated with "traces" of transformations has been proposed (Chomsky, 1976). But Chomsky (1975, pp. 18ff.) is still adamant in regard to most substantive contentions, for example: "there is no reason to suppose that grammatical theory can make use of the notion of 'semantic relatedness' " (which, I suggested above, is the ONLY relationship that decides in practice what sentences are derivable from others); or "a surface structure is in interesting respects analogous to an expression in conventional systems of logic"; or the "thesis of 'autonomy of syntax' " is "surely not refuted or supported by recent discussion"; and so forth. The Dresher and Hornstein (1976) quote cited above shows the unbroken insistence on studying language independently of language use.

All the same, mentalism is no more deserving of a wholesale repudiation than is behaviorism. Some mentalist tenets should also be upheld, such as:

1. "Linguistic theory is concerned with discovering a mental reality underlying actual behavior [Chomsky, 1965, p. 4]." This reality need not be manifest in the overt behavior studied in old-style laboratories.
2. "Linguistic theory" presents certain empirical hypotheses . . . [that] aim to characterize the schematism that the mind imposes in examining the data of sense and acquiring knowledge of language [Chomsky, 1975, p. 13]."
3. "A grammar of a language" should "provide an explicit analysis" of the speaker's "contribution [Chomsky, 1965, p. 4]."
4. "It is questionable whether the theory of meaning can be divorced from the study of other cognitive structures [Chomsky, 1975, p. 23]."
5. "The normal use of language characteristically involves new sentences [Chomsky, 1972b, p. 171]"; thus, "the most striking aspect of linguistic competence . . . [is] "the creativity of language [Chomsky, 1966b, p. 11]."
6. What speakers say at a single moment need not reflect the totality of the knowledge and ability in their language.

What should be repudiated is the cavalier distrust of empirical evidence, namely the actual activities of humans in natural communicative situations. That attitude only entrains us in continual uncertainties about the status of theories and concepts whose technical usage is at variance with their commonsense implications. That variance leaves us wondering whether—to paraphrase Chomsky's (1959, p. 30) rebuke of Skinner—linguistics creates the illusion of a rigorous scientific theory with a very broad scope, although in fact the terms used in the description of real life and of abstract grammar may be mere homonyms, with at most a vague similarity of meaning.

COGNITIVE SCIENCE

A New Research Program

Cognitive science is a recently emerging field at the crossroads of psychology, linguistics, philosophy, computer science, anthropology, sociology, and education. Its goal is to create a unified science of cognition and communication, with the specific concerns of the several sub-disciplines forming an integrated whole. That undertaking might appear utterly utopian, were it not for the growing realization that the individual questions of each discipline may well be unanswerable without the framework of a far broader theory. For example, the attempts to derive both semantics and pragmatics from syntax have been a notorious weakness of linguistics; what is needed is rather a theory of how knowledge is utilized (psychology) and how humans interact in society (sociology).

Cognitive science offers the only solution I can envision to the central crisis of both physicalism and mentalism: the correlation between theory and observation. Physicalist theories were highly impoverished through disallowing all pheonomena not subject to direct outward observation. Mentalist theories were elaborate, but largely unsupported by observable language behavior. More generally, this crisis confronts EVERY scientific theory, precisely because the theory itself so strongly influences our inclination to observe some aspects of a domain and to disregard the rest (Hanson, 1958). We need only consult the various behaviorist or transformational studies to notice the importance of this consideration: Both sides designed experiments that confirmed their totally contradictory standpoints. The theory versus observation crisis is egregiously acute in the scientific exploration of complex human capacities that may themselves be affected by our own beliefs regarding them (just as a child whose peers or teachers consider him or her stupid soon comes to act stupidly).

To escape this general quandary, I have proposed to redefine the conception of TESTING THEORIES BY OBSERVATION as one of the **functional diversification** and **consensus of models** (Beaugrande, 1981a, 1981b). Here, any theory about a domain of cognition or communication is expressed as a working model of what humans are doing in that particular regard. That model must provide orientation and explanation such that observable and nonobservable aspects can be seen to interact in a powerful way—where **power** is defined as the ability to work with a high-plane set of general strategies that can be specified for a wide range of incidental operations and data types (cf. Minsky & Papert, 1974, p. 59). A model meeting this requirement is likely to offer **functional consensus,** that is, a working agreement among scientists about how the domain can be envisioned and investigated.

In many cases, a specialized domain will be expressible in more than one model. The next test should be **functional diversification,** where one model is expanded to cover steadily greater domains (e. g., a model of discourse production that also fits the literature on the capacities of working memory). If the model can offer functional consensus for that wider range, it is preferable to a model that cannot. In each new domain of application, the points where scientists can inject their theoretical predispositions and the means for doing so are structurally and functionally altered. Entirely artifactual findings biased by the investigator's own theory thereby become much harder to uphold and are more likely to be suspected. The significance of these considerations is being slowly recognized all throughout science. William Estes, a well-known psychologist, concludes: "the measure of success in moving toward a scientific explanation is the degree to which a theory brings out relationships between otherwise distinct and independent clusters of phenomena [1979, p. 47]."

The importance of **antecedence** (where a particular theory is founded by specification or specialization of a general, subsuming one) as opposed to **extrapolation** (where a theory is simply borrowed elsewhere without any such overarching theoretical framework) (cf. pp. 211–212) is quite conspicuous in this context. If a theory of knowledge is needed to found a theory of linguistic meaning (as even Chomsky suggests), then the semanticist will have to consult the psychologist. However, to escape the dangers of a vague, unqualified extrapolation, a more general theory of cognition and communication is required in order to provide corresponding concepts and methods in both disciplines. The failure of Skinner and Chomsky to explain human language was due in no small degree to their decision to extrapolate from domains highly removed from language without any conceptual apparatus to clarify the conditions of the transfer; and to their refusal to diversify, for instance, by dispassionately examining and incorporating the evidence brought forward by the other side. Thus, Skinner (1978, pp. 101 and 97) disallows all "introspection" as "dubious" and "defective," leading only to groundless "inventions." Chomsky (1965, p. 4) in his turn pontificates that "observed use of language or hypothesized dispositions to respond, habits, and so on ... cannot constitute the actual subject matter" of any "serious discipline."

In cognitive science, functional diversification and consensus are highly respected pursuits. In my estimation, the attractive tenets I enumerated from both behaviorism (p. 212–222) and mentalism (p. 222–228) are shared in some form by most of us in the discipline, though we might phrase them differently. We do not see them as mutually incompatible because of a priori allegiances to established dogma. On the contrary, it is widely accepted that mental events are a class of ACTIONS whose execution involves both cognitive processing and social behavior. Any borderline between the two must be fuzzy in comparison to their concerted interactions.

Some major tenets of cognitive science might be:

1. Interdisciplinarity is superior to fragmentation in the construction of theories (cf. Anderson, Spiro, & Montague, 1977; Beaugrande, 1980, 1982a; Chafe, 1980; Freedle, 1977, 1979; Kintsch & Vipond, 1979; Rumelhart, 1977; Schank & Abelson, 1977).

2. We must "make a greater effort to understand cognition as it occurs in the ordinary environment and in the context of natural purposeful activity [Neisser, 1976, p. 7]."

3. "What sort of information processing system a human becomes depends intimately on the way he develops"; "many constraints upon the nature of the fully developed system arise from the requirement of self-organization [Newell & Simon, 1972, p. 7]."

4. "To understand what it takes to be intelligent," we need "a science of cognition" that "deals with all cognitive processes—whether real or imaginary, concrete or abstract, human or machine [Norman, 1979, p. 142]."

5. "Experiments aimed at existing theories should be designed to find out how, where, and in what sense these theories need revision of why they should be rejected, not to provide additional support for them [Tulving, 1979, p. 30]."

6. "What we hope for primarily from models is that they will bring out relationships between experiments or sets of data that we would not otherwise have perceived [Estes, 1975, p. 271]."

7. "Premature formalization" "provides a sense of false security. Our intellectual resources are misplaced if they are spent on the construction of elaborate and unwieldy logical and mathematical structures to explain experimental findings in situations in which the facts are soft and the basic concepts still be invented [Tulving, 1979, p. 30]."

8. "Thinking seriously about intelligent behavior of any sort requires thinking seriously about what representation is best suited to the domain in which the intelligent behavior is exhibited [Winston, 1977, p. 15]."

9. We should "describe the objects in a domain in a way that uncovers useful constraints on how the objects interact with one another [Winston, 1977, p. 45]."

10. "Language," "visual perception," "problem solving," and "education" are all linked under "the single unifying concept" of "the representation of information within human memory [Norman & Rumelhart, 1975, p. 3]."

11. "In every domain of human experience, perception, comprehension, and interpretation involve an interaction of input with existing knowledge [Anderson, 1977, p. 417]."

Tenets such as these set decisive priorities for studying the production and comprehension of discourse (cf. general survey in Beaugrande, 1980). For example, grammatical rules should be stated as **procedures** for using the rules in real time (Rumelhart, 1977, p. 122). A representation or notation should suggest how the entities under consideration are built, controlled, and accessed Anderson, 1977; Findler, 1979; Rumelhart & Norman, 1975; Rumelhart, 1977). Theories of meaning should reflect how human beings acquire, store, recover, and apply knowledge of the world (Brachman, 1978; Fahlman, 1979; Hörmann, 1976; Kintsch, 1977; Miller & Johnson-Laird, 1976). Communication must be seen in relation to human plans and goals (Allen, 1979; Cohen, 1978; McCalla, 1978; Schank & Abelson, 1977; Wilensky, 1980).

Such a multi-disciplinary science of discourse would in turn be properly antecedent to a **science of composition,** that is, a discipline devoted to the investigation of human writing processes (cf. Beaugrande, 1982a). A cognitive science research program for that discipline might include: (*a*) a model of the operations and controls involved in writing; (*b*) an account of how writing conditions differ systematically from speaking conditions; (*c*) an explication of strategies of decision and selection; (*d*) a means for decomposing the entire writing process into manageably small subtasks; (*e*) a prediction of the most preponderant difficulties in writing, that is, of the normal weak points in the production system; and (*f*) a set of criteria for evaluating and revising written texts.

The program cannot be met unless steady compromises are drawn between the extremes of physicalism and mentalism. We must view language in the broader, livelier context of the total event in which writer and reader influence each other's behavior; and we must start from the "here-and-now behavior" of the students and work forward through successive approximations (see "Physicalism," pp. 212–222). On the other hand, we must explore the students' "mental reality," including their internal predispositions, their cognitive structures, their creativity, and their underlying competencies (see "Mentalism," pp. 222–228).[9]

In the context of the total event, writing cannot be seen in isolation from communicative skills in general. It entails the application of more powerful skills such as learning, planning, memory, interaction, and problem solving (cf. Beaugrande, 1980; Bruce, Collins, Rubin, & Gentner, 1978; Flower & Hayes, 1980; Gregg & Steinberg, 1980). A theory of writing must be formulated in close contact with current theories of reading (cf. Flower, Hayes, & Swarts, 1980; Hirsch, 1977; Meyer, 1979a; Tierney & LaZansky, 1980); what writers do depends on what they hope or expect their readers to do. Writing and reading skills must be stipulated in co-ordination with

---

[9]This research outlook has already become firmly established in studies of reading (cf. Beaugrande, 1981a), and composition should follow soon.

research on speaking and listening skills (cf. Beaugrande, 1982a, 1982b, 1982c; DeVito, 1965; Durell, 1969; Perfetti & Goldman, 1976; Rubin, 1980; Ruddell, 1965; Sticht, 1972; Tatham, 1970).

These interdependencies are vital because writing itself has seldom been studied in its own right. For one thing, researchers found it far more congenial to study language comprehension—usually construed as identical with "sentence comprehension" (survey in Levelt, 1978)—than language production. No doubt the design of experiments seems unduly complex and unreliable in the latter domain. In comprehension, test subjects need merely be shown a sentence and asked to perform a brief task: pressing a button when they feel they have understood the sentence (the favorite tactic of Herbert Clark), recalling the sentence, distinguishing the sentence from similar versions, and so forth. I have suggested on occasion that these data are softer than researchers suppose (see especially Beaugrande, 1981a). When test subjects carry out operations such as reporting the form or content of some presentation, they are of course engaging in discourse production; yet the latter activity is usually taken for granted by the same experimenters who laboriously trace out the comprehension of every word or phrase. The large literature on story understanding (see for example van Dijk, 1980), much of which is based on readers' accounts of a story, should be more consistently integrated with attempts to model story TELLING, surely a matter of equal importance (cf. survey in Applebee, 1978; simulation model in Beaugrande & Colby, 1979).

Under these circumstances, the cognitive science literature on discourse production is still sparse. We have a number of studies on the computer generation of sentences, largely concerned with defining the role of a grammar in regard to operations of expression (e.g., Beaugrande, 1979c; Davey, 1974; Goldman, 1975; McDonald, 1978, 1979; McGuire, 1980; Simmons & Chester, 1979; Simmons & Slocum, 1971; Wong, 1975). Only a few address issues like the global coherence of stories (Meehan, 1976) or the pursuit of communicative goals (Cohen, 1978).

Within psychology proper, a number of sketches are available on production, following various orientations: linguistic syntax (Boomer, 1965; Garrett, 1975; Jarvella, 1977; Kempen, 1977; Lackner & Levine, 1975; MacKay, 1974); semantic units (O'Connell, Kowal, & Hörmann, 1969; Rosenberg, 1977b); neurological and physiological processes (Lashley, 1951), or, more specifically, motor activity (Ertel, 1977; McNeill, 1975; MacNeilage, 1970; Selnes & Whitaker, 1977; Sussman, 1972); mental disorders (Gosnave, 1977; Rochester, Thurston, & Rupp, 1977); speech hesitations (Goldman-Eisler, 1961, 1972; Rochester, 1973); speech rhythms (Jaffe, 1977); and speech errors (Boomer & Laver, 1968; Fromkin, 1973; MacKay, 1972).

Several main points can be made about this psychological literature (which I undertake to survey elsewhere, Beaugrande, 1982a). First, many of the studies were concerned not with speech production as an interesting object in its own right, but with finding support for some particular theory. Linguists, for example, especially transformational grammarians, hoped to demonstrate the primacy of syntax over other language aspects. A debate ensued about whether (as the standard grammar suggests) people select syntactic formats BEFORE deciding what words to use—a view espoused by Chomsky (1959, p. 54, appealing to Goldman-Eisler, 1958, and work in progress by Osgood [Maclay & Osgood, 1959; cf. Boomer, 1965]), Nooteboom (1969), and Fromkin (1971), but rejected no less emphatically by Schank, Goldman, Rieger, and Riesbeck (1975), Clark and Clark (1977), Kempen (1977), Rosenberg (1977b), and Schlesinger (1977). Though highly speculative, the view naturally arose from linguistic methods and declined only as more flexible research procedures evolved.

The second point may be evident from this illustration. Research that explores speech production only as an incidental demonstration of other issues is not prone to yield any comprehensive or unified picture of the activity as such. Rosenberg (1977b, p. 223) pessimistically concludes:

> There is little to be learned about the speech production process from the results of large-scale correlative studies of speech errors, and although experimental methods hold more promise of helping us identify the organization and operation of the speech production processes, most of the available experimental literature suffers from serious methodological and conceptual problems.

One of these problems, I suspect, is the hope of showing that THE PRODUCTION PROCESS ALWAYS WORKS THE SAME WAY. It is far more likely that the process is adapted to tasks and contexts, for example, that neither syntax nor word selection MUST come first; or that speech pauses have many causes, not just a single one. We would do better to design experiments that test comprehensive models rather than isolated hypotheses.

The third point is that virtually none of this literature concerns the writing process as distinct from that of speaking. The very factors that experimental psychologists prefer to manipulate, such as time allotment, forced choices, and distractions, apply very differently to writing. Pauses, hesitations, and errors may have a distinctive distribution in writing, and may go undetected both by the investigator and the writer. The organization of the discourse itself is clearly different as well, most notably perhaps in regard to the consistency and distinctness of structural units and boundaries. Unequal degrees of facility in speaking and writing are very frequent, as every composition teacher knows.

In the remainder of this chapter, I shall pursue this third point as a largely unmapped but essential domain for both theory and pedagogy of writing. I shall offer an outline model of language production and consider some properties of speaking versus writing. I shall analyze some comparative data samples and draw some implications for developmental composi-

tion as tested in my own projects. For a broader discussion of this work and its place in a general science of composition, see Beaugrande (1982a).

An Outline Model and Some Specializations

The simplest view of discourse production is often embodied in what we can call **sequential-stage relay models**. The overall action is seen as a series of independent phases passing their results along in a fixed chain (e. g., Fromkin, 1971). In generative semantics, for example, a "logical form," that is, a predication, is generated and passed to a syntactic interpreter and finally to a phonological interpreter, resulting in the spoken utterance. Among the most stringent advocates of this model type is Eleanor Gibson (1971), who insists that during comprehension graphemic–phonemic, syntactic, and semantic stages are entirely independent, each one extracting steadily more complex "features" of the input.

In simulations of discourse comprehension, sequential-stage relay models have been found to be **combinatorially explosive**: They proliferate alternative readings for each stage in a geometrical progression because the stages cannot consult each other's analyses. Researchers have therefore been impelled to develop **parallel-stage interaction models** in which the various aspects of the message are analyzed in mutual co-operation (Walker *et al.*, 1978; Woods & Brachman, 1978). Explosion is precluded by discarding alternatives that another stage of analysis has shown to be improbable. For instance, many syntactically possible ambiguities are at once disallowed if we consult the meaning and purpose of a discourse. The same considerations will undoubtedly emerge as discourse production is simulated in more comprehensive models.

Another argument against sequential-stage relay models is largely anecdotal, but nonetheless compelling. During the act of speaking or writing, we often find that some decisions we made were not in our best interests after all. We are then impelled to shift away from the uttering stage to such stages as plan construction and idea search. In sequential models, we could presumably only loop back and run all the way through the entire production process in the same fixed order. But it seems plausible that we may well be juggling plans, ideas, expressions, syntactic formats, and so on even during the moment we speak or write. Speech errors should manifest conflicting directives issuing from these various stages at about the same time. In parallel models, shifts and consultations in all directions are allowable, leading to a savings in pathways of search and access. Moreover, the surface structure of the discourse could be construed not simply as syntax, but also as signalings of ideas, plans, propositions, and so forth. On occasion, syntax per se might be partially bypassed—a conception suggested for comprehension by studies of skim-reading for a gist (cf. DeJong, 1977; Masson, 1979; Schank, Lebowitz, & Birnbaum, 1978).

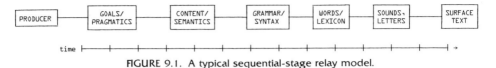

FIGURE 9.1. A typical sequential-stage relay model.

The popularity of sequential-stage models is surely due to their simplicity of **design.** Everything runs through a clear series of black boxes with invariable circuiting. And the experimenter conveniently supposes that the test subject is doing only one thing at any time, so that every stage shows up as a distinct linear increment of time on task. Parallel-stage models, on the other hand, present dire problems of **scheduling,** that is, of determining what steps should be done in any order, and how much is going on concurrently. Worse yet, the stages may well not show up as linear time increments; instead, time on task may only represent activities performed with **attention,** while **automatic** processes run alongside, undetected by our stop watches (Beaugrande, 1981a). This circumstance is disturbing for experimental psychologists whose tests routinely rely on time as the dependent variable.

Figures 9.1 and 9.2 illustrate these considerations. In Figure 9.1, we see the familiar chain of control, making allowances for looping back, but upholding the requirement that after re-entry, the entire chain must be traversed again. In Figure 9.2, we see the much messier kind of shifting, restarting, and consulting that parallel-stage models would enable.[10] Notice that I am replacing the conventional terminologies, for example, "semantics," "syntax," "phonology," with operational process notions. The goal level subsumes setting up a general discourse goal and the steps or subgoals that should be achieved along the way. Ideation occurs through the initiating of global configurations of conceptual content, for example, setting the main topic. Conceptual development comprises the elaboration, specification, and interconnection of ideas. Expression is the matching of cognitive content with language expressions. Phrase linearization arranges words in groups such that linear production can be achieved in real time (as compared to psychological time). The actual formation of written symbols is carried out by an **executor** during the phase of **sound/letter linearization.** (For a discussion and elaboration of this model, see Beaugrande, 1982a.) Though these five stages interact, they cannot be identical with each other; there must be considerable **asymmetry** (where a single entity of

---

[10]The justification for this multi-level design is presented in terms of a large number of experimental findings on memory, attention, and learning in my paper, "Text, attention, and memory in reading research," in R. J. Tierney *et al.* (Eds.), *Understanding Readers' Understanding* (Hillsdale, N.J.: Lawrence Erlbaum, in press). A comparable analysis for writing is given in Beaugrande (in preparation).

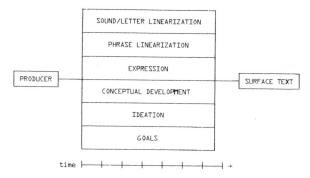

FIGURE 9.2. A parallel-stage interaction model.

one stage correlates with multiple choices in another) and **redundancy** (where a single decision in one stage is signaled with multiple elements in another).

This flexible model seems to be the only escape from the endless debates over "content versus form" or "thought versus expression." Some philosophers (e.g., Robinson, 1976; Vendler, 1970) assert that thought and expression are identical. Linguists, on the other hand, draw a radical demarcation, often for the purpose of studying form or expression and ignoring content. Psychologists allow for a division, but along various lines. Rosenberg (1977a, pp. 3f.) sketches the main viewpoints as follows. First, thought precedes the formatting of clauses, but happens to be "best expressed" in linguistic units. Second, thought precedes the formatting of clauses, but the strategic usefulness of syntactic units such as clauses is due to constraints on "information processing load, communicative effectiveness, output monitoring, and the like." Third, the linguistic formatting itself gives rise to "speech planning and execution strategies" that work back to constrain ongoing thought. Fourth, thought is made possible by speech capacities in the first place, so that units of speech and units of thought are simply externalized and internalized versions of the same thing.

The multi-directional parallel-stage model I am advocating allows for all four viewpoints without insisting on any one as correct. The most crucial, in my view, is the second: that syntax is present in natural languages largely as a repertory of conventions for respecting and managing the contingencies of ongoing communication. Since the repertory of conceptual relations (e. g., "agent of action," "location of object") is large and sometimes highly specialized, a much more limited, general organization system is needed for the formatting of the surface text. Thus, syntax offers a modest number of grammatical relationships (e. g., "subject of verb," "modifier of head"), each of which constrains the quantity of conceptual relations that language users will preferentially consider. Despite frequent asymmetry (e. g., "subject of verb" can correspond to many other things besides "agent of action") between syntax and semantics, these constraints normally suffice for rapid, reasonably accurate processing. Syntax acts as a kind of "distant early-warning system" for signaling meanings and intentions—in light of which consideration the "independent" or "autonomous syntax" of Chomsky's "standard theory" seems singularly absurd.

Learning experiments (e. g., the massive study of Friedman *et al.*, 1963) show that humans regularly strive for increased efficiency by adapting their expectations about what occurrences are likely to be encountered. No doubt many syntactic patterns come to be handled as quasi-automatic routines for everyday expression and thereby influence the organization of thoughts (as assumed in the first and third viewpoints cited above). The apparent identity of thought and expression would be an effect due to the relatively infrequent cases where no noticeable asymmetry or redundancy obtains, or where pre-packaged content has become fully habitual through constant repetition. Conceivably, people might even run through these habituated expressions without paying attention to the content conveyed, for example, when giving everyday commands within a team of workers. But this special case, which the behaviorists believed to be the general case, can hardly act as a model for the far more variegated contingencies of communication.

One consequence of the multi-directional parallel-stage model is that text production has no clearly built-in conclusion, no point at which cognitive processes are definitively accomplished. Instead, the processor would assign **dominance** to a stage until some approximative threshold of satisfaction is attained, and would then impose a termination by shifting dominance elsewhere. However, subsequent processing may reveal that a revision of an earlier stage is strategically called for—not necessarily the stage that would normally be immediately adjacent. One could then back-shift and restart operations or re-open decisions until the new contingencies have been met.[11]

It follows from here that text production is essentially probabilistic and approximative. Strict rules, though common in linguistic and logic-based grammars, are far less vital than flexible strategies. Given a particular communicative situation, the producer makes the most of available time and resources and accepts whatever inconsistency or inexactness may ensue. The conditions of speech production are in many ways disadvantageous, due largely to the demand for continuous flow of utterances with few long silences within or between them. Time is greatly limited, and attention may be diverted away from the more heavily linguistic stages of expression and parsing. In most settings, conversational participants tolerate

---

[11]Flower & Hayes (1979) propose a model that is in some ways comparable, but they suggest that dominance is shifted for whole blocks of text, whereas I surmise that these stages ALL run for EACH stretch of the text under normal conditions.

considerably higher approximativeness than they would in written communication: uncertain correlations between content and expression, structural shifts, needless repetitions, and so forth.

An essential criterion of textuality is **informativity**: the extent to which the presented test is new, unexpected, or unpredictable (Beaugrande, 1980; Beaugrande & Dressler, 1981). Though downplayed both by the behaviorist reliance on "conditioning" and the mentalist insistence on "categorical rules," this factor is one major impetus that drives communication forward: the removal and restoration of cognitive stability. A highly predictable text is **efficient** for processing but not **effective,** because it stimulates little interest. Conversely, a highly unpredictable text may impose unreasonable processing demands and thereby engender confusion or resentment. Text producers must find a workable balance for each situation and audience.

To reflect the dynamics of communication, we can say that all aspects of a message (sound script patterns, syntax, meaning, purpose) constitute ORDERED SETS OF HYPOTHESES ABOUT APPROPRIATE PROCESSING ACTIONS. These actions may or may not be oriented toward language itself, for instance, building syntactic patterns, expanding or revising one's knowledge stores, and carrying out a physical act. A speaker can guide these actions more directly than a writer, for example, by eliciting feedback, interfering, answering objections, or applying force. The writer must devise far more circumspect plans and arrangements that can be expected to guide a wider and often inaccessible audience, especially when the text material itself is densely informative.

The average college freshman possesses reasonable speaking skills, but underdeveloped writing skills. The natural consequence is to project the production conditions of speech onto the act of writing. The student discounts inconsistencies and redundancies that, though perfectly tolerable in conversation, are quite disturbing to readers (cf. the factoring later on in this section). In the past, teachers not infrequently denounced student usage as intrinsically "incorrect," "inferior," or even "illiterate." The students failed to recognize their own abilities to communicate in a particular type of system, so that previously available skills were not properly applied in the learning of new ones. At best, the red markings made by teachers as "corrections" might somehow be generalized into powerful strategies for self-help, but usually only by exceptional learners. The majority relied on a hit-or-miss, fix-it approach that attained isolated cosmetic improvements without engendering a reliable operating repertory of strategies conducive to good writing as such.

Studies sketched in the next sections indicate that writing proficiency can be measured most adequately in terms of the factors that differentiate speaking and writing. By the same token, composition instruction can profitably focus on training which encourages an awareness of these factors and a set of methods for controlling them. My results lead me to believe that at least some learners experience an increase in both text quality and personal confidence that is quite remarkable in the short space of one course. But even the slow learners are aided through step-by-step procedures that take their current skills as a serious foundation: They experience a processing overload (or "cognitive strain" in terms of Bruner, Goodnow, & Austin, 1956) when trying to write under the habits of speaking, but they can compensate through explicit revision techniques, addressing just one factor at a time. Of course, the main ideas and the general direction of the discourse are settled; but the immediate formatting of phrases and clauses has to be navigated all over again, and many inconsistencies or redundancies can be eliminated.

Speech Characteristics

A useful mode for gathering data relevant to the speculations in the foregoing section is to elicit oral and written versions of the same content from the same language user. I have been asking basic writers to "tell me in their own words" about some experience or topic which they can select on their own. These sessions are recorded on tape and later transcribed. The same students are also assigned to write on the same material, usually within a week's time. Interestingly enough, the resulting sample pairs are not significantly different if the written version is prepared BEFORE the spoken one: having the content firmly in mind is no direct elimination of all local organizational problems.

The case studies on pp. 253–259 arose from an investigation presented by Wallace Chafe (Note 1). He discussed two versions of a narrative produced by his student, Deborah Tannen, concerning a foreign sojourn stemming from a research project (cf. Chafe, 1980; Tannen, 1979a, 1979b). I reproduce these two versions as samples (10) and (11). Unlike Chafe's transcription, mine is not organized into sentences with conventional punctuation, since this notation would be my own (or Chafe's) addition. I merely note pauses with three dots; the numbering serves for citation and merely suggests where conceptual units might be found.

> (10.1) Um... I was staying with George's family... in Crete... (10.2) and um ... we were sitting around you know... (10.3) we were sitting around the dinner table... (10.4) all of them... all of us you know his his parents ... a-and... George and me... (10.5) and... um... for dessert ... they brought out this big plate of grapes... these big purple... (10.6) you you heard the story when I told the thing... (10.7) this big plate of grapes... (10.8) and I said no cause it wasn't the kind of grapes that I liked... (10.9) they were... purple ones... with seeds in them... (10.10) and I don't like that kind [portion omitted; she decided to eat them after all] (10.11) and then of course I had eaten them... (10.12) and I thanked

them . . . cause they'd gone to so much trouble . . . (10.13) so I got them again the next night [laughs] . . . the next night [laughs] . . . and every night I was the-ere [another speaker says: you had purple grapes] . . . (10.14) there were these grapes yeah [another portion omitted] . . . (10.15) and every morning [another speaker says: you got . . .] (10.16) for the rest of my stay [laughs] . . . (10.17) no matter what time I got up . . . (10.18) there were eggs sitting on the table for me . . . scrambled . . . scrambled . . . (10.19) [another speaker says: do you like scrambled eggs?] (10.20) no I hate 'em [laughs]

Contrast (10) with the written account (from Tannen, 1979b, numbering added):

(11.1) While staying with a family on the island of Crete, (11.2) I found that no matter how early I awoke, (11.3) my hostess managed to have a plate of scrambled eggs sitting on the table for me (11.4) by the time I was up and dressed. (11.5) And at dinner every evening, (11.6) dessert included a pile of purple seeded grapes. (11.7) Now I don't happen to like seeded grapes or scrambled eggs, (11.8) but I had to eat them both (11.9) because they had been set out—(11.10) at great inconvenience to my hosts—(11.11) especially for me.

Chomsky's (1965, p. 4) disdain of "observed use of language" can be readily appreciated from sample (10): It appears as if casual English conversation is not composed of well-formed sentences with recognizable boundaries. The question is whether we have any grounds for postulating that all the utterances in samples like (10)—which is typical of all the data I can gather—are somehow derived from underlying well-formed sentences (suggested by Brown, 1973, p. 209). Linguists and psycholinguists routinely assume that such is the case and do not deem it worthwhile to gather solid evidence. However, some evidence is available that people have substantial difficulty recognizing sentence boundaries of recorded speech (Broen, 1971, Note 2); and in deciding what underlying sentences should be assumed for many texts (Beaugrande, 1980a, p. 58). Thus, sentencehood should be regarded, pending evidence to the contrary, as a useful heuristic for language formatting, but certainly not as the most basic notion of "competence" (cf. O'Connell, 1977).

Using parallel samples like (10) and (11), I have tried to factor out the effects of speech production conditions that are disadvantageous for the inexperienced writer, hoping to identify specific areas for training in the classroom. These factors fall into three major classes: (*a*) bridging over moments where some stage of the production processes is still running and holding up the rest; (*b*) inconsistencies arising from sudden decisions whose effects do not exactly fit the current point of the discourse stream; and (*c*) redundancies arising from trying to keep needed items in working storage for further treatment. The processing load upon speaking is relaxed somewhat in that spelling and punctuation are not required, whereas pronunciation and intonation are generally managed by well-practiced habits.

The following speech characteristics would be damaging if incorporated directly into writing:

Fillers

Fillers maintain or support continuity without conveying useful or informative content. Some important types are: **non-words** that simply keep the stream of sound going, for example, *um* (10.1, 2, 5); **feedback signals** that reassure the speaker of the audience's continuing attention and understanding, for instance, *you know* (10.2, 4); and **connectors** marking the speaker's intent to keep talking, for example, *and* (10.2, 5, 8, 10, 11, 12, 15). I use the term "filler" because the other functions of these types seems less essential than their use in keeping the speaking turn, so that other participants will not cut in—what Harvey Sacks (cited in Coulthard, 1977, p. 57) calls "utterance incompletors." The feedback signal *you know* is not normally designed as an express question asking if the audience knows, nor as an assertion to that effect. Hence, when our speaker really needs to probe background knowledge, she says *you heard the story when I told the thing* (10.6). Similarly, the connector *and* is not essential, because it serves to signal **additive** relationships among stretches of discourse; and addition is the default anyway (Beaugrande, 1980a, p. 160). Nothing would be lost by deleting these numerous *ands* that introduce so many stretches in our sample. [12]

Lexical Variants

Lexical variants are words or word forms more characteristic of speaking than of writing, for example, *yeah* (10.14) and *cause* (10.8, 12) for *because*. The form *yeah* allows the speaker to lengthen the vowel and lend it a variety of intonation curves, so that different modes of agreement (e. g., emphatic, reserved, skeptical, hesitant, sarcastic) can be signaled—an instance where goals from the planning stage emerge in the surface text without passing through any stages related to semantics or syntax. The form *cause* seems to obey Zipf's (1935) law that frequent words tend to be short; a common conceptual signal (at least in English), namely causality, has lost a syllable. In the written version, we of course find *because* (11.9) in the same context as that of (10.12).

Though these lexical variants might be treated as examples of dialect interference (see Hartwell's [1980] review essay), they seem better understood as rooted in production conditions than in alternative linguistic codes. That is, these problems reflect what Hartwell calls "an imperfectly developed neural coding system, . . . a layered set of cognitive abilities,

---

[12]The usage *his parents and George and me* (10.4) is also conversational; in writing, there should be only one *and* to announce the final member of a list, whereas the speaker may not foresee the end of the list in time.

stretching from matters of surface detail to abstract expectations and strategies for processing print as reader and writer [1980, p. 109]."

Simple Restarts

Simple restarts are found where one or more initial elements are uttered by way of introducing a phrase, and then re–uttered when the whole phrase is run as a unit, for example, *his his parents* (10.4) or *you you heard* (10.6). Maclay and Osgood found that restarts typically (89% in their study) involve the repetition of function words (articles, prepositions, conjunctions, and pronouns) such as *his* and *you* in my examples. Such findings suggest the usefulness of phrase units, along the lines of operational syntax suggested in the section, "An Outline Model and Some Specializations": production operations characteristically output a phrasal load in a single pass. The repetition of the content word *scrambled* (10.18), on the other hand, does not lead to any new phrase, though it may be emphatic. The tape indicates that the intonation curve was revised the second time to show the end of an utterance.

Revised Restarts

Revised restarts occur when one or more initially produced items is replaced or altered, and the phrase then goes on. In sample (10), we have only the restart in the loosely–knit appositive phrase *all of them . . . all of us* (10.4) that specifies *we* and is in turn further specified by a listing (*his parents . . . a-and . . . George and me*). In another study (Beaugrande, 1982b), I note such cases as *I found there was . . . I could not slip it off.* Maclay and Osgood (1959) reported that most such corrections affect content words rather than function words; if the latter were involved, the speaker usually did not restart the whole phrase. My own findings does not bear these results out in any comparable proportions. Indeed, a sequence such as *all of them . . . us* hardly seems plausible.

An interesting borderline case is present in *we were sitting around you know . . . we were sitting around the dinner table* (10.2–10.3). It could be a simple restart, interrupted with a filler; or it could be a revised restart in which *sitting around* has its own designation (i. e., *relaxing, doing nothing*) and *sitting around the dinner table* is a different kind of action. Quite possibly, the speaker herself remained undecided between these two intentions as the direction of the discourse only gradually took on distinctness.

Shifts

The term **shifts** can designate cases where the phrasing takes a new direction without any restarts. This category is also not clearly represented here; in my previous study, an illustration was *I started by . . . took off the air filter.* According to Maclay and Osgood, these occurrences should usually affect content words but they observed a preponderance of restarts.

Post-completions

Post-completions form an intriguing class of occurrences where the speaker discovers after finishing the phrase that some items have been left out and proceeds to supply them. In our sample, post completion affects modifiers: a single modifier in *there were these eggs sitting on the table for me . . . scrambled* (10.19), and a whole string in *they brought out this big plate of grapes . . . these big purple* (10.5). The latter blends with a revised restart or a reusage through *this –these* and *big –big,* though the reference is different. Notice that we could normalize (10.19) by moving the modifier in front of its head *eggs,* but that the same procedures would yield the oddly repetitive phrasing *this big plate of these big purple grapes* for (10.5). If another phrase intervenes, the speaker might tend to perform post–completion with complete phrases, since the the previous structure would normally have decayed from working storage (cf. "Further Directions," pp. 253–259). For example, our speaker wants to modify *grapes* still further to explain her dislike; following the intervening phrase of (10.8), she prefers to say *they were purple ones with seeds in them* (10.9) rather than a version without placeholders like *purple with seeds.* Rather oddly, studies of pronouns within linguistic grammar (e.g., Postal, 1968) seldom appeal to memory limitations. Note also that the version *purple with seeds* could be ambiguous, describing either the *grapes she liked* (most recent previous phrase) or the *grapes they brought* (the intended antecedent, but appearing at considerable distance).

Though post–completions may seem awkward, they could offer a peculiar advantage. It has often been remarked that the final stretch of English clauses is a good slot for placing material in the focus of attention (e.g., Chafe, 1970; Firbas, 1964; Halliday, 1967–1968). Perhaps post-completion is a handy device in spontaneous speech for getting modifiers to the end of an utterance and thereby drawing attention to them. In our examples here, the modifiers are certainly important as explanations of the speaker's discomfort. Also, it seems odd that such important content would not have been available for uttering at the grammatically appropriate moment before the head.

Non-agreements

Non–agreements are a familiar class of "errors" for the composition teacher, namely, inconsistencies in the grammatical inflections within subject–verb dependencies. Our sample has no instances, but less practiced speakers, especially in certain dialects, are prone to such usage, for example, *there's some bars* from Beaugrande (1982b). The most decisive mechanism here can be called **attraction:** the verb agrees with the nearest previous noun rather than with the subject. My students' papers contain such illustrations as: *In the background is two mechanics;* or *the team with the* *most goals win.* Attraction strikingly signals the tendency to build grammatical dependencies in a heavily linear series, rather than as structural derivations from some top "sentence node" being "rewritten" as "noun phrase plus verb phrase" and so on. The parsing stage of production clearly depends on the capacity of working memory and suffers disturbances either if attention is needed in another stage or if too many items must be held until a clause structure is completed. The notion of a **hold stack** in working storage might help to model the latter consideration (cf. Rumelhart, 1977, p. 131). During attraction, the order of adjacency on the stack overrides larger-scale dependencies and outputs erroneous commands to the inflectional execution programs.

Vagueness

Vagueness is tolerated in conversation because the situational setting and the paralinguistic systems (voice contours, gestures, etc.) support a reasonable degree of determinacy. Problematic usage can be handled with further explanation if the audience appears puzzled. One type of vagueness seems to ensue when the expression phase returns no clear correlate for some concept or idea. In (10.6), *the thing* is little more than a evasive place-holder for some such expression as *the incident* or *my experience.* The audience's expected prior knowledge (at least that of the addressee of *you*) will compensate.

Vagueness is also frequent in **co–reference** with **pro–forms** (cf. Beaugrande & Dressler, 1981, chap. IV). In (10.11–10.13), the third-person plural pronouns are deployed in rapid alternation for both *family* and *grapes* with no attendant announcement. The audience should simply conclude that *grapes* are more likely to be *eaten* or *gotten* for dinner, whereas a family is more likely to be *thanked* or to *go to trouble.* In writing, this kind of usage would be more noticeable and possibly construed as a sign of laziness or indifference in the writer.

Vagueness can be structural as well as semantic. It is not always clear exactly where one sentence ends and another begins. The filler-like *ands* might be taken as linking long stretches of discourse, for example, (10.1– 10.5) into lengthy compounded ("run-on") sentences. On the other hand, there are fragmentary sequences whose membership in a sentence is left undecided, for instance, in (10.4–10.7), where we may have a loose string of appositives, first for *we* and then for *plate of grapes.* The borderline between the domain of *got them again* (10.13) and *there were these grapes* (10.14) is not marked, leaving *the next night and every night I was there* hanging loosely in between. Many beginning writers do evince considerable uncertainty in recognizing and punctuating the boundaries of sentences and clauses precisely because conversation tolerates so much structural vagueness.

So far, we have considered some characteristics of speech that manifest themselves as minor disturbances of cohesion and coherence, usually in the on-line execution of the linear utterance. Evidently, there are bottlenecks in processing resource distribution now and then, notably at the boundaries of major segments like phrases, clauses, conceptual units, plan steps, and the like. The text producer is then confronted by either too few or too many options, and selections are not retained under full control. However, text receivers are seldom unduly disoriented, chiefly because they are intent on getting at the gist of the discourse and its situational relevance, both of which are processed on more powerful planes than local cohesion and coherence. Significantly, speakers often stop and "repair" their utterances (or hearers interpose a demand for repair) during a stretch of discourse that initiates a new **topic** (Schegloff, 1977 Note 3, pp. 15ff.). It would be plausible that such junctures would be especially sensitive to disturbances that would be unimportant when the topic is clearly established.

We shall now survey a class of speech characteristics whose inadequacy for written communication is due not to disturbance, but to **redundancy.** Speakers apparently attempt to keep working memory in some kind convenient order by rehearsing ongoing material of both content and expression. Since the spoken text decays rapidly, conversation contains considerable padding whose function is more to remind than to inform.

Simple Recurrence

Simple recurrences provide a direct rehearsal of previously uttered material. In (10.7), the speaker repeats what she said in (10.5) in order to proceed after a brief digression in (10.6). Restatements are also used to lend emphasis, especially when the second uttering is given a high intensity of information (cf. Beaugrande & Dressler, 1981, chap. IV; Brazil, 1975). If the repetition of *scrambled* in (10.18) were in a high key, the speaker would be stressing her indignation or repulsion.

Revised Recurrence

Revised recurrences use the same expressions, but in a slightly different parsing, for example, *it wasn't the kind that I liked* (10.8) versus *I don't like that kind* (10.10). The effects are much the same as for simple restatement, for instance, returning to the topic or showing emphasis. It would be intriguing to learn what processing differences obtain between the two kinds of restatement. On the one hand, the simple kind would be easiest to execute; on the other, the rearranged kind can fit the material to a different structural setting (see examples of "partial recurrence" in Beaugrande & Dressler, 1981, chap. IV). For instance, the rearrangement *they were purple ones* brings the attribute *purple* in a prominent predicate slot, as contrasted to the modifier sequence *these big purple* (10.9 versus 10.7).

Self-Paraphrases

Self-paraphrases rehearse the same conceptual material, but with different expressions. In (10.14), *there were these grapes* merely paraphrases what was already said by *I got them* in (10.13); in this case, another speaker had interposed a preview of what would be said, so that (10.14) also stands in a restatement relationship to that interpolation.

Reusages

Reusages can designate the return of the same expressions for different content (e.g. with different reference). For example, the *grapes* of (10.8) are of a kind the speaker *likes,* not the *purple ones* of (10.9); the *grapes* of (10.14) are purple, but not identical with those eaten the first night. Similarly, the reference of the three reusages of *night* in (10.13) is distinct each time. If we postulate that production involves a mapping of content onto form, then the implications of reusage are not the same as for restatement or paraphrase; but all these occurrences no doubt profit from similar strategies to reduce the load on processes of memory, expression, parsing, and articulation, at least in comparison to a constant presentation of new content in new form.

Needless Wordage

Needless wordage is common in conversational speech, though sample (10) has no unequivocal illustrations. Some illustrations from my other data include the expansion of statements like *X is Y* into ones like *X is kind of–sort of–pretty much–basically–just about Y;* or *X did Y* into *X started to–began to do Y.* Such usage is akin to fillers in adding little to the content, particularly when deployed in virtually every statement. The speaker gains time while uttering heavily habituated modifiers whose function is at most one of hedging: If a statement elicits objections, one can fall back on reservations such as *sort of* or *started to* as limitations on the force of an assertion (*X isn't really Y, just sort of; X didn't really do Y, but merely started;* etc.). Otherwise, many needless word sequences seem to serve only to consume space or time while decisions are being made. A case in point is my students' fondness for formats such as *This X is one that is Y* rather than *This X is Y;* or *There are many W who do Z* rather than *Many W do Z;* and numerous comparable formats. The linkage of the major concepts (X to Y or W to Z) is thereby circuitously expressed.

Proficiency Measures and Revision Strategies

The simplest hypothesis would be that basic writers simply commit to paper the identical language that they would produce in the casual conversational style they know best. In practice, this direct transfer is rather exceptional and sometimes barely feasible. Instead, most papers from basic writers are situated along a gradation between the poles represented by samples (10) and (11). I have found that my factoring of speech characteristics as outlined in the section, "Speech Characteristics," offers two advantages. First, I can construct an individual proficiency profile for each student based on the extent to which his or her writing reveals these characteristics, whereas the traditional measures (e.g., "error" tabulation or "wholistic grading") often suppress or overlook the cognitive operations underlying text production. Second, I obtain a reasonably detailed starting point from whence the student's training program can commence—the student's "actual here-and-now behavior" (to borrow Zoellner's phrase)—whereas traditional instruction routinely held forth remote ideals many learners at once concluded to be unattainable.

For the basic writer, success depends crucially on being able to factor out one's own problems until they become obvious and tractable, according to the technique of solving problems by decomposing them into sub-problems (Newell & Simon, 1972). The leap from speech habits to writing habits is not usually navigable any other way. I have accordingly been developing classroom programs whose major principle is **selective focus:** suspending other considerations until the learners gain confidence regarding one major problem. I have found it expedient to begin with tests where the planning and ideation stages are relaxed, for example, having students describe a visual scene or narrate events presented through picture sequences or short silent films. The next step is oral presentation of a text to be retold with whatever embellishments or changes the writers care to make. As prose learning research attests (cf. Beaugrande, 1981a; Meyer, 1979b) the danger that students will merely parrot back the exact words they heard is not acute. Instead, a gist is formed during the presentation and utilized later as a partial (but by no means complete or definitive) outline. The shift from a visual to a verbal presentation has interesting implications in view of recent speculations on the interaction of language and vision (cf. Minsky, 1975; Paivio, 1975; Waltz, 1978). For one thing, my students evince striking personal variations in the situations or event sequences they envision from my presented text.

A further step is to negotiate with each student a topic about which he or she possesses a reasonable expertise: notably hobbies, sports, recent experiences, major field of study, or professional employment. The usual plan is to assume a naive, uninformed audience who must be told how to play a game, build an apparatus, carry out a job, etc., in a clear fashion. By grounding the content in a prior domain of knowledge, basic writers are less beset by difficulties of anxiety and low motivation than when a topic is dictated from outside. Many of my students undergo substantial surprise at the discoveries that (contrary to what their high school teachers told them) they do have something to say after all, and that writing does help to get it set down.

Proceeding through this gradual progression, I obtain a spectrum of samples from each student, most of them indicative of at least some speech characteristics. During classroom meetings or on home assignments, specific revision strategies are practised upon representative illustrations culled from student papers of past courses. I have essayed to organize these exercises in such a way as to reflect the essential differences between samples like (10) and (11). Let us suppose for the sake of demonstration that (11) was not composed directly from knowledge store, but obtained by revising (10). The following tasks would be required:

Simple Deletion

Simple deletion would remove fillers, the first run of restarts, the more obvious restatements of self-paraphrases, and the needless words. In (11), *um* and *you know* disappear, whereas of the seven utterance-linking *ands* of (10), only one remains (11.5): precisely at a strategic point for signaling that the next episode is prefigured by the foregoing one. No restarts such as *his his parents* (10.4) are seen in (11). The restatements involving *grapes* (10.5–10.9), *not liking* (10.8, 10), *night* (10.13), or *scrambled* (10.18) have no counterparts in the written version. However, *happen to like* (11.7) is a mild case of needless words as contrasted with *like*.

Rearrangement

Rearrangement would apply to both small-scale and large-scale cases where material was not presented at the most strategic juncture. A significant contrast between (10) and (11) is that the episodes have been reordered to match their chronological sequence in the day, with breakfast before dinner. This tendency belongs to what we could call "normal ordering strategies," the preference for utilizing real-world organization in arranging discourse (Beaugrande, 1980a, pp. 114ff.).[13]

On a smaller scale, rearrangement picks up post–completions and any elements left stranded by deletion. Thus, we have *a plate of scrambled eggs sitting on the table for me* (11.3) rather than *there were eggs sitting on the table for me scrambled* (10.18). The sequence *this big plate of grapes these big purple . . . they were purple ones with seeds in them* (10.5–10.9) corresponds to merely *a pile of purple seeded grapes* (11.6).

Consolidation

Consolidation compacts the extent of surface expressions deployed to convey content from the ideation and development stages of text production. Interactions with deletion and rearrangement are commonplace, but

---

[13]To gain support for his independent syntax, Chomsky (1965, pp. 6ff.) attacks Diderot's highly vulnerable arguments about "a 'natural order of thoughts' that is mirrored by the order of words." However, the correlations are certainly not randon, as shown by a rich experimental literature (cf. Clark & Clark, 1977).

the focus here is on retaining the content while streamlining the text. The entire sequence *we were sitting around the dinner table . . . they brought out . . . so I got them again the next night the next night and every night that I was the-ere* (10.3, 10.5, 10.13) is now compacted to *at dinner every evening, dessert included* (11.5–11.6). Notice how consolidation reaches to very scattered points of the original spoken version, presumably because the writer has a more powerful perspective on the large-scale organization of ideas. We have just one clause for *I don't happen to like seeded grapes or scrambled eggs* (11.7), whereas the spoken text contains *it wasn't the kind of grapes that I liked they were purple ones with seeds in them and I don't like that kind . . . there were eggs sitting on the table for me scrambled . . . scrambled . . . I hate 'em* (10.7–10.10, 10.18–10.20).

The striking role of consolidation in our demonstration is due to the close organizational resemblance between the two experiences with grapes and eggs, respectively. Free from the demands for continuous flow of discourse in a tightly interactive situation, the writer makes skillful use of parallel aspects, for example, the *not liking* but *having to eat* both foods out of respect for the *hosts' inconvenience* (11.7–11.10). The ability to detect and exploit such commonalities, rather than treating each instance as peculiar only unto itself, is essential for powerful communicative strategies.

Moreover, consolidation should apply also to surface structuration. Version (11) has only three well-integrated sentences, as contrasted with the numerous, loosely-knit clauses and phrases of (10). If, as many researchers claim (cf. literature cited in regard to "post-completion"), the latter stretch of a sentence is expected to contain important information, a writer should be extremely cautious about the number and arrangement of sentences. A lot of short sentences will dilute the audience's focus across many slots whose content is not really so crucial. For example, we find frequent subject–verb dependencies in version (10) that contribute little and in fact have no correlates in (11): *I was staying* (10.1), *we were sitting* (10.2, 3), *they brought out* (10.5), *I said* (10.8), *it wasn't* (10.8), *they'd gone* (10.12), *I got* (10.13), and *I was* (10.13). Whatever is preserved of the content underlying these dependencies now appears in modifiers: *while staying* (11.1) versus *I was staying* (10.1); *at dinner* (11.5) versus *we were sitting around the dinner table* (10.3); *every evening* (11.5) versus *every night that I was there* (10.13); *purple seeded grapes* (11.6) versus *they were purple ones with seeds in them* (10.9); and *at great inconvenience to my hosts* (11.10) versus *cause they'd gone to so much trouble* (10.12). The clause-final material of (11) thereby springs into more prominent focus: *a plate of scrambled eggs* (11.3), *a pile of purple seeded grapes* (11.6), and *eat them both* (11.8) all occupy predicates with direct–object constructions, where their importance for the narrative is well brought out. Here, we see the most essential motivation for using "sentence-combining" when a series of short sentences (or clauses) spreads audience attention unduly thin; but occasions also arise where new, unexpected, or momentous content should be presented in small steps, justifying short simple sentences over long complex ones.

Differentiation

Differentiation is a tendency opposed to those we have observed so far: it routinely adds or expands rather than removes or compacts. The spoken version only reports: *no matter what time I got up* (10.17). The written version differentiates between *no matter how early I awoke* (11.3) and *by the time I was up and dressed* (11.4); apparently, the intervening time, during which the hostess was speedily preparing the eggs, has been recognized as an essential aspect. The motives might be the same for distinguishing *up and dressed* (11.4) as compared to *up* (10.17)—the hostess heard the *getting up* and carried out her task during the *dressing*.

Although she took advantage of shared material in the two episodes (already noted above), the writer makes a difference between *a plate of scrambled eggs* (11.3) and *a pile of purple seeded grapes* (11.6); in the spoken version the *grapes* were on a *plate* (10.5) and the *eggs* merely *on the table* (10.18). Several motives could apply here. The written version may be intended to respect the distinct shapes of the two comestibles, one lying flat and the other in a heap. Or the introduction of *eggs* in a context where dining has not yet been mentioned (in contrast to the spoken text) would encourage a reference to a *plate*.

Finally, the permanence of the written text makes it advantageous to vary surface expressions for the same content, lest informativity sink and interest be lost. "Elegant variation" was Fowler's famous term. In (11), it would be unwise to simply re-use a stretch of (11.3) in (11.6), for example, *my hostess managed to have a pile of purple seeded grapes sitting on the table for me*. Conceivably, the differentiation of *plate* versus *pile* may also be due to such variation.

Specification

Specification is a tendency related to differentiation, involving an account of useful details that, in speech, might be taken for granted. In (10), vague reference is made to *George's family, his parents,* and *they–them* (10.1, 10.4, 10.5, 10.12) as the agents responsible for the offering of the foods. In (11), the agent is specified to be *my hostess* (11.3) for the egg episode; in (10.18), the *eggs* were simply *sitting* there and agency was taken for granted. The further details of the offering are indicated by *managed*, that is, *prevailed in the face of difficulties*. The writer's obligation to be polite is brought to the fore by specifying how it had all been done *especially for me* (11.11).

Differentiation and specification overlap to some extent, depending on what we construe to be members of a class or constituents of a situation or event, and so on. The same two processes apply to surface structuring as well. For instance, most conceptual relations among the content of clauses are levelled in (10) by the routine, filler-like use of *and* (cf. "Speech Characteristics" on fillers). There were only two markers or causality, *cause* (10.8, 10.12) and *so* (10.13), both of which are typical of conversation in this usage; and only one marker of time, *when* (10.6), included in an aside to the audience. Even though the written version has far fewer clause boundaries, a greater variety of connectives helps to differentiate and specify conceptual relationships (cf. Beaugrande, 1980, pp. 159ff.). We have now only a single *and* (11.5) whose placement, as I already remarked, is strategically planned. Time relations are much clearer: The inclusion of the whole narrative sequence in a *stay with a family* is signaled by *while* (11.1). *No matter what time* (10.17) is localized in the day as *no matter how early* (11.2). The simultaneity of actions is emphasized with *by the time* (11.4).

The connective *now* (11.7) introduces a missing presupposition essential for appreciating the story: a condition prevailing at all times, but suddenly relevant here. The other connectives set up the point of the story. The *but* (11.8) announces that the writer's actions were not expected in view of her dislikes. The motivation is supplied in a clause preceded by *because* (11.9).

Parallelism

Parallelism entails reusing the same surface structuration for a new block of content. My data so far suggest that most reusage in speech is essentially of the restatement type, such that particular words and/or concepts are repeated before anything new is set forth. Basic writers also show some little resistance to parallelism. This technique apparently demands both prior training and on-line attention, especially for elaborate structures. In (10), we are not surprised that *there were eggs sitting on the table for me* (10.18) is not parallel to any structure dealing with getting grapes: *they brought out this big plate of grapes* (10.5), *I got them again* (10.13), or *there were these grapes yeah* (10.14). In (11), the food items are both expressed in direct object slots (a good focus position, as was noted above) and within parallel phrases: *a plate of scrambled eggs* and *a pile of purple seeded grapes* (11.3, 11.6) (also discussed above). Compare the fully nonparallel phrasings of *this plate of grapes these big purple* and *eggs sitting on the table for me scrambled* (10.5, 10.18).

Generalized Perspective

Generalized perspective is a possible designation for the tendency of writing to move back from the immediate experiential flow, that is, from the momentary impressions of the text producer at the time of the narrated happenings. We step onto the scene of *staying with a family* and of *sitting around the dinner table*; the enumeration of the people present (*parents, George, me*) is reminiscent of being there sweeping the group with a moving gaze (10.1–10.4). The entire scene is recounted in terms of what happened that particular night; only in retrospect do we learn that the same events devolved *every night I was there* (10.13). In the written version, we are alerted right away that the grapes were *included* (and eaten despite the narrator's dislike) *at dinner every evening* (11.5); we are given no direct entry onto any individual scene.

I doubt that the gradation at stake here should be identified with that of concreteness of speech versus abstractness of writing. Both samples seem to be quite concrete even though shared materials in the episodes are better exploited in writing. More likely, the production conditions of speech influence the producer's perspective in the direction of steady, small-range flow, and away from time-independent classifications and consolidations. Basic writers certanly suffer from uncertainties about the most advantageous points for introducing details, and about the appropriate extent of specialization. In a story such as (10), the enumeration of people *sitting around the dinner table* is not essential for the point of the story, and details of this kind creep into many freshman papers.

Further Directions

In the second week of an experimental writing course, I gave my basic learners this assignment:

Imagine you were staying with a family in a foreign country, and after dinner one night they brought out a big plate of purple grapes with seeds. You didn't like that kind, but you felt you had to eat them anyway because your hosts had gone to a lot of trouble to get them for you. Now imagine you also got scrambled eggs for breakfast, which you didn't like either. You tried getting up earlier in the morning, but no matter how early you got up, you'd find the scrambled eggs waiting for you.

I concluded by saying, "Now tell the story back to me." I gave no further details about content, length, or amount of incidents. The assignment was due a week later.

I correctly predicted that no student would be able to tell me the story back in my own words, but that the individual stories would vary in diverse and revealing ways. I designed a **story schema** with two parallel episodes (Figure 9.3) to serve as the global organizational framework all of the stories should share. I also tried to predict the slots where details would most often be supplied, thus arriving at Figure 9.4: name of country and family, feelings of the narrator, and so on. If stories center around problem solving (Beaugrand & Colby, 1979; Meehan, 1976; Rumelhart & Ortony, 1977), narrators might envision plans for escaping the act of eating the disfavored foods.

Of the 19 stories I obtained, only 3 followed the assignment rather closely, omitting and adding little. All the rest offered substantial changes or embellishments, most often regarding the slots stipulated in Figure 9.4.

STORY SCHEMA

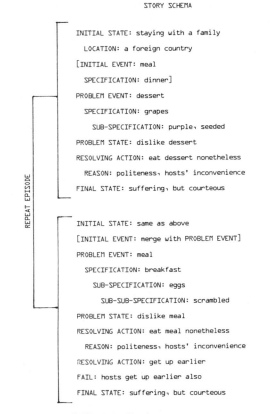

FIGURE 9.3. The basic story.

For example, the country was stipulated as Germany and Italy by 3 students apiece, and Mexico, Czechoslovakia, Spain, England, France, Sweden, and "Fantasy Island" (the last from the television show) each figured in one paper. Another addition was the reason for being away from home (important for young learners just now leaving their families for college). Five narrators were *exchange students;* one attended *college;* one visited *relatives,* and one *old friends;* and two were simply *on vacation.*

The original story has fuzzy boundaries: It jumps into the middle of a *stay in a foreign country* and ends with the narrator suffering from reluctant eating. Most student stories also started off with little introduction, for example: *Here I am, a guest in a foreign land; I am staying in France; While on summer vacation in Czechoslovakia;* or *I am an American living in Europe with a problem.* Some opened with a time indicator: *Years ago, Last year, Three weeks ago,* etc. Interestingly enough, three narrators chose the start of the day as content for their opening sentences: *My famous trip starts early one morning;*

The early morning light peered its way through the venetian blinds; and *I awoke at 7:00 on July 2.* The tendency to follow normal temporal ordering in a narrative was already cited in the discussion of "rearrangement."

On the other hand, the students felt the need for a more conclusive, obvious ending. Only five left the protagonist stuck in the unresolved problem state, for instance, *grinning and bearing it* or *getting up earlier and earlier.* Two learned to like the foods after all, and one *became a better person* by suffering for the sake of other people's feelings, but these were exceptional. Six narrators resolved to enlighten their hosts, though only two actually got around to it, and one of them was hit with a skillet by a morbidly sensitive housewife. Two fabricated an allergy to eggs, one accompanied by skin rash, the other by violent sneezing (that *blew the eggs right off the table*). Less effective (because temporary) solutions included secretly disposing of the foods in a napkin, or claiming to be too rushed to eat. More drastic ones included trying to assassinate the chicken and going beserk enough to be incarcerated in a padded cell, drawing pictures of grapes and eggs for 10 years.

The **turning points** of stories (events deciding whether the resolution will be positive or negative) are often embellished with **evaluations** and

BASIC STORY SCHEMA	OPTIONAL SLOTS
INITIAL STATE: staying with a family	SPECIFICATION: name of family
LOCATION FOREIGN COUNTRY	SPECIFICATION: name of country
	REASON: why narrator is abroad
[INITIAL EVENT: meal	SPECIFICATION: what was served
SPECIFICATION: dinner]	REACTION: how the narrator liked it
PROBLEM EVENT: dessert	NIL
SPECIFICATION: grapes	NIL
SUB-SPECIFICATION: purple, seeded	NIL
PROBLEM STATE: dislike dessert	REASON: why disliked
RESOLVING ACTION: eat dessert nonetheless	SPECIFICATION and REACTION: how eaten, results
REASON: politeness, host's inconvenience	SPECIFICATION: how politeness manifested
	OTHER RESOLVING ACTIONS: complain, escape, etc.
FINAL STATE: suffering, but courteous	SPECIFICATION: how suffered
INITIAL STATE: same as above	INITIAL ACTION: get up and dressed
[INITIAL EVENT: merge with PROBLEM EVENT]	
PROBLEM EVENT: meal	NIL
SPECIFICATION: breakfast	NIL
SUB-SPECIFICATION: eggs	SUB-SPECIFICATION: other items as well
SUB-SUB-SPECIFICATION: scrambled	NIL
PROBLEM STATE: dislike meal	REACTION: why disliked
RESOLVING ACTION: eat meal nonetheless	SPECIFICATION AND REACTION: how eaten, results
REASON: politeness, hosts' inconvenience	SPECIFICATION: how politeness manifested
RESOLVING ACTION: get up earlier	OTHER RESOLVING ACTIONS: complain, escape, etc.
FAIL: hosts also get up earlier	OTHER FAILURES
FINAL STATE: suffering, but courteous	SPECIFICATION: how suffered
	REACTIONS: conclusions drawn from the experience

(REPEAT EPISODE — bracket spanning both episode blocks at left margin)

FIGURE 9.4. Story schema with optional slots.

motivational statements (cf. Labov & Waletzky, 1967; Beaugrande & Colby, 1979). In my student's stories, the moment of anguish was of course the eating: an *agony, ordeal, onslaught,* or *nightmare,* endured in the face of *aversion, heartburn, nauseousness,* and *a turned stomach.* All the while, the protagonists revelled in a show of hypocrisy: they *heartily, smilingly,* and *greatfully downed the mess, pretending to enjoy it.* Their motivations were often adduced: not *hurting feelings* (three stories), *not having the heart to protest* (two stories), *wanting to cause the least amount of trouble* (one story), and so on; five stories praised their narrator's own *politeness.* On occasion, the well-meaning but deluded hosts were also given motivations, for example, believing that the foods in question were dear to Americans (4 stories).

While these broad narrative lines were fairly consistent in all stories, there was a wide spread in the extent to which the speech characteristics depicted on pp. 240–247 were present in individual cases. I was thereby able to draw personal proficiency measurements that correlated well with the student's level of skills revealed throughout the course. The traits of writing suggested on pp. 247–253 also yielded a positive scale, for instance, consolidation, differentiation, parallelism, and generalized perspective. For example, some students exploited the structural similarity of the two episodes, though less skillfully than version (11).[14]

The preponderance of the diverse speech characteristics was quite varied. Restarts and post–completions were extremely rare, at least in their pure form.[15] In writing, restarts appear more usually as appositives, for example:

(12)   *Snacks are always ready when I want them. They, the family that I live with,* [. . .]

where misleading reference was corrected. Postcompletions can yield follow-up sentences:

(13)   *The grapes weren't the worst part of it. No, it was the scrambled eggs.*

Fillers, shifts, and nonagreements were more common. Fillers included *well, now,* and *you see.* Shifts revealed some bizarre structural mixtures, for example:

(14)   *They had gone out to great expense and effort and purchased a large supply.*

---

[14]Lexical variants are not considered here, since the narrative was given in an essentially informal style to begin with.

[15]However, student papers often contain later insertions, arrows, and strikeovers that signal the same mechanism. The writer can always suppress or alter restarts and post–completion by copying over, so the data are not reliable unless the act of writing is carefully observed throughout.

(15)   *Jerry had really nice parents and were very hospitable.*

The notorious dangling modifier is a type of shift:

(16)   *Being very pleased with themselves for obtaining these things, all I felt I could do was close my eyes and eat.*

Shifts in content can disrupt a chain of causality:

(17)   *It is considered not polite to refuse their hospitality. And if you do refuse, they consider that an insult. They then interpret it that if you eat as much as you do, you must enjoy it, so they increase the portions.*

Nonagreements appear not only in combining singulars and plurals (cf. examples on pp. 244–245), but also in confusing subject and object pronouns:

(18)   *They gathered around and handed me grapes, which me not really liking, accepted.*

Perhaps the *me* has been attracted into the object form via proximity to *which.*

By far the most frequent difficulties were vagueness, restatements of all kinds, reusages, and needless wordage. Vagueness of pronoun reference was rife:

(19)   *These people were so very hospitable I had to eat them.*

Vague notions about sentence boundaries engender the well-known "comma splice" (19) and the "sentence fragment" (20):

(20)   *They feed me a "american breakfast" scrambled eggs, I hate eggs.*
(21)   *I'm trying to avoid another scrambled egg breakfast. Basically, because I hate them.*

Such cases could well be treated by informal sentence-combining for consolidation, rather than just changing punctuation marks. In the domain of content, vagueness can create unintentionally comic ambiguities:

(22)   *That first night was a pleasant one filled with meeting new people.*

Though composition handbooks (e.g., Gula, 1980) dwell almost entirely on these structural disturbances,[16] redundancies are, in my own experience, a most prevalent and serious matter in basic writing. We noted that restarts and post–completions appear in writing as redundancies such as

[16]Of his 36 chapters, Gula devotes 15 to grammatical structures and 21 to punctuation and mechanics. Redundancies figure only very marginally on pp. 108–110, where we are told: "try to avoid a series of similar sounding sentences"; "don't use language that is unnecessarily complex"; and "don't use unnecessary words." Each precept is accompanied by two examples that do NOT resemble what I would consider spontaneous student writing.

(12) and (13). Restatements can be distressing obstacles to progress through the line of a narrative or a description, for instance:

(23)   *To cause the least amount of trouble, you eat the eggs; even though you don't like them. Throughout the week, you continue to eat the eggs. Even if you attempt to avoid eating the eggs by awaking one hour earlier, they insist on preparing the eggs.*

No less tedious are reusages, for instance that of *consider* in (17), and needless wordage cropping up in passages like:

(24)   *My famous trip startes out by early one morning I moved into a strange house. The reason for it being strange is because I am from a foreign country.*

Similarly, the lack of generalized perspective leads to unduly detailed sequences with many irrelevant incidents:

(25)   *At the conclusion of the meal, grapes were presented. I rose and proceeded to leave the room. When questioned, I made an idle excuse that I could not eat them because of their cost. The hostess insisted I eat them. I told her I did not care for the taste of grapes. She understood my opinion. I went to my room.*

Following the proportions of these difficulties, I instituted revision training. At first, each aspect (such as shifts and needless wordage) was subjected to intensive single scrutiny until learners were fairly capable of recognizing and revising it through techniques outlined in "Proficiency Measures and Revision." Gradually, several aspects were gathered into single exercises, until, toward the end of the course, test samples are presented with all representative difficulties. I list the presentation and two student revisions (both from writers who began the course in a mode close to my presented test) in the Appendix to show how basic learners can develop impressive revision skills in a short training program.

However, I must review in closing some important questions that still demand extensive future research. First, I have found a marked variance in the ability of individual students to work through only a few drafts as opposed to a great many. Even if writers must revise over and over, they eventually obtain a reasonable version; yet their abilities documented on special tests (like that in the Appendix) remain hard to apply spontaneously. We must uncover further factors beyond speech habits that impede trouble-free on-line production. Lack of confidence or interest regarding their own topics has been reported by some students whose papers vacillate so extremely.

Second, we must learn if overloads and bottlenecks are really built into human language production systems, for example, by contingencies separated in real time. Or, appropriate training might overcome or at least attenuate these degredation tendencies; if so, at what age and with what incentives can this be done? Will the danger of backsliding always persist?

Third, we must explore whether complex production strategies normally deployed automatically (or at least with little conscious focus of attention) can in fact be synthesized in the brief time span of a composition course— rather than gradually habituated during the many years of writing practice that today's students do not command. Will conscious exercises eventually affect unconscious behavior, and how reliably?

Fourth, we must determine the extent to which writing habits may be viewed as an extension or modification of speech habits. My tasks and experiments deal only with college-age learners much more skilled in speaking than writing; at this age, transfer from the one domain to the other via specific training has been shown to be feasible. But it is far from clear that the language-learning child undergoes any similar procedures of transfer; or, even if this is so, that the transfer would occur at the same level of awareness or abstraction for every individual child. The observable variations both in naturally acquired writing skills and in abilities to re- spond to classroom instruction suggest rather the opposite.

Fifth, we must learn to explain the relevant problems and solutions to a population that is extremely naive about language. On the one side, tech- nical jargon is intimidating and exacting; on the other, traditional ter- minologies are notoriously hard to convert into actions, for instance, "good style." So far, I have managed with a small set of well-defined terms like "repeated words" supported by a continual stream of examples for active revision.

The literacy crisis has been long in coming and will not evaporate quickly. But optimism may not be out of place at a time when serious research into realistic, diverse language activities is finally beginning with some directly relevant explorations.

APPENDIX

The Following Sample Was Distributed with Instructions to Revise. Time: 30 minutes

One of the many things that are hard when you leave high school and go to college is the fact that your in college not high school any more. This being a major change. Untill now they treated you like a little tiny baby and your on you're own now and you have responsibilities and you gotta be responsible about them.

For example registering. You register by going to registration at the time they give you to register. So you start to go there and there are zillions of problems and no courses anyone would want except unless their outa there mind or something, you know?

You take youre card and you write down on the card the courses you wanna take. Hoping their still open, that is. When it gets to be youre turn you give it to them and they punch it into the computer, it says it won't work. So you have to start changing it. When your done changing it it gets punched in again, it says the same thing again. Finally it turns out that you get some courses that just happen to be the ones that are open.

Now you are finished and your just started. Because now you have to try going around and add the courses you really wanted in the first place.

In conclusion let me finish by saying that's all I got to say.

The Following Are Two Revised Versions
Turned in by First-Quarter Freshmen

One difficult thing you encounter when leaving high school for college is change. You were treated like a baby, but in college you are given many new responsibilities.

A good example is being present for registration at an assigned time. There are millions of problems you must solve, and the courses offered wouldn't be wanted by the most desperate of freshmen.

You write down the courses wanted and hope they are still open. The card with your choices is given to a person who tells the computer what you picked. If the computer rejects your information, you must change your selections until the machine accepts them.

When finished with registration, all that is left to do is follow this procedure during the drop/add period to attain what you really want.

Let me finish by saying that registration is a good test of how responsible one can be.

A major change in college is knowing that you are no longer in high school and you now have responsibilities.

Registering can present many problems in course selection. You fill out a card with your desired courses. If the computer does not accept the schedual being punched in, then you make changes until you get open courses. This is just the beginning of a frustrating cycle for your desired courses.

It is a difficult proceedure.

ACKNOWLEDGMENT

I am indebted to Wallace Chafe for samples (10) and (11), and to the following students for the participation in my project: Ken Brodsky, Doyle Bush, Del Kelley, Amy Shaff, Nadine Schochet, Michael Weiss, Stacey Wenzel, and Sandra Whitehead.

REFERENCE NOTES

1. Chafe, W. *Spoken and written language.* Paper presented at the Second Congress of the Internation Association for Semiotics, Vienna, 1979.
2. Broen, P. *A discussion of the linguistic environment of the young language-learning child.* Paper presented at the American Speech and Hearing Convention, Chicago, 1971.
3. Schegloff, E. *Six themes on a conversational variation of "syntax and discourse": The case—uh,*

some aspects of same-turn repair. Paper presented at the Conference on Syntax and Discourse, Los Angeles, 1977.

REFERENCES

Allen, J. *A plan-based approach to speech-act recognition.* Toronto: University of Toronto Computer Sciences Technical Report 139/79, 1979.

Anderson, R. The notion of schemata and the educational enterprise. In R. Anderson, R. Spiro, & W. Montague (Eds.), *Schooling and the acquisition of knowledge.* Hillsdale, N.J.: Lawrence Erlbaum, 1977. Pp. 415–431.

Anderson, R., Spiro, R., & Montague, W. (Eds.) *Schooling and the acquisition of knowledge.* Hillsdale, N.J.: Lawrence Erlbaum, 1977.

Anttila, R. Formalization as degeneration in historical linguistics. In J. M. Anderson & C. Jones (Eds.), *Historical linguistics.* Amsterdam: North-Holland, 1974. Pp. 1–32.

Applebee, A. N. *The child's concept of story: Ages two to seventeen.* Chicago: University of Chicago Press, 1978.

Bateman, D., & Zidonis, F. *The effect of a knowledge of generative grammar upon the growth of language complexity.* Columbus: The Ohio State University, 1964.

Beaugrande, R. de. Toward a general theory of creativity. *Poetics,* 1979, *8,* 269–306. (a)

Beaugrande, R. de. Moving from product toward process. *College Composition and Communication,* 1979, *30,* 357–363. (b)

Beaugrande, R. de. Theoretical foundations for the automatic production and processing of technical reports. *Journal of Technical Writing and Communication,* 1979, *9,* 239–268. (c)

Beaugrande, R. de. *Text, discourse, and process.* Norwood, N.J.: Ablex, 1980.

Beaugrande, R. de. Design criteria for process models of reading. *Reading Research Quarterly,* 1981, *16,* 261–315. (a)

Beaugrande, R. de. Linguistic theory and meta-theory for a science of texts. *Text,* 1981, *1,* 113–160.

Beaugrande, R. de. *Text production: Toward a science of composition.* Norwood, N.J.: Ablex, 1982. (a)

Beaugrande, R. de. Cognitive processes and technical writing: Developmental foundations. *Journal of Technical Writing and Communication,* 1982, 12. (b)

Beaugrande, R. de. Linguistic and cognitive processes in developmental writing. *International Review of Applied Linguistics,* 1982. (c)

Beaugrande, R. de & Colby, B. N. Narrative models of action and interaction. *Cognitive Science,* 1979, *3,* 43–66.

Beaugrande, R. de., & Dressler, W. *Introduction to text linguistics.* London: Longman, 1981.

Bierwisch, M. Strukturalismus: Geschichte, Probleme und Methoden. *Kursbuch,* 1966, *5,* 77–152.

Bloomfield, L. *Language.* New York: Holt, 1933.

Boomer, D. S. Hesitation and grammatical encoding. *Language and Speech,* 1965, *8,* 148–158.

Boomer, D. S., & Laver, J. D. Slips of the tongue. *British Journal of Disorders of Communication,* 1968, *3,* 2–11.

Boyle, C. G. On "talk–write." *College English,* 1969, *30,* 648–652.

Brachman, R. *A structural paradigm for representing knowledge.* Cambridge: Bolt, Beranek, & Newman Technical Report 3605, 1978.

Brazil, D. *Discourse intonation.* Birmingham: English Language Research, 1975.

Brown, R. *A first language.* Cambridge: Harvard, 1973.

Bruce, B., Collins, A., Rubin, R., & Gentner, D. *A cognitive science approach to writing.* Urbana, Ill.: ERIC Report EC 157 038, 1978.

Bruner, J., Goodnow, J., & Austin, G. *A study of thinking.* New York: Wiley, 1956.

Chafe, W. *Meaning and the structure of language.* Chicago: University of Chicago, 1970.
Chafe, W. (Ed.) *The pear stories: Cognitive, cultural, and linguistic aspects of narrative production.* Norwood, N.J.: Ablex, 1980.
Chomsky, N. *Syntactic structures.* The Hague: Mouton, 1957.
Chomsky, N. Review of *Verbal behavior,* by B. F. Skinner. *Language,* 1959, *35,* 28–58.
Chomsky, N. *Aspects of the theory of syntax.* Cambridge: M.I.T. Press, 1965.
Chomsky, N. *Cartesian linguistics.* New York: Harper and Row, 1966a.
Chomsky, N. *Topics in the theory of generative grammar.* The Hague: Mouton, 1966b.
Chomsky, N. *Studies on semantics in generative grammar.* The Hague, Mouton, 1972a.
Chomsky, N. *Language and mind.* New York: Harcourt, Brace, and Jovanovich, 1972b.
Chomsky, N. *The logical structure of linguistic theory.* New York: Plenum, 1975.
Chomsky, N. Conditions on rules of grammar. *Linguistic Analysis,* 1976, *2,* 303–351.
Christensen, F. The problem of defining a mature style. *English Journal,* 1968, *57,* 572–579.
Clark, H., & Clark, E. *Language and psychology.* New York: Harcourt Brace Jovanovich, 1977.
Cohen, P. *On knowing what to say: Planning speech acts.* Toronto: University of Toronto Computer Sciences Technical Report 118, 1978.
Coulthard, M. *An introduction to discourse analysis.* London: Longman, 1977.
Davey, A. *The formalization of discourse production.* Edinburgh: University of Edinburgh dissertation, 1974.
Deese, J. On the structure of associative meaning. *Psychological Review,* 1962, *69,* 161–175.
Deese, J. *The structure of associations in language and thought.* Baltimore: Johns Hopkins University, 1965.
Deese, J. The psychology of learning and the study of English. In C. Reed (Ed.), *The language of learning.* New York: Appleton-Century-Crofts, 1971. Pp. 157–185.
DeJong, G. *Skimming newspaper stories by computer.* New Haven: Yale Computer Science Research Report 104, 1977.
DeVito, J. A. Comprehension factors in oral and written discourse of skilled communicators. *Speech Monographs,* 1965, *32,* 124–128.
Dijk, T. van (Ed.) Special issue on story comprehension. *Poetics,* 1980, *9/1–3,* 1–332.
Dresher, E., & Hornstein, N. On some supposed contributions of artificial intelligence to the scientific study of language. *Cognition,* 1976, *4,* 321–398.
Durell, D. D. Listening comprehension versus reading comprehension. *Journal of Reading,* 1969, *12,* 455–460.
Ertel, S. Where do subjects of sentences come from? In S. Rosenberg (Ed.), *Sentence production: Developments in research and theory.* Hillsdale, N.J.: Lawrence Erlbaum, 1977. Pp. 141–167.
Ervin, S. M. Changes with age in the verbal determinants of word-association. *American Journal of Psychology,* 1961, *74,* 361–372.
Estes, W. K. Some targets for mathematical psychology. *Journal of Mathematical Psychology,* 1975, *12,* 263–282.
Estes, W. K. On the descriptive and explanatory functions of theories of memory. In L. G. Nilsson (Ed.), *Perspectives on memory research.* Hillsdale, N.J.: Lawrence Erlbaum, 1979. Pp. 35–60.
Fahlman, S. *NETL: A system for representing and using real-world knowledge.* Cambridge: M.I.T. Press, 1979.
Findler, N. V. (Ed.) *Associative networks: Representation and use of knowledge by computers.* New York: Academic Press, 1979.
Firbas, J. On defining the theme in functional sentence perspective. *Travaux linguistiques de Prague,* 1964, *1,* 267–280.
Flower, L., & Hayes, J. R. *A process model of composition.* Pittsburgh: Carnegie-Mellon Document Design Project Technical Report 1, 1979. Also in L. Gregg and E. Steinberg (Eds.), *Cognitive processes in writing.* Hillsdale, N.J.: Lawrence Erlbaum, 1980. Pp. 3–30.

Flower, L., Hayes, J. R., & Swarts, H. *Revising functional documents: The scenario principle.* Pittsburgh: Carnegie-Mellon Document Design Project Technical Report 10, 1980.

Fodor, J. Could meaning be an r_m? *Journal of Verbal Learning and Verbal Behavior,* 1965, *4,* 73–81.

Fodor, J., Bever, T., & Garrett, M. *The psychology of language.* New York: McGraw-Hill, 1974.

Freedle, R. (Ed.) *Discourse production and comprehension.* Norwood, N.J.: Ablex, 1977.

Freedle, R. (Ed.) *New directions in discourse processing.* Norwood, N.J.: Ablex, 1979.

Friedman, M., Burke, C., Cole, M., Estes, W., Keller, L., & Millward, R. Two-choice behavior under extended training with probabilities of reinforcement. In R. Atkinson (Ed.), *Studies in mathematical psychology.* Palo Alto: Stanford, 1963. Pp. 250–291.

Fromkin, V. A. The non-anomalous nature of anomalous utterances. *Language,* 1971, *47,* 27–52.

Fromkin, V. A. (Ed.) *Speech errors as linguistic evidence.* The Hague: Mouton, 1973.

Gantt, W. H. Principles of nervous breakdown—schizokinesis and autokinesis. *Annals of the New York Academy of Sciences,* 1953, *56,* 143–163.

Garrett, M. The analysis of sentence production. In G. Bower (Ed.), *Advances in learning theory and motivation.* (Vol. 9). New York: Academic Press, 1975.

Gibson, E. J. How perception really develops. In D. LaBerge & S. J. Samuels (Eds.), *Basic processes in reading: Perception and comprehension.* Hillsdale, N.J.: Lawrence Erlbaum, 1977. Pp. 155–173.

Goldman, N. Conceptual generation. In R. Schank, M. Goldman, C. Rieger, & G. Riesbeck, *Conceptual information processing,* Amsterdam: North-Holland, 1975. Pp. 289–371.

Goldman-Eisler, F. Speech analysis and mental processes. *Language and Speech,* 1958, *1,* 67–75.

Goldman-Eisler, F. Hesitation and information in speech. In C. Cherry (Ed.), *Information theory.* London: Butterworth, 1961, 162–174.

Goldman-Eisler, F. Pauses, clauses, sentences. *Language and Speech,* 1972, *15,* 103–113.

Gosnave, G. Sentence production test in sensory aphasic patients. In S. Rosenberg (Ed.), *Sentence Production: Developments in research and theory.* Hillsdale, N.J.: Lawrence Erlbaum, 1977. Pp. 37–50.

Gregg, L., & Steinberg, E. (Eds.) *Cognitive processes in writing.* Hillsdale, N.J.: Lawrence Erlbaum, 1980.

Gula, R. J. *Precision: A reference handbook for writers.* Cambridge, Mass.: Winthrop, 1980.

Halliday, M. A. K. Notes on transitivity and theme in English. *Journal of Linguistics,* 1967, *3,* 37–81 and 199–244; and 1968, *4,* 179–215.

Hanson, N. R. *Patterns of discovery.* Cambridge, England: Cambridge University Press, 1958.

Hartwell, P. Dialect interference in writing: A critical view. *Research in the Teaching of English,* 1980, *14,* 101–118.

Hirsch, E. D. *The philosophy of composition.* Chicago: University of Chicago, 1977.

Hörmann, H. *Meinen und Verstehen.* Frankfurt: Suhrkamp, 1976.

Jackendoff, R. *Semantic interpretation in generative grammar.* Cambridge: M.I.T. Press, 1972.

Jaffe, J. The biological significance of Markovian communication rhythms. In S. Rosenberg (Ed.), *Sentence production: Developments in research and theory.* Hillsdale, N.J.: Lawrence Erlbaum, 1977. Pp. 51–63.

Jarvella, R. J. From verbs to sentences: Some experimental studies of predication. In S. Rosenberg (Ed.), *Sentence production: Developments in research and theory.* Hillsdale, N.J.: Lawrence Erlbaum, 1977. Pp. 275–306.

Johnson, N. F. The influence of associations between elements of structured verbal responses. *Journal of Verbal Learning and Verbal Behavior,* 1966, *5,* 369–374.

Katz, J., & Postal, P. *An integrated theory of linguistic description.* Cambridge: M.I.T. Press, 1964.

Keller, F., & Schoenfeld, W. *Principles of psychology.* New York: Appleton-Century-Crofts, 1950.

Kempen, G. Conceptualizing and formulating in sentence production. In S. Rosenberg (Ed.),

Sentence production: Developments in research and theory. Hillsdale, N.J.: Lawrence Erlbaum, 1977. Pp. 259–274.

Kintsch, W. *Memory and cognition*. New York: Wiley, 1977.

Kintsch, W., & Vipond, D. Reading comprehension and readability in educational practice and psychological theory. In L. G. Nilsson (Ed.), *Perspectives on memory research*. Hillsdale, N.J.: Lawrence Erlbaum, 1979. Pp. 329–365.

Kuhn, T. S. *The structure of scientific revolutions*. Chicago: University of Chicago, 1970.

Labov, W., & Waletzky, J. Narrative analysis: Oral versions of personal experience. In J. Helm (Ed.), *Essays on the verbal and visual arts*. Seattle: University of Washington, 1967. Pp. 12–44.

Lackner, J. R., & Levine, K. B. Speech production: Evidence for syntactically and phonologically determined units. *Perception and Psychophysics*, 1975, *17*, 107–113.

Lashley, K. S. The problem of serial order in behavior. In L. A. Jeffress (Ed.), *Cerebral mechanisms in behavior*. New York: Wiley, 1951. Pp. 112–146.

Levelt, W. J. M. A survey of studies in sentence perception: 1970–1976. In W. J. M. Levelt & G. B. Flores d'Arcais (Eds.), *Studies in the perception of language*. New York: Wiley, 1978. Pp. 1–74.

Lounsbury, F. G. Transitional probability, linguistic structure, and systems of habit–family hierarchies. In C. E. Osgood & T. A. Sebeok (Eds.), *Psycholinguistics: A survey of theory and research problems*. Bloomington: Indiana University, 1965.

MacKay, D. G. The structure of words and syllables: Evidence from errors in speech. *Cognitive Psychology*, 1972, *3*, 210–227.

MacKay, D. G. Aspects of the syntax of behavior: Syllable structure are speech rate. *Quarterly Journal of Experimental Psychology*, 1974, *26*, 642–657.

Maclay, H., & Osgood, C. E. Hesitation phenomena in spontaneous English speech. *Word*, 1959, *15*, 19–44.

MacNeilage, P. F. Motor control of serial ordering of speech. *Psychological Review*, 1970, *77*, 182–196.

Masson, M. E. *Cognitive processes in skimming stories*. Boulder: University of Colorado Institute for the Study of Intellectual Behavior Technical Report 84-ONR, 1979.

McCalla, G. *An approach to the organization of knowledge for the modelling of conversation*. Vancouver: University of British Columbia Computer Sciences Technical Report 78-4, 1978.

McDonald, D. A simultaneously procedural and declarative data structure and its use in natural language generation. *Proceedings of the Second National Conference of the Canadian Society for Computational Studies of Intelligence*, 1978, 38–47.

McDonald, D. *Steps toward a psycholinguistic model of language production*. Cambridge: MIT Artificial Intelligence Laboratory Working Paper 193, 1979.

McGuire, R. *Political primaries and words of pain*. New Haven: Yale Computer Science Research Report, 1980.

McNeill, D. Semiotic extension. In R. L. Solso (Ed.), *Information processing and cognition*. Hillsdale, N.J.: Lawrence Erlbaum, 1975.

Meehan, J. *The metanovel: Writing stories by computer*. New Haven: Yale Computer Science Research Report 74, 1976.

Mellon, J. C. *Transformational sentence-combining: A method for enhancing the development of syntactic fluency in English composition*. Champaign, Ill.: NCTE, 1969.

Meyer, B. J. F. *Research on prose comprehension: Applications for composition teachers*. Tempe: Arizona State University Prose Learning Series Research Report 2, 1979. (a)

Meyer, B. J. F. *A selected review and discussion of basic research on prose comprehension*. Tempe: Arizona State University Prose Learning Series Research Report 4, 1979. (b)

Miller, G. A., & Johnson-Laird, P. N. *Language and perception*. Cambridge: Harvard University Press, 1976.

Minsky, M. A framework for representing knowledge. In P. Winston (Ed.), *The psychology of computer vision*. New York: McGraw-Hill, 1975. Pp. 211–277.

Minsky, M., & Papert, S. *Artificial intelligence: Condon lectures.* Eugene: Oregon State System of Higher Education, 1974.

Moffett, J. *Teaching the universe of discourse.* Boston: Houghton Mifflin, 1968.

Mowrer, O. H. The psychologist looks at language. *American Psychologist,* 1954, *9,* 660–694.

Neisser, U. *Cognition and reality.* San Francisco: Freeman, 1976.

Newell, A., & Simon, H. *Human problem solving.* Englewood Cliffs, N.J.: Prentice-Hall, 1972.

Nilsson, L. G. (Ed.) *Perspectives on memory research.* Hillsdale, N.J.: Lawrence Erlbaum, 1979.

Norman, D. A. Perception, memory, and mental processes. In L. G. Nilsson (Ed.), *Perspectives on memory research.* Hillsdale, N.J.: Lawrence Erlbaum, 1979. Pp. 121–144.

Norman, D. A., & Rumelhart, D. E. *Explorations in cognition.* San Francisco: Freeman, 1975.

Nooteboom, S. G. The tongue slips into patterns. *Leyden studies in linguistics and phonetics.* The Hague: Mouton, 1969.

O'Connell, D. C. One of many units: The sentence. In S. Rosenberg (Ed.), *Sentence production: Developments in research and theory.* Hillsdale, N.J.: Lawrence Erlbaum, 1977. Pp. 307–313.

O'Connell, D. C., Kowal, S., & Hörmann, H. Semantic determinants of pauses. *Psychologische Forschung,* 1969, *33,* 50–67.

Osgood, C. E. On understanding and creating sentences. *American Psychologist,* 1964, *18,* 735–751.

Osgood, C. E. Meaning cannot be an r_m? *Journal of Verbal Learning and Verbal Behavior,* 1966, *5,* 402–407.

Osgood, C. E. Where do sentences come from? In D. D. Steinberg & L. A. Jakobovits (Eds.), *Semantics.* London: Cambridge University Press, 1971. Pp. 497–529.

Osgood, C. E., & Bock, J. K. Salience and sentencing: Some production principles. In S. Rosenberg (Ed.), *Sentence production: Developments in research and theory.* Hillsdale, N.J.: Lawrence Erlbaum, 1977. Pp. 89–140.

Osgood, C. E., & Tannenbaum, P. H. The principle of congruity in attitude change. *Psychological Review,* 1955, *62,* 42–55.

Paivio, A. Perceptual comparisons through the mind's eye. *Memory and Cognition,* 1975, *3,* 635–647.

Perfetti, G., & Goldman, S. Discourse memory and reading comprehension skill. *Journal of Verbal Learning and Verbal Behavior,* 1976, *14,* 33–42.

Piaget, J. *The child and reality.* New York: Penguin, 1976.

Pike, K. L. Language as particle, wave, and field. *Texas Quarterly,* 1959, *2,* 37–54.

Pike, K. L. *Language in relation to a unified theory of the structure of human behavior.* The Hague: Mouton, 1967.

Postal, P. Cross-over phenomena. In W. Plath (Ed.), *Specification and utilization of a transformational grammar.* Yorktown Heights, N.Y.: Watson Research Center, 1968.

Robinson, I. *The new grammarians' funeral.* London: Cambridge University Press, 1976.

Rochester, S. R. The significance of pauses in spontaneous speech. *Journal of Psycholinguistics,* 1973, *2,* 51–81.

Rochester, S. R., Thurston, S., & Rupp, J. Hesitations as clues to failures in coherence: A study of the thought-disordered speaker. In S. Rosenberg (Ed.), *Sentence production: Developments in research and theory.* Hillsdale, N.J.: Lawrence Erlbaum, 1977. Pp. 68–87.

Rosenberg, S. Introduction and overview. In S. Rosenberg (Ed.), *Sentence production: Developments in research and theory.* Hillsdale, N.J.: Lawrence Erlbaum, 1977. Pp. 1–13. (a)

Rosenberg, S. Semantic constraints on sentence production: An experimental approach. In S. Rosenberg (Ed.), *Sentence production: Developments in research and theory.* Hillsdale, N.J.: Lawrence Erlbaum, 1977. Pp. 195–229. (b)

Rosenberg, S. (Ed.) *Sentence production: Developments in research and theory.* Hillsdale, N.J.: Lawrence Erlbaum, 1977. (c)

Rubin, A. D. A theoretical taxonomy of the differences between oral and written language. In

R. Spiro, B. Bruce, & W. Brewer (Eds.), *Theoretical issues in reading comprehension.* Hillsdale, N.J.: Lawrence Erlbaum, 1980. Pp. 411–438.

Ruddell, R. B. The effect of the similarity of oral and written patterns of language structure on reading comprehension. *Elementary English,* 1965, *42,* 403–410.

Rumelhart, D. E. *Introduction to human information processing.* New York: Wiley, 1977.

Rumelhart, D. E., & Ortony, A. The representation of knowledge in memory. In R. Anderson, R. Spiro, & W. Montague (Eds.), *Schooling and the acquisition of knowledge.* Hillsdale, N.J.: Lawrence Erlbaum, 1977. Pp. 99–135.

Schank, R., & Abelson, R. *Scripts, plans, goals, and understanding.* Hillsdale, N.J.: Lawrence Erlbaum, 1977.

Schank, R., Goldman, N., Rieger, C., & Riesbeck, C. *Conceptual information processing.* Amsterdam: North-Holland, 1975.

Schank, R., Lebowitz, M., & Birnbaum, L. *Integrated partial parsing.* New Haven: Yale Computer Science Research Report 172, 1978.

Schlesinger, I. M. *Production and comprehension of utterances.* Hillsdale, N.J.: Lawrence Erlbaum, 1977.

Selnes, O. A., & Whitaker, H. A. Neurological substrates of language and speech production. In S. Rosenberg (Ed.), *Sentence production: Developments in research and theory.* Hillsdale, N.J.: Lawrence Erlbaum, 1977. Pp. 15–35.

Shutt, P. R. After wrap-around blackboards, what? *College English,* 1969, *30,* 662–667.

Sidman, M. Operant techniques. In A. Bachrach (Ed.), *Experimental foundations of clinical psychology.* New York: Basic Books, 1964. Pp. 170–210.

Simmons, R. F., & Slocum, J. *Generating English discourse from semantic networks.* Austin: University of Texas Computer Sciences Technical Report NL-3, 1971.

Simmons, R. F., & Chester, D. *Relating sentences and semantic networks with clausal logic.* Austin: University of Texas Computer Sciences Technical Report, 1979.

Skinner, B. F. Are theories of learning necessary? *Psychological Review,* 1950, *57,* 193–216.

Skinner, B. F. *Verbal behavior.* New York: Appleton-Century-Crofts, 1957.

Skinner, B. F. Why I am not a cognitive psychologist. In B. F. Skinner, *Reflections on Behaviorism and Society.* Englewood Cliffs, N.J.: Prentice-Hall, 1978. Pp. 97–112.

Sticht, T. Learning by listening. In J. Carroll & R. Freedle (Eds.), *Language comprehension and the acquisition of knowledge.* Washington, D.C.: V. H. Winston & Sons, 1972.

Sussman, H. M. What the tongue tells the brain. *Psychological Bulletin,* 1972, *77,* 262–272.

Tannen, D. What's in a frame: Surface evidence for underlying expectations. In Freedle (Ed.), *New directions in discourse processing.* Norwood, N.J.: Ablex, 1979. Pp. 137–181. (a)

Tannen, D. *Ethnicity and conversational style.* Austin: Southwest Educational Development Laboratory Working Paper 55, 1979. (b)

Tannenbaum, P. H., Williams, F., & Hillier, C. S. Word predictability in the environment of hesitations. *Journal of Verbal Learning and Verbal Behavior,* 1965, *4,* 134–140.

Tatham, S. M. Reading comprehension of materials written with select oral language patterns: A study at grades two and four. *Reading Research Quarterly,* 1970, *5,* 402–426.

Tierney, R., & LaZansky, J. *The rights and responsibilities of readers and writers: A contractual agreement.* Urbana, Ill.: Center for the Study of Reading Education Report 15, 1980.

Tulving, E. Memory research: What kind of progress? In L. G. Nilsson (Ed.), *Perspectives on memory research.* Hillsdale, N.J.: Lawrence Erlbaum, 1979. Pp. 19–34.

Underwood, B. J., & Schultz, R. W. *Meaningfulness and verbal learning.* Philadelphia: Lippincott, 1960.

Vendler, Z. Say what you think. In J. J. Cowan (Ed.), *Studies in thought and language.* Tucson, University of Arizona, 1970. Pp. 79–98.

Walker, D. E., Grosz, B. J., Hendrix, G. G., Robinson, A. E., Robinson, J. J., Slocum, J., Fikes, R. E., & Paxton, W. H. *Understanding spoken language.* Amsterdam: North-Holland, 1978.

Waltz, D. On the interdependence of language and perception. *TINLAP-2*, 1978, 149–156.

Watson, J. B. *Behaviorism*. Chicago: University of Chicago Press, 1924.

Weinreich, U. *Languages in contact*. New York: Linguistic Circle, 1953.

Wilensky, R. *Understanding goal-based stories*. New York: Garland, 1980.

Winston, P. H. *Artificial intelligence*. Reading, Mass.: Addison-Wesley, 1977.

Wong, H. *Generating English sentences from semantic structures*. Toronto: University of Toronto Computer Science Technical Report 84, 1975.

Woods, W., & Brachman, R. *Research in natural language understanding*. Cambridge, Mass.: Bolt, Beranek, and Newman Technical Report No. 3963, 1978.

Young, R., Becker, A., & Pike, K. L. *Rhetoric: Discovery and change*. New York: Harcourt Brace Jovanovich, 1970.

Zipf, G. K. *The psycho-biology of language*. Boston: Houghton Mifflin, 1935.

Zoellner, R. Talk–write: A behavioral pedagogy for composition. *College English*, 1969, *30*, 267–320.

Zoellner, R. Lucy's dance lessons and accountability in English. *College Composition and Communication*, 1971, *22*, 229–236.

Chapter **10**

Explorations in the Real-Time Production of Written Discourse

Ann Matsuhashi

OBSERVING WRITING AS A REAL-TIME PROCESS

Writers portrayed through film often serve to fulfill a popular, if illusory, image of how a writer works. Consider, for instance, Jane Fonda's portrayal of young Lillian Hellman in the movie *Julia*. Seated before a black enamel manual typewriter—its clickety–clack sound magnified for effect—she peers nearsightedly at the completed page. Visibly dissatisfied, she rips it from behind the platen and hurls the crumpled mass toward an already overflowing wastebasket. This dramatic scene is intended to captivate the viewer, to create a sense of having witnessed an event: the writer at work. In fact, this highly technical cinematic product does not display a writer at work, but a paid professional actress executing the directions of the filmmaker.

Although film is often used to create fiction, it can also be used to great advantage to record an event or to observe a process more carefully than had been possible before. A film can be made—not to portray a filmmaker's image of a writer—but to document what a writer actually does. Watching a writer begin to work can be truly dramatic. Imagine a slow motion film of a high school student, John, just beginning to write. His shoulders bend forward; his forehead dips. His pen, hovering above the page, silently traces a letter in the air. Words, sentences, then paragraphs emerge. The desk becomes a stage: a composition of time, movement, and space.

The process in motion; the writer engaged. What happens in the mind of this writer as he propels the text forward through space and time? What sorts of decisions, plans, strategies lie behind the final, physical inscription of the written product? How can we render transparent the cognitive architecture of writing, an architecture of which the writer is largely unaware?

Close observation of a writer at work makes one aware that these questions are not easily answered. The process is invisible, hidden. The only tangible evidence of its occurrence is the series of black marks as they appear on the page and the obvious symptoms of a writer hard at work. From these black marks, we must move backwards to reconstruct the production process. To learn about this complex and creative behavior, we must operate like a detective, speculating backward from the event, reconstructing the pieces of the puzzle, constantly asking what each piece means in terms of the whole scenario.

One of the most obvious clues to the writing process is that it takes time. What makes writing a time-consuming activity is less obvious: It is not just the time used to write words, but also the TIME USED BY THE WRITER TO PAUSE BETWEEN WORDS. Yet, the move from this casual observation to a more systematic investigation of the writing process presents a significant challenge, given the pioneering state of current writing process research.

To study the temporal aspects of the writing process, I videotaped four skilled high school writers producing several kinds of writing. To learn how pause time varied for writing produced for different purposes, I studied long pauses in particular linguistic and discourse contexts (Matsuhashi, 1981). The assumption throughout all of this chronographic analysis is that pauses—moments of scribal inactivity during writing—reflect time for the writer to engage in cognitive planning and decision-making behavior.

This chapter continues my exploration of the cognitive processes underlying the real-time production of written discourse. Broadly conceived, the question is: How—as time continually presses forward—does a writer maneuver the complexities of planning and developing the ideas, insights, and memories to be expressed in language and written in accordance with the linear text format of conventional English syntax? One approach to learning about how the mind works to produce written discourse is to build a model that characterizes some essential features of the process (see Black, Wilkes-Gibbs, & Gibbs, Chapter 12 in this volume). Because much research in written discourse production is pretheoretical, that is, because it lacks a coherent theory from which to generate and test hypotheses, a useful psychological process model must, at least, locate regularities or patterns in observational data from ordinary experience. Thus, a major goal in building a model of the production process is to construct an abstract system that tentatively characterizes the process and then to categorize approximately the salient operations within the system (Diesing, 1971).

Because the search for a model of the writing process is part and parcel of a search for a methodology to verify that model, I have included as a preface a review of research on pauses in speech production that—in a loosely historical fashion—traces a trend away from narrow explanations of planning behaviors and toward explanations that take into account the influence of goal-directed, purposeful behavior on global as well as local planning and on semantic issues as well as on syntactic ones. This review supports my own exploration of pausing behavior as an index of planning activity during written discourse production.

The central portion of this report is, in effect, an exercise in model building. Relying on pause data from one writer and additional observational data from his hand movements, gazing and rereading activity, I looked for behavioral patterns that were associated with language choices in the text and that suggested planning activity. What result from an interpretation of this observational data are some speculations on the character of writing as an instrumental, planful, and purposeful act. These speculations touch on the kind and complexity of decisions writers must make even before language is assigned to ideas and experiences. In addition, these speculations characterize how the writer accommodates the serially organized, real-time physical process of inscribing words to the shifting circumstances and constraints posed by the writer's developing conceptual knowledge and by the text as it accumulates on the page.

PAUSE RESEARCH IN SPEECH PRODUCTION

Whereas the study of speech production rests on well over a quarter century's research and criticism (Appel, Dechert, & Raupach, 1980; Boomer, 1970; O'Connell & Kowal, in press; Rochester, 1973; Rosenberg, 1977), the study of written discourse production—with the exception of one anachronistic study (van Bruggen, 1946)—is a relatively recent enterprise. Consequently, the purpose of this review is to identify in the oral pause research tradition important issues for the study of planning activity during written discourse production. (For a review of other possible sources of pausing behavior, e.g., anxiety, see Rosenberg, 1977.)

Much of the early work, remains preoccupied with the search for a SINGLE SYNTACTIC UNIT—the phrase, the clause, the sentence—that could then be interpreted as a FUNCTIONAL UNIT for planning and encoding speech. Later studies, no longer able to ignore the importance of suprasentential units such as the paragraph or whole texts, began to look beyond the sentence for explanations of planning processes. Some of these studies focused on semantic planning throughout the entire discourse, whereas others explored the relationship between syntactic and semantic planning. These concerns represent a crucial development for research in the production of spontaneous speech: Certainly this research left behind the constraints of narrowly behavioristic theories, but it also left behind conceptions of planning limited only to constituent structures. Now pauses could be interpreted in the context of the whole discourse, resulting in conclusions which could involve potentially the full range of cognitive processes contributing to discourse production. This research trend—in oral pause research specifically but also generally in the field of psycholinguistics—has had a powerful impact on research on and ideas about writing processes (e.g., Beaugrande, 1980; Clark & Clark, 1977; Dressler, 1978; Kintsch & van Dijk, 1978; van Dijk & Kintsch, 1978). No longer preoccupied with only sentence-level syntactic concerns, composition researchers have begun to consider text production in light of pragmatic and semantic as well as syntactic concerns.

Encoding Lexical and Syntactic Units

The idea that there is a single unit for encoding speech has dominated and perhaps limited pause research (Rochester, 1973). This notion originated as a category in a theory of grammar that accounted for meaningful segments of texts and that offered, originally, a way to describe the surface structure of natural language. According to Frederiksen (1977), category based units could be ordered in a hierarchical fashion from superordinate and inclusive levels (the topmost unit being the sentence) to a subordinate level, the lowest of which is the phoneme or the grapheme.

In the service of pause research, these descriptive units were often interpreted as processing or encoding units. Typically, researchers asked questions such as: What is the size of the encoding unit? How far ahead does a speaker plan? What is the nature of lexical, syntactic, and semantic planning? The goal of much of the early pause research was to determine whether "pauses function in terms of phrases, intonation units, [or] major grammatical constituents in the surface or deep structure [Rochester, 1973, p. 54]."

The earliest pause studies adopted a model of speech production that examined single words as a functional unit for encoding. Goldman-Eisler (1958, 1968) suggested that key words in a discourse are often selected independently, not necessarily in the context of an already formed syntactic or semantic unit. To test this notion, Goldman-Eisler relied on Lounsbury's (1954) hypothesis that messages are planned and produced from left to right in a sequence and that the transitional probabilities of individual words would explain the presence of long pauses during speech. Several further studies were designed to challenge or replicate Goldman-Eisler's study "based on the belief that a systematic account of hesitation phenomenon may require a unit larger than the word [Boomer, 1965, p. 149]."

Boomer (1965), for instance, refuted Goldman-Eisler's word-by-word production model, yet replaced it with another, only slightly more inclusive encoding unit—the phonemic clause, a phonological unit very similar to the written clause. Other studies refuted the word-by-word production model by substituting a hierarchical model with an "emphasis on major constituents as encoding units, [relegating] lexical choice to a lower level of decision-making [Rochester, 1973, p. 58]." Maclay and Osgood (1959), for instance, used Fries's (1952) descriptive scheme to identify patterns of long pauses prior to words in lexical and function categories. They found that pauses occurred at the phrase boundary and then again prior to the lexical choices within the phrase. For example, in the phrase, *in the house,* a speaker in Maclay and Osgood's study might have paused prior to *in* and then again before *house.* On the basis of this pattern, Maclay and Osgood suggested that the encoding unit—at some level of organization—is "phrase-like, a lexical core with its tightly bound grammatical context [p. 41]."

The hierarchical production model received additional support from later studies by Hawkins (1971) and Goldman-Eisler (1972). Testing children, Hawkins found that 76% of his subjects'—children ages 6 : 5 to 7 : 0—pause time was located prior to clause boundaries, 18% at phrase boundaries and the remaining 6% at word boundaries. Goldman-Eisler, examining the speech of academics during a radio show, found a decreasing hierarchy of pause time for sentence, then coordinate clause, then subordinate clause, and finally, relative clause.

Beyond Syntax

All of these studies are limited by the grammatical boundary of the sentence—a wall beyond which many researchers could not see (O'Connell, 1977). Even so, Hawkins (1971)—in the context of a sentence-level analysis—found that two-thirds of all pauses and three-quarters of all pause time were located at clause boundaries, he looked beyond the sentence boundary for an explanation: "It is no coincidence that 90% of the long pauses (5 seconds or more) are located [at clause boundaries], and in all probability they mark the end of an episode in the story, at which point a major decision . . . is necessary [p. 286]." He accounts for the clustering of pause time at clausal boundaries by suggesting that the clause is a decision point for structuring the information content within the text as it relates to the writer's overall purpose for the discourse. My point in recounting Hawkin's post-research musings is to note that any attempt to uncover global planning, the planning that affects the meaning of entire segments of the text, must rely on a production model capable of explaining the complex types of decisions that oversee lexical and syntactic choices.

Recognizing that the linear progression of word choices during speech could only account for limited planning activity, Goldman-Eisler (1968) broadened her model to include three discrete choices: lexical choice, construction of syntax, and conception of content. Although this view of cognitive processes attempts to account for a broader range of planning, it is limited by Goldman-Eisler's conclusion that syntactic and semantic decisions are independent, resulting from discrete, sequential operations during production. By contrast, lexical and semantic plans, she concludes, result from willful, pause-laden operations whereas syntactic operations—particularly the embedding of clauses—are a fluent, proficient, independent operation.

These conclusions stem from a series of experiments in which Goldman-Eisler (1968) first examined semantic planning in two contrasting contexts and subsequently attempted to assess the significance of syntactic planning. To learn how semantic decisions are reflected in pause patterns throughout the spontaneous production of entire discourse, Goldman-Eisler asked subjects to respond to a cartoon in two distinct rhetorical contexts—first for the purpose of describing the cartoon and second for the purpose of interpreting it. (See Rosenberg's critique of the research design, 1977, pp. 203–204). The fact that the ratio of total pause time to total speech time was nearly twice as high for interpretation as for description suggested that interpreting—abstracting meaning from events and assigning a general meaning—presents a greater cognitive challenge than describing sequentially related concrete events. In a later post hoc analysis, Goldman-Eisler compared the syntactic complexity of sentences in three contexts: describing, interpreting, and in an interview situation. Her measure of complexity was the subordination ratio (the number of subordinate clauses divided by the total number of clauses). Goldman-Eisler found that even though sentences in the interview situation were as heavily embedded as those in the interpretation context, speakers used even less pause time than for simple sentences in description. Syntax, Goldman-Eisler concluded, is independent of pausing and, therefore, irrelevant to the speaker's planning processes.

Rochester and Gill (1973) in a replication of Goldman-Eisler's study, challenged her conclusions, arguing that the subordination ratio is too gross a reflection of syntactic complexity. Consequently, in addition to testing the subordination ratio, Rochester and Gill identified sentences that contained relative clauses and noun phrase complements. (They examined spoken hesitations, not silent pauses, in two contexts: monologues and dialogues. I will discuss results from the monologues only). Rochester and Gill found, as did Goldman-Eisler, no relationship between general syntactic complexity and speech disruptions. However, when they looked at the two specific types of modification, a definite relationship appeared: Speech disruptions were far more frequent in sentences with noun phrase complements than in those with relative clauses. Rochester and Gill suggest that general syntactic complexity scores are inadequate because of an underlying semantic difference that makes the production of a relative clause different from the production of a noun clause. According to one linguistic argument, the relative clause is tied directly to the noun it modifies, whereas the noun phrase complement introduces a new concept.

Implications for an Integrative Model of the Production Process

Goldman-Eisler's separation of lexical, syntactic, and semantic operations fits neatly into a sequential stage model of speech production. Sequential stage models analyze speech production in terms of a fixed sequence of subprocesses. They oversimplify language processes by assuming that language production always works the same way regardless of tasks and contexts (see Beaugrande, Chapter 9, this volume). The fixed sequence typically begins with idea generation followed by a linguistic translation of ideas culminating in verbal or written expression. A stage analysis assumes that if psychological processes during language behavior can indeed be separated into component subprocesses, then carefully designed experimental investigations ought to support distinctions among the stages.

In an effort to refute a stage model approach to the study of speech production, Danks (1977) designed a study that—using the logic of stage analysis—would separate the idea generation stage from the verbal expression stage. Danks' evidence convinced him that the separation did not, in fact, exist. He concluded that "idea generation and sentence construction are not discrete stages," and further, that "sentence production is a unitary, integrated process. In the mind of a real speaker, producing ideas and sentences are one and the same process [Danks, 1977, pp. 247–248]."

Taken together, Hawkin's comments, the Goldman-Eisler studies, the Rochester and Gill replication, and Danks' conclusions suggest the need for a production model that integrates syntactic and semantic operations with other text-creating operations, rather than a model that separates the process into discrete stages. This need is also suggested by the work of O'Connell, Kowal, and Hörmann (1969) and O'Connell and Kowal (1972). They found that when speakers retold paragraph length stories containing one semantically incongruous sentence, changes in pause patterns were evident throughout the entire retelling of that paragraph. Results such as these suggest that the speaker is operating under the influence of a task-oriented schema: an internal representation or set of expectations that guides speaking and writing behavior.

An integrative model of the production process ought to emphasize the task-oriented nature of the writing process. If writing is indeed an intentional, purposeful activity, then the decisions a writer makes throughout the process must be appropriate to the demands of the particular task. In fact, Goldman-Eisler's cartoon experiment comparing description with interpretation as well as my own comparison of reporting, persuading, and generalizing (Matsuhashi, 1981) suggests that planning requirements vary for different discourse purposes. The problem remains, however, to develop a model which accounts for some of these task-related plans. The remainder of this chapter is devoted to this effort.

DOCUMENTING WRITING BEHAVIORS

An Elementary Taxonomy of Writing Behaviors

Over and over again writers tell us that they discover what they think as they write—that it is the activity of writing itself that sparks creativity during writing. Donald Murray (1978, pp. 101–103) makes this point, offering for support the testimony of well-known writers:

Edward Albee: *Writing has got to be an act of discovery. . . . I write to find out what I'm thinking about.*

Thomas Williams: *A writer keeps surprising himself, . . . he doesn't know what he is saying until he sees it on the page.*

The observations of these writers suggest that much of the process of writing is not available to conscious introspection. Under normal circumstances, writers are unconscious of motor control during writing: that is, they inscribe words automatically from sense or content. However, when the writer confronts a particularly difficult decision, such as the decision to begin a new paragraph or even the realization that a word is spelled incorrectly, conscious attention may return (Weigl, 1975; Scardamalia, Bereiter, & Goelman, Chapter 8, this volume). Similarly, Nisbett and Wilson (1977) have argued that even though informants often claim to be aware of higher mental processes, this information is actually unavailable to consciousness during the operation of complex systems such as language production. Thus, if writers are, for the most part, unaware of their own mental processes during discourse production and if, as plans and decisions become difficult, conscious attention returns, then one way to study writing processes is to observe ways in which pauses reflect decision-making activity.

Pauses—periods of apparent motor inactivity during writing—reflect the elapsed time between the close of one word and the start of the next. To say, however, that motor activity ceases during a pause is misleading; WHAT CEASES IS ONLY SCRIBAL ACTIVITY, NOT OTHER HAND AND EYE MOVEMENTS. In this chapter I will take a broader look at the motor activity that accompanies pauses during writing. I assume not only that pauses reflect planning, but also that patterns of body language associated with pauses will corroborate notions about the functions of pauses. Furthermore, I assume that patterns of body language (unless used for communicative gestures as is sometimes the case in speech) occurring coterminously with long pauses represent the integration of planning processes in a dynamic central cerebral mechanism. For instance, Lashley (1951) correlated tongue movements during silent mathematical problem-solving with the progress of the subject's computations. Chafe (1980) reported a study in which eye movements were coordinated with verbal descriptions of a statue. And McNeill (1979) documented that noncommunicative gestures were synchronized with ideational content during spoken messages. In all of these studies the coordination of physiological actions with verbal efforts suggests the existence of highly general schemas integrating and coordinating both motor and mental activity simultaneously.

The coordination of hand and eye movements with long pauses at various locations in the text creates a new perspective for studying writing behaviors. This concern with body language and long pauses, however, fits into a larger theoretical context that emphasizes the writer's purpose (to report or to generalize) and that suggests how these different tasks impose different planning requirements on the writer. In addition, this perspective stresses the integrated nature of decisions during writing. Texts produced for the purpose of reporting concrete events characteristically differ from texts produced for the purpose of generalizing about how people behave (Jones, 1977). Also, planning processes required to produce these texts differ (Goldman-Eisler, 1968; Matsuhashi, 1981). One such difference is in the use and placement of highly abstract statements (Matsuhashi, 1981).

My purpose in this chapter is to locate some patterns or regularities in observational pause data that will suggest how planning requirements for **generalizing** and **reporting** differ. To identify patterns of planning and important points of decision making during writing I have singled out the 10 longest pauses in approximately the first 100 words of a piece of generalizing and the first 100 words of a piece of reporting from one writer's work. Because the reporting piece is produced much more rapidly than the generalizing piece—both in the 100-word samples and in the compositions from which the samples were taken—I intend to explore how these two tasks influence the writer's production processes.

For each of the 10 longest pauses, I noted whether it was at a sentence boundary (**S**) or an internal pause (**I**), and I coordinated the available information describing the writer's body language. This information does not include the sort of sophisticated eye fixation data developed and used in the context of reading research. Instead, from the videotapes I was able to single out points where the writer's general visual focus changed sharply from a location in the text to either reread (**RR**) sections of the text or to gaze (**G**) away from the text. I also noted points where the writer shifted his entire body posture. Perhaps the most interesting measure was the location of the pen: At the location of each of the longest pauses I noted whether the writer's hand and the pen stayed in the immediate proximity of the previously written word (noted as **PD** for pen down) or whether the writer removed the pen from the area (noted as **PR** for pen removed). What follows is a description of body language during long pauses in each of two discourse tasks as well as some tentative claims about the cognitive processes at work.

Writing for Two Discourse Purposes

Generalizing (Refer to Figure 10.1 and Table 10.1)

At all but one of the sentence boundaries where pauses fall into the longest 10, John removed his pen from the proximity of the previous word. In several cases John either reread, gazed away, or shifted his entire body posture. This physical distancing from the text was accompanied by a cognitive distancing that allowed John to foreground an abstract representation of the information in the text. To illustrate this claim, I'll refer to the 3 longest pauses in the generalizing paragraph. A pause of 16.6 seconds (line 5) occurred after John wrote the word *self-centeredness*. More specifically, he terminated the sentence with a period, paused for 16.6 seconds, revised his decision by changing the period to a colon and then paused again for 5.5 seconds (line 5) before continuing on. Both the length and location of the pause suggest that this writer was facing several time-consuming decisions.

First, the fact that the writer ended the sentence and then reread the passage suggests that he was evaluating the existing text against a set of expectations for it. John was also probably concerned with evaluating the

1   Truly$^{.6}$successful$^{1.1}$person$^{.5}$-to$^{.8}$-person$^{2.3}$communi-
2    $^{1.8}$cation$^{3.5}$is$^{1.9}$difficult$^{1.3}$because$^{6.9}$people$^{.6}$in$^{.9}$general$^{1.1}$are$^{.9}$poor
3    $^{1.0}$listeners. $^{7.0}$They$^{1.0}$would$^{.7}$rather$^{1.4}$listen$^{.5}$to$^{.9}$themselves$^{1.9}$speaking
4    $^{2.1}$than$^{.4}$someone$^{.7}$else$^{.5}$. $^{4.7}$It$^{.9}$is$^{.7}$my$^{.7}$feeling$^{1.9}$that$^{9.7}$this$^{.8}$occurs
5    $^{1.6}$because$^{1.1}$of$^{1.2}$a$^{.8}$basic$^{2.7}$self-centeredness.$^{16.6.}$ $^{5.5}$people$^{4.8}$tend$^{1.2}$to
6    $^{1.9}$be$^{.6}$more$^{.5}$interested$^{.7}$in$^{.7}$their$^{.9}$own$^{.7}$lives$^{1.5}$to$^{1.2}$bother$^{1.0}$exposing
7    $^{1.3}$themselves$^{.7}$to$^{.5}$how$^{.7}$others$^{.8}$live.
8        $^{13.3}$Communication$^{1.2}$is$^{.7}$successful$^{.8}$only$^{.8}$when$^{2.9}$there
9    $^{2.2}$is$^{2.4''.5}$give$^{.6}$and$^{.8}$take''$^{1.1}$between$^{3.7}$the$^{.7}$parties$^{1.1}$. $^{3.7}$Each$^{.7}$one
10   $^{1.9}$should$^{.9}$contribute$^{1.2}$equally$^{2.1}$,$^{1.0}$as$^{.8}$well$^{.7}$as$^{2.0}$accepting$^{.7}$the
11   $^{2.2}$contributions$^{5.3}$of$^{.6}$the$^{.7}$others. $^{12.8}$The$^{.6}$situation$^{.7}$I$^{1.0}$have
12   $^{1.8}$described$^{6.6}$above$^{3.2}$leads$^{.6}$to$^{.6}$poor$^{.8}$communication$^{1.7}$,$^{1.0}$since
13   $^{1.9}$everyone$^{.8}$wants$^{.9}$to$^{.6}$''give''$^{1.2}$and$^{.8}$no$^{1.0}$one$^{.6}$wants$^{.9}$to
14   $^{1.2}$''take.''

FIGURE 10.1. Pause times for a segment of generalizing.

TABLE 10.1
Body Language During Long Pauses in Generalizing

Line #	Pause length (in seconds)	Location of pause: S or I	Location of Pen: PD or PR	Visual focus: RR, G	Other nonverbal movements
			Body language		
5	16.6	S	PR	RR	
8	13.3	S (paragraph)	PR	G	Shifts in seat, leans back
11	12.8	S	PR	G	Shifts in seat
4	9.7	I	PR	RR (entire text)	
3	7.0	S	PD, PR (scribbles)	No change	
2	6.9	I	PD (moves forward slightly on same line)	No change	
12	6.6	I	PD	G	
5	5.5	S	PD	No change	
11	5.3	I	PR (retraces previous line)	RR (previous line)	
5	4.8	I	PD	No change	

statement in terms of its abstraction level within the passage, as well as considering how it contributes to the general topic he has chosen to discuss. His change from a period to a colon reflected his decision that the underlying idea expressed in the previous sentence needed elaboration. Furthermore, the use of the colon allowed John to insert his detailed elaboration, *people tend to be more interested. . .*, into the left-to-right sequence as a complete sentence whose logical relationship to the previous sentence is established implicitly via the punctuation mark. It is important to note that there is nothing sacrosanct about sentence boundaries during the production process: John could have expressed the same information in one sentence using subordinate or reduced clauses. Even so, the fact that throughout all of his writing John revised rarely is conducive to this left-to-right, add-on choice for his elaboration. Finally, John may have also been influenced by audience considerations, thinking that his reader (perhaps a teacher) expected more information, perhaps a definition for self-centeredness.

Following the 16.6 second pause, John kept his pen close to the page and his hand in readiness prior to pauses of 5.5 seconds prior to *people* and for 4.8 seconds (line 5) prior to *tend*. These two words provide the central propositional relationship underlying the sentence and probably subsume most of the planning time since the next 16 words, the rest of the sentence, spill rapidly out, using remarkably little pause time.

John's comments from a retrospective interview conducted immediately after writing suggest that he was more concerned with what to say than how to say it. Although John's insights into his own composing process are most likely a reconstruction of what he was aware of at the time of writing, they nevertheless buttress the information available from the written compositions and from the videotapes. The question he responded to was a standard opener for the postwriting interviews and simply encouraged the writer to tell everything he could remember about the writing experience. John explained that even though he was writing about something he believed was true, he had never really thought much about it. Thus, he concluded, "It was actually a learning experience while I was writing. And I was learning about how I thought and how I analyzed the situation." John was aware of a great deal of difficulty composing the third sentence. He explained:

> *Now, talking about . . . basic self-centeredness . . . I hate to be that negative about people . . . I realized I had committed myself to a certain view point and in a way I felt guilty because as I was writing I realized my position was not really that strong in some places and, I wasn't sure if that's what I wanted to say.*

John was certainly judging the coherence of his arguments, questioning whether his reasoning followed and whether it seemed to be an accurate representation of events in the world. The fact that he wondered whether or not he was being too negative suggests the presence of a powerful editor–evaluator. This concern may have prompted the additional elaboration (*people tend . . .*) to soften the impact of what he considered too strong an assertion.

Like the 16.6-second pause, the next two longest pauses—13.3 seconds (line 8) and 12.8 seconds (line 11)—were accompanied by similar planning considerations. John removed his pen from the page, shifted his posture and, in the case of the 12.8 second pause gazed away. The paragraph opener, *Communication is successful . . .* represents a conceptual boundary between the new paragraph and the previous paragraph's *communication is difficult* theme. The statement is a general one, at a high level of abstraction, and one that provides the gist for the immediate paragraph. During the 12.8-second pause, John gazed away. Judging from the next six words, *The situation I have described above . . .*, John may have used the time to review a schematic representation of the communication situation he had just described.

Although it is a fact that the longest pauses in the data occurred at sentence boundaries, long pauses regularly occurred within sentence boundaries and involved equally complex planning decisions. For instance, in line 2, John paused for 6.9 seconds prior to completing the adverbial clause *because.* . . During this pause the pen stayed close to the page and moved forward slightly along the unfinished line of print. Because this was the first sentence and one that introduced the topic of the entire discourse, John's choice to complete the causal proposition with an explanation for WHY people are poor listeners had far-reaching effects on what followed. Not only was the decision a local one that required slotting information into an existing constituent structure, in this case the adverbial clause; it was also a decision involving the development of the underlying logical and conceptual relationships that gave rise to the information needed to complete the sentence. In addition, because of the role of the sentence within the discourse, its content maintained the highly abstract nature of the statement.

Other pauses during discourse production reflected the more limited demands of fitting information into an existing informational and syntactic framework. For instance, during the 5.3 second (line 11) pause, John retraced with his pen and reread the entire sentence in order to insert the information that established WHOSE *contributions.* This pause seemed to be used to solve the relatively simple problems of syntactic formatting because the content of the phrase must have been implicitly established in the earlier context of the *parties;* thus *one* must be complemented by *the others.*

Two other interesting pauses occurred in the generalizing paragraph. In line 12, John began a sentence with *The situation I have described* . . ., then paused for 6.6 seconds during which time he gazed away, again perhaps reaching for a schematic representation of the text rather than rereading for content. Another interesting pause is a 9.7-second pause in line 4. During this pause, John reread the entire text up to that point. He had begun the sentence with a neutral filler, *It is my feeling that* . . ., which could have been followed by nearly anything. John chose to continue by referring to the entire previous sentence with the reference item *this* (Halliday & Hasan, 1976). During rereading he may have been evaluating the gist of what he had said thus far to choose among several possible alternatives for the distribution of information throughout that portion of the text.

Reporting (Refer to Figure 10.2 and Table 10.2)

An obvious difference between the reporting and generalizing pieces is that the reporting piece was produced much more efficiently. The majority of the longest pauses in reporting occurred within sentence boundaries and not between them. This efficiency might have resulted from John's reliance on a pattern that suited the event-based narrative format and that provided slots into which an agent was followed immediately by an action. With the exception of an introductory adverbial phrase in the first sentence and a prepositional phrase in the second, all five sentences followed this agent–action pattern:

. . . I managed
Students . . . were
My co-conspirator and I chose . . .
We wanted . . .
We discussed . . .

During the first sentence, John paused twice for long periods of time. Prior to the word *project,* John paused for 4.5 seconds (line 2) during which time he held the pen close to the page drawing circles in the air directly above the spot where the next word would appear. It is possible that John was searching for or reviewing alternatives for the precise term that would name the subject of his narrative. The next long pause, 6.1 seconds (line 2), followed the word *was* and answered the question WHAT. Again the pen stayed down, close to the previous word until John reeled off a nine-word series of qualifiers, *a little more than just run-of-the-mill.* Although each of these two pauses preceded choices constrained in the surface structure by immediate constituents, each choice contributed globally to the organization of the discourse as a whole. The first pause preceded the name for the topic of the paper—a project. The second preceded an evaluative qualifier through which John tells the reader, albeit modestly, that the project was a success and is a worthwhile topic for his essay.

After an initial sentence that provided an orientation for the reader, John began the narrative by telling about the original class assignment. The longest pause, 6.8 seconds (line 5), occurred in the midst of the infinitive *to do* during which John removed the pen from the page, leaned back, and reread the entire piece. His decision at this point was limited by the constituent context: completing the infinitive and adding whatever may complement it. Yet what followed was clearly more than a surface structure decision; it involved answering the question WHAT, telling the reader more about the project.

Prior to the third sentence, John removed his pen from the paper, shifted

1   Back·^{8}during·^{8}my·^{6}junior·^{7}year·^{6}in·^{7}high·^{7}school
2    $^{2.1}$I$^{3.2}$managed$^{1.0}$to·^{8}get$^{1.1}$myself·^{9}involved$^{1.1}$in·^{6}a$^{4.5}$project
3    $^{1.6}$that$^{1.5}$was$^{6.1}$a·^{8}little·^{7}more·^{4}than·^{8}just$^{1.0}$run-of-the-mill.
4    $^{5.1}$Students$^{1.0}$in·^{7}my$^{1.7}$AP·^{9}American·^{8}History$^{2.3}$class·^{7}were
5    $^{1.7}$to$^{1.2}$pair·^{7}off$^{1.6}$in·^{6}order·^{8}to$^{6.8}$do$^{1.1}$a$^{1.0}$report$^{2.3}$on·^{9}some
6    $^{1.5}$aspect·^{9}of·^{8}the$^{1.0}$Jacksonian·^{9}era·^{9}. $^{6.3}$My$^{2.3}$co-conspirator
7    $^{1.6}$and$^{1.8}$I$^{1.4}$chose$^{3.2}$Daniel·^{8}Webster,·^{6}who·^{4}as$^{1.6}$we·^{7}soon
8    $^{7.1}$found·^{6}out$^{1.8}$,·^{7}was$^{2.2}$a·^{7}most·^{8}fascinating·^{7}figure·^{6}in·^{7}U.S.
9    $^{1.9}$history·^{8}. $^{4.6}$We$^{1.0}$wanted$^{2.1}$to$^{1.4}$make·^{8}our·^{8}report$^{1.0}$stand
10   $^{2.2}$out$^{1.1}$from·^{9}the·^{8}rest$^{4.7}$by·^{8}giving·^{7}it$^{1.3}$some$^{1.1}$interesting
11   $^{1.8}$format·^{7}. $^{2.4}$We·^{7}discussed$^{1.3}$the·^{8}possibility·^{8}of$^{3.3}$making·^{7}it
12   $^{1.8}$an$^{1.8}$interview$^{3.6}$or·^{7}talk·^{9}show$^{1.1}$or$^{2.0}$maybe$^{1.1}$even·^{9}a
13   ·^{6}trial.

FIGURE 10.2. Pause times for a segment of reporting.

TABLE 10.2
Body Language During Long Pauses in Reporting

Line #	Pause length (in seconds)	Location of pause: S or I	Body language		
			Location of pen: **PD** or **PR**	Visual focus: **RR, G**	Other nonverbal movements
8	7.1	I	**PD**	No change	
5	6.8	I	**PR**	RR/No change	Leans back
6	6.3	S	**PR**	No change	Shifts in seat
3	6.1	I	**PD**	No change	
4	5.1	S	**PD**	No change	
10	4.7	I	**PR**	**RR** (immediate location)	
9	4.6	S	**PR**	No change	
2	4.5	I	**PD** (draws circles at location)	No change	
12	3.6	I	**PD**	No change	
11	3.3	I	**PD**	No change	

in his seat, paused for 6.3 seconds (line 6), and began to write a sentence in which he identified the actors in a bit more detail (*My co-conspirator and I...*) and continued to elaborate on the events of the project. During the transition from line 7 to line 8 John paused for 7.1 seconds (line 8). His pen remained close to the page and he continued to gaze down at the page—perhaps planning for the information that would complete the sentence.

One interesting fact about this reporting piece is that John did not gaze away from the text as he did several times during the generalizing piece. One explanation is that in the generalizing pieces, the schematic representation of the idea network (macrostructure) underlying John's piece on communication was not readily available. His comments support this notion: "It was actually a learning experience while writing." By contrast, John's comments about his experience writing the reporting piece suggested that his major concern was recalling the actual details of the event: "It was a little tough to remember the details.... There were some parts where I got stuck trying to think about.... I had this feeling there was something important I left out." It is likely that the events of the Daniel Webster play were more readily translated from episodic memory into the language that appeared in the surface structure of the text and that this sort of text production problem is more easily solved than the type of problem presented by a generalizing task which is based primarily on semantic-conceptual memory.

TOWARD A TASK-SPECIFIC MODEL OF DISCOURSE PRODUCTION

Schematic Differences: Drawing on Memory and Experience

Comparing pause patterns in reporting and generalizing reflects an assumption about the nature of the underlying processes required by each of these discourse types. Whatever the range of plans—whether local or global, conceptual or syntactic—the writer is operating under the rubric of a schematic representation of knowledge and experience that informs text production at all times.

Remembering events and ideas, abstracting them into schemas in memory, and recalling them into consciousness are activities crucial to producing a written discourse. Beaugrande likens this activity to "a beam of light sweeping across an enormously elaborate network of knowledge [1980, p. 202]." Our knowledge of the world—what we perceive and how we remember it—creates the conceptual landscape of consciousness. This conceptual landscape from which a writer identifies ideational content is the result of an active, interpretive construction of perceptual and remembered material (Greene, 1979). Ideational content is created through a largely abstractive process; the load of incoming material on memory is reduced by a stripping away of onion-like layers of unnecessary detail. Salient material usually based on a large number of personal experiences forms a **schema:** a highly abstract mental pattern that may be recalled, revised, and reinterpreted to serve the needs of new situations (Baddeley, 1971; Bartlett, 1932; Chafe, 1977).

How, then, did John solve the problem of remembering events and developing ideas presented by the reporting and generalizing tasks? Each of the two tasks, in their most typical form, characteristically requires a different ordering of content. The reporting task generally requires a linear ordering of content something like the step-by-step progress of following a road map. The organization of content for the generalizing taks is more matrix-like, requiring that the writer keep the entire road map—or at least sections of it—in mind at one time. The matrix-like mix of abstraction with detail creates an internal logic focused on the information carried by the piece (Jones, 1977).

To produce the piece of reporting, John relied primarily on episodic memory, memory for events and experience (Tulving, 1972). The task was a good deal more straightforward than that required by the generalizing one. John moved the discourse forward by relying on an agent–action pattern pausing only to plan for new content in the sentence. Note that the only two times John stopped to reread (for 6.8 seconds in line 5 and for 4.7 seconds in line 10) he was well into the sentence and appeared to be planning for new content that would move the discourse forward. In the first instance, he paused to plan the remainder of the infinitive and to supply information that answered the question WHAT. During the other incidence of rereading John paused to answer the question HOW. John's retrospective self-report supports this notion: He seemed most concerned with remembering the details of the event.

By contrast, generalizing required that John abstract ideas and information from a wealth of personal experience. Acquiring and developing these ideas results from a gradual feeding of episodic memory into semantic memory, memory that systemizes one's knowledge of the world (Beaugrande, 1980, pp. 71–72). The longest pauses in this segment of generalizing appeared at sentence boundaries—locations where a shift in the abstraction level was likely to occur. When John removed his pen from the page and gazed away for 13.3 seconds (line 8) before beginning a new paragraph, he had reached an important conceptual boundary in the production of this piece. A decision at this moment during production certainly hinged on what had been written up to that point, but it also depended on a schematic representation of knowledge that may not, in this case, have been readily available. Creating meaning, organizing what he knows about the world in a new way, and placing that information in the context of a draft that he has begun and to which he is committed requires time-consuming mental effort (Cooper & Matsuhashi, forthcoming). By contrast, a schema for the reporting task is well-practiced and readily available: John must simply fit the events to a chronological line and inscribe the text, detail by detail. Though not the only influence on planning patterns, a writer's purpose or task wields a weighty influence on production processes.

Flexibility in Planning and Production

Throughout the speech production literature a common tactic has been to represent planning processes as units of language—most often the clause of the sentence—that are subsumed in hierarchical order. This hierarchical view results from a preoccupation with the static nature of finished products: (*a*) written text or (*b*) transcribed speech. For example, a hierarchical description of planning and execution forms the basis for an entire chapter on speech production in *Psychology and Language* (Clark & Clark, 1977, p. 224). According to Clark and Clark, production processes involve the following five hierarchical levels: discourse plans, sentence plans, constituent plans, articulatory program, and articulation. During discourse plans the speaker chooses a particular kind of discourse with its appropriate structure. In the context of this choice the speaker plans for the sentence, identifying the speech act, the subject, given and new content, and deciding how content will be subordinated. Likewise, to plan for constituents the speaker chooses the words and phrases that complete the sentence plan. Such a description aligns the entire production process, much of which is hidden, with the surface structure of the finished text. Consequently, analyses based on such descriptions often result in summary data from descriptive linguistic analysis that, understandably, does not take into account the real-time aspects of the process (See "Encoding Lexical and Syntactic Units" pp. 272–273). Moreover, in my own early work with pauses during writing, I found decreasing pause times prior to hierarchically ordered textual units (Matsuhashi & Cooper, 1978, Note 1).

The crucial question for learning about production processes is not how surface structures should be analyzed to account for decision making, but rather HOW UNDERLYING CONCEPTUAL CONTENT CORRESPONDS LEXICAL AND GRAMMATICAL CHOICES. Wallace Chafe (1979) explains how plans and decisions are made in terms of the interdependence of ongoing thought and ongoing speech. When Chafe examined stretches of spoken narrative, rather than summary data, he observed that speakers seemed to be deciding on a particular focus, or basic unit of information, as they spoke. The **focus,** the smallest unit of cognitive integration in Chafe's model, becomes the central unit or 'building block' in discourse production. He suggests that as a speaker moves from focus to focus the continuous revisions, hesitations, and garbles as well as pauses of various lengths represent transitions of varying difficulty.

My own observations of writers at work support Chafe's view of speech production. The psychological processes during discourse production are flexible; writing is produced at the same time it is organized. During text production, the writer responds to multiple demands with varying emphases: searching memory and consciousness, identifying and elaborating the underlying conceptual content, evaluating ideas and details in terms of their coherence and appropriateness, choosing which ideas will achieve dominance in the discourse, representing the conceptual content in syntactic structures, and managing the graphomotor activity necessary to inscribe the text. Finally, the fact that writing proceeds as an integral system is evident in the interleaving of long pauses and accompanying body language with the decision to produce substantial and complex segments of language.

From the real-time production data in Figures 10.1 and 10.2, I will make two broad claims about the flexible nature of planning and decision making during writing.

1. PLANNING DOES NOT CORRESPOND TO GRAMMATICAL UNITS; RATHER, IT CORRESPONDS TO PSYCHOLOGICAL PROCESSING UNITS BASED ON UNDERLYING CONCEPTUAL CONTENT. Surface structure constituents are seldom produced as a unit. Many times part of a constituent is produced with a preceding constituent. For example:

communication is difficult because... people (Gen, line 2)
"give and take" between... the parties (Gen, line 9)
managed to get myself involved in a... project (Rep, line 2)

One way to think about how time is used during writing is to conjecture that long pauses occur when the relationship between ideational content and final expression in syntax is most incongruous (Beaugrande, 1980). The underlying ideational or semantic content—often characterized as propositions (Kintsch, 1974)—does not necessarily depend on language, nor does it depend on real time. By contrast, producing the grammatical surface structure is a serially organized behavior that DOES depend on real time (Lashley, 1951; Miller, Galanter, & Pribram, 1960). Beaugrande (1980) suggests that "the selection of lexical and grammatical options tends to remain largely episodic [p. 72]." Thus, the long pauses that seem to interrupt constituents may represent a disjunction between the underlying psychological process of making meaning and the constraints of expressing meaning in the surface structure.

2. LONG PAUSES, ACCOMPANIED BY GAZING OR REREADING ACTIVITY AND BY REMOVING THE PEN FROM THE PAGE, CORRESPOND TO MULTIPLE DECISIONS, GENERALLY ONES WHICH ENCOMPASS GLOBAL ISSUES AS WELL AS LOCAL ONES. The taxonomy of body language during long pauses suggests a distinction between global decisions and local ones. When the hand holding the pen remains tense, close to the previously written word, the decision is, most likely, a local one, one that the writer expects to resolve quickly. The material for such a decision may reside in the immediate portion of the text, in short term memory store, or in a choice between several relatively accessible options. By contrast, when the writer relaxes his hand, removes it from the vicinity, and gazes away, he is involved in a substantially more complex, global decision concerning the writer's knowledge base or the overall semantic structure of the developing text.

Consider, for instance, the very different locations and body movements associated with the 13.3-second pause (Gen, line 8) and the 5.3-second pause (Gen, line 11). During the 13.3-second preparagraph pause, John leaned back, removed his pen from the vicinity and gazed away. By contrast, during the pause before *of the others,* John's pen followed his eyes as he reread the previous line preparing to complete the sentence with the appropriate information. The very different constellations of writing behavior surrounding these two pauses suggest very different operations: In the first instance John gazed away and distanced himself from the text to attend to a schematic representation of his knowledge of communication. In the second instance, John was attending to a surface structure decision based on material available from the already inscribed text.

This chapter stressed the need for an integrative model of production processes during writing. Relying on observational data—pause time accompanied by hand and eye movement—I have illustrated how such a model must account for the flexibility needed to plan and produce written discourse without oversimplifying the process. I have also suggested that a useful model of the writing process ought to account for the way that underlying meaning is identified, developed, and finally, expressed within the constraints of real time. This chapter provides a point of departure for further observational analysis of the writing process and further attempts at developing a sound theoretical model of the writing process.

ACKNOWLEDGMENTS

The research reported in this chapter was partially supported by a grant from the Graduate College Research Board of the University of Illinois at Chicago Circle. I am grateful to Cheryl Baunbach for the time she spent typing several drafts of this chapter. I am also grateful for the assistance of Karen Spittle for the many hours we spent discussing the issues underlying the research reported here.

REFERENCE NOTE

1. Matsuhashi, A., and Cooper, C. R. *A video time-monitored observational study: The transcribing behavior and composing processes of a competent high school writer.* Buffalo: State University of New York at Buffalo, 1978. (ERIC Document Reproduction Service No. ED 155 701)

REFERENCES

Appell, G., Dechert, H., & Raupach, M. (Eds.). *Selected bibliography on temporal variables in speech.* Tübingen: Gunter Narr Verlag, 1980.

Baddeley, A. D. *The psychology of memory.* New York: Basic Books, 1976.

Bartlett, F. *Remembering.* Cambridge: Cambridge University Press, 1932.

Beaugrande, R. de *Text, discourse and process: Toward a multidisciplinary science of texts.* Norwood, N.J.: Ablex, 1980.

Boomer, D. S. Hesitation and grammatical encoding. *Language and Speech,* 1965, *8,* 148–158.

Boomer, D. S. Review of Psycholinguistics: Experiments in spontaneous speech by F. Goldman-Eisler *Lingua,* 1970, *25,* 152–164.

van Bruggen, J. Factors affecting regularity of the flow of words during written composition. *Journal of Experimental Education,* 1946, *15,* 133–155.

Chafe, W. Creativity in verbalization and its implications for the nature of stored knowledge. In R. O. Freedle (Ed.), *Discourse production and comprehension.* Norwood, N.J.: Ablex, 1977.

Chafe, W. The flow of thought and the flow of language. In T. Givon (Ed.), *Discourse and syntax.* New York: Academic Press, 1979.

Chafe, W. The deployment of consciousness. In W. Chafe (Ed.), *The pear stories: Cognitive, cultural, and linguistic aspects of narrative production.* Norwood, N.J.: Ablex, 1980.

Clark, H., & Clark, E. *Psychology and language.* New York: Harcourt Brace Jovanovich, 1977.

Cooper, C. R., & Matsuhashi, A. A theory of the writing process. In M. Martlew (Ed.), *The psychology of writing*. New York: Wiley, forthcoming.

Danks, J. H. Producing ideas and sentences. In S. Rosenberg (Ed.), *Sentence production: Developments in research and theory*. Hillsdale, N.J.: Lawrence Erlbaum, 1977.

Diesing, P. *Patterns of discovery in the social sciences*. Hawthorne, N.Y.: Aldine, 1971.

Dijk, T. A. van, & Kintsch, W. Cognitive psychology and discourse: Recalling and summarizing stories. In W. Dressler (Ed.), *Current trends in textlinguistics*. New York: de Gruyter, 1978.

Dressler, W. V. (Ed.). *Current trends in textlinguistics*. New York: de Gruyter, 1978.

Frederiksen, C. H. Semantic processing units in understanding text. In R. O. Freedle (Ed.), *Discourse production and comprehension*. Norwood, N.J.: Ablex, 1977.

Fries, C. C. *The structure of English: An introduction to the construction of English sentences*. New York: Harcourt and Brace, 1952.

Goldman-Eisler, F. Speech production and the predictability of words in context. *Quarterly Journal of Experimental Psychology*, 1958, *10*, 96–106.

Goldman-Eisler, F. *Psycholinguistics: Experiments in spontaneous speech*. New York: Academic Press, 1968.

Goldman-Eisler, F. Pauses, clauses, sentences. *Language and Speech*, 1972, *15*, 103–113.

Greene, M. Language, literature, and the release of meaning. *College English*, 1979, *41*, 123–135.

Halliday, M., & Hasan, R. *Cohesion in English*. London: Longman, 1976.

Hawkins, P. R. The syntactic location of hesitation pauses. *Language and Speech*, 1971, *14*, 277–288.

Jones, L. *Theme in English expository discourse*. Lake Bluff, Ill.: Jupiter Press, 1977.

Kintsch, W. *The representation of meaning in memory*. Hillsdale, N.J.: Lawrence Erlbaum, 1974.

Kintsch, W., & van Dijk, T. A. Toward a model of text comprehension and production. *Psychological Review*, 1978, *85*, 363–395.

Lashley, K. S. The problem of serial order in behavior. In L. P. Jeffress (Ed.), *Cerebral mechanisms in behavior: The Hixon symposium*. New York: Wiley, 1951.

Lounsbury, F. Transitional probability, linguistic structure, and systems of habit family hierarchies. In C. E. Osgood and T. A. Sebeok (Eds.), *Psycholinguistics: A survey of theory and research problems*. Baltimore: Waverly Press, 1954.

Maclay, H., & Osgood, C. E. Hesitation phenomena in spontaneous English speech. *Word*, 1959, *15*, 19–44.

Matsuhashi, A. Pausing and planning: The tempo of written discourse production. *Research in the Teaching of English*, 1981, *15*(2), 113–134.

McNeill, D. *The conceptual basis of language*. Hillsdale, N.J.: Lawrence Erlbaum, 1979.

Miller, G. A., Galanter, E., and Pribram, K. H. *Plans and the structure of behavior*. New York: Holt, Rinehart, and Winston, 1960.

Murray, D. M. Internal revision: A process of discovery. In C. R. Cooper & L. Odell (Eds.), *Research on composing: Points of departure*. Urbana, Ill.: National Council of Teachers of English, 1978.

Nisbett, R. E., & Wilson, T. D. Telling more than we can know: Verbal reports on mental processes. *Psychological Review*, 1977, *84*, 231–259.

O'Connell, D. C. One of many units: The sentence. In S. Rosenberg (Ed.), *Sentence production: Developments in research and theory*. Hillsdale, N.J.: Lawrence Erlbaum, 1977.

O'Connell, D. C., & Kowal, S. Cross-linguistic pause and rate phenomena. *Journal of Psycholinguistic Research*, 1972, *1*(2), 155–164.

O'Connell, D. C., & Kowal, S. Pausology. In W. Sedelow & S. Sedelow (Eds.), *Computer uses in the study of language* (Vol. 3), *Cognitive approaches*. The Hague: Mouton, in press.

O'Connell, D. C., Kowal, S., & Hörmann, H. Semantic determinants of pauses. *Psychologuische Forschung*, 1969, *33*, 50–67.

Rochester, S. The significance of pauses in spontaneous speech. *Journal of Psycholinguistic Research*, 1973, 2, 51–81.

Rochester, S., & Gill, J. Production of complex sentences in monologues and dialogues. Journal of Verbal Learning and Verbal Behavior, 1973, *12*, 203–210.

Rosenberg, S. Semantic constraints on sentence production: An experimental approach. In S. Rosenberg (Ed.), *Sentence production: Developments in research and theory*. Hillsdale, N.J.: Lawrence Erlbaum, 1977.

Tulving, E. Episodic and semantic memory. In E. Tulving and W. Donaldson (Eds.), *The organization of memory*. New York: Academic Press, 1972.

Weigl, E. On written language: Its acquisition and its lexicographic disturbances. In E. H. Lenneberg and E. Lenneberg (Eds.), *Foundations of language development* (Vol. 2). New York: Academic Press, 1975.

Chapter 11

Speech–Act Theory
and Writing

Martin Steinmann, Jr.

Perhaps the chief focus of rhetoric, both classical and modern, has been on writing well (let us set speaking aside)—on effective expression, on writers' causing readers to experience the effects they intend them to experience. As Quintilian (1921, vol. 1, p. 388) said, "rhetorice . . . erit bene dicendi scientia." **Speech–act theory**—a theory of linguistic communication—makes two contributions to rhetoric as the study of effective expression. First, it makes a principled distinction between two kinds of effective expression. One kind is writing clearly, writing readable discourse—in other words, writing so that readers easily experience the effect of understanding the discourse (in speech–act terms, **the illocutionary effect**). The other kind of effective expression is writing persuasively—writing so that readers experience other intended effects (**perlocutionary effects**), such effects as believing a statement, granting a request, and answering a question. Second, implicit in speech–act theory is part of a rhetorical theory—in particular, **a theory of illocutionary-effectiveness competence,** a theory of what writers who write clearly know that enables them to write that way.

Effective expression, however, is a rather vague notion; and, before turning to speech-act theory, I want to clarify it.

EFFECTIVE EXPRESSION

First, effective expression is not merely correct expression; writing well is not merely writing correctly. Writing correctly is like playing a game according to the rules; writing well is like winning games. As someone has observed,[1] there is a great difference between books entitled *How to play chess* and ones entitled *How to Win at Chess*. **Correct expression** is the object of grammatical (or linguistic) research, of research into a theory of grammatical competence. Such a theory formulates the grammatical rules of a language—the syntactic and the graphemic rules, for example. Grammatical competence is knowledge of these rules. It is the ability to write the language correctly. **Effective expression,** on the other hand, is the object of rhetorical research, of research into a theory of rhetorical competence (discussed later, pp. 295–297). The ultimate goal of such a theory is to formulate rhetorical laws, empirical laws causally relating written discourse to effects on readers. Rhetorical competence is knowledge of these laws. It is the ability to choose, from an indefinitely large number of sequences of grammatical (correct) sentences, a sequence that, when written and read, causes readers to experience the effects intended (cf. Steinmann, 1976).

Second, what about the five parts of classical rhetoric: *inventio, dispositio, elocutio, memoria,* and *pronuntiatio*? Are they included in the notion of effective expression? I exclude the last two with no hesitation, because, though relevant to speaking, they are irrelevant to writing. The first three, however, are problematic. The domain of *inventio* is choice (or discovery) of things to say; of *dispositio,* choice of ways to organize them; of *elocutio,* choice of sentences to say them. There are principled ways of distinguishing these three choices. Choice of things to say, unlike the other two choices, is not in itself expressive but cognitive or affective. A writer has some knowledge and makes a statement about it, for example, or has a desire and makes a request that it be satisfied. Making a statement or a request is an expressive act (in speech–act terms, an illocutionary act), but having knowledge or desires is not an act at all.[2] And choice of ways of organizing things to say, unlike choice of sentences to say them, is semantic (or propositional) rather than lexical and syntactic. A certain organiza-

---

[1]Who I have unfortunately forgotten, but it is neither de Saussure (1959, pp. 22–23) nor Wittgenstein (1964, 43, 45), each of whom uses a language–chess analogy in his own way, each way different from my forgotten source's.

[2]This is not to dismiss epistemological questions about the relationships between making assertions and having knowledge. If the ancient distinction between knowing-HOW and knowing-THAT (elaborated in "Competence," pp. 294–295) is valid, perhaps no one ever knows THAT something is the case without having asserted, at least subvocally, that it is: "One does not conceive a theory and then express it; he conceives it by expressing it; and, if he cannot express it, he doesn't have it [Steinmann, 1966, pp. 19–20]."

tion does not entail a certain language. The three choices, nevertheless, coalesce in effective expression. Choice of sentences embodies the other two choices, and it is the only choice that has direct EFFECTS on readers. Rhetorical research in writing may sometimes wish to isolate these three choices from one another, but all contribute to effective (or ineffective) expression.

Three matters that I have only glanced at also require some clarification: the distinction between a rule and an empirical law; competence, or knowledge; and rhetorical theory.

Rules Versus Empirical Laws

An empirical law is a part of nature, human or otherwise; but a rule is a human creation. A **law** is simply a regularity: under conditions of a certain kind (the cause), an event of a certain kind (the effect). The regularity may be universal: if the temperature rises to 212°F, and if atmospheric pressure is normal, then water ALWAYS boils. Or it may be statistical: if a writer uses a polite form of request (*Would you please send me . . . ?*) rather than a direct form (*Send me. . . .*), then readers are MORE LIKELY to comply with the request. But a **rule** is, in effect, a decision made by a human group: a decision that, under conditions of a certain kind, each member of the group engage in behavior of a certain kind in order to serve some purpose. Often, though not always, a rule is arbitrary in the sense that a different decision (though not just any different decision) would serve the purpose just as well. Among drivers in England, it is a rule to drive on the left; among drivers in America, to drive on the right. One rule serves the purpose of coordinating traffic as well as the other (though a rule to drive in the middle would not). Among speakers of English, it is a rule, under conditions of a certain kind, to count an utterance (either one's own or another's) of *my mother* as a reference to the writer's mother; among speakers of French, to count an utterance of *ma mère*. One rule serves the referential purpose as well as the other (though a rule to so count an utterance of *Rumpelstiltskin,* perhaps, would not). (Both rules and laws differ, of course, from their formulations: Formulations are sentences; rules and laws are not.)

Though an empirical law is a regularity of behavior, human or otherwise, it does not regulate behavior; it IS behavior—regular (but not regulated) behavior. A rule, on the other hand, regulates behavior (but only human behavior), not in the way a tap on the patella jerks the knee but by prescribing it. Members of the group—drivers in England, for example, or speakers of French—expect one another to follow the rule; that is, they believe that, under conditions of the requisite kind, they not only usually do, but ought to, engage in behavior of the requisite kind. But the possibility of following a rule implies the possibility of breaking it: to say that such and such is a rule but that so and so broke it is not a contradiction. In the sense of *law* sketched here, however, a law is not the sort of thing that can be either followed or broken: Whatever is, is.

A rule may be either **regulative** or **constitutive** (Searle, 1969, pp. 33–42). If regulative, it regulates behavior of a kind that would exist even if the rule did not. The traffic rule to drive on the right, for instance, is regulative, because car driving exists independently of traffic rules. If a rule is constitutive, it constitutes (creates, defines) behavior of the very kind it regulates. Under conditions of the requisite kind, a hostess's extending her hand counts as a greeting; writing *Would you please... ?*, as a polite form of request; writing *my mother,* as a reference to the speaker's mother. Without a constitutive rule, a hostess can extend her hand, but not as a greeting; someone can write (or utter the sounds represented by) *Would you please...?* , but not as a polite form of request; someone can write *my mother,* but not as a reference to that person's mother. Greeting, requesting, and referring do not exist independently of the rules that constitute behavior of these kinds.

Human behavior is, of course, guided by both **law competences** (knowledge of laws) and **rule competences** (knowledge of rules), not to mention knowledge of historical facts. Any knowledge can guide behavior. The cook who avoids close contact with red pepper surely knows the law causally relating red pepper to sneezing. The writer who, in making a request, writes *Would you please... ?* surely knows both the law causally relating that form to reader compliance and the rule that utterance of that form counts as a polite form of request. Certainly linguistic behavior is guided by knowledge of both laws and rules—specifically, by knowledge of rhetorical laws (causally relating written discourse to effects upon readers) and grammatical rules (regulating the creation and the interpretation of discourse). There are, of course, grammatical laws as well as grammatical rules. There seems, for instance, to be a statistical grammatical law causally relating a vowel's position before a nasal consonant to its nasalization. But knowledge of grammatical laws seems not to guide linguistic behavior (though grammatical rules perhaps evolve in accordance with grammatical laws). On the other hand, though there are rhetorical laws, there are no rhetorical rules. There is, for example, no rule—though there is, perhaps, a law—that, if a written discourse contains many familiar (high-frequency) words, then its readers will easily experience the effect of understanding it. If readers do easily experience this effect, they do so, not because they have decided or agreed to, but because their knowledge and minds are so structured that they must.

Competence

I have said that writers can have both **rhetorical competence** (knowledge of rhetorical laws) and **grammatical competence** (knowledge of grammatical rules). If, however, all knowledge consists of the knowers' having justified true beliefs—of their knowing THAT something is the case—then my claim is very implausible. This **theoretical,** explicit, and (often) formulated **knowledge** of language and its uses is what (some) linguists, philosophers, and psycholinguists have. But obviously few writers have it; and, of course, qua writers, they don't need it. What writers do have, I postulate, is **practical,** implicit, intuitive, unconscious, unformulated **knowledge** of rhetorical laws and grammatical rules. They don't know THAT; they know HOW—how to perform in certain ways. Linguists have long postulated grammatical competence—practical knowledge of grammatical rules—to explain CORRECT linguistic performance (e.g., Bach & Harnish, 1979, pp. 8–9, 93; Chomsky, 1965, p. 8). It is, I suggest, equally plausible to postulate rhetorical competence—practical knowledge of rhetorical laws—to explain EFFECTIVE linguistic performance.

Rhetorical Theory

Finally, before outlining speech-act theory and showing how it makes a principled distinction between two kinds of effective expression and how implicit in it is a rhetorical theory, I must sort out some of the things that might be called rhetorical theories, show how they are related to one another, and say to which of them speech-act theory can contribute.

One kind of rhetorical theory tries to explain how writers can acquire rhetorical competence through formal instruction. This is **a pedagogical theory of rhetoric,** a theory of teaching written composition. What methods of instruction—lecture, discussion, drill, guided practice, and so on—are best for instilling rhetorical competence? What are the best ways to prepare teachers to instill it? These are among the general questions that a pedagogical theory of rhetoric might try to answer. Most rhetorical research in writing in our century (as reported in *College Composition and Communication,* for example) has tried to answer such questions.

Another kind of rhetorical theory tries to explain how writers with rhetorical competence produce the effective product: the process of effective expression—the physical, the psychological, or even the neurological mechanisms that operate when writers express themselves effectively. This is **a theory of rhetorical performance** or of the rhetorical or composing process. What goes on—physically, psychologically, or neurologically—when writers express themselves effectively? What is the role of memory or the role of intelligence in effective expression? These are among the questions that such a theory might try to answer. In recent years, much rhetorical research in writing has turned to such questions, often mixing them with pedagogical questions. As Donovan and McClelland (1980, p. x) put it, "Today we have begun to ask, how is good writing performed?"

Finally, yet another kind of rhetorical theory tries to explain what writers must know in order to express themselves effectively. This is, in the strictest sense, **a theory of rhetorical competence** (including, as we shall see, both a theory of illocutionary-effectiveness competence and a theory of perlocutionary-effectiveness competence). It might also be called a theory of the effective product, of effective discourse, or a theory of what linguistic choices are effective. But a bit misleadingly, for a theory of this kind must go beyond describing the effective product or effective choices. Effectiveness is not a property of the product; it is a relation—a causal relation—between the product and readers. Effective choices are choices that—once they are transformed into writing and, so transformed, are read—cause readers to experience the effects writers intend. And what writers must know—practical knowledge, not theoretical—in order to make effective choices is rhetorical laws, empirical laws causally relating the product or linguistic choices to effects on readers. A theory of rhetorical competence is, then, a theory of competence (rather than a pedagogical theory or a theory of performance) in precisely the sense that a grammar of a language is a theory of grammatical competence (rather than a pedagogical theory of grammar or a theory of grammatical performance) (cf. Chomsky, 1965, pp. 3–9). The differences between a theory of rhetorical competence and a theory of grammatical competence spring from their different objects: knowledge of rhetorical laws and knowledge of grammatical rules, respectively.

Because a theory of rhetorical competence formulates laws causally relating written discourse to readers' responses to it (relating the product to consumers' acceptance of it) it is also a theory of readers' responses to discourse. But its focus is the product: What must writers know about readers' responses to discourse in order to produce a product that causes readers to have the responses writers intend?

How are these three kinds of rhetorical theory related to one another? In two ways, I believe.

First, the difference between (*a*) pedagogical theories of rhetoric and (*b*) theories of performance and theories of competence is like the difference between horticulture and botany or between animal husbandry and zoology or between engineering and physics. It is a difference between a technology and the science that the technology presupposes. As I have argued elsewhere (Steinmann, 1965, 1966, 1967), a valid theory of rhetorical performance and a valid theory of rhetorical competence are basic; without them, a valid pedagogical theory of rhetoric is impossible; and the almost universally acknowledged failure of freshman composition in America is chiefly due to its lack of any basic theoretical support. Until recently, no one knew much, except in an intuitive way, about what goes on when writers make effective choices or about what choices are effective; and what little was known had little effect on the teaching of writing. On the whole, this teaching has been a technology without—though hardly in search of—a science.

My point is not, of course, that in order to learn how to write effectively, students must be acquainted with a valid theory of rhetorical performance or rhetorical competence or even that, in order to teach writing successfully, teachers must be acquainted with it. My point is that, to the extent that good teaching of writing must depend on pedagogical research, it must depend also on basic research.

Second, just as a theory of grammatical performance presupposes a theory of grammatical competence (cf. Chomsky, 1965, pp. 10–15), a theory of rhetorical performance presupposes a theory of rhetorical competence. In other words, a theory of what goes on—physically, psychologically, or neurologically—when writers make effective choices must incorporate a theory of what choices are effective. In recent years, scorning the product and embracing the process have become fashionable; there has, we are told (Donovan & McClelland, 1980, pp. x–xii), been a Kuhnian paradigm shift. Indeed, some researchers (e.g., Emig, 1978) find investigation of the product intellectually disreputable, if not morally reprehensible. But it makes no sense to investigate a process without knowledge of its product. How can researchers investigate a means without knowing what end it is a means to? How can they ask, as Donovan and McClelland (1980, p. x) do, "how is good writing performed?" without first asking what good writing is?

SPEECH–ACT THEORY

Speech-act theory is a comprehensive theory of linguistic communication—a theory, that is, of what a writer (or a speaker) and a reader (or a listener) have to know and to do if the former is to communicate with the latter through written (or spoken) discourse. This theory is not monolithic or static but various and dynamic. The original speech-act theory was advanced by the late J. L. Austin (1962) in his William James Lectures at Harvard in 1955 and elaborated by his student J. R. Searle (1969, 1979). Later theories—notably, Sadock's (1974) and Bach and Harnish's (1979)—rival Austin and Searle's as well as one another in numerous and important ways. These rival theories, however, agree about fundamentals. They all agree, for example, that linguistic communication is more than merely saying something; it is saying something in a certain context, with certain intentions, and with the reader's (or the listener's) recognition both of what is said and of these intentions. This is not the place to go into the differences among these rival theories, nor is it the place for a full exposition of any of them. I shall confine myself to a brief and greatly simplified exposition of Bach and Harnish's theory, the most comprehensive, elaborate, and technical of these rival theories. I choose their theory not only because I believe it to be the best but partly because I also believe it to contribute most to rhetoric as the study of effective expression.

Here is Bach and Harnish's theory in a nutshell. Linguistic communication is a cooperative venture between a writer (or a speaker) and one or more readers (or listeners). The writer performs certain speech acts, and readers interpret them. Linguistic communication occurs when two conditions are satisfied. First, the writer says something to readers, intends them to take it as a sign that he (or she)[3] has a certain attitude (a certain belief or desire, say), and further intends them to recognize that he has this intention. Second, readers recognize the writer's intentions.

In speech-act terms, what the writer does in this cooperative venture is to perform three different communicative speech acts simultaneously—an **utterance act,** a **locutionary act,** and an **illocutionary act**—and what readers do is to infer what these acts are. The writer also, and simultaneously, performs a fourth speech act—a **perlocutionary act.** Like the other three acts, this act is intentional. Unlike them, however, it is not communicative. It is, rather, a consequence or result of one or more of the communicative acts.

Utterance Act

In a certain context of utterance, the writer intentionally utters to readers an expression (usually a sentence) from some language; that is, he performs an **utterance act.** For example, he writes,

(1)   *The boy next door likes Hazel better than Joan.*

In performing an utterance act, the writer intends and expects readers to know **the linguistic meaning** of his expression (that is, the meaning that it has by virtue of the grammatical rules of its language) or, if it is (even though he does not realize that it is) ambiguous, at least one of its linguistic meanings. To explain how he can reasonably expect them to know this, the theory postulates **the linguistic presumption:** the mutual belief in the language-speaking community (of which he and they are members) that its members share grammatical competence in the language and consequently that, if the writer takes an expression to have a certain linguistic meaning, then readers will too. (A **mutual belief** is a belief, not only that both writer and readers have, but also that both believe both to have and both believe both to believe both to have.) But an ambiguous expression is a special case. In a sense, all members of the community know its multiple meanings: If the meanings are pointed out, they will at once be recognized. But, if they are not, they may not. An ambiguous expression is like the now-it's-a-duck, now-it's-a-rabbit, ambiguous drawings so dear to experimen-

---

[3]To avoid prolixity, I henceforth use the pronouns *he, him,* and *his* in their generic senses to refer to any writer of either sex.

tal psychologists. Quite possibly, therefore, both the writer and readers may fail to recognize multiple meanings, and the sole meaning he recognizes may well be different from the one they recognize. Sentence (1), for example, has two linguistic meanings: First, 'The boy next door likes Hazel better than he likes Joan'; second, 'The boy next door likes Hazel better than Joan likes Hazel.' Both the writer and readers may fail to recognize both of these; he may recognize only the first, say, while they recognize only the second.

As for readers, they infer the linguistic meaning or meanings of the expression because they share the linguistic presumption with the writer and because they in fact have grammatical competence in the language.

Locutionary Act

In performing an utterance act in a context, usually the writer also performs a **locutionary act**—that is, an act of intentionally saying something to readers. In writing sentence (1), for instance, the writer is, let us suppose, saying that the boy next door likes Hazel better than he likes Joan (rather than saying that he likes Hazel better than Joan likes her).

What is the difference between merely uttering an expression (merely performing an utterance act) and, in uttering it, saying something (performing a locutionary act)? The difference is in the writer's intentions. In merely uttering an expression, the writer intends and expects readers to know the linguistic meaning or meanings of the expression. But, in saying something in uttering the expression, the writer intends and expects readers to know not only that but also (*a*) the operative meaning of the expression, (*b*) its propositional content, and (*c*) its type of saying. The **operative meaning** is the meaning the writer intends the expression to have. The operative meaning of sentence (1), for example, is (we have supposed) 'The boy next door likes Hazel better than he likes Joan.' The **propositional content** consists of (*b.1*) the referents (people, objects, places, times, etc.) that the writer is referring to and (*b.2*) the predication (the properties or the relations he is predicating of these referents). The propositional content of sentence (1), for instance, consists of (*b.1*) the referents some boy, next door, the boy next door, Hazel, and Joan and (*b.2*) the predication of a certain relation of some boy and next door (some boy's LIVING next door) and a certain relation of the boy next door, Hazel, and Joan (his LIKING Hazel BETTER THAN he LIKES Joan). The **type of saying** is such a thing as saying that it is the case that (*b.1*) plus (*b.2*) (for example, that the boy next door likes Hazel better than he likes Joan) or as saying whether it is the case that (*b.1*) plus (*b.2*) (for example, whether the boy next door likes Hazel better than he likes Joan). In these two examples, the referents are identical (some boy, next door, the boy next door, Hazel, and Joan), and so is the predication (the relation predicated of some boy and next door and the one predicated of the boy next door, Hazel, and Joan). The types of saying, however, are different.

Perhaps the best way to see the difference between merely uttering an expression and, in uttering it, saying something is to notice that a writer can, as I have done here in writing sentence (1), perform an utterance act without performing a locutionary act. In writing (1), I intended and expected my readers to know the linguistic meaning of (1) but nothing more—neither operative meaning, propositional content, nor type of saying. Indeed, there is no operative meaning for my readers to know. For I intended neither of the linguistic meanings of (1). Nor is there any propositional content for them to know. For there is no boy, no next door, no boy next door, no Hazel, no Joan that, in writing (1), I was referring to; and nothing can be predicated of nothing. And, since there is no propositional content, there is no type of saying either.

To infer what the writer is saying (that is, the operative meaning, the propositional content, and the type of saying), readers do a variety of things, making tentative inferences until everything seems to hang together.

First, operative meaning. Readers need infer it only if the expression is, like sentence (1), ambiguous; otherwise, the operative meaning is identical with the (sole) linguistic meaning (which readers already know, from the utterance act). Once readers know the operative meaning, they know the predication, and they may know something about the referents as well. Operative meaning completely determines predication but never completely determines the referents of referring expressions (such expressions as *the boy, next door, the boy next door, Hazel,* and *Joan*). For one thing, referring expressions that are proper names (*Hazel, Joan*) seem to have no meaning at all, either linguistic or operative (cf. pp. 312–313); and, to determine their referents, readers must use **mutual contextual beliefs,** mutual beliefs about the context of utterance. To determine the referent of *Hazel* in (1), for instance, readers might use the mutual contextual belief that the writer's sister is the only person named Hazel that he knows and thereby infer that the referent of *Hazel* is the writer's sister. For another thing, even to determine the referents of referring expressions that do have meaning—pronouns (*he, she*) and definite descriptions (*the boy, next door, the boy next door*)—readers must supplement knowledge of their meaning with mutual contextual beliefs. For example, to which next door (of an indefinitely large number of next doors) is the writer using *next door* to refer? Only a mutual contextual belief can guide readers to a plausible answer.

If the expression is ambiguous—has two or more linguistic meanings—readers must determine which one is the operative meaning by using mutual contextual beliefs; and, of course, these beliefs may cause readers to recognize only one linguistic meaning (namely, the one identical with the operative meaning). To determine which linguistic meaning of sentence (1), for instance, is operative, readers might use the mutual contextual belief that Joan does not even know that Hazel exists (and therefore can have no feelings about her) and thereby infer that the operative meaning of (1) is 'The boy next door likes Hazel better than he likes Joan' rather than 'The boy next door likes Hazel better than Joan likes Hazel.'

Finally, using the linguistic presumption and grammatical competence, readers determine the type of sentence (declarative or interrogative, say) and therefore the type of saying—determining, for example, that sentence (1) is declarative and therefore that the type of saying is saying-THAT-it-is-the-case-that rather than saying-WHETHER-it-is-the-case-that.

Illocutionary Act

In performing a locutionary act—that is, in intentionally saying something to readers, usually the writer also performs an **illocutionary act**—that is, an act of doing such a thing as stating, requesting, promising, greeting, or apologizing. In saying that the boy next door likes Hazel better than he likes Joan, for instance, the writer is stating (affirming, alleging, asserting, avering, claiming, maintaining, submitting) that the boy next door likes Hazel better than he likes Joan.

Like the difference between performing an utterance act and performing a locutionary act, the difference between performing a locutionary act and performing an illocutionary act is solely a difference in the writer's intentions. In merely saying something, the writer intends and expects readers to know not only the operational meaning of the expression but also the propositional content and the type of saying. But, in doing something (stating, requesting, promising, greeting, apologizing) in saying something, he expresses at least one **attitude,** and for him to express an attitude is for him to **reflexively intend** readers to take the locutionary act as a sign that he has that attitude.

But what is an attitude? It is a state of mind such as a belief, an intention, a desire, or a feeling. In performing the illocutionary act of stating, for example, the writer expresses both belief in a certain proposition (that is, belief that such and such is the case) and the intention that readers believe that proposition. In performing the illocutionary act of requesting, he expresses both the desire that readers do a certain thing and the intention that they do it because (or partly because) of his desire. In performing the illocutionary act of promising, he expresses three attitudes: the belief that the locutionary act creates an obligation for him to do a certain thing, the intention to do that thing, and the intention that readers believe that that act creates that obligation and that he intends to do that thing. In performing the illocutionary act of greeting (sincerely rather than perfunctorily), he expresses both pleasure at meeting readers and the intention that they believe that he is so pleased. In performing the illocutionary act of apologizing (sincerely), he expresses both regret for having done a certain thing to readers and the intention that they believe that he regrets having done that thing.

And what is a reflexive intention? It is an intention that its intender intends someone to recognize as intended to be recognized: the writer, for instance, intends readers to recognize that he intends them to recognize that he has a certain attitude. In performing the illocutionary act of stating, for instance, the writer intends readers to recognize that he intends them to recognize both that he believes a certain proposition and that he intends them to believe that proposition.

In performing an illocutionary act, the writer has, then, a reflexive intention. But—and this *but* is crucial—his reflexive intention is of a special kind known as an illocutionary intention. His illocutionary intention is a reflexive intention whose achievement or fulfillment consists solely in readers' recognizing that intention. Communication is complete as soon as (if ever) readers recognize his reflexive intention, as soon as they identify the illocutionary act that he is performing—in speech-act terms, as soon as they experience (what Searle named) **the illocutionary effect** or (what Austin named) **uptake.** If the writer performs the illocutionary act of making a statement, for example, communication is complete as soon as readers recognize that he intends them to recognize both that he believes a certain proposition and that he intends them to believe it. Nothing further is necessary for communication. Readers need not, for instance, actually believe either that he believes the proposition (they may believe him to be lying) or that he intends them to believe it (*Surely he doesn't expect us to believe that*); and they certainly need not believe it, not even if they believe that he believes it (they may believe him to be mistaken in believing it). (Anything further—readers' forming these beliefs, for instance—is, as we shall see, perlocutionary: the writer's performing a perlocutionary act and readers' experiencing a perlocutionary effect.)

To recognize the writer's reflexive intention (to identify the illocutionary act that he is performing, to experience the illocutionary effect or uptake), readers must make three correct inferences.

First, they must infer that the writer has some illocutionary intention, that he is performing SOME illocutionary act. What act (if, indeed, any) he is performing is a question to be answered by the other two inferences. As readers' basis for this first inference, the theory postulates **the communicative presumption:** the mutual belief in the language-speaking community (of which the writer and readers are members) that, if the writer is performing a locutionary act (saying something), then he is also performing some illocutionary act, unless readers have reason to believe otherwise. Readers might, for example, believe that, in saying that the boy next door likes Hazel better than he likes Joan, the writer was just kidding or was telling a joke (*It seems that the boy next door* . . .) or was setting down the first sentence of a novel (cf. Brown & Steinmann, 1978; Searle, 1979, pp. 58–75). Believing that, readers believe that, though performing a locutionary act, the writer is not performing any illocutionary act at all; and, therefore, they abandon inference-making.

Once readers have inferred that the writer is performing SOME illocutionary act, they must make two further inferences: what kind of illocutionary act (stating, requesting, promising, greeting, apologizing—whatever) he is performing and what its content is (what he is stating, requesting, promising . . .).[4] The bases for these two inferences are, the theory postulates, various—notably, what the writer says (the type of saying and the propositional content of the locutionary act), but also mutual contextual beliefs and other mutual beliefs. Making these two inferences can be a very complicated activity, and I cannot go very far into it here. But I want to briefly discuss two facts that especially complicate it. One is that the writer's illocutionary act may be either literal or nonliteral (that is, figurative—ironical, say, or metaphorical). The other is that, whether literal or nonliteral, his act may be either direct or indirect as well.

The difference between a literal and a nonliteral illocutionary act is determined by the relationship that the writer intends between the act and what he says. If his act is literal, then what he says limits but does not fully determine that act; it must be compatible with that act but may be compatible with other acts as well. For example, his saying that the boy next door likes Hazel better than he likes Joan is compatible not only with his stating that but also with his suggesting or conceding it. To infer what kind of literal illocutionary act he is performing, readers cannot, therefore, rely solely upon what he says. They must use mutual contextual beliefs too. If, on the other hand, his act is nonliteral, then what he says does not limit (is incompatible with) that act, though what he says must, if readers are to correctly infer what that act is, have some recognizable connection with it. For example, his saying that the boy next door likes Hazel better than he likes Joan is incompatible with his asking readers whether the boy next door likes Hazel better than he likes Joan. It is also incompatible with his stating that the boy next door likes Joan better than he likes Hazel.

To decide whether the writer's illocutionary act is literal or figurative, readers rely upon two (among other) mutual beliefs. One is a set of presumptions, first formulated by Grice (1975), called **conversational presumptions.** Some of these presumptions are relevant only to communication between speakers and listeners: the presumption, for instance, that

---

[4]Some kinds of illocutionary act seem to have no propositional content: greeting (*Hi!*), for example, and pure expressions of such attitudes as surprise (*Ah!*), sorrow (*Alas!*), joy (*Hurrah!*), and pain (*Ouch!*) (cf. Steinmann, 1978).

the speaker's illocutionary act is relevant to the conversational exchange at a given stage—that it is, say, of a kind appropriate at the stage (for instance, an answer to a question). But most of these presumptions are relevant to communication between writers and readers as well: the presumption, for example, that the writer's statement is, given mutual contextual beliefs, as informative as readers need or want it to be but no more informative than that or that his statement is true or that his request is such that they have the ability to comply with it. If what he says seems to accord with (or satisfy) these conversational presumptions, then they decide that his illocutionary act COULD be literal. By relying upon another mutual belief, they decide that his act IS literal: **the presumption of literalness,** the mutual belief in the language-speaking community that, if the writer's illocutionary act COULD be literal, then it is. If, for example, the writer and readers mutually believe that they want to know whether the boy next door likes Hazel better than he likes Joan, and if the writer says that the boy does, readers will decide that his act is literal. In other words, if what he says is something that they obviously want to know, then the act is literal. If, on the other hand, he and they mutually believe that they know that the boy next door hates Hazel and loves Joan and if he says that the boy likes Hazel better than he likes Joan, readers decide that the writer's act is nonliteral. In other words, if what he says is obviously false, then the act is nonliteral.

Once readers decide that the writer's illocutionary act is nonliteral, they must then decide what kind of act it is and what its content is. Usually the kind of act is not at issue, and they need decide only what its content is. To decide this, they may consider many kinds of hypothesis. I mention only one. If the kind of illocutionary act is statement-making, they may consider the hypothesis that the act is ironical—that is, that what the writer SAYS is the opposite of what he is STATING. Though he says that the boy prefers Joan to Hazel, perhaps he is stating that the boy prefers Hazel to Joan. If this hypothesis seems to fit mutual contextual beliefs better than rival ones do, readers decide that the writer's act is ironical.

Just a few words about the other fact that complicates readers' inferring both what kind of illocutionary act the writer is performing and what its content is: the fact that, whether literal or nonliteral, his act may be either direct or indirect as well. If his illocutionary act is indirect, he performs it while, and as a consequence of, performing another (direct) illocutionary act; and, to identify the indirect act, readers must first identify the other (direct) act. For instance, while stating (a direct act) that the readers' mother is suffering from malnutrition, the writer is requesting (an indirect act) that they give her food. Often, as in this example, the direct and the indirect acts differ both in the kind of act performed (here: stating versus requesting) and in content (here: mother-suffering-malnutrition versus readers-giving-mother-food). The readers first identify the direct act as a certain statement and then, by using conversational presumptions and mutual contextual beliefs, identify the indirect act as a certain request. Using a conversational presumption, they expect the writer's statement to be no more informative than they need it to be, but he and they mutually believe that they know perfectly well that their mother is suffering from malnutrition and therefore do not need to be so informed. He and they further mutually believe that they have an obligation to relieve her suffering but that, unlike him, are indifferent to it and will not relieve it unless he requests them to. Perhaps he makes an indirect request rather than a direct because an indirect one is more polite—they can save face by pretending that his statement is news—and because he can avoid the possible unpleasantness that a direct request might provoke. (If so, his intentions—to be polite and to avoid unpleasantness—are, as we shall see, PERLocutionary.)

Perlocutionary Act

BY performing an utterance act, a locutionary act, or an illocutionary act, the writer may, but need not, perform a **perlocutionary act,** an act of producing a certain effect—a perlocutionary effect upon readers. He performs a perlocutionary act if and only if (*a*) he intends (a perlocutionary intention) to produce an effect (the INTENDED perlocutionary effect) upon readers that is different from the communicative effect of their recognizing his utterance, locutionary, or illocutionary act (different, notably, from the illocutionary effect), (*b*) he produces some such effect (the ACTUAL perlocutionary effect) upon them, and (*c*) he produces the perlocutionary effect by producing the communicative effect of their recognizing his utterance, locutionary, or illocutionary act (that is, this communicative effect is a necessary, though not a sufficient, condition of the perlocutionary effect).

Some examples of perlocutionary acts: By performing the utterance act of writing, *Sic transit gloria mundi,* the writer intends (his perlocutionary intention) to impress readers with his knowledge of Latin (the INTENDED perlocutionary effect) but causes them to think him pretentious (the ACTUAL perlocutionary effect). By performing the utterance act of writing, *Ron called me yesterday,* and, in performing it, performing the locutionary act of saying that President Reagan called him yesterday, the writer intends (his perlocutionary intention) readers to believe (and—a reflexive intention—intends them to recognize that he so intends) that he believes that letting people know that one is on a first-name basis with the mighty is rather gauche (the INTENDED perlocutionary effect) and causes them to believe that he so believes (the ACTUAL perlocutionary effect). IN performing the illocutionary act of stating that the boy next door likes Hazel better than he likes Joan, the writer intends (his ILlocutionary intention) readers to recognize that he intends them to recognize both that he believes this and that he intends them to believe it. BY performing this illocutionary act, he intends (his PERlocutionary intention) both (*a*) that they believe that he believes this (one INTENDED perlocutionary effect) and (*b*) that they believe it (the other INTENDED perlocutionary effect) and causes them to experience (*a*) but not (*b*). In other words, he (as he intends) causes them to believe him to be sincere (*a*) but (as he does not intend) does not cause them to share his belief (*b*).

These examples suggest four conclusions about the relationship between a perlocutionary act and one or more of the other three speech acts. First, the writer typically, but not necessarily, performs an utterance, a locutionary, or an illocutionary act with a perlocutionary intention—an intention to produce a certain perlocutionary effect (the intended perlocutionary effect). Second, his perlocutionary intention is different from—it is over and above—his communicative intention (that is, his intention that readers recognize his utterance, locutionary, or illocutionary act). Notably, his perlocutionary intention is different from his illocutionary intention. His illocutionary intention is merely that readers recognize that he intends them to recognize his attitudes (including, usually, an attitude that is an intention that they believe something or do something). His illocutionary intention is solely a communicative intention: once readers recognize it (the communicative effect), communication is complete. His perlocutionary intention, however, is, by performing one of the other three speech acts (notably, an illocutionary act) and getting readers to recognize that act, to affect them in some further way—to get them to believe something, for example, or to do something. Third, unlike his communicative intention (notably, his illocutionary intention), the writer's perlocutionary intention is not achieved or fulfilled solely by readers' recognizing it. Like his illocutionary intention, his perlocutionary intention may (but need not) be reflexive (that is, he may or may not intend readers to recognize it). But, even when it is reflexive, its achievement does not depend solely upon their recognizing it. They can recognize the INTENDED perlocutionary effect without experiencing it: the ACTUAL perlocutionary effect can be different. Indeed, their recognizing his perlocutionary intention (his intention, say to hoodwink them) may be fatal to its achievement or fulfillment. Fourth— and this conclusion is closely related to the third—the ACTUAL perlocutionary effect (that is, the perlocutionary effect upon readers) depends much more upon them than the communicative effect (notably, the illocutionary effect) does; consequently, the ACTUAL perlocutionary effect varies more from reader to reader than the communicative effect does. The communicative effect depends solely upon readers' grammatical competence, mutual beliefs, and ability to use this competence and these beliefs to infer the writer's communicative intention. The ACTUAL perlocutionary effect, however, depends upon much more: not only upon the communicative effect (and all that it depends upon) but also upon other things in readers' nature and nurture. Their intelligence and temperament; their beliefs (other than mutual beliefs) about the writer or his subject; their values, tastes, and affections; their mood; the state of their digestion—all these and thousands of other factors can conspire with the communicative effect to determine the ACTUAL perlocutionary effect. Not surprisingly, even though the communicative effect of the writer's speech act upon one reader may well be much the same as upon another reader, the ACTUAL perlocutionary effect is likely to vary widely from reader to reader.

SPEECH-ACT THEORY AND EFFECTIVE EXPRESSION

Rhetoric as the study of effective expression has usually distinguished two kinds of effective expression. One kind is writing clearly; the other, writing persuasively. These two kinds of effective expression correspond to the two problems of effective expression that writers have. One problem is to communicate with readers: for instance, to make a statement to them, to ask them a question, to make a request of them, or to welcome them. The other problem is to get them to do something: to believe the statement or answer the question or comply with the request or feel welcome.

Speech-act theory makes two contributions to rhetoric as the study of effective expression—in particular, to research into the theory of rhetorical competence. First of all, in distinguishing between communicative effects (notably, illocutionary effects) and perlocutionary effects, speech-act theory permits a principled distinction between writing clearly and writing persuasively and thus between the problem of communicating with readers and the problem of getting them to do something. In speech-act terms, it permits a distinction between **illocutionary effectiveness** and **perlocutionary effectiveness** (cf. Steinmann, 1976). Second, implicit in speech-act theory is a theory of rhetorical competence—in particular, a theory of illocutionary-effectiveness competence.

Illocutionary Effectiveness

What is illocutionary effectiveness? Or—much the same question—how is illocutionary effectiveness measured? Loosely speaking, a written discourse is illocutionarily effective to the extent that it is readable; the easier it is to read, the greater its illocutionary effectiveness. But this loose definition leaves three important questions unanswered. First, easier than what? All possible discourses? Some? If some, which ones? Second, easier for whom? All readers? Some? If some, which ones? Third, easier how? More precisely, then, and in speech-act terms, a discourse written with a certain illocutionary intention is more illocutionarily effective than another discourse (actual or possible) written with that same intention if and only if intended readers can experience the illocutionary effect (infer that intention) faster by reading it than by reading the other. Easier, then, than another discourse written with the same illocutionary intention. Easier for readers that the writer intends. And easier because readers experience the illocutionary effect (or infer the illocutionary intention) faster.

This measure of illocutionary effectiveness ranges all possible discourses written with the same illocutionary intention and for the same intended readers along a scale of increasing illocutionary effectiveness—each discourse owing its place along this scale to its illocutionary-effectiveness characteristics—to their number, their strength, their relative weight, their mix, and so on. As we shall see, discourses written with the same illocutionary intention need not be, and often are not, synonymous with one another; in particular, corresponding referring expressions may have different meanings. And an analogous measure ranges all possible writers along an analogous scale, each writer owing his or her place to (no doubt among other things) knowledge of such aspects of these characteristics.

To achieve illocutionary effectiveness, a writer must know something and must do something. One thing the writer must know—practical, implicit, intuitive, unconscious, unformulated, knowing-HOW knowledge—is illocutionary-effectiveness laws. An **illocutionary-effectiveness law** is an empirical law, probably statistical, relating certain conditions to a certain effect: Given condition$_1$, . . . , condition$_n$, then the effect. One set of conditions consists of characteristics of the discourse; these conditions are within the writer's control. The other set consists of characteristics of the intended reader or readers—notably, readers' discourse-processing capacities and their beliefs, including mutual contextual beliefs; these conditions are not within the writer's control. The effect is speed of illocutionary effect, its values ranging upward from zero (no effect at all). The other thing the writer must know is when both sets of conditions are satisfied. The thing the writer must do to achieve illocutionary effectiveness is, of course, to write in accordance with these laws—that is, so that, given the characteristics of the intended readers, the characteristics of the discourse are such as to maximize the speed of illocutionary effect (cf. Kintsch & Vipond, 1979, p. 362; Miller & Kintsch, 1980, p. 348).

A written discourse—whether only a single sentence or an extended sequence of sentences such as an essay—may be characterized at three levels. At the least abstract level, a discourse is a sequence of graphs: letters (capital or lower case, roman or italic, boldface or lightface, with or without diacritics), punctuation marks, and spaces. At a more abstract level, a discourse is a sequence of morphological and syntactic forms: morphemes, words, phrases, clauses, and sentences, some units hierarchically ordered. At a still more abstract level, a discourse is a sequence of propositions, each with reference and predication and each associated with a type of saying. Some propositions in the sequence are embedded within and in some sense presupposed by other propositions. For example, the proposition that the boy next door likes Hazel better than he likes Joan embeds and presupposes the proposition that there is a boy next door. In terms of classical rhetoric, this last, most abstract level is the domain of both *inventio* (choice of things to say) and *dispositio* (choice of ways to organize them), while the other two levels are the domain of *elocutio* (choice of sentences to say them). As we shall see, at any level a characteristic of discourse can affect speed of illocutionary effect.

If this account of illocutionary effectiveness is roughly correct, then the ultimate goal of research into the theory of illocutionary-effectiveness competence (one of the two branches of the theory of rhetorical competence) is to formulate illocutionary-effectiveness laws. Writers who are illocutionarily effective—who know how to smooth the way for their intended readers to infer their illocutionary intentions—know these laws; their practical, implicit knowledge of them constitutes their illocutionary-effectiveness competence. And the goal of research is to make this implicit knowledge explicit.[5]

To put the matter in another way, research into the theory of illocutionary-effectiveness competence tries to discover which discourse characteristics at any of the three levels of discourse facilitate, and which impede, speed of illocutionary effect; and whether a characteristic facilitates or impedes the speed of this effect depends on characteristics of readers.

But facilitation or impedance can depend both on characteristics common to all possible readers and on characteristics peculiar to the reader or readers that the writer intends. Common to all possible neurologically normal readers are, it seems, genetically determined ways of processing, or reading, discourse. These are ways of inferring linguistic meaning. They are, therefore, a necessary though not a sufficient condition of inferring what writers are saying (locutionary intentions) and what attitudes they are expressing (illocutionary intentions). And common to all possible readers who are speakers of a given language are, no doubt, learned ways, or strategies, of processing discourse. Speakers of English, for example, learn to expect most sentences to be ordered subject–verb–object; speakers of Japanese, subject–object–verb. These ways of processing discourse— whatever the ultimate truth about them may turn out to be—are rhetorical universals; all illocutionary and all perlocutionary effects seem to depend on them. On the other hand, peculiar to a given intended reader or given intended readers are certain other characteristics relevant to their inferring illocutionary intentions. Some readers—good readers—have learned strategies of inference that enable them to readily cope with such things as

---

[5]In this research, comprehension (experiencing illocutionary effects, inferring illocutionary intentions) is a constant, and what is measured is speed of comprehension.

English sentences ordered object–subject–verb. Others have knowledge or other beliefs relevant to their inferring linguistic meaning and such things as intended referents.

Implicit in speech–act theory is a theory of the relationship between characteristics of discourse and knowledge that intended readers have. Let me first say something about this relationship and then say something about the relationship between characteristics of discourse and the way all possible readers process discourse.

Speech-Act Theory and Intended Readers

First, some explication of the notion of **the intended reader** or **readers.** Surely few writers write with all possible readers in mind, not even all readers who have grammatical competence in their language. A writer generally writes with certain readers in mind—writes a letter to a friend with the friend in mind, a memorandum to the staff with the staff in mind, an article commissioned by *Scientific American* with its readers in mind. The readers that a given writer has in mind vary from discourse to discourse: Bertrand Russell writing for other philosophers, but elsewhere for other pacifists; Margaret Mead writing for other anthropologists, but elsewhere for the educated laity. The readers that a given writer has in mind are intended readers; they are the readers that a given writer intends and expects to read a given discourse.

Intended readers are different not only from all possible readers but also from actual readers and ideal readers. For a given discourse, the intended readers are the readers that the writer intends and expects to read it; the actual readers, the readers who, intended or not, actually read it; the ideal readers, the readers who—intended or not, actual or not—are such that, if they read it, they experience the illocutionary effect with maximum speed and also experience the intended perlocutionary effect. Suppose, for example, that a woman writes a letter to her brother with a certain illocutionary intention (to express the belief, say, that her husband is a bounder and the intention that her brother believe that he is a bounder) and with a certain perlocutionary intention (that her brother feel sorry for her). Her intended reader is her brother, but both the actual reader and the ideal reader may be different. The actual reader may be her brother, but may—either instead or in addition—be an agent of the FBI. And, if the actual reader is her brother, her brother may not be the ideal reader: her brother may fail to experience the illocutionary effect at all or, experiencing it, fail to experience the intended perlocutionary effect (that is, fail to feel sorry for her).

Writers who are illocutionarily and perlocutionarily effective—writers whose intended readers are also both actual and ideal—manage to suit their discourse not only to their illocutionary intentions and to the way (discussed in the next section) that all possible readers process discourse but also to characteristics of their intended readers. Given a certain illocutionary intention, these effective writers suit their discourse to what they know (or, at least, believe) about these readers. In achieving illocutionary effectiveness, they suit it to their knowledge of these readers' knowledge. In achieving perlocutionary effectiveness, they suit it not only to that but to their knowledge of these readers' values. Postponing discussion of perlocutionary effectiveness, here I say something about how illocutionarily effective writers suit their discourse to their knowledge of their intended readers' knowledge.

One of the things that these writers know is, of course, that their intended readers know the language of the discourse, that they have grammatical competence in that language. The linguistic presumption entitles them (so to speak) to this knowledge. But grammatical competence is not the fixed body of knowledge shared by all speakers of the language that this presumption suggests. Perhaps every speaker knows what every other speaker knows about syntax, though even this is doubtful. But certainly not every speaker has the same vocabulary as every other speaker; no speaker possesses the entire vocabulary (or lexicon) of a language. Some speakers have larger vocabularies than others; some have more specialized vocabularies. All speaker of English have *girl, tree,* and *chair* in their vocabularies. But only linguists are likely to have *hypercorrection;* only lawyers, *tort;* only physicists, *neutrino;* only jazz musicians, *gig* ('one-night engagement'); only crooks, *paper-hanger* ('check forger'). Indeed, learning the jargon of a profession, a discipline, a coterie, or a mob is usually the chief part of members' apprenticeship or initiation, setting them apart from outsiders. Consequently, illocutionarily effective writers suit their discourse to their intended readers' vocabularies. At best, readers' ignorance of the meaning of a word impedes speed of illocutionary effect, for they must pause to speculate or guess. At worst, it blocks the full illocutionary effect.

The other thing that illocutionarily effective writers know is what other relevant knowledge or beliefs—including, but not restricted to, mutual contextual beliefs and conversational postulates—their intended readers have; and these writers suit their discourse to this relevant knowledge. The inferences that most depend on intended readers' knowledge of things other than language are (*a*) inferring that an illocutionary act is nonliteral and then what kind of act it is and what its content is; (*b*) inferring that an illocutionary act is indirect, first inferring the direct act of which it is a consequence and then inferring its kind and content; and (*c*) inferring what referents the writers are, by using referring expressions, referring to. The earlier discussion of literal and nonliteral and of direct and indirect illocutionary acts well suggests how inferences of the first and the second kind depend on intended readers' knowledge of this sort. Let me focus here on how inferences of the third kind depend on it and on how illocutionarily effective writers suit their discourse—especially, but not only, their referring expressions—to knowledge of this sort.

Writers use referring expressions to refer their readers to the referents (people, objects, events, times, places) of which they intend to predicate properties or relations. In writing (2) in a letter to Marie—

(2) *The man with the red beard we met in Nice is a spy.*

—George uses the referring expression *the man with the red beard we met in Nice* to refer Marie to a certain person of whom he intends to predicate the property of being a spy (by using the predicating expression *is a spy*). The information contained in the referring expression (that Marie and George met such a man in Nice) is said to be **given;** the information added by the predicating expression (that the man is a spy) is said to be **new** (Clark & Clark, 1977; see also Glatt, chapter 4 this volume). To discover whom George is referring her to, all that Marie has to do is, with the given before her, to search her long-term memory for a referent that matches it. If, however, while trying to connect her new stereo turntable to her amplifier, Marie reads (3)—

(3) *Connect the black wire with the split lug on its end to the ground terminal.*

—she may well have to search, not her long-term memory, but her turntable and her amplifier for referents that match the given (that there is such a black wire and that there is such a terminal). Until she finds these two referents, she cannot do what the predicating expression (*connect . . . to*) instructs her to do (connect them).

Corresponding to a given referent (Andrew Jackson, say) to whom a particular writer might wish to refer intended readers is an indefinitely large number of referring expressions: proper names (*Andrew Jackson, Old Hickory*), pronouns (*he, him, his*), and definite descriptions (*the seventh president of the United States, the general who defeated the Creek Indians in the battle of Horseshoe Bend, the governor of the Florida Territory in 1821, the president who introduced the spoils system*). Indeed, any proposition true of a referent can become the content of a definite description: that the United States has had at least seven presidents, that some general defeated the Creek Indians in the battle of Horseshoe Bend, and so on. (These rival referring expressions are not, it is worth noting, synonymous with one another. The definite description *the seventh president of the United States,* for example, has a linguistic meaning different from that of the description *the general who defeated the Creek Indians in the battle of Horseshoe Bend.* Indeed, some referring expressions—proper names—seem to have no meaning at all. The essential points are that the meaning of a referring expression is different from the referent that it is used to refer to and that referring expressions with different meanings, or with no meaning at all, may be used to refer to the same referent.)

From this indefinitely large number of referring expressions, a writer must make a small selection—often just a proper name and pronouns compatible with it but sometimes, instead of or in addition to these, one or more definite descriptions. An illocutionarily effective writer selects these expressions, not randomly, but wisely.

The factor determining a wise selection is the writer's knowledge of the intended readers' knowledge or ignorance of the referent. If the intended readers are historians of American history, then *Andrew Jackson, he, him,* and *his* will do very nicely to refer them to Andrew Jackson. From the initial *Andrew Jackson,* they will instantly infer the intended referent; and *he, him,* and *his* will continue to so refer them. If, on the other hand, the intended readers know very little (though, necessarily, something) about American history, then an illocutionarily effective writer does one of two things. One is to include, early on in the discourse, a good many propositions about Jackson (beginning, perhaps, with *The seventh president of the United States was Andrew Jackson,* and going on with *Born in Waxhaw, South Carolina, in 1767, he went west to Nashville, Tennessee, in 1788 and opened a law office there*) and later to use only the referring expressions *Jackson, he, him,* and *his.* The other is to use a long referring expression or combination of expressions (say, *Andrew Jackson, the seventh president of the United States as well as the general who defeated the Creek Indians in the battle of Horseshoe Bend*) for the first reference and then to use *Jackson, he, him,* and *his.* Use of a referring expression longer and more informative than *Andrew Jackson* may puzzle intended readers who are historians: Why, they may wonder (invoking the conversational presumption that writers are only as informative as intended readers need them to be), should the writer use this expression in a discourse intended for us to read? Use of this expression may even insult them (an unintended perlocutionary effect). In any event, its use is likely to impede speed of illocutionary effect. On the other hand, use of a referring expression as short and uninformative as *Andrew Jackson* will puzzle intended readers who know very little about American history, but puzzle them in a different way: Who, they will ask, is Andrew Jackson? Not knowing, they will not experience the illocutionary effect at all, let alone speedily.

Discourse Processing

Facilitation or impedance of speed of illocutionary effect depends, I have hypothesized, not only on characteristics of discourse but on characteristics of readers. Common to all readers are ways, probably genetically determined, of **processing discourse**—ways of reading, of experiencing illocutionary effects, of inferring illocutionary intentions. And common to all possible readers who are speakers of a given language are, no doubt, learned ways of processing discourse. Peculiar to given intended readers are, as we have just seen, a certain vocabulary and certain other relevant knowledge. Actually, there is a good deal of evidence (Dillon, 1978; Kintsch & Vipond, 1979) that there are other relevant characteristics peculiar to some readers (good readers): some have learned—or created—strategies of inference that others have not; and some have more advantageous short-term memory characteristics than others. Here, however, my focus is the relationship between characteristics of discourse and characteristics common to all possible readers (cf. Miller & Kintsch, 1980). Given a certain theory of the discourse-processing capacities of all possible readers, which characteristics of discourse facilitate, and which impede, speed of illocutionary effect? This is a question for what is generally known as **readability research.**

Readability research has, of course, been going on for a long time, since the early 1920s at least. But, until fairly recently, this research has been severely practical, methodologically unsound, theoretically uninteresting, and therefore unfruitful—revealing symptoms of illocutionary effectiveness and ineffectiveness but not the underlying causes. (For surveys and critiques of research, see, e.g., Felker, 1980; Hirsch, 1977; Kintsch & Vipond, 1979; Schlesinger, 1968.) The chief methodology of this research has been correlations between readability of extended discourses as variously measured (by reading speed, comprehension, recall, etc.) and certain variables—notably, sentence length and word length—rather than controlled experimental manipulation of variables. Its chief product has been readability formulas, rather than theories of illocutionary-effectiveness competence or theories of reading performance. Guided by no theories of grammatical competence, it has been unable to identify and consider variables less obvious than sentences and words. And guided by no theories about the human mind—notably, no theories about its discourse-processing capacities—it has been unable to distinguish symptoms of reading ease or difficulty from underlying causes. The point is not that readability formulas—there are now about fifty of them (Kintsch & Vipond, 1979, p. 335)—have no practical uses; they are, surprisingly, valid predictors of the readability of extended discourse (Klare, 1974–1975). The point is that they do not reveal why some discourse is easier or harder to read than other.

An abnormally high ratio of words to sentences, for instance, is probably only the rash that often symptomizes a syntactic virus that causes reading difficulty. Though many long sentences are hard to read, not all are; and not all short sentences are easy to read. This is the view confirmed by recent readability research, guided by a theory of grammatical competence and a theory of discourse processing and by a theory of illocutionary-effectiveness competence based on them. The theory of grammatical competence—structural theory enriched by transformational—I shall not discuss (cf. Chomsky, 1965). But, simply to suggest how recent readability research differs from older, I shall outline and illustrate a shard of a theory of discourse processing and also a shard of a theory of illocutionary-effectiveness competence.[6]

First, **the theory of discourse processing:**

1. READERS PROCESS DISCOURSE LINEARLY—on the whole from left to right in the writing system used by European languages.

2. AS THE FIRST STEP IN DECIDING WHAT THE PROPOSITIONAL CONTENT (the referents and the predication) OF A SENTENCE IS, READERS PARSE THE SENTENCE—that is, decide (unconsciously, of course) what the boundaries of phrases and clauses are, what syntactic category each word, phrase, and clause belongs to, and what syntactic function each has.

For example, in (4)—

(4) *Obviously, the bagels John disliked.*

—parsing reveals that *obviously* is an adverb functioning as modifier of all the rest of the sentence; *the bagels,* a noun phrase functioning as direct object; *John,* a noun phrase functioning as subject; and so on.

3. IN MOVING FROM LEFT TO RIGHT WHILE PARSING, READERS AIM FOR **closure**—that is, they try to make tentative boundary, category, and function decisions about each word or string of words they encounter. Until they achieve closure of a word or string, they must store it in **short-term memory,** which has a capacity of from five to seven chunks (words or strings, say). If they cannot at once achieve closure, they move on to the next word or string, trying to achieve its closure while storing the first in short-term memory and trying to find syntactic or semantic clues for achieving its closure. Sometimes these clues do not turn up until (if ever) the very end of the sentence.

4. IF, AT SOME POINT IN THE SENTENCE, READERS SUSPECT THAT A TENTATIVE DECISION (perhaps, though not necessarily, now in long-term memory) IS INCORRECT, THEY REVIEW THAT DECISION AND PERHAPS CHANGE IT.

In parsing (4), for instance, readers may tentatively decide that *the bagels* functions as subject and store it in either short- or long-term memory so labeled. Getting to *John,* they may suspect that it, not *the bagels,* functions as subject, review that decision, and tentatively decide that *the bagels* functions as direct object (tentatively, because the possibility remains that

[6]I do not want to father these shards on anyone else. Nor, on the other hand, do I want to claim paternity; but see, for example, Clark and Clark, 1977, especially chap. 2; Dillon, 1978; Gibson and Levin, 1975; Hirsch, 1977, especially chap. 5; Kintsch and Vipond, 1979; Miller and Kintsch, 1980; Just and Carpenter, 1980; and Haviland and Clark, 1974.

John functions as subject of a relative clause: *The bagels John disliked were stale*, say). Not until they get to the end of the sentence (and find that *disliked* is the last word) are they sure that *the bagels* functions as direct object. Another example, this one from a book of philosophy:

(5) *Matthew's point . . . seems to me a useful correction to the claim that Ryle was attacking a basic human intuition. . . .*

In parsing (5), readers may tentatively decide that *that* is a relative pronoun functioning as direct object of a relative clause (*that Ryle was attacking*). Getting to *a basic human intuition,* they are sure that this decision is incorrect (if the clause is relative, its last word must be *attacking*; for, if *that* functions as direct object, *a basic human intuition* cannot); they review this decision; and they decide that *that* is a subordinating conjunction introducing a noun clause (*that Ryle was attacking a basic human intuition*) in apposition with *the claim.*

5. HAVING PARSED ONE SENTENCE (and therefore having decided what its propositional content is), READERS BEGIN TO PARSE THE NEXT ONE BY TRYING TO RELATE THE TWO—that is, by trying to integrate the emerging propositional content of the latter into the propositional content of the former—and in this way they try to store a coherent sequence of propositions in long-term memory. If the two sentences do not cohere, readers must, by drawing on their knowledge of the subject of the discourse, make a **bridging inference,** that is, create a proposition that makes the two sentences cohere.

The two sentences in (6), for example, do not cohere:

(6) *Herbert looked at the picture. The woman was beautiful.*

To make them cohere, readers must make a bridging inference, create a proposition—say that the picture depicts a woman. The two sentences in (7), however, require no bridging inference:

(7) *Herbert looked at the picture. The woman **depicted in it** was beautiful.*

Second, based on this theory, **the theory of illocutionary-effectiveness competence:**

1'. ANY INDECISION IN MAKING TENTATIVE DECISIONS—any consideration of rival boundaries, categories, or functions—DELAYS CLOSURE, TAKES ADDITIONAL PROCESSING TIME, AND THEREFORE IMPEDES SPEED OF ILLOCUTIONARY EFFECT.

Take, for instance, the following newspaper headline:

(8) *Action against rape program set for January 14.*

Perhaps readers will decide at once that *action against rape program* is a noun phrase functioning as subject. But they may well consider rival boundaries, categories, and functions within this noun phrase. One constellation of boundaries, categories, and functions makes this ambiguous noun phrase mean 'an action that is against a rape program': *action* (a noun functioning as head noun); *against rape program* (a prepositional phrase functioning as modifier of *action*); and *rape program* (a noun phrase functioning as object of the preposition *against*). A rival constellation makes the phrase mean 'A program that somehow involves action against rape': *program* (a noun functioning as head noun); *action against rape* (a noun phrase functioning as modifier of *program*); *action* (a noun functioning as head word of this phrase); *against rape* (a prepositional phrase functioning as modifier of *action*); and *rape* (a noun phrase functioning as object of the preposition *against*). Considering these rivals takes processing time. In the end, readers will doubtless decide that the first is incorrect and the second correct. But that end is not the end of the sentence. This sentence, unlike (4), has no point where they can discover what is incorrect and what is correct. To discover that, they must either read the article below the headline or use their beliefs about what actions civic-minded people are likely to take regarding rape. It is worth noting that an illocutionarily effective headline writer could (at the least abstract level of discourse, where discourse is a sequence of graphs) have avoided this syntactic ambiguity by using a hyphen or two. The first constellation: "Action against rape-program." The second: "Action-against-rape program."

2′. ANY REVIEW AND CHANGE OF A TENTATIVE DECISION TAKES ADDITIONAL PROCESSING TIME AND THEREFORE IMPEDES SPEED OF ILLOCUTIONARY EFFECT.

In parsing (9), a sentence from a newspaper story—

(9) *Parkhurst said that Evans, Ward and McCray were overheard discussing a plan to beat the inmates at a New Year's Eve party in the kitchen of another guard's home the night before the beating.*

—some readers must, when they get to *the night before the beating*, correct their tentative decision that the beating was planned to take place at a New Year's Eve party in the kitchen of another guard's home (or that the inmates were at that party?). It's the overhearing (or the discussing?), not the beating, that takes place at the party. And this correction takes processing time. It is worth noting that nothing in the SYNTAX of the sentence forces this correction on readers; it is the SEMANTIC incongruity between *a plan to beat* and *before the beating*: if the beating is planned, it cannot take place before it is planned. At the level where discourse is a sequence of morphological and syntactic forms, there is obviously much grist here for an illocutionarily effective reviser's mill.

3′. ANYTHING THAT DELAYS CLOSURE MAY OVERLOAD SHORT-TERM MEMORY, TAKE ADDITIONAL PROCESSING TIME, AND THEREFORE IMPEDE SPEED OF ILLOCUTIONARY EFFECT.

In parsing (10), for example—

(10) *That the boy and the girl the snake the zoo owns bit are in Memorial Hospital, just off the freeway on Harper Drive, morning papers reported.*

—readers must, just for a start, aim at closure of the string beginning with *that*—a string that is clearly a noun clause (and therefore a noun phrase as well) and that, when readers at long last achieve its closure (when they get to *morning newspapers*), turns out to end with *Drive* and to function as direct object. But, while trying to achieve closure of this noun clause, readers must achieve closure of (among other things) a noun phrase (*the boy and the girl the snake the zoo owns bit*), a relative clause embedded in it (*the snake the zoo owns bit*), and a second relative clause embedded in the first (*the zoo owns*) and must in short-term memory store (among other things) this closure within a closure within a closure. They must, that is, store one closure (of the second relative clause) while trying to achieve a second closure (of the first relative clause) while trying to achieve a third closure (of the noun phrase *the boy . . . bit*) while trying to achieve a fourth closure (of the noun clause). Not surprisingly, this hierarchical delay of the fourth closure may well overload short-term memory, causing readers to forget one of the other three closures or something else (that, for instance, the first relative clause modifies the coordinate head nouns *boy* and *girl* or even indeed that the noun clause is a noun clause, rather than the main clause). If readers forget something, they must look back to the left to retrieve it, and looking back takes processing time.

4′. CREATING BRIDGING INFERENCES TAKES ADDITIONAL PROCESSING TIME AND THEREFORE IMPEDES SPEED OF ILLOCUTIONARY EFFECT.

Thus, at the most abstract level of discourse, where discourse is a sequence of propositions, (6) is less illocutionarily effective than (7):

(6) *Herbert looked at the picture. The woman was beautiful.*
(7) *Herbert looked at the picture. The woman **depicted in it** was beautiful.*

For (7), unlike (6), does not require readers to make the bridging inference that the picture depicts a woman.

It is now, I think, apparent why one of the villains (and darlings too) of readability formulas—high ratio of words to sentences—is, at best, only a symptom of underlying causes of reading, or processing, difficulty. One of the 5 difficult single sentences is only 5 words long (4), another only 8 (8); and the longest, but by no means the most difficult is 34 (9). And here are the first 59 words of a sentence 139 words long that is far easier to process than any of these 5. It is almost the last sentence of Jonathan Swift's *A Modest Proposal* (1729):

(11) *Therefore let no man talk to me of other expedients: of taxing our absentees at five shillings a pound; of using neither clothes nor household furniture except*

what is of our own growth and manufacture; of utterly rejecting the materials and instruments that promote foreign luxury; of curing the expensiveness of pride, vanity, idleness, and gaming in our women;. . . .

Once readers get beyond the prepositional phrase *of other expedients* (no arduous journey), the rest is easy. All they need do is to achieve closure of each of a series of eight prepositional phrases, each coordinate with *of other expedients* and each beginning with *of*. Since these phrases, unlike the clauses and the phrases in (10), are coordinate rather than hierarchical, readers are not obliged to store one closure while trying to achieve another. This sentence could be so extended indefinitely without overloading short-term memory or in any other way increasing the ratio of processing time to words and therefore without impeding speed of illocutionary effect.

Perlocutionary Effectiveness

Guided by a theory of grammatical competence and also by a theory of discourse processing, research into a theory of illocutionary-effectiveness competence has achieved impressive results. Unfortunately, but not surprisingly, research into a **theory of perlocutionary-effectiveness competence** has not.

To achieve perlocutionary effectiveness, writers must (as they must to achieve illocutionary effectiveness) know something and do something. What they must know—practical, implicit knowledge—is both **perlocutionary-effectiveness laws** (relating causes or conditions to intended perlocutionary effects) and when the relevant conditions are satisfied. What they must do is to write in such a way as to satisfy these conditions.

But achieving perlocutionary effectiveness is obviously much more difficult than achieving illocutionary effectiveness. Every writer knows that it is much easier to achieve illocutionary effects than to achieve intended perlocutionary effects. It is easier to get readers to understand statements than to believe them, to understand requests than to grant them, and so on. Perlocutionary-effectiveness laws are, it seems likely, much more complex than illocutionary-effectiveness laws: the number of conditions per law much greater. A necessary condition of any perlocutionary effect, intended or not, is, of course, that readers experience some communicative effect, an illocutionary effect or at least an utterance or a locutionary effect: no communicative effect, no perlocutionary effect. But, once readers experience the communicative effect, any characteristic whatsoever of the readers—anything in their nature or nurture—can condition the perlocutionary effect, can play a role in what might be called the **perlocutionary process,** the end point of which is the readers' experiencing a perlocutionary effect. Clearly, it is not easy for writers to know perlocutionary-effectiveness laws or, knowing them, to know in a given case when the relevant conditions are satisfied. What is a given reader's intelligence? Temperament? Beliefs about the writer or the subject? Values? Tastes? At best, it would seem, writers can only make informed guesses.

Nor—equally clearly—is it easy for researchers to discover these perlocutionary-effectiveness laws and to formulate them, as those who have tried have found out. Research into a theory of perlocutionary-effectiveness competence is one aspect of a broader field of research in social psychology known as **attitude-change research.** The question this research asks is broader than the question of which characteristics of discourse facilitate, and which impede, intended perlocutionary effects. It asks what factors condition changes in attitude. Like most terms, *attitude* is theory laden; that is, both its conceptual and its operational definitions vary from theory to theory. But in practice the term is as broad and vague in attitude-change research as it is in speech–act theory. Conceptually, an attitude is a state of mind such as a belief, an intention, a desire, or a feeling. It has an object; that is, it is an attitude TOWARD something (a belief ABOUT, an intention TO, a desire FOR, and so on). And it is an **intervening variable;** that is, it mediates between antecedent conditions and consequent behavior. For example, reading a certain discourse written by a certain writer (antecedent conditions), a reader forms or modifies a certain belief (a value of an intervening variable) about a certain common stock (the object of this attitude—here, of a belief) and buys 10 shares of it, urges friends to buy some shares, and so on (consequent behavior). In any case, production of intended perlocutionary effects—persuasion—is clearly one kind of attitude change (cf. Himmelfarb & Eagly, 1974, pp. 3–6).

Attitude-change research has not been—probably it could not possibly have been—so successful as readability research, but in many other ways its history has been much like the history of readability research. (For critical surveys, see Eagly & Himmelfarb, 1974; Himmelfarb & Eagly, 1974.)

In its first stage, in the 1920s and 1930s, attitude-change research was on the whole severely practical and untheoretical (cf. Hovland, Janis, & Kelley, 1953, p. 4). For example, comparing two particular discourses written with the same perlocutionary intention but differing from one another in numerous other ways, it asked which one better achieved the intended perlocutionary effect. The answer, while of practical importance (to Madison Avenue, say), revealed little or nothing about the underlying causes of the difference in effect. Like a readability formula, it was a valid predictor (which discourse will sell more soap?) but no explainer (why?) at all.

In its second stage, in the 1950s and the early 1960s, attitude-change research spawned numerous theories and theories of numerous kinds but of overlapping scopes: cognitive-consistency theories (people abhor inconsistency as nature abhors a vacuum, and attitude change can reduce inconsistency), learning-theory theories (attitudes are learned), social-judgment theories (people's initial attitude affects their judgments of discourse that attempts to change it), functional theories (attitudes serve such functions as maximizing pleasure and minimizing pain, maintaining a satisfactory representation of the world, and protecting the ego against threats from the world or the unconscious), and innoculation theories (resisting persuasion is like resisting disease: innoculation with a small dose of the virus of discourse that attacks an attitude is better protection against its change than large doses of the preventive medicine of discourse that supports it) (cf. Himmelfarb & Eagly, 1974, pp. 9–47).

Indeed, there proved to be an embarrassment of theoretical riches. For one thing, though there was much variety, there was no unity, no unifying theory or even framework; in the Kuhnian sense (Kuhn, 1970; Kuhn, 1977), there was no paradigm (Eagly & Himmelfarb, 1974, p. 609). For another thing, no theory even claimed to account for all the phenomena of attitude change; all were of limited generality. Consequently, research was guided, not by a theory, but by a great variety of theories. Finally, to make matters worse, some theories inspired very little research, partly because they were hard to test (what function, for instance, does a given attitude of a given person serve?); and much research, perhaps most, was inspired by no theories—findings-oriented research, designed simply to discover the effects of independent variables on attitude change (Himmelfarb & Eagly, 1974, p. 48).

In the latest stage of attitude-change research, from the middle 1960s on, these theories have, as Eagly and Himmelfarb (1974, pp. 609–610) put it, "merely faded away"—not because a new theory of great generality has replaced them, but because, for reasons I have just sketched, they were not very fruitful. And research is now pretty much findings oriented, guided by no theories.

What explains the lack of success of attitude-change research? I can only speculate. The scope of attitude-change research in general, even of perlocutionary-effectiveness research in particular, is so great—the number of factors conditioning any change in attitude is so astronomically large—that what is surprising is that this research has had any success at all. A highly general, unified theory of attitude change, even of discourse-related attitude change only, would come close to being a theory of all social interaction. The conclusion that Eagly and Himmelfarb (1974, p. 594) draw is rightly dismal:

> After several decades of research, there are few simple and direct empirical generalizations that can be made concerning how to change attitudes. In fact, one of the most salient features of recent research is the great number of studies demonstrating that the empirical generalizations of earlier research are *not* general, but contingent on conditions not originally apparent.

Should perlocutionary-effectiveness research be abandoned? Perhaps. What might encourage it to go on is our gut belief that there is such a thing as perlocutionary-effectiveness competence. There are, we believe, writers (and speakers) who are very good at achieving the perlocutionary effects they intend, and not just when writing on one subject or for one kind of reader. Presumably they know something that the rest of us don't know: perlocutionary-effectiveness laws. And what they know research can try to discover and formulate.

REFERENCES

Austin, J. L. *How to do things with words.* Oxford: Clarendon Press, 1962.

Bach, K., & Harnish, R. M. *Linguistic communication and speech acts.* Cambridge: M.I.T. Press, 1979.

Brown, R. L., Jr., & Steinmann, M., Jr. Native readers of fiction: A speech–act and genre–rule approach to defining literature. In P. Hernadi (Ed.), *What is literature?* Bloomington: Indiana University Press, 1978. Pp. 141–160.

Chomsky, N. *Aspects of the theory of syntax.* Cambridge: M.I.T. Press, 1965.

Clark, H. H., & Clark, E. V. *Psychology and language.* New York: Harcourt Brace Jovanovich, 1977.

Dillon, G. L. *Language processing and the reading of literature: Toward a model of comprehension.* Bloomington: Indiana University Press, 1978.

Donovan, T. R., & McClelland, B. W. (Eds.) *Eight approaches to teaching composition.* Urbana, Ill.: National Council of Teachers of English, 1980.

Eagly, A. H., & Himmelfarb, S. Current trends in attitude theory and research. In S. Himmelfarb & A. H. Eagly (Eds.), *Readings in attitude change.* New York: Wiley, 1974. Pp. 594–610.

Emig, J. Review of *The philosophy of composition* by E. D. Hirsch, Jr. *Rhetoric Society Quarterly,* 1978, *8,* 145–148.

Felker, D. B. *Document design: A review of research.* Washington: National Institutes for Research, 1980.

Gibson, E. S., & H. Levin. *The psychology of reading.* Cambridge: M.I.T. Press, 1975.

Grice, H. P. Logic and conversation. In P. Cole & J. L. Morgan (Eds.). *Syntax and semantics* (Vol. 3), *Speech acts.* New York: Academic Press, 1975. Pp. 41–58.

Haviland, S. E., & Clark, H. H. What's new? Acquiring new information as a process in comprehension. *Journal of Verbal Learning and Verbal Behavior,* 1974, *13,* 512–521.

Himmelfarb, S., & Eagly, A. H. Orientations to the study of attitudes and their change. In S. Himmelfarb & A. H. Eagly (Eds.), *Readings in attitude change.* New York: Wiley, 1974. Pp. 2–49.

Hirsch, E. D., Jr. *The philosophy of composition.* Chicago: University of Chicago Press, 1977.

Hovland, C. I., Janis, I. L., & Kelley, H. H. *Communication and persuasion: Psychological studies of opinion change.* New Haven: Yale University Press, 1953.

Just, M. A., & Carpenter, P. A. A theory of reading: From eye fixations to comprehension. *Psychological Review,* 1980, *87,* 329–354.

Kintsch, W., & Vipond, D. Readability comprehension and readability in educational practice and psychological theory. In Lars-Göran Nilsson (Ed.), *Perspectives on memory research.* Hillsdale, N.J.: Lawrence Erlbaum, 1979. Pp. 329–365.

Klare, G. R. Assessing readability. *Reading Research Quarterly,* 1974–1975, *10,* 62–102.

Kuhn, T. S. *The structure of scientific revolutions.* (2nd ed.) Chicago: University of Chicago Press, 1970.

Kuhn, T. S. *The essential tension: Selected studies in scientific tradition and change.* Chicago: University of Chicago Press, 1977.

Miller, J. R., & Kintsch, W. Readability and recall of short prose passages: A theoretical analysis. *Journal of Experimental Psychology: Human Learning and Memory*, 1980, *6*, 335–354.

Quintilian. [*Institutio oratoria.*] Translated by H. E. Butler. London: Heinemann, 1921. 4 vols.

Sadock, J. *Toward a linguistic theory of speech acts.* New York: Academic Press, 1974.

Saussure, de, F. [*Course in general linguistics.*] Edited by C. Bally & A. Sechehaye, translated by W. Baskin. New York: Philosophical Library, 1959.

Schlesinger, I. M. *Sentence structure and the reading process.* The Hague: Mouton, 1968.

Searle, J. R. *Speech acts: An essay in the philosophy of language.* Cambridge: Cambridge University Press, 1969.

Searle, J. R. *Expression and meaning: Studies in the theory of speech acts.* Cambridge: Cambridge University Press, 1979.

Steinmann, M., Jr. Freshman English in America. *Universities Quarterly*, 1965, *19*, 391–395.

Steinmann, M., Jr. Freshman English: A hypothesis and a proposal. *Journal of Higher Education*, 1966, *37*, 24–32.

Steinmann, M., Jr. Rhetorical research. In M. Steinmann, Jr. (Ed.), *New rhetorics.* New York: Charles Scribner's Sons, 1967. Pp. 16–32.

Steinmann, M., Jr. Rule competences and rhetorical competences. In S. S. Mufwene, C. A. Walter, & S. B. Steever (Eds.), *Papers from the twelfth regional meeting Chicago Linguistic Society.* Chicago: Chicago Linguistic Society, 1976. Pp. 610–616.

Steinmann, M., Jr. Expressives. In D. M. Lance & D. E. Gulstad (Eds.), *Papers from the 1977 Mid-America Linguistics Conference.* Columbia, Mo.: University of Missouri, 1978.

Wittgenstein, L. *Philosophische bemerkungen* (R. Rhees, Ed.) Oxford: Blackwell, 1964.

Chapter **12**

What Writers Need to Know
That They Don't Know
They Need to Know

John B. Black
Deanna Wilkes-Gibbs
Raymond W. Gibbs Jr.

INTRODUCTION

A good writer is able to think of ideas to write about, organize those ideas, and convey them to the reader with a minimum of detail. Much of this skill is unconscious. Ideas seem to pop into consciousness automatically, it is "obvious" that some ideas are related whereas others are not, and it is "clear" that some details can be omitted whereas others are crucial. Underlying these seemingly automatic processes is a great deal of tacit knowledge. How are we to investigate such well-hidden aspects of human behavior? Computer modeling methods used in the field of **artificial intelligence** (AI) provide the needed tools. AI researchers investigate theories about the tacit knowledge needed for intelligent behavior by constructing experimental computer implementations of the theories. Specifically, a theory is tested by designing a computer program to contain knowledge that the theory says is necessary for the behavior, then executing the program to see if it actually exhibits the desired ability. The necessary kinds of tacit knowledge are discovered by noting how the behavior of the computer program that implements the theory departs from the desired behavior.

In this chapter we describe kinds of knowledge necessary for story writing that have been discovered using these AI research methods (for a more general survey of writing research see Black, in press). In the next section we describe an early attempt at writing stories by computer, then go on to discuss in more detail the kinds of knowledge necessary for story production and comprehension. An additional section covers the critical role that memory organization plays in writing stories. Our focus here is primarily on story writing, only because almost all of the AI research thus far has dealt with stories. We emphasize, however, that the same research methods can also be used to study other kinds of discourse production—in fact, work on arguments has begun recently (Birnbaum, Flowers & McGuire, 1980). [See also Cooper's discussion of FRAMES and IMPLICATURES in writing, Chapter 5 this volume.]

WRITING AND MISWRITING STORIES BY COMPUTER

An early AI program that writes stories is Meehan's (1976) TALE-SPIN program. Meehan was interested in what you need to know to make up a story. The emphasis of his program was on the knowledge needed by a storyteller, not on the style of expression or the ultimate structures of the stories themselves.

TALE-SPIN has three active components. There is a PROBLEM SOLVER that, given a specific goal, produces other goals (subgoals) and plans events that could possibly satisfy the goal. There is an ASSERTION MECHANISM that takes an event and adds it to the program's world model. This world model contains the static description of each knowledge area in the program. Thus, when an event is given to the assertion mechanism, it updates each knowledge area according to what the physical world looks like at that instant, what social relationships exist between the characters at that moment, etc. This collection of different knowledge areas is referred to as the program's **memory,** and represents the storyteller's true knowledge of the world—basically analogous to the perspective of an omniscient observer. Finally, there is an INFERENCE MAKER that takes an event and computes its consequences. The result of this simulation takes the form of a story, which can be used to determine adequacy of the general models upon which the simulation is based.

Let us now look at an example of a story written by TALE-SPIN. The program can run in any one of three modes, each of which demonstrates to a different degree the application of **tacit knowledge structures** to the composition process. In one mode, the point of the story is chosen at the beginning. The program produces the story using the Conceptual Dependency representation of meaning (Schank, 1972, 1973), and the production output is fed to a different part of the program that translates it into English. Specifying the story's point at the beginning helps determine what some of the world knowledge will look like for a particular story. If the point for the story is "Never trust flatterers," then the storyteller knows that the story must have a character who flatters, a character who is flattered, and a situation where someone loses because of the flattery. In addition, of course, it must understand the concept of flattery. Thus, if we want Bill to trick John out of some possession, then certain things about their individual personalities and their relationship are already defined. Here is an example of a story produced given various characters, a setting, and the moral "Never trust flatterers."

> Once upon a time there was a dishonest fox named Henry who lived in a cave, and a vain and trusting crow named Joe who lived in an elm tree. Joe had gotten a piece of cheese and was holding it in his mouth. One day, Henry walked from his cave, across the meadow to the elm tree. He saw Joe Crow and the cheese and became hungry. He decided that he might get the cheese if Joe spoke, so he told Joe that he liked his singing very much and wanted to hear him sing. Joe was very pleased with Henry and began to sing. The cheese fell out of his mouth and down to the ground. Henry picked up the cheese and told Joe Crow that he was stupid. Joe was angry, and didn't trust Henry anymore. Henry returned to his cave.

The story is written by having the characters themselves make the appropriate inferences, connecting the goal of possessing an object to some action on the part of the owner. The information about the owner's personality is then used to find a reason why the owner should perform that action. Thus, Henry Fox knew that Joe Crow was vain and might be persuaded to sing. This demonstrates the effective use of knowledge about plans and goals in producing a story. Without this general knowledge about people (or talking foxes and bears), their goals, and the plans they use to attain those goals, it would be impossible to construct such a story.

While developing TALE-SPIN, however, Meehan would continually build into the program all the knowledge he thought was necessary for a certain kind of story, but then be surprised at the results when the program was executed. For example, the following story was produced by an early version of TALE-SPIN:

> One day Joe Bear was hungry. He asked his friend Irving Bird where some honey was. Irving told him there was honey in the oak tree. Joe threatened to hit Irving if he didn't tell him where some honey was.

Here TALE-SPIN knew about bargaining between story characters (e.g., first ask, then threaten, etc.), but it did not know that bargaining (or any plan) can be abandoned once the goal has been attained. Another related story generated at an early stage was:

> One day Joe Bear was hungry. He asked his friend Irving Bird where some honey was. Irving told him there was a beehive in the oak tree. Joe threatened to hit Irving if he didn't tell him where some honey was.

Now TALE-SPIN knew about when to stop pursuing plans, but it did not know enough about conversations. In particular, it did not know that answers to questions can take many forms so that a statement describing the location of a beehive can be the answer to a question about honey.

Later in its development, TALE-SPIN was becoming more sophisticated but was still producing incorrect stories. For example, one of the stories TALE-SPIN generated at a later stage in its development was:

> One day Henry Crow sat in his tree, holding a piece of cheese in his mouth, when up came Bill Fox. Bill saw the cheese and was hungry. He said, "Henry, I like your singing very much. Won't you please sing for me?" Henry, flattered by his compliment, began to sing. The cheese fell to the ground. Bill Fox saw the cheese on the ground and was very hungry. He became ill.

Notice that a great deal of knowledge about the world is necessary to write such a story. Some of the knowledge used in generating this story was:

1. If a story character sees a piece of food, then that character becomes hungry—that is, the goal of hunger is placed on the character's "goal stack."
2. A character cannot hold something in his mouth and sing at the same time.
3. If one character wants to get another to do something, then he must bargain with him.
4. One type of bargaining is flattery.
5. If a story character's hunger passes a certain threshold, then that character becomes ill.

Thus, Bill Fox sees the cheese that Henry Crow is holding and, since seeing food makes one hungry, Bill becomes hungry. When someone is hungry they have the goal of alleviating that hunger, so Bill now wants to eliminate his hunger. He adopts the plan of obtaining the cheese by using flattery to get Henry to sing and therefore drop the cheese. Henry sings and drops the cheese because he cannot sing with his mouth and hold cheese in it at the same time. But then the story takes a wrong turn because Bill sees the cheese on the ground, which causes more hunger to be added to his "goal stack." Now Bill is overly hungry and that causes him to become ill. Therefore, the program needed to know the difference between psychological hunger induced by seeing food and the actual physical state of food deprivation. This story continued and ran into even more trouble:

> Henry Crow saw the cheese on the ground, and he became hungry, but he knew that he owned the cheese. He felt pretty honest with himself, so he decided not to trick himself into giving up the cheese. He wasn't trying to deceive himself, either, nor did he feel competitive with himself. But he did dominate himself, and was very familiar with himself so he asked himself for the cheese. He trusted himself, but he remembered that he was also in a position of dominance over himself, so he refused to give himself the cheese. He couldn't think of a good reason why he should give himself the cheese, so he offered to bring himself a worm if he'd give himself the cheese. That sounded okay, but he didn't know where any worms were. So he said to himself, "Henry, do you know where any worms are?" But of course, he didn't, so he . . .

Here Henry has seen the cheese so he also gets hungry and hence develops the goal of eliminating that hunger. A character in the story possesses the piece of food he wants, so he determines how to bargain with that character (to get the food) by examining their relationship. He decides to bargain for the food by offering to trade another object (a worm that he knows the other character likes) for the desired food.

All of this reasoning seems correct, but the story generated from it is ridiculous because two subtle details were omitted from the store of knowledge that the program used. One detail is that if a character drops something then he no longer physically possesses it because it is at a different location than he is, so the kind of plan that will regain it involves a change in location. The second detail is that if the story character who owns an object is yourself, then you do not have to bargain for the object because you already own it. Similar details are needed at the end of this story excerpt to keep Henry from bargaining with himself to discover the location of a worm to offer himself in exchange for the cheese.

Meehan (1976) gives an entire chapter full of these humorous "mis-spun tales," but the important point here is that it is hard to imagine any other research methodology discovering that such subtle pieces of knowledge were needed to write reasonable stories. In the next section we describe some of the kinds of knowledge that have been uncovered since the TALE-SPIN program.

KNOWLEDGE NEEDED FOR WRITING STORIES

Scripts

The type of knowledge that has received the most attention is the **script** (Schank & Abelson, 1977). As used here, this term refers to THE CHAIN OF EVENTS IN A COMMONPLACE EXPERIENCE, such as that involved in going to a restaurant, having a birthday party, and going to the dentist. For example, in the script that represents going to a restaurant for dinner, a person may enter, be seated at a table by the maitre-d', get a menu, read the menu, order from the waiter, eat dinner, pay the check, and leave. Consider the following story episode:

> John went into a restaurant. He ordered lobster and thought it tasted great. After finishing his dessert he went home.

Although this simple episode follows the restaurant script, there are a number of events that we know probably occurred despite the fact that they were not mentioned explicitly. For example, it is likely that John sat down at a table, read the menu, ate the lobster, paid the bill, and left a tip. The main point here is that, because of scriptlike knowledge about going to a restaurant, it is not necessary to state all the details in order to have a reader understand what happened in the story. The restaurant script establishes various expectations about typical activities in a restaurant from the customer's perspective, so that readers can expect that a critical event took place even when it is not mentioned. Recently a number of psychologists have shown that such scriptlike knowledge is actually used by people when understanding stories (Bower, Black, & Turner, 1979; Gibbs & Tenney, 1980; Graesser, Gordon, & Sawyer, 1979).

This type of tacit knowledge about commonplace situations is also important in writing stories. The writer's goal is to describe only what is necessary to activate our script knowledge about a situation. If too much of the script is made explicit, the story will seem dull. Thus, writers must utilize their script knowledge when determining the best level of detail to use in describing a routine activity. Leaving out mundane details allows the writer to focus on more interesting aspects of the story. Consider the following example:

> John went into a restaurant. He ordered lobster and thought it tasted very good. After he finished dessert, he left without paying the check.

In this episode our expectations have been violated. Using the restaurant script, we expected that John would pay the check before leaving. Violating this expectation focuses the reader's attention on this deviation and arouses his or her curiosity about why it occurred. Thus, writers can exploit scriptlike knowledge to focus attention and create interest.

Similarly, writers can exploit such taken-for-granted knowledge to cause humorous mistakes on the reader's part. A riddle-maker utilized the hospital script to manipulate readers of the following:

> A badly injured boy was brought by ambulance to the emergency room of a large metropolitan hospital. Recognizing the seriousness of the unconscious boy's injuries, the nurse on duty immediately called for an attending physician. Upon entering the boy's room, the doctor cried out, "My God! That's my son!" and collapsed. The astonished nurse frantically called for another doctor. The second physician rushed into the room but suddenly froze in mid-stride. "Oh my God," groaned the doctor. "That's my son."

How can this be? Of course, the two doctors are husband and wife, but why does the situation seem paradoxical at first? This puzzle arises because of the riddle-maker's realization that our hospital script includes a default assumption that doctors are male. Exploiting this tacit assumption leads to the apparent paradox, baffling many over the years. Perhaps as future patients find that their typical medical experience can include either a male or a female physician, their "doctor scripts" will not allow such a potentially misleading inference.

Plans

We often encounter situations that do not have a conventional routine or set of actions associated with them. For such situations, we have a form of knowledge more abstract and flexible than rigid scripts. Schank and Abelson (1977) termed these more general knowledge structures **plans.** In particular, plans are GENERAL OR ABSTRACT ACTIONS ASSOCIATED WITH GENERAL GOALS. For example, if we want to use some object, then we have to discover its location, go to that location, get control over the object and prepare for using it, then finally we can use it to do what we wanted. Using this plan, we can generate the following episode:

> John wanted a video recorder to record TV movies [goal of using object]. He found the address of a Video Store in the telephone book [determined location of object] and drove his car there [goes to location of object]. He bought a video recorder [got control over object] and the clerk taught him how to use it [prepared to use object]. Now he was ready to record his favorite movie from the Late Show [now can use object to do what he wants].

The knowledge used here is not a buy-video-recorder script, or even a going-to-the-store script, because we can change the specific actions and the plan remains the same. For example, it makes little difference whether John looked in the telephone book or asked a friend about the store location; whether he drove his car, took the bus or walked to the store; etc. Thus, critical to generating this coherent episode is abstract information about changes in knowledge, location and control (i.e., planning knowledge), rather than knowledge about specific actions (i.e., script knowledge).

In the previous example, we explicitly stated all of the plan but typically omitted the easily inferred parts. Thus, plans also tell writers what to make explicit in a text and what can be left for the reader to infer. Take, for example, the following brief passage (from Schank, 1975):

> John wanted to become supervisor at the plant. He went out and got some arsenic.

This story fragment is clearly dramatic. We understand what John's goal is and we know his basic plan to attain it—namely, getting some arsenic and poisoning whomever is presently supervisor so that the position will become vacant and John can then get it. If the writer did not know that readers have the planning knowledge necessary to understand this elliptical passage, then he or she would have had to make explicit any inferences necessary to connect these fragments. If this were the case, the same passage would become the following ponderous text:

> John wanted to become supervisor at the plant. Since someone already was the supervisor, the only way he could get the job was if the man who held the job was no longer able to perform the job. One way of bringing this situation about would be to kill the man. John thought he could do this by secretly poisoning the man. John decided that the best way to do this would be to get some arsenic and give it secretly to the supervisor so that it would kill him, thus enabling John to get the man's position as supervisor.

This particular version of the episode is not as dramatic or interesting as the first one. Because the writer has the appropriate knowledge about people's plans and goals, and because it is possible to assume that the reader will also share similar knowledge, the writer can compose an understandable story without being ponderous and prosaic.

Goals

Knowing about plans and scripts is not enough, however—a writer must also know when they are appropriate. Since both plans and scripts are methods for accomplishing **goals,** such goals become the key to when various plans and scripts are brought to mind. Consequently, we also need a classification of goals. Schank and Abelson (1977) found that the following categories of goals were useful for organizing the plans and scripts they discussed:

1. Satisfaction goals arising from recurring biological needs that must be pursued (e.g., hunger and thirst)
2. Enjoyment goals that are pursued optionally for enjoyment or pleasure (e.g., hearing music)
3. Achievement goals (e.g., achieving a particular social position)
4. Preservation goals that involve preserving some desireable state that may be threatened (e.g., one's health)
5. Instrumental goals that arise in the pursuit of other goals (e.g., to buy something at a store, you must first go to the store).

As an example, the USE plan we discussed previously is particularly appropriate for satisfaction goals. Thus, whenever a writer assigns a satisfaction goal to a story character, the USE plan could be implemented to determine what the character should do next.

But, as Wilensky (1978, 1980) has correctly observed, merely having a character executing a plan in pursuit of a goal does not a story make. For example, in the following excerpt John has a goal and pursues a plan that results in its fulfillment:

John loved Mary. He asked her to marry him. She agreed, and soon after they were wed. They were very happy.

But it is hard to imagine anyone bothering to write such a story, let alone wanting to read it. Of much more interest is the following account:

John loved Mary. He asked her to marry him. She agreed, and soon after they were wed. Then one day John met Sue, a new employee in his office. He soon fell in love with Sue . . . .

The basic difference between these two passages is that the second one involves more than just a character who has a goal and takes some steps to achieve it. The second story expresses a human dramatic situation; that is, a sequence of goal-related events that contain some problem for a character. Wilensky found that most problematic situations involve more than one goal at a time. Thus, in addition to knowing what kinds of goals exist in the world and how any given one may be achieved, writers must also be able to handle more complicated goal situations. Specifically, they must also know about relationships between goals, such as when a character like John has conflicting goals (e.g., to maintain his relationship with Mary but do something about his love for Sue), or when several characters have goals that are in competition. As an example of the latter, consider the following:

> John told Bill he would break his arm if Bill didn't give John his bicycle. Bill got on the bicycle and rode away.

To understand why it is appropriate that Bill should leave, one must realize that Bill had goals of his own and that they were incompatible with John's. In this story, Bill is trying to avoid losing his bicycle to John and is also trying to avoid getting hurt. His means of trying to accomplish these goals is running away from John. Thus, to understand the story, readers must not only infer what Bill's goals were, but also recognize the relationship between his goals and John's. These two characters' goals are in competition: If Bill succeeded in preserving his possession of the bicycle, then John would have failed to fulfill his goal, and vice versa.

Wilensky (1978) proposed three ways to cause goal competition. The first is having a shortage of some consumable resource that both characters need in their plans for achieving their respective goals. The following passage is an example of **goal competition** resulting from such resource limitations:

> John and Bill were driving across the desert when their car broke down. They had only enough water left for one of them to make it to the nearest town. . . .

Likewise, characters' goals can compete because achieving them would require mutually exclusive states to come into existence, as in:

> John wanted to win the race but so did Bill . . . .

The problem here is obviously that a race can have only one winner. Finally, consider the following situation:

> John wanted to go to the track, but his wife didn't want him to go because she thought gambling was immoral . . . .

This example illustrates how the goal of one character can induce an incompatible goal in another character—e.g., John's desire to gamble induced his wife's goal of stopping him.

Wilensky discussed two other kinds of multiple-goal situations that lead to problems. In the preceding example, the incompatible goals were desired by different characters (goal competition), but similar problems arise when the incompatible goals are desired by the same character (**goal conflict**). There is much overlap in the methods of resolving goal conflict and competition, but there are also differences. For example, if two characters are traveling together but differ in their opinions on where to go next, then a fistfight can settle the disagreement. However, if the same character wants to go to two different places next, he cannot settle the conflict by hitting himself. The other problematic situation discussed by Wilensky is a **goal subsumption** failure. Here, a state of affairs that subsumed many goals is terminated, so the goals are activated again. For example, the state of marriage subsumes so many goals (e.g., friendship, sex, financial security) that if a writer begins a story with a divorce, the story almost writes itself.

Themes

The categories of goals described in the preceding section are based on differences in how the goals can be achieved. But where do these goals come from in the first place? That is, how do we know when to expect that certain goals will become active in a story?

Schank and Abelson (1977) proposed a kind of knowledge they termed **themes.** These themes contain the BACKGROUND INFORMATION ON WHICH WE BASE OUR PREDICTIONS THAT AN INDIVIDUAL WILL HAVE A CERTAIN GOAL. When a theme is established, it allows a writer to motivate a story character's behavior by providing a prior context for his or her actions.

Schank and Abelson discussed three types of themes, each representing knowledge about a particular type of predisposition that a character may have. One example is a **role theme.** Once a theme of this type is invoked it establishes expectations about a particular character's goals and actions based on his or her role in the story.

Some role goals are quite straightforward and their associated plans have a scriptlike representation. For example, one of a chambermaid's goals is to keep things clean, and it would therefore be reasonable to have a character in that role execute the scour-a-bathroom script. Thus, a writer could easily include the following sentence in a story:

> *Ruth, the chambermaid, had to clean all the toilets in the building once a week as part of her routine.*

On the other hand, if the story included

> *Mary, the dentist, had to clean all the toilets in the building once a week as part of her routine . . . ,*

then the writer would have a lot of explaining to do. Clearly, the role of a dentist does not evoke goals for which cleaning toilets is a probable plan of achievement.

Some roles have more flexible plans associated with them, however. Take, for example, the role of a Wild-West sheriff (Schank & Abelson, 1977). If someone tells the sheriff that all his cattle have been stolen, we have very strong expectations that the sheriff will then have the goal of finding the rustling-victim's herd. In general, role goals are triggered by actions of other "players" when these actions become known to the character in the role. Once such a goal is successfully triggered, the character's plans are much more predictable than if a non-role person had the same goal. If our Wild-West sheriff has the goal of catching someone, then it is very likely that he will choose horseback to satisfy his goal of getting to where the "bad guy" is "holed-up," and perhaps he will enlist the help of a posse to achieve his goal of gaining control over the nasty "hombre." Thus, we can write:

> Jake told the sheriff, "My cattle are gone!" The sheriff went to the saloon to find his pals Slim, Ernie, Baldy and Pete . . . ,

and be confident the readers will infer that the sheriff intends to round up a posse. On the other hand, we would only confuse the reader if we wrote:

> Jake told the chambermaid, "My cattle are gone!" The chambermaid went to the saloon to find her pals Slim, Ernie, Baldy and Pete . . . .

When a role member performs his or her unique functions, then other characters will respond in predictable ways, thereby allowing us to make further thematic predictions about their goals and actions.

Another very useful type of theme is **interpersonal** in nature. Social relationships can be represented by this type of theme. Thus, invoking the theme that Michael LOVES Anne allows us to predict what Michael will probably do if Anne is sick, if her life is threatened, if another man shows interest in her, and so on; that is, we can predict what goals Michael might have in particular situations. All this information is part of the LOVE theme.

The thematic context that has been established can make a big difference in how readers interpret the same statements. Consider how you would interpret the following passage if you knew that Michael and Anne were soon to be married.

> One evening Michael walked into the local bar and saw Anne in the passionate embrace of a stranger. So involved were they that she didn't even see Michael pull out a gun. An instant later she lay dead on the floor.

You might guess that Michael was extremely impulsive, perhaps crazed by his jealousy, and in a fit of passionate anger shot his unfaithful betrothed. The ability to generate such an explanation for Michael's behavior is based on what we know about people in love; that is, the information that Michael and Anne were engaged is likely to invoke a LOVE theme which then activates his goals.

On the other hand, what if you were aware that Michael was actually engaged to Susan, whose life Anne was seriously threatening for one reason or another. This information, too, might invoke a LOVE theme, but your subsequent reasoning might be based on another feature of it; namely, that if someone harms a loved one, the lover wants to harm the harmer. If someone threatens to harm a loved one, that person can become an ENEMY—another interpersonal theme in which one goal might be removing the enemy from the face of the earth. Clearly, one plan to achieve such a goal is premeditated murder, and we would consequently have a somewhat different interpretation of Michael's behavior in the preceding episode.

A third kind of theme describes the general aim that a person has in life. Thus, in such **life themes** individuals can aspire to reach the top of their professions, to live lavishly, or to be rich. These themes generate goals continuously in a variety of situations, and tend to incorporate expectations about the general character of everything a person does. In this sense, they are different from the other types of themes because they are continuous in nature, rather than active only in situations involving certain other specific actors.

If we assign some story characters the life theme of LUXURY LIVING, then we can have them live in a huge and lavish house, own yachts, and buy fancy new cars each year. Some goals packaged into such a theme are having large amounts of money, owning desirable objects, getting rich people to like you, establishing a credit rating, etc. Some expectations we might consequently have are (a) that if there's an opportunity to get money, this person will take it, (b) that if a valuable object can be obtained, this person will try to get it, and so on. Such knowledge of goals is established by evoking the LUXURY LIVING life theme. People can and do operate under a multitude of life themes at any given moment, and any story character that did not would seem one-dimensional and unrealistic. What distinguishes life themes (and the other themes as well) from goals themselves is that the THEMES ARE PACKAGES OF GOALS. Life themes are important for writing stories in that they establish long-range tendencies in a character's actions. Establishing a story character's life themes means establishing what that character wants most and what he or she is likely to do to get it.

Putting It All Together

Although there is an AI program that integrates all these kinds of knowledge to understand stories (see Dyer & Lehnert, 1980), there is no program at this time that uses all of this knowledge to generate stories. However, a simple example will illustrate how they can be utilized by a writer when composing a story. First, the writer would establish the themes. For example, John and Rita are in love and they are married (i.e., they are in husband and wife roles). Next the writer would establish the interesting problem using one of the multiple-goal situations—for example, a goal subsumption failure. Thus, John and Rita get divorced after an argument. This goal subsumption failure unleashes all the goals that had been subsumed by the marriage, so the story characters start pursuing plans to attain those reactivated goals. Thus, John and Rita start dating others. Since the LOVE theme is still in effect between them, however, these dates with others are doomed to be dismal failures. Finally, an old friend reunites them and they settle their differences, thus resubsuming all those bothersome goals. They live happily ever after except for a few goal competitions—for example, he wants to watch football on TV (thus fulfilling his macho role) whereas she wants to watch ballet on TV (thus fulfilling her feminine role). In this case, they resolve their goal competition by eliminating their TV resource limitation (i.e., they buy another TV). Actually this story would be more memorable if the husband wanted to watch ballet and the wife wanted to watch football. In the next section, we discuss why adding such twists make stories more memorable.

WRITING MEMORABLE STORIES

What makes a story memorable? There are two conditions that make this possible: one is that the story remind the readers of experiences from their own lives, and the other is that the readers be reminded of the story at appropriate times during their lives. Thus, the key to writing memorable stories is determining how one experience reminds people of another. Reminding occurs when people classify experiences into the same memory category, so the important issue here is determining how experiences are organized in people's memories. In fact, the organization of memory determines both how writers generate ideas from their own experiences, and how writers use these ideas to remind their readers of the right associations. The writer's task is to bring experiences to the consciousness of the readers that will shed light on what they are reading. To do this requires a memory organization that can be indexed so that the appropriate experiences can be accessed easily when needed.

Kintsch (1980) and Dehn (Note 1) have recently stressed the importance of memory organization for writing. In addition, Schank (1980) and Schank and Abelson (Note 2) have proposed a general theory of memory that emphasizes the importance of reminding. We will consider the memory organization proposed by Schank and Abelson, but will apply it to writing as suggested by Kintsch and Dehn. A good writer can utilize memory organization to facilitate understanding by reminding the readers of their own experiences or of ones they have experienced vicariously. In this sense, truly understanding a story means understanding it in terms of our own experiences. A good writer, therefore, is one who facilitates that integration by skillfully tapping existing memories.

Consider the following reminding experience reported by Schank (1980). There is a restaurant in Boston called Legal Seafood that is abnormal because you first pay and then eat. If you had been to Legal Seafood, then going into another restaurant where you paid immediately after ordering should normally cause you to be reminded of Legal Seafood. A script-based view of comprehension would suggest that the restaurant script is called into play here to help us understand the experience of going into a place where you pay immediately after ordering. In addition, however, when we come upon a deviation from our normal expectations, we also activate more specific relevant experiences. The restaurant script, in this case, is the memory category under which our various restaurant experiences are stored. General memory categories like this one have an enormous number of experiences stored under them, so a new experience that is a typical instance of this category is not particularly memorable. What makes a restaurant experience distinctive is if it deviates from the typical one. In fact, if another experience that deviates in the same way is encountered later, then it reminds you of the earlier deviate. Thus, although experiences seem to be organized in memory by the general memory category to which they belong, they are also indexed under that category according to how they deviate from it.

The memory category we used in our Legal Seafood example was a script, but all the types of knowledge we described in the last section (i.e., goals, plans, and themes) act as general memory categories for organizing experience. For example, goal-based reminding occurs simply when our understanding of someone's goals reminds us of someone pursuing a similar goal. Thus, seeing someone wait in line for a long time just to buy one stamp reminds us of the time when someone waited in line a long time just to buy a dollar's worth of gas. Both of these experiences are slightly unusual because the person in question failed to think about the future. Each person could have saved themselves considerable time by buying more stamps or gas at an earlier time. But each person failed to subsume this goal. In this manner, the predicament of the person in the post office is understood in terms of the goal-subsumption failure of the person in the gas station. Thus, just as there are specific memories indexed under script-based situations, there are also memories indexed under episodes of goal-subsumption failures.

Plan-based reminding is common because we focus on not only the goals that people pursue, but also on their methods of attaining those goals. So, seeing someone trying to find a contact lens in a big pile of sand may remind you of the classic needle-in-a-haystack problem. This reminding occurs not just because you are thinking about a plan to find something that is lost, but because it is a rather futile plan. This futility provides the deviation from normalcy needed to make this plan situation distinctive.

Similarly, patterns of affectively evaluated events and mental states can serve as general memory categories. Lehnert (1980) has described a number of these. For example, if a negative event (e.g., flunking a midterm exam) motivates a mental state (e.g., determination to do well in the course) that in turn causes a positive event (e.g., getting an A on the final exam), then we have a "success born of adversity" experience. As with the other memory categories, a highly memorable "success born of adversity" experience would be one that basically matches the general pattern but deviates from it in an interesting way (e.g., success on the final exam is caused by taking a memory-boosting drug). Because of this uniqueness, the experience becomes separately indexed in memory by its deviation from the general pattern.

Another high-level type of reminding that often takes place is mediated by patterns of themes, goals, and outcomes. Schank and Abelson (Note 2) call this phenomenon "thematic sequence reminding." For example, many who have seen or read *Romeo and Juliet* and are seeing *West Side Story* for the first time realize that it is just *Romeo and Juliet* in a modern setting with music. To be reminded of *Romeo and Juliet* when seeing *West Side Story*, one must recognize that, although the content is different, the overall pattern of goals, outcomes, and themes is the same. The mediating pattern here seems to be something like:

> *Two people try to get together, but are thwarted by outside opposition. This opposition eventually results in a report of a tragedy for one of them that actually results in a tragedy for the other.*

Here again, what makes *Romeo and Juliet* sufficiently distinctive that *West Side Story* reminds us of it is the departure of their (similar) patterns of goals, outcomes, and themes from what we normally expect. Typically, two people trying to get together have little trouble doing so, but in these stories the attempts become very involved and, in the end, result in failure.

No AI program has yet been designed to test the utility of these ideas about reminding and memory organization for writing, but they have been shown to be of value in designing AI programs that understand (Lebowitz, 1980) and answer questions about (Kolodner, 1980) stories. However, a simple example should illustrate how these ideas can facilitate the writing of memorable stories. The writer would start with a standard memory category and fill in details using the knowledge about scripts, plans, goals, and themes described in the last section. For example, two young people are in love and decide to get married. Their parents are excited and plan a large church wedding for them. Considering this general knowledge about weddings reminds the writer of some weddings she has attended, so she also draws material from these personal experiences to make the story more vivid. Thus, the writer might describe a particularly picturesque church she remembers and also include a few humorous anecdotes she recalls about weddings (e.g., the bride insists on finishing a soap opera before she will get dressed for the wedding).

Now the writer adds a twist to this normal wedding scenario to make the story distinctive and therefore memorable. For example, just as the new-lyweds are about to leave the wedding reception and start their honeymoon, a discussion among two of the parents reveals that the bride and groom might actually be brother and sister. It seems that the bride's mother and the groom's father had an affair 9 months before the bride was born. Hence, the bride and groom may have had the same father. The rest of the story would then describe the story characters' attempts to deal with this aberration. This story is quite distinctive so it would remind readers of any weddings they may have experienced where the bride and groom were not what they seemed. In addition, any experiences of this kind that the readers have subsequently would remind them of this story. Thus we have a memorable narrative.

APPLICATIONS TO WRITING INSTRUCTION

We have described some of the kinds of tacit knowledge that are necessary for producing and understanding stories. These theories of the knowledge needed for such ability have been investigated and elaborated through research methods from the field of artificial intelligence—namely, by considering how to construct computer programs that use such knowledge to model human behavior.

One of the motivations underlying this quest to understand written discourse composition is a serious, real-world problem—how can we use our knowledge to improve a student's writing abilities? We believe that the approach we describe can yield valuable information when applied to the study of just such complex, real-world phenomena. Trying to get a computer to do something intelligent is difficult. The task forces us to be very specific when designing our theories. If we overlook some needed tacit knowledge, then the computer program that implements the theory will simply not exhibit the desired behavior. Observing how test programs perform erroneously directs us to specific problem areas in our overall conception of the process under study.

The experience of Brown and Burton (1978) with a similar problem will serve to illustrate how the methods of AI can aid educational practice. These researchers were interested in how one might improve a student's ability to solve arithmetic problems. In their view, a student's error might be thought of as evidence for a "bug" in some procedure he or she used in applying his or her overall knowledge of arithmetic to solve the problem. To aid the student, the teacher must form an accurate picture of the student's misconception(s) on the basis of his or her errors. Thus a prerequisite to correcting the student's mistakes is having a detailed model of his or her knowledge, including the misconceptions. Such a model can then be used to diagnose exactly where the student makes his or her mistakes.

Brown and Burton used the methods of AI to develop a diagnostic model for arithmetic in the form of a computer program named BUGGY that can simulate the problem student. Some of the insights they gained by using the model are enlightening. For example, they were able to demonstrate that some common assumptions among math teachers were fallacious. These assumptions were that students are poor at following procedures and that erratic behavior is the primary cause of a student's inability to perform each problem-solving step correctly. Rather, experience in diagnosing problems with BUGGY showed that students are remarkably competent procedure followers, but that they often follow the wrong procedures. Brown and Burton described one case in which a student went through the entire school year with his teacher thinking he had absolutely no knowledge of addition—that is, that his answers to problems seemed to be completely random numbers. However, using their diagnostic computer model, Brown and Burton were able to discover that this student had only one simple bug in a procedure for applying his knowledge. All along he had a complete and consistent procedure for doing arithmetic and, far from being random, his answers showed that he followed that procedure almost perfectly.

Furthermore, BUGGY can be used to develop teachers' intuitions by presenting them with examples of "buggy" behavior and having them try to diagnose the underlying causes of the errors. Feedback is then provided by having BUGGY give a trace of how it produced the errors, so teachers can use BUGGY to gain experience in forming theories about the relationship between the symptoms of a bug and the underlying bug itself. Thus BUGGY provided two aids to arithmetic instruction: It provided a detailed model of the learning difficulties of the student, and it provided a method for increasing the accuracy of teachers' perceptions of students' problems.

The importance of BUGGY for writing, however, is that its success was made possible by having a detailed model of the phenomenon—exactly the kind of model that AI methodology is especially good at providing. Imagine the possibilities if a similar AI program could be developed for diagnosing the bugs that students with writing difficulties have. Combining such a program with a similarly detailed AI model of teaching (for example, see Collins, Warnock, & Passafiume, 1975) would promote a major increase in the effectiveness of writing instruction. Certainly we do not claim that the existence of a writing diagnosis program is just around the corner, for writing is much more complicated than addition and subtraction. However, developing and testing specific models of human text production and understanding, using the methods of AI, brings us closer and closer to realizing this exciting prospect.

REFERENCE NOTES

1. Dehn, N. *Story generation.* Manuscript in preparation, Department of Computer Science, Yale University, New Haven, Conn.
2. Schank, R. C., & Abelson, R. P., *Representation, generalization, organization and explanation,* book in preparation.

REFERENCES

Birnbaum, L., Flowers, M., & McGuire, R. Towards an AI model of argumentation. *Proceedings of the First Annual National Conference on Artificial Intelligence,* 1980, 313–315.

Black, J. B. Psycholinguistic processes in writing. In S. Rosenberg (Ed.), *Handbook of Applied Psycholinguistics.* Hillsdale, N.J.: Lawrence Erlbaum, in press.

Bower, G. H., Black, J. B., & Turner, T. J. Scripts in memory for text. *Cognitive Psychology,* 1979, *11,* 177–220.

Brown, J. S., & Burton, R. R. Diagnostic models for procedural bugs in basic mathematical skills. *Cognitive Science,* 1978, *2,* 155–192.

Collins, A. M., Warnock, E. H., & Passafiume, J. J. Analysis and synthesis of tutorial dialogs. In G. H. Brower (Ed.), *The psychology of learning and motivation* (Vol. 9). New York: Academic Press, 1975.

Dyer, M. G., & Lehnert, W. G. *Memory organization and search processes for narratives.* Research Report No. 175, Department of Computer Science, Yale University, New Haven, 1980.

Gibbs, R. W., & Tenney, Y. J. The concept of scripts in understanding stories. *Journal of Psycholinguistic Research,* 1980, *9,* 275–284.

Graesser, A. C., Gordon, S. E., & Sawyer, J. D. Recognition memory for typical and atypical actions in scripted activities: Tests of a script pointer plus tag hypothesis. *Journal of Verbal Learning and Verbal Behavior,* 1979, *18,* 319–332.

Kintsch, W. *Psychological processes in discourse production.* Technical Report No. 99, Institute of Cognitive Science, University of Colorado, Boulder, Col., 1980.

Kolodner, J. L. *Retrieval and organization strategies in conceptual memory: A computer model.* Research Report No. 187, Department of Computer Science, Yale University, New Haven, 1980.

Lebowitz, M. *Generalization and memory in an integrated understanding system.* Research Report No. 186, Department of Computer Science, Yale University, New Haven, 1980.

Lehnert, W. G. *Affect units and narrative summarization.* Research Report No. 179, Department of Computer Science, Yale University, New Haven, 1980.

Meehan, J. R. *The metanovel: Writing stories by computer.* Research Report No. 74, Computer Science Department, Yale University, New Haven, 1976.

Schank, R. C. Conceptual dependency: A theory of natural language understanding. *Cognitive Psychology,* 1972, *3,* 552–631.

Schank, R. C. Identification of conceptualizations underlying natural language. In R. C. Schank and K. M. Colby (Eds.), *Computer models of thought and language.* San Francisco: Freeman, 1973.

Schank, R. C. *Conceptual information processing.* Amsterdam: North-Holland, 1975.

Schank, R. C. Language and memory. *Cognitive science,* 1980, *4,* 243–284.

Schank, R. C., & Abelson, R. P. *Scripts, plans, goals and understanding.* Hillsdale, N.J.: Lawrence Erlbaum, 1977.

Wilensky, R. *Understanding goal-based stories.* Research Report No. 140, Department of Computer Science, Yale University, New Haven, 1978.

Wilensky, R. *Points: A theory of story content.* Memo No. M80/17, Electronics Research Laboratory, University of California, Berkeley, 1980.

Chapter 13

Learning to Revise: Some Component Processes

Elsa Jaffe Bartlett

In this chapter, I describe results of some recent studies of editing and revision. The data were obtained over a 2-year period from some 250 elementary and junior high school students in grades four through seven. The research was intended to assess certain claims, based on current models of revision processes, about difficulties that students might encounter in detecting and correcting text problems. For reasons that will become clear, it seemed desirable to focus on problems of syntactic anomaly and referential ambiguity. The results, however, should be readily applicable to a range of revision problems.

I will begin with a general discussion of current research, focusing on some of the problems inherent in current formulations. I will then discuss three distinct components of revision processes, illustrating the discussion with results from my own research.

WHAT IS REVISION?

Revision seems to be an essential component of virtually every attempt to construct a model of the writing process. Depending on the model, it is viewed as a separate activity, performed on completed drafts (e.g., Murray, 1978) or as a recursive activity, performed at any point in the writing process on any type of text segment (e.g., Collins & Gentner, 1980). But

WHAT WRITERS KNOW
The Language, Process,
and Structure of Written Discourse

whatever its place in the writing process, revision is invariably distinguished from text generation by the fact that it involves some fairly explicit processes of comparison, generally between some segment of a text (a word, phrase, sentence, paragraph, etc.) and some representation of a writer's knowledge or intention, which results in some attempt to change existing text.

There is no doubt that writers can deliberately initiate revision processes and further, that writers can specify a type of revision in advance. For example, a writer might decide to review a text for transcription problems or problems of interpretability. However, for many writers (and especially beginners), detection seems to be a fairly haphazard process, often proceeding without well-planned goals or strategies. For example, Shaughnessy (1977) claims that her adult beginners often seemed to initiate revision processes prematurely, after production of no more than a sentence or two. Calkins (n.d.) has noted that beginners often have difficulty maintaining a plan for a revision.

Professional writers and writing teachers are fond of pointing out that writing is essentially rewriting (e.g., Murray, 1978) and that students tend to do precious little of it. Moreover, when students revise at all, they generally focus on changes at the level of individual words or phrases, often dwelling on problems of transcription, syntactic form (e.g., subject–verb agreement) or lexical choice. This appears to be as true of college freshmen (e.g., Sommers, 1978) as elementary and high school students (e.g., National Assessment of Educational Progress, 1977; Stallard, 1974).

More important, perhaps, is the finding that revisions do not always result in appreciably better text. For example, although researchers such as Beach (1979) and Bamberg (1978) report that revisions of their high school and college freshman subjects did result in qualitatively better drafts, data from 9-, 13- and 17-year-old subjects in a recent National Assessment of Educational Progress show that revisions did not reliably improve the holistic ratings of texts. Similarly, Scardamalia, Bereiter, Gartshore and Cattani (n.d.), and Bracewell, Bereiter and Scardamalia (n.d.) found no reliable differences in the quality of original and revised versions of essays produced by elementary and high school students.

In a recent review of the literature, Gantry (1980) attributes these inconsistent results to differences in the complexity of measures used in evaluating students' drafts. However, most evaluations appear to be based on comparable holistic schemes that take into account complex aspects of intersentence organization as well as aspects of vocabulary choice and mechanics. It seems to me more likely that differences in results can be attributed to characteristics of the editing tasks themselves. In particular, those studies that report gain in quality seem to involve situations where revisions are based on the evaluations of peers or teachers. When evaluations are generated by the writers themselves, improvement in quality is much less likely.

Accounting for Student Difficulties

Researchers have attempted to account for students' difficulties in a number of ways. For one thing, as Murray and others have noted, students are rarely required to revise their compositions. Most get away with first-draft copy and even when revision is demanded, it usually amounts to little more than corrections of mechanical errors. Research by Calkins (1979) has indicated that when elementary students are given ample opportunity to practice, they can eventually develop sophisticated revision skills. However, research based on Piagetian theories of cognitive development suggests that there may be certain cognitive limits on the skills that even these practiced youngsters are able to acquire.

In his original observations, Piaget (1926) was able to demonstrate striking ambiguities and omissions in elementary-age children's attempts to describe or explain events and in their retellings of stories. These children often failed to supply sufficient information for listeners to determine word referents and intended logical relations, and in general Piaget concluded that they seemed unable to adjust the content of their messages to meet the needs of listeners who did not share their knowledge of a topic. Piaget attributed the difficulty to children's inability to represent an event from two points of view (their own and a listener's), claiming that childish "egocentrism" would eventually diminish as children learn to maintain two representations and make rapid "decentered" comparisons between them.

As characterizations of cognitive aspects of revision, Piagetian notions of egocentrism and decentered perception are attractive because they attempt to describe limits of children's comparison processes—processes that are certainly at the very heart of revision. However, attempts to invoke Piagetian explanations of students' difficulties have had only limited success. In most attempts, beginners' problems are characterized as stemming from some failure to represent an "audience's point of view," but unfortunately, the meaning of audience in this context remains somewhat vague. Although experienced writers certainly take pains to shape their texts to suit the knowledge and expectations of their intended readers, it is not clear how a failure to represent the viewpoint of intended readers can account for more than a small proportion of students' revision failures.

Interpreting Piaget more broadly, Bracewell, Bereiter and Scardamalia have suggested that students' difficulties stem from an inability to compare any two representations of the same event, claiming that for elementary students, revision will be ineffective regardless of the circumstances:

> Central to Piaget's concept of decentration is back-and-forth comparison, not simple shifting of viewpoint and . . . this lack of comparison may lie behind much that appears egocentric in children's behavior. Without comparison, of course, revision is impossible and what appears instead is pseudo-revision, generation of new material using old as stimulus. With a time lag (between composition and revision) or with an unfamiliar

composition to work with, the new material produced may be different from the old, but it will not necessarily be better [p. 1].

Attempts to test this notion, however, have met with mixed success. When authors' original and revised drafts were compared holistically, these researchers did indeed find that revision resulted in no improvement, regardless of whether revision occurred immediately after composition or after a week's delay. However, contrary to these authors' predictions, attempts by nonauthors to revise these same texts resulted in appreciable improvement, provided that an editor was sympathetic to the content and point of view expressed by an author.

One problem in interpreting these results is the lack of details concerning students' actual revisions. For example, differences may have been due to the fact that nonauthors were better able to detect text problems or, alternatively, despite equivalent detection, that nonauthors were better at formulating an effective correction. Unfortunately, these questions cannot be addressed by the holistic ratings reported in these studies. To approach them, more fine-grained analyses based on more precise definitions of components of revision processes are necessary.

COMPONENTS OF REVISION PROCESSES

How can we characterize different components of revision?

We might begin with the observation that revision seems to involve both evaluation and correction, with correction being motivated by the detection and identification of some malfunction or discrepancy in existing text. For example: "The Editing process examines any material that the writer puts into words. . . . Its purpose is to detect and correct violations in writing conventions and inaccuracies of meaning and to evaluate materials with respect to the writing goals [Hayes and Flower, 1980, p. 16]." Under most circumstances, these processes are carried out together, but it is easy to see that difficulties might develop somewhat independently in any one. For example, most teachers can recall students—particularly beginners—who notice that something is wrong with a text without being able to identify the problem, complaining only that it "sounds funny" or "isn't right." Similarly, students may be able to identify a problem but produce an ineffective change. The point, then, is that these different processes are likely to require different sorts of skills while at the same time presenting students with different sorts of difficulties. We will consider each in turn.

Detection Processes

Revision is generally triggered by awareness (however inchoate) of some malfunction or discrepancy—perhaps a violation of writing convention, an ambiguity or logical inconsistency. This awareness must surely involve contact (at some more or less conscious level) between existing text and some body of knowledge from which text alternatives might be formulated (i.e., knowledge of text conventions or recollection of original goals or intended meanings). The nature of that contact may be more or less explicit and may involve more or less elaborate processes of comparison, depending on the skill of the writer and the difficulty of a particular problem. For example, skilled writers may find some problems so routine that they are hardly aware of the process by which the need for alternative text is formulated, whereas other problems may require lengthy comparison and deliberation.

In any case, if (as seems likely) detection processes require some contact between existing text and a body of knowledge from which alternative texts might be constructed, then it is easy to see that revision tasks may be characterized in terms of the ease with which such contact can be effected—for example, the ease with which relevant knowledge can be recollected or represented. For example, detection of some malfunctions may draw on knowledge of well-practiced skills that have become highly automatic and thus easy to recollect. For the most part, these will involve highly conventional aspects of language that remain more or less invariant in form from one composition to the next. Other text revisions may involve knowledge that is more ad hoc: aspects of content and language assembled to meet the needs of a particular composition. These may be more inchoate and thus difficult to recollect during revision, making it more difficult for students to detect discrepancies between existing text and some originally intended meaning, as well as between existing text and some previously unrecognized and potential meaning.

These examples suffice to indicate that detection of different types of malfunctions is likely to involve somewhat different types of knowledge. It may also be the case that knowledge may be much more accessible under some conditions than others. For example, we might imagine that although most conventional linguistic knowledge (e.g., correct syntax, punctuation, spelling) might be readily available across a broad range of revision situations, other types of knowledge might be less accessible. For instance, it might be fairly difficult for students to make judgments about text interpretability when evaluating their own texts. To appreciate how this might occur, consider once again the task facing a writer who sets out to reread his or her own text for revision. Generally, when we read, we actively seek to understand a text: We attempt to fill in missing information, draw inferences and predict intended meanings. Revision, however, requires a somewhat different approach. As one writer and writing teacher has observed: "Writers perform a special, significant kind of reading when they read their own writing in process. Writers must achieve a detachment from their work that allows them to see what is on the page, not what they hope will be on the page [Murray, 1978, p. 95]."

Of crucial importance is a writer's ability to inhibit interpretations based on knowledge of the writer's own intentions. Thus, for example, although a writer may know an intended referent for a word, in evaluating the interpretability of the particular text, a writer must inhibit any tendency to use this "privileged" knowledge in computing a meaning, limiting his or her interpretative activities to whatever can be constructed from the information actually available on the page. For example, a writer may know (and intend to say) that Sam Smith is the husband or Sue and the brother of Sarah, but if this information has not already been established in the discourse, then a phrase such as "her husband" or "her brother" will be difficult to interpret.

Initially, at least, this may require that writers develop some explicit awareness of the kinds of processes (inferencing, expecting, etc.) through which their interpretations are accomplished, and it may well be the case that there are large individual differences in the ease with which explicit knowledge of these processes is acquired (Gleitman & Gleitman, 1979).

The notion of privileged information, of course, refers only to writers' knowledge of their own intentions. Obviously, writers will not have such information about texts composed by others and will not be faced with the problem of inhibiting certain interpretive activities. This suggests (as the folklore would have it and contrary to the hypotheses of Bracewell *et al.* n.d.) that student writers may find it considerably easier to detect problems in texts of others than in their own, but only those problems that can be masked by interpretive activity based on the use of privileged information. Thus, although we might expect students to be more adept at detecting logical inconsistencies or referential ambiguities in the texts of others, we would expect to find no difference in their detection of spelling errors or faulty syntax or other problems related to knowledge of language conventions.

These hypotheses were investigated in a series of studies designed to assess students' abilities to detect various types of problems in their own texts and in texts composed by others. Given the above hypotheses it seemed important to investigate problems whose presence in an author's text might be masked by use of privileged knowledge. For this, referential ambiguity seemed ideal, especially since results of previous research indicated that ambiguities were likely to occur fairly often in the first drafts of narratives by elementary students (Bartlett & Scribner, in press). Additionally, it seemed important to study a type of problem less likely to be masked by privileged knowledge. Although we might have examined problems of spelling or punctuation, we have chosen to focus on detection of certain syntactic anomalies—missing subjects, predicates, or prepositions—partly because detection of these seemed to involve larger segments of text than would be the case with spelling and partly because these also have been found to occur fairly frequently in children's narrative texts.

Two studies were carried out involving a total of 110 fourth and fifth graders. In each, our main purpose was to compare children's detection of these problems in their own texts with detection of comparable problems in the texts of others. In both studies, children composed and (one week later) edited a short narrative for publication in a class anthology. (Original texts were xeroxed prior to editing so that original and edited versions could be compared and so that children could edit from their own original copy.) In addition, a week after editing their own texts, children were asked to edit a series of eight short paragraphs adapted by a researcher from texts produced by children in a previous study. Of these, six contained faulty referring expressions and two, a missing subject or predicate (see examples in Table 13.1).

Data from the fifth-grade study will be described in detail. Seventy-nine children drawn from four public school classrooms participated.

In analyzing the data, we were primarily interested in comparing children's detection of the two types of problems in their own texts and texts prepared by the experimenter. As a first step, each first draft was examined by two trained raters, working independently, for instances of these two problems. In all, raters found 34 texts with at least one instance of syntactic anomaly and 30 with some referential ambiguity (representing 49% and 43% of the total, respectively). A student was given credit for detecting a text problem if both raters agreed that anomalous or ambiguous portions of text had been altered during revision, regardless of whether the writer succeeded in correcting the problem. For example, if a child had changed the second text in Table 13.1 to:

One day a man left his house. Another man was standing outside. The man took out a letter and gave it to the other man. . . .

that child would be credited with detection, despite the fact that the ambiguity was not corrected.

We had predicted that children would be more likely to detect syntactic anomalies than referential ambiguities in their own texts and this was strikingly confirmed. Of the 34 students producing syntactic anomaly, 18 (53%) managed to detect at least one anomaly during revision—not a high percentage, but one that indicates some level of skill. By contrast, of the 30 students producing referential ambiguity, only 5 (17%) managed to detect the problem. The difference between these percentages is statistically reliable ($z = 3.00$; $p < .01$).

These results are quite different from those obtained on the experimental texts. Here we found that of the 30 students making referential ambiguities, 22 (73%) detected at least one referential ambiguity in these texts and in all, managed to detect 57% of the total number of problems presented. Similar results were obtained from the 34 students producing syntactic anomalies: 30 (88%) managed to detect at least one anomaly in the experimental texts and over all, they managed to detect a total of 69% of

TABLE 13.1
Examples of Experimental Revision Texts

Single referent problems

Policemen sometimes have special jobs. Once there was a policeman who was supposed to chase robbers. One day he got into a policecar and drove to the city to catch a robber. They had a big fight. He was killed.

Double referent problems

One day a man left his house. Another man was standing outside. The man took out a letter and gave it to him. They talked for a while and then they got into a car. They were both policemen. They were going to catch a thief.

Syntactic anomaly

A man was going to the movies. Later was going to meet his wife. They were going to have a Chinese dinner and then take the subway home. But when the man got to the movies he saw that he had no money. He had left it at home.

these problems. Although the syntactic anomalies were somewhat easier to detect, the difference in the percentage of detected problems was not statistically reliable ($z = 1.71$; $p > .05$). Additionally, when we compare children's detection of problems in their own and another's text, we find that children were better at detecting both types of problems in another's text and these differences were highly reliable. (See Table 13.2.) Finally, we might also note that similar results were obtained with our sample of 40 fourth graders, although (as we might expect) scores on most measures tended to be somewhat lower.

Taken together, these results indicate that for children in this age range, both types of problems are substantially easier to detect in the texts of others than in their own. Nor does the difference seem due to any general reluctance on the part of these young writers to make changes in their first drafts. Of the fifth graders producing referential ambiguity, 57% made some text change during revision, whereas 53% of those making syntactic anomalies did so. These percentages are quite comparable to the 61% found for the sample as a whole. (Fourth graders were a little less likely to make changes: 49% of those producing a target text problem made some change, as compared with 56% for the sample as a whole.) Finally, we might note that very few children were able to detect referential ambiguities in their own texts. Since these same children were able to detect a fair percentage of comparable problems in the texts of others, it seems unlikely that the difficulty is due to some general lack of knowledge concerning ambiguity. Rather, this pattern of results suggests that the ability to detect ambiguity and (to a somewhat lesser extent) syntactic anomaly may require some additional skills. In the case of referential ambiguity, at least, this may include an ability to inhibit the use of privileged knowledge when reviewing text.

TABLE 13.2
Detection of Text Problems

Detection of referential ambiguities
$N=30$

	Own text	
	Detects none	Detects at least one
Experimental texts		
Detects at least one	17	5
Detects none	8	0
		$z = 4.13, p < .01$

Detection of syntactic anomalies
$N=34$

	Own text	
	Detects none	Detects at least one
Experimental texts		
Detects at least one	15	15
Detects none	4	0
		$z = 3.88, p < .01$

Contrary, then, to the conclusions of Bracewell *et al.*, it appears that children's revision difficulties are not simply due to some general inability to make rapid comparisons. Nor is it the case that, as these writers seem to imply, all text comparisons draw on roughly the same types of cognitive skills. Rather, it appears likely that different skills are involved, depending on the type of knowledge required and the circumstances under which that knowledge must be assembled.

Identification Processes

Under most circumstances, detection and identification of a text problem occur together, but as we have noted, there are undoubtedly times when students are aware that something is wrong with a text without being able to identify the difficulty. What a writer identifies will, of course, depend on how that writer conceptualizes the task of writing. Presumably, in setting out to compose a text, writers entertain some definition of the dimensions of the task—goals, strategies, skills, and knowledge that together constitute the range of things-to-be-done and things-that-can-go-wrong.

At present, very little can be said about the range of malfunctions that can be identified by students at various levels of development. Reports by Graves and his colleagues (Calkins, 1979; Graves, 1974, 1979) suggest that even very young beginners seem to identify problems at the level of text transcription and sentence syntax. The National Assessment of Educational Progress (1977) data suggest that elementary-age students are also able to identify problems of vocabulary choice, whereas some older students may also be able to identify problems relating to intersentence coherence (e.g., coreferencing and use of logical connectives). There is virtually no information concerning children's ability to identify structural problems at the paragraph or whole-text level, although current research concerning the structural properties of children's narratives and essays suggests that children show at least tacit appreciation of certain discourse features in their compositions (see discussion in Bartlett, 1979; in press).

Identification of problems need not involve an ability to name or define them. Indeed, there is no doubt that much revision is accomplished so swiftly that writers could not possibly have had a chance to articulate or reflect on the nature of the problem. Nonetheless, it is possible that the development of revision skill is accompanied by an increasing ability to articulate and reflect on specific text problems and that in fact development of new revision skills begins with an ability to reflect on a new type of problem.

Researchers have speculated on the mechanisms by which such abilities might be developed but, again, few data are available. Sinclair (1978) reports that surprising events—successes or failures—can sometimes trigger conscious awareness of relations in nonverbal tasks and she suggests that knowledge of success and failure may also aid in the development of awareness in language, with comments and questions from teachers and peers serving to provoke that knowledge. However, we might note that in Sinclair's research, conscious awareness was provoked at times when children were actively involved in trying to solve particular problems. Often, comments and questions about text reach a writer long after the immediate struggle to communicate is over and it is unclear how knowledge of success or failure will affect a problem solver once the immediate desire to solve the problem has "cooled off."

In any case, at the moment it seems reasonable to expect that students' skill in revision will be related to their skill in articulating various text problems and that this, in turn, will be related to their skill in articulating various plans and goals. For example, we might expect that students with better articulated initial text plans are also better able to identify text malfunctions in first-draft copy and similarly, that training in goal articulation might lead to more effective identification of first-draft problems. However, data to test these notions have yet to be collected, and they remain only intriguing hypotheses.

Correction Strategies

Success in correcting a text problem depends on adequate detection and identification processes. However, good detection and identification need not necessarily lead to an appropriate correction. Consider, for example, the ambiguity in this sentence and a fifth grader's attempt at revision:

ORIGINAL TEXT: *One day three boys went ice skating. He was showing off and he didn't see....*

REVISION: *One day, David Bill and Harry went ice skating. The boy was showing off and he didn't see....*

Clearly, the writer was able to identify the malfunctioning language even though he was unsuccessful in correcting it.

Choice of a revision strategy depends on many factors. No doubt a choice will reflect knowledge of the semantic and syntactic properties of a particular linguistic device together with knowledge of the effects of context on its use. Stylistic judgments will also play a large role in mature writers' choices. By contrast, beginners may lack knowledge of the full range of candidate devices for accomplishing a given function and may consequently rely on certain familiar devices regardless of their appropriateness in particular contexts. Additionally, students may make choices on the basis of other, more mechanical constraints. For example, we know from the observations of Graves, Calkins, and their colleagues that young elementary-age beginners have difficulty handling the physical mechanics of revision—erasing, inserting, making room, copying over. This suggests that these students are most likely to attempt only those changes involving a minimum of physical rearrangement. A need to reword text may also play an important role in their strategy choice: For instance, the rewording involved in inserting new material into existing text may be substantially greater than that required to delete, substitute or add new material to the end of a passage. Indeed, Calkins (n.d.) has observed that coherent integration of new content into ongoing text is one of the principal problems plaguing novice writers as they attempt to move from proofreading and the refining of text to revisions that involve more extensive reworking.

Questions of revision strategy have received virtually no attention in the existing literature and as a result, we know little about the range of solutions for various text problems available to children at different ages and levels of development. In an attempt to explore some possible factors in development, therefore, we have begun to investigate the range of children's solutions to problems of ambiguous coreferencing in narrative texts.

Generally, both child and adult writers accomplish coreferencing in narratives by using pronouns or by repeating an antecedent referring expression, as in the examples of Table 13.3. For example, analyses of referring

TABLE 13.3
Examples of Coreferencing Devices

Pronouns

___

*One day a man went to the beach. The day was hot and **he** needed a cool swim.*

Repetitions

___

*Shortly after Christmas a young woman moved into the house. The **young woman** had few possessions and she settled in quickly.*

---

expressions in about 900 narratives produced by 300 third through eighth graders indicate that 52% of the coreferencing is accomplished by pronouns and another 40% by repetition. Occasionally, however, these strategies will not work: Pronouns and repetitions fail to differentiate among referents and other strategies, such as those in Table 13.4, must be used. One question addressed by our current research concerns the types of solutions adopted by older elementary and junior high school students in these more unusual contexts.

In one study, we analyzed students' revisions of the set of eight experimental paragraphs described in Table 13.1. One hundred and twenty students participated, 20 above- and 20 below-average writers in each of grades five through seven. Of particular interest were their responses to the three double referent problems in Table 13.1, in which referents for two noun phrases were in doubt. We were curious to know how above- and below-average writers would cope with situations requiring more than the

TABLE 13.4
Examples of Referencing

Ambiguous coreferencing

___

One day two girls set out for the park. She had a bike . . .
One day two girls set out for the park. The girl had a bike . . .

Definite referencing through the addition of new information

One day two girls named Sandy and Karen went to the park.
Sandy had a bike . . .
One day two girls set out for the park. One was very athletic and the other hated sports. The athletic one had a bike . . .

Indefinite referencing

___

One day two girls went to the park. One had a bike . . .
One day two girls went to the park. They had a bike . . .

TABLE 13.5
Results of Experimental Revision Task: Percentage total problems

	Above-average writers		Below-average writers	
	Detected	Corrected	Detected	Corrected
Grade level				
Fifth	62%	17%	37%	06%
Sixth	72%	32%	57%	17%
Seventh	75%	36%	59%	21%

usual referencing strategies. Hence we designed texts where neither pronouns nor repetitions of antecedent referring expressions (e.g., *a man, another man*) would accomplish unambiguous referencing in these contexts.

When we examined students' attempts to revise these paragraphs, we found that students were fairly good at detecting the double-referent ambiguities, although they had considerable difficulty correcting them. As we might expect, above-average writers were more successful in their attempts, but even so, the percentage of solutions was not high. (See Table 13.5.)

Writers can correct these ambiguities by adding new differentiating information, by resorting to some type of indefinite reference, or by deleting the ambiguous sentence altogether. The range of solution types actually adopted is presented in Table 13.6.

As we can see, below-average writers were somewhat more likely to solve these problems by avoiding definite reference but the distribution of nondefinite and definite solution types did not differ significantly in the

TABLE 13.6
Distribution of Solution Types: Percentage of Total Solutions

Definite reference	Above-average writers	Below-average writers
1. Adding descriptive information		
a) about both referents	33%	09%
b) about one referent	10%	41%
2. Naming characters	29%	05%
Total definite reference	72%	55%
Nondefinite reference		
1. Indefinite noun phrases	23%	27%
2. Plural noun phrases	06%	18%
Total nondefinite reference	29%	45%

two groups ($\chi^2 = 1.91$; $df = 1$; $p > .05$). On the whole, when below-average writers attempted to construct a definite reference, they did so by adding new information about only one of the referents in question; whereas above-average writers tended to characterize both, either by giving them names or by providing descriptive information. It is possible that preference for this strategy by below-average writers reflects their difficulties in integrating new information into ongoing texts, with these students preferring to integrate only minimal amounts. However, given the relatively small number of solutions (particularly by the below-average writers) these differences may prove to be artifactual. For the moment it is probably best to conclude that when above- and below-average writers do manage to solve these problems, they seem to draw on a comparable range of strategies.[1]

Perhaps even more interesting than students' successful strategies, however, are their unsuccessful attempts since these are likely to provide information about earlier phases of skill development. As we can see from Table 13.5, more than half of students' correction attempts proved unsuccessful; this was true at all skill and grade levels.

Generally, when children failed, their failures involved some attempt to use the familiar strategy of repeating an antecedent noun phrase. For example, consider these attempts to revise the double referent text in Table 13.1:

One day a man left his house. Another man was standing outside. The man took out a letter and gave it to the other man. . . .

. . . The other man took out a letter and gave it to him. . . .

. . . The other man took out a letter and gave it to the other man. . . .

It seems likely that the choice of *other man* represents some attempt to repeat the antecedent *another man*, without regard for the fact that *other* generally requires contexts in which alternatives are clearly designated. Overall, about 60% of children's poor solutions could be characterized in this way.

Another 25% involved recopyings of miscellaneous antecedent information that also failed to differentiate among characters. For example:

[1]When a group of 20 graduate-student adult controls attempted to solve these problems, their solution strategies showed a similar distribution, indicating that the strategies adopted by our elementary and junior high school samples are fairly adult-like in their range. Distribution of Solution Types Adult and Child Subjects Percentage Total Solutions

	Adult controls	Above-average students	Below-average students
Definite reference	75%	72%	55%
Nondefinite reference	25%	28%	45%

. . . The man that was standing outside took out a letter and gave it to the other man. . . .

. . . The man that was standing outside took out a letter and gave it to the other man outside. . . .

Although these involve repetitions of antecedent wordings, the repetitions do not involve nouns and so may represent rudimentary attempts at differentiating among characters by supplying descriptive information.

At a somewhat more advanced level were attempts to introduce new information that failed primarily because the writer did not use the information in a differentiating way:

EXPERIMENTAL TEXT: *A boy lived on Elm Street. Another boy lived next door. The boy had a new bike and he wouldn't let the other boy ride it. . . .*

STUDENT'S REVISION: *Joe lived on Elm Street. Another Joe lived next door. Joe had a new bike and he wouldn't let the other Joe ride it. . . .*

STUDENT'S REVISION: *The boy had a new bike and wouldn't let anyone ride it. . . .*

STUDENT'S REVISION: *Tommy had a new bike and wouldn't let him ride it. . . .*

Attempts such as these accounted for the remaining 15% of children's poor solutions.

Children's difficulties are no doubt related to a number of factors, including the mechanics of physically inserting new material into text (see Graves, 1979). But one problem may have proved overwhelming: the task of integrating information regarding the contexts of two ambiguous noun phrases. Scardamalia (in press) has suggested that elementary students have particular difficulty integrating information about two discrete ideas into a single coherent text. Using similar arguments, we might propose that students' difficulties are due in large part to their difficulties generating and coordinating information about two sets of ambiguous noun phrases.

This possibility was assessed in another study, in which students revised six double referent problems, identical in referential structure but differing in the amount of potential differentiating information available in their contexts. Three problems, identical to those of the first study, provided no differentiating information whereas three others provided information about character names which could readily serve to differentiate the two (Table 13.7). Thirty-nine children participated, 20 sixth and 19 seventh graders.

The results are clear cut. Of the texts containing potential disambiguating information, 62% of the problems were detected and of these, 95% were successfully corrected. As we might expect, these correct solutions almost invariably involved a strategy of repeating the character names. Of the texts without disambiguating information, 52% of the problems were detected but of these, only 55% were successfully corrected. (Analyses of variance for the detection data show a main effect for grade ($F(1,35) =$

TABLE 13.7
Examples of Experimental Texts

With differentiating context information

A girl named Linda lived on State Street. Another girl named Jane lived next door. The girl had a new sled and wouldn't let her ride it. They argued about it for a long time. Finally, they agreed to share the sled. After that they became best friends.

Without differentiating context information

A boy lived on Elm Street. Another boy lived next door. The boy had a new bike and wouldn't let him ride it. They had a big fight about it. They were so mad they didn't speak for a whole week. They should have shared that bike!

6.6966, $p = .014$) but none for problem type and no interactions. Analyses of variance for the correct solution data show main effects for grade ($F(1,35) = 10.8875$, $p = .002$) and problem type ($F(1,35) = 16.389$, $p < .0001$) with no interactions.

The point, then, is that while these children were able to recognize and use disambiguating information when it was provided in a text, they had considerable difficulty generating the same type of disambiguating information on their own. The difficulty is all the more striking when we realize that children worked on both types of problems in a single session and might have adopted our use of named characters as a model for solving referential problems in the texts without character names. That so few apparently did this suggests that the tasks of generating and recognizing disambiguating information draw on rather different sets of skills.

CONCLUDING COMMENTS

The main points of our discussion can be briefly summarized. We began with the observation that revision involves detection skills as well as knowledge of how text works to convey an intended meaning. We noted that detection involves comparison and that text problems may be more or less easy to detect, depending on the ease with which a segment of text and potential alternatives can be represented. In some cases, representation of alternatives may be highly automatic but in others, considerable effort may be required. We noted, also, that comparison may be more or less difficult, depending on the extent to which evaluation requires some monitoring or alteration of normal interpretive activity. In particular, we demonstrated that some text problems may be more readily detected in texts composed by others than in one's own.

We also noted that effective revision depends on effective correction strategies and that generation of effective strategies is likely to depend on a number of factors. For elementary students, at least, choice is likely to depend less on the constraints of a particular context than on the ease with which a strategy can be executed, particularly on the amount of physical text rearrangement and content integration required. This does not mean that elementary students ignore the effects of context altogether. Indeed, children in our studies were able to detect text problems that they could not correct, indicating that some knowledge of context constraints—or at least their violation—was available for detection purposes. However, these same constraints often appeared to be ignored when children generated their corrections. Among other things, this suggests that knowledge available to comprehension and detection processes need not be equally accessible for production and correction and raises important questions about the special task requirements of each.

We have emphasized differences between normal processes of text comprehension and processes of text review and error detection, pointing out that the two draw on rather different interpretive activities. In particular, we have suggested that in reviewing their own texts, authors must sometimes inhibit interpretive use of certain privileged information and we speculated that development of this skill may require development of fairly explicit knowledge concerning interpretive activities (e.g., inferring, expecting).

At this point, it is also important to emphasize certain differences between production of first-draft copy and text corrections. For one thing, corrections are generated in the context of an existing text and must be integrated into that textual environment. At the same time, corrections are generated in response to an awareness (however vague or explicit) that something is wrong or at least discrepant in that existing text. This suggests that skills and knowledge available for generation of first draft copy need not necessarily be available for use within the constraints of revision. We know little about how skills become available for use within the constraints of the revision task. It is tempting to speculate that the burden of accommodating language to the constraints of an existing text environment may foster explicit awareness of how text functions and conversely, that explicit knowledge is (initially, at least) required for meeting these various demands. At present, however, this remains only an interesting hypothesis. What is clear, however, is the fact that revision is a complex and difficult process, distinct from generation of first-draft text in its task demands and its development.

ACKNOWLEDGMENTS

Research reported in this chapter was generously supported by grant number 78-0170 from NIE and grant number 785-0310 from The Ford Foundation to The Rockefeller University. The author is grateful to William Hirst, George A. Miller, Katherine Miller, and Sylvia Scribner for their comments and advice at various stages of the research and to Jay Wilson for her assistance in data collection and analysis.

REFERENCES

Bamberg, B. Composition instruction does make a difference: A comparison of college freshmen in regular and remedial English courses. *Research in the Teaching of English*, 1978, *12*, 47–59.

Bartlett, E. Learning to write a story. Paper presented at the Twelfth Annual Conference, Canada Council of Teachers of English, Carleton University, Ottawa, Canada, May, 1979.

Bartlett, E. *Learning to write: Some cognitive and linguistic components*. Washington, D.C.: Center for Applied Linguistics, in press.

Bartlett, E., & Scribner, S. Texts in context. In C. Frederiksen, M. Whiteman, & J. Domonic (Eds.), *Writing: The nature, development and teaching of written communication (Vol. 1)*. Hillsdale, N.J.: Lawrence Erlbaum, in press.

Beach, R. The effects of between-draft teacher evaluation versus student self-evaluation on high school students' revising of rough drafts. *Research in the Teaching of English*, 1979, *13*, 111–119.

Bracewell, R. J., Bereiter, C., & Scardamalia, M. A test of two myths about revision. Unpublished manuscript, The Ontario Institute for Studies in Education, n.d.

Calkins, L. M. Andrea learns to make writing hard. *Language Arts*, 1979, *56*, 569–576.

Calkins, L. M. Children's rewriting strategies. Unpublished manuscript, University of New Hampshire, Durham, n.d.

Champagne, M., Scardamalia, M., Bereiter, C., & Fine, J. Children's problems with focus and cohesion in revising. Unpublished manuscript, The Ontario Institute for Studies in Education, n.d.

Collins, A., & Gentner, D. A framework for a cognitive theory of writing. In L. W. Gregg & E. R. Steinberg (Eds.), *Cognitive processes in writing*. Hillsdale, N.J.: Lawrence Erlbaum, 1980.

Flower, L. S., & Hayes, J. R. The dynamics of composing: Making plans and juggling constraints. In L. W. Gregg and E. R. Steinberg (Eds.), *Cognitive processes in writing*. Hillsdale, N.J.: Lawrence Erlbaum, 1980.

Gantry, L. A. Textual revision: A review of the research. Southwest Regional Laboratory Technical Note. TN 2-80/11. Los Alamitos, Cal., SWRL, 1980.

Gleitman, H., & Gleitman, L. Language use and language judgment. In C. Fillmore, D. Kempler & W. S. Y. Wang (Eds.), *Individual differences in language ability and language behavior*. New York: Academic Press, 1979.

Graves, D. H. *Children's writing: Research directions and hypotheses based upon an examination of the writing processes of seven year old children*. Ann Arbor: University Microfilms, 1974, No. 7408375.

Graves, D. H. Patterns of growth in the writing processes of young children. Paper presented at the Canadian Council of Teachers of English Twelfth Annual Conference, Carleton University, Ottawa, Canada, May, 1979.

Hayes, J. R., & Flower, L. S. Identifying the organization of writing processes. In L. W. Gregg and E. R. Steinberg (Eds.), *Cognitive processes in writing*. Hillsdale, N.J.: Lawrence Erlbaum, 1980.

Murray, D. M. Internal revision: A process of discovery. In C. R. Cooper & L. Odell (Eds.), *Research on composing*. Urbana, Ill.: National Council of Teachers of English, 1978.

National Assessment of Educational Progress. *Write/rewrite: An assessment of revision skills*. Writing Report No. 05-W-04. Denver, Col.: National Assessment of Educational Progress, 1977.

Piaget, J. *The language and thought of the child*. London: Routledge & Kegan Paul, 1926.

Scardamalia, M. How children cope with the cognitive demands of writing. In C. Frederiksen, M. Whiteman, & J. Dominic (Eds.), *Writing: The nature, development and teaching of written communication* (Vol. 1). Hillsdale: N.J.: Lawrence Erlbaum, in press.

Scardamalia, M., Bereiter, C., Gartshore, S., & Cattani, C. Locating the source of children's revision difficulties. Unpublished manuscript, The Ontario Institute for Studies in Education, n.d.

Shaughnessy, M. P. *Errors and expectations*. New York: Oxford University Press, 1977.

Sinclair, H. Conceptualization and awareness in Piaget's theory and its relevance to the child's conception of language. In A. Sinclair, R. J. Jarvella, & W. J. M. Levelt (Eds.), *The child's conception of language*. New York: Springer-Verlag, 1978.

Sommers, N. Revision in the composing process: A case study of college freshmen and experienced adult writers. Doctoral dissertation, Boston University, 1978.

Stallard, C. K. An analysis of the writing behavior of good student writers. *Research in the Teaching of English*, 1974, *8*, 206–218.

Chapter 14

Writing and Learning in School Settings

Arthur N. Applebee

INTRODUCTION

Any careful examination of student writing in American secondary schools leads quickly to fundamental questions about what students must be able to do in order to demonstrate that they "know" a subject. In this chapter, we will begin by examining some of the types of knowledge that ordinarily become relevant in a writing situation. We will then examine the knowledge drawn on in schools through an examination of results from a recent study of writing in the secondary school. This will lead us to conclude that the kinds of things students are asked to do with written language are narrow and ultimately unproductive, having negative effects not only on students' writing abilities but also on their subject-area learning. In any given writing situation, there are at least three domains of knowledge that interact in powerful ways to shape the text: knowledge of language, knowledge of the topic, and knowledge of audience. We will consider each of these in turn.

Knowledge of Language

The knowledge of language that is relevant during the writing process exists at several different levels. At the simplest level, it is knowledge of the conventions governing words and sentences—the rules of spelling and

WHAT WRITERS KNOW
The Language, Process, and Structure of Written Discourse

syntax. This knowledge has a very wide range of application and is tapped whenever we write. Simply being able to write correct sentences, however, is not enough to ensure that a person will be able to write coherently at any greater length. Longer stretches of writing require a range of language skills that give shape to the text as a whole; in Michael Halliday's (1977) terms, these skills give a segment of discourse unity and **texture,** a sense that the text "coheres" (Halliday & Hasan, 1976). Some aspects of texture derive from patterns of lexical and pronominal reference (**thematic progressions:** see Glatt, Chap. 4 this volume). Others derive from conventional, formal patterns that shape a text representing a particular genre—the narrative conventions of storytelling, for example, or the logical conventions of exposition and argument. These conventional rhetorical patterns operate on a variety of levels, from general expectations about overall form (that a fable will end with a moral, for example) to the local but powerful expectations set up by such words as *however, if, but, although,* or *in addition* (Bereiter & Scardamalia, in press).

Such expectations help to make language a powerful heuristic device, an instrument for clarifying as well as presenting our knowledge of the topic being discussed. In essence, our knowledge of how to create texture provides us with sets of possible relationships among items of information. These relationships can in turn be judged for reasonableness and coherence within our knowledge set as a whole.

Another level of a writer's knowledge of language has to do with strategies for organizing and monitoring the writing task itself. These skills have recently begun to be investigated under the label of "metacognition" (Flavell, 1978); basically, metacognitive skills provide the language user with ways to recognize (and avoid) problems in comprehension and production. In reading tasks, for example, metacognitive skills monitor comprehension of text and provide ways to cycle back through the text when comprehension falters (Brown, 1978, 1980). In writing, metacognitive skills have been less thoroughly investigated, but experienced writers are likely to have developed a series of specific strategies both for monitoring the development of the text as a whole and for directing the production of various text segments (e.g., Flower & Hayes, 1980). (For example, experienced writers will monitor whether they "said what they meant," and will have strategies for revising when they discover that they did not.)

Knowledge of the Topic

The second major body of knowledge drawn on in a writing task involves the writer's knowledge of the topic chosen for writing about. This knowledge will have a number of features that affect the writing task, such things as whether the knowledge is based on direct experience or from listening to what others have had to say; whether it is extensive or fragmentary; and whether it is fresh in memory or buried deeply in the past. For the purposes of the present argument, the most important of these features has to do with the extent that the concepts that make up the background of relevant information and experience have been integrated with one another, and with other aspects of experience. When a subject is known very thoroughly, the component concepts will be well enough integrated that any writing about the subject will involve primarily **routine** learning, a transcription into language of an already well-ordered set of relationships. In such cases, the writing that results is usually very fluent, with few pauses or changes of direction because there is little need for the writer to reformulate or rethink.

When the topic being written about raises questions that have not been fully explored in the past, the written language may become a tool for ordering and clarifying relevant knowledge and experience. In this case, the writing task becomes a **heuristic** one, a process of discovery and reformulation that will in all likelihood be halting and somewhat uncertain. Here, relationships among concepts are being discovered rather than recited; when the writing is over, we can say that the writer has learned something new (cf. Polanyi, 1958).

Knowledge of Audience

The third body of knowledge that the writer brings to bear involves the audience for whom the text is being written. Although there are a number of ways in which **audience** can be approached, we will concentrate here on awareness of the overlap in relevant knowledge between reader and writer. This includes the extent to which the writer expects the reader to make sense of experience in the same way; that is, the extent to which the reader is likely to embrace or resist a particular argument or interpretation.

When authors share (or believe that they share) a common knowledge base with prospective readers, it is possible to leave a great deal unsaid (Applebee, 1977; Britton, 1969, 1970). In the extreme case of writing for oneself, the language may even reduce to a set of notes intelligible only to the notetaker. A shopping list, for example, is likely to consist only of reminders of the needed items—toothpaste, milk, fruit, bread. In using the list, the shopper must mentally reconstruct a fuller text around each item, knowing that the words were meant to imply a family-size tube of Crest toothpaste, a quart of homogenized milk, a dozen eating apples, and a 1-pound loaf of unsliced cracked-wheat bread.

At the other extreme, a text meant to introduce a reader to a new domain of knowledge or experience can assume very little. The text is likely to contain many new concepts that need to be defined and related to one another in systematic and nontrivial ways; in order to do this, the author must work out from an initially limited body of overlapping knowledge, using a variety of linguistic techniques to guide the reader's response rather than assuming initial understanding. To accomplish this, writers use two quite different sets of linguistic conventions. One set relies on "objectification" through traditional methods of deduction and induction. These techniques are represented most fully in symbolic logic, where a text will be based on a specific set of axioms and permissible transformations upon them. The second approach to guiding reader response relies on an increasingly tightly textured set of relationships among the elements of a presented experience—the poetic control that is part of any literary art form. (These two sets of conventions, and their basis in fundamental aspects of human experience, are discussed in more detail in Applebee, 1978.)

The extent to which a writer will rely on such methods for guiding reader response will depend on (*a*) the extent of shared prior knowledge and (*b*) the extent to which the writer assumes the reader will agree with what is being said.

Audience–Text Interactions

There is another aspect of audience that is at work in any language situation, and that will turn out to be important in the school context. This has to do with our natural tendency to make sense of what we hear or read. We can gain insight into this phenomenon by examining Louise Rosenblatt's (1978) helpful analysis of the nature of literary experience. She argues that a literary work is not

> an object or an ideal identity. It happens during a coming-together, a compenetration of a reader and a text. The reader brings to the text his past experience and present personality. Under the magnetism of the ordered symbols of the text, he marshalls his resources and crystallizes out from the stuff of memory, thought, and feeling a new order, a new experience, which he sees as a poem [p. 12].

Shorn of their rhetoric, Rosenblatt's words offer a useful insight into the nature of the audience for all types of linguistic expression, not just for literature. There is an important sense in which the words on the page do not exist as text except as they are assimilated and made sense of by the interested reader (including the writer in the role of reader). During this assimilation—the marshalling of resources and crystallizing out from memory that Rosenblatt speaks of—readers create their own personal versions of the text, versions that make "best sense" in terms of their own experience. If their experience is inadequate, the text in the end may NOT make sense; but if the experience of the reader is greater than that of the writer, it is quite possible for the text to make MORE sense to the reader than it does to the writer.

WRITING IN SCHOOLS

Knowledge of language, knowledge of topic, and knowledge of audience are drawn on in any attempt to write; they shape the task facing the writer as well as the text that results from the process as a whole. As we have seen, each of the three domains has a number of components that may be stressed or ignored in a particular writing task. The emphases placed on different types of relevant knowledge become especially important in school situations, where the emphases are usually determined by the teacher (as audience) rather than by the student (as writer). Implicitly, these emphases determine what will be considered "valuable" knowledge; as a result, they have a direct effect on what will be learned.

The National Study

To examine the types of knowledge currently stressed in school writing, we will be considering data drawn from a recent study of writing in ninth- and eleventh-grade classrooms, in six subject areas: English, science, social science, foreign language, business education, and math (Applebee, in press). One strand of the study consisted of case studies of instruction in two high schools over the course of an academic year. Project staff visited classes, interviewed teachers and students, and collected writing samples for later analysis. Some 13,293 minutes of instruction were observed in all.

For the second strand of the study, some 200 principals in a national sample were asked to nominate one good teacher in each of 6 subject areas to complete a questionnaire about the ways writing was being used in their classes. Some 83% of the principals agreed to participate; of the teachers they nominated, 754 teachers (68%) returned useable questionnaires.

The results from these strands of research can be used to examine the kinds of knowledge that are required—and implicitly valued—in undertaking school writing tasks. In most cases, as we will see, the issue is not whether a particular kind of knowledge is drawn on, but the degree to which it is encouraged and emphasized. The evidence available includes the types of writing that occur, the forms of instruction that surround each writing task, the time for and length of typical writing assignments, and postwriting activities, including teachers' written remarks and marking practices.

Knowledge of Language

Word and Sentence Level

Written language skills at the word and sentence level are emphasized by teachers in all subject areas. This is evident in the amount of writing required and in teachers' marking practices.

For research purposes, we adopted a broad definition of **writing** that included any task in which information or experiences were being written down for later reference. Table 14.1 summarizes the categories that we developed to describe uses of writing. (The categories are an extension and reformulation of a categorization proposed by James Britton, 1971.) The major categories include writing without composing (in which only word- and sentence-level skills are needed), informational uses, personal uses, and imaginative uses.

In the observational studies, just over 40% of the lesson time observed involved one or another of the activities in Table 14.1. Results from English and science classes illustrate the general emphases that we found. In En-

TABLE 14.1
Uses of School Writing

10 Writing without composing (mechanical uses of writing)
   11 Multiple-choice exercises
   12 Fill-in-the-blank exercises (answered with less than a sentence)
   13 Short-answer exercises (brief, one or two sentences per question)
   14 Math calculations
   15 Transcription from written material (copying)
   16 Transcription from oral sources (dictation)
   17 Translation
   18 Other mechanical uses
20 Informational uses of writing
   21 Notetaking
   22 Record of ongoing experience (This is what is happening.)
   23 Report. Retrospective account of particular events or series of events (This is what happened.)
   24 Summary. Generalized narrative or description of a recurrent pattern of events or steps in a procedure. (This is what happens; this is the way it is done.)
   25 Analysis. Generalization and classification related to a situation, problem, or theme, with logical or hierarchical relationships among generalizations implicit or explicit.
   26 Theory. Building and defending at a theoretical level, including implicit or explicit recognition that there are alternative perspectives. Hypotheses and deductions from them.
   27 Persuasive or regulative uses of writing. (Any instances in which the attempt to convince overrides other functions or in which rules are given and compliance assumed.)
   28 Other informational uses
30 Personal uses of writing
   31 Journal or diary writing, for own use
   32 Personal letters or notes, where main purpose is "keeping in touch"
   33 Other personal uses
40 Imaginative uses of writing
   41 Stories
   42 Poems
   43 Play scripts
   44 Other imaginative uses

glish, 41% of class time involved one or another of these written language activities; in science, 48% of the observed class time involved activities requiring at least word- or sentence-level language skills.

The national survey did not provide a comparable measure of percentage of time, but it did ask teachers about the frequency of various writing-related activities. Virtually all of the teachers reported frequent use of one or another task requiring word- or sentence-level skills. (We will consider subject-area variations in these tasks in the next section, on text-level skills.)

Finally, teachers who asked students for writing of at least paragraph length were asked about their marking practices. Some 70% reported that they "routinely" indicated problems in word- or sentence-level skills (spelling, grammar) when responding to student writing. Though English teachers were the most likely to make such responses (88% claiming to do so routinely) teachers in all of the subject areas that made much use of longer writing assignments made this sort of correction. Among science teachers, for example, 63% reported routinely indicating word- and sentence-level errors in student writing.

Text Level

Text-level language skills received much less emphasis. Of the uses of writing listed in Table 14.1, those labeled "writing without composing" require only word- and sentence-level skills. In these tasks, the overall text structure (if there is any) is provided by the teacher, and the students respond with an appropriate word, phrase, or sentence. (Direct translation from one language to another is similar, in that the text to be translated provides the global structure, within which the translator can operate at a sentence-by-sentence level.)

In the observational studies, just over half of the written language activities that occurred were classified as writing without composing, requiring few if any text-level skills. Results from English and science classes again illustrate the range of results. In English, 39% of the writing activities were at the mechanical level (e.g., filling in the blanks or providing one- or two-sentence responses). In science classes, 53% of the observed writing activities required only sentence-level skills.

Of the remaining activities, notetaking (a subcategory within informational uses of writing) is in an intermediary position. It usually involves longer stretches of text, but the text need not be very explicitly developed; in some cases it can remain as fragmentary as the grocery list we mentioned earlier. To get a clear picture of the emphasis on writing skills beyond the word and sentence level, we can look at the amount of class time devoted to writing of at least paragraph length. (In terms of Table 14.1, this excludes all mechanical writing tasks, and the subcategory of notetaking under informational writing.) Computed in this way, writing requiring text-level skills was emphasized during 3% of lesson time over-all; it was at its height in English classes, where 10% of lesson time was devoted to writing requiring text-level skills.

Patterns of emphasis in the national sample were very similar to those observed in the two case-study schools. Overall, only about a third of the teachers reported "frequently" asking students for paragraph-length or greater writing. Over half reported that students frequently took notes; 40% asked for short-answer responses; and 32% made frequent multiple-choice or fill-in-the-blank assignments.

Again, English and science teachers illustrate the range of responses. Fully 82% of the English teachers reported frequent use of writing of at least paragraph length, compared with only 15% of the science teachers. Stress on multiple-choice and fill-in-the-blank activities was reversed: Only 23% of the English teachers reported frequent use, compared with 51% of the science teachers. Over half of both groups reported frequent use of notetaking and of short-answer exercises (requiring a sentence or two to complete).

Most of these variations in emphasis follow predictable subject-area lines. Even the third of the sample who reported frequent assignments of at least paragraph length, however, were not necessarily placing much stress on students' ability to apply text-level language skills. This is a topic we will return to later, when we consider the effects of knowledge of audience on school writing tasks, but some preliminary evidence is avail-able in the teachers' reports of emphases in marking student work. We have already noted that teachers in all subject areas tend to indicate errors routinely on the word and sentence level. Comments on text-level skills, such as lapses in logic or organization, are somewhat less likely to be used routinely. Overall, such comments were reported by some 58% of the teachers, about 15% fewer than made routine use of comments on sentence-level skills. Again, English teachers were more likely than science teachers to comment on text-level problems (76% versus 52%).

Clearly, those teachers who assign writing of at least paragraph length do value students' ability to construct coherent text, but they seem to place less emphasis upon the requisite skills than they do on sentence- and word-level knowledge.

Metacognitive Level

Overall, attention to metacognitive skills was haphazard and accidental. This is partly to be expected, in that scholarly attempts to define those skills are just getting underway, and exist mostly in the technical literature of psychology. At another level, however, this neglect is surprising, in that concern with metacognition is really only a way to formalize a concern with what students must learn to do in order to organize and revise their writing—and such problems have long been a central concern for teachers.

Before beginning to write, a writer needs strategies to retrieve and organize information and experiences relevant to the writing topic, as well as strategies for narrowing and focusing the subject to be discussed. The emphasis teachers place on these skills is best illustrated by a simple measure of amount of time: In the observational studies, the time devoted to preparation for writing averaged just over 3 minutes. Typically, that 3 minutes was devoted to reading the assignment, passing out materials, and answering procedural questions about length and due date. Except for occasional brainstorming sessions reported by about a fifth of the teachers, there is no systematic attempt to provide students with strategies for recognizing what information might be relevant, or assessing the extent to which more information might be needed before beginning to write.

There is even less attention to strategies that might help a student while actually writing. The typical instructional pattern is one of write–react, the first phase involving only the student and the second involving only the teacher. For the most part students are simply confronted with the fact that something is wrong, or does not make sense. This is a very negative instructional approach, one that tells a student that the process has gone wrong without providing strategies to avoid similar problems in the future.

Systematic attention to rewriting offers one way around this dilemma. Here the teacher's comments can suggest ways to improve the writing (and help the student recognize places where the meaning is unclear) as part of the process of shaping the work, rather than as an evaluation of a completed product. This approach is not used very frequently, however. Though 59% of the English teachers in the national survey reported regularly asking for more than one draft, only 7% of the science teachers asked students to rework their writing.

Knowledge of the Topic

In the school context, knowledge of the topic to be written about usually involves some aspect of a specific subject area and is specified by the teacher in the course of making the assignment. Here the teacher has a choice between asking students to engage in a routine task, repeating back familiar material, or to engage in a heuristic one, extending their grasp of less familiar material. In all subject areas, the major emphasis was on demonstrating mastery of familiar material. This manifested itself both in the ways in which tasks were structured and in the ways they were evaluated.

In the national survey, teachers were asked directly about their reasons for asking students in particular classes to write at all; the items were designed to illustrate the relationships teachers expected between a writing task and progress within the subject area. Results for English and science teachers indicate both differences between subject areas and some common concerns. For English teachers, the item that was most consistently chosen was, "To test students' ability to express themselves clearly" (61%). No other item was chosen by even 50% of the English teachers. For science teachers, on the other hand, the most popular item was, "To test whether students have learned relevant content." Three other items were also chosen by 50% or more of the science teachers: "To help students remember important information" (67%); "To clarify what has been learned by applying the concepts to new situations" (60%); and "To force students to think for themselves" (58%).

Both the English teacher and the science teacher seem to view writing as primarily a tool to evaluate learning. They differ in that the relevant domain of knowledge for the science teacher has to do with scientific information and concepts, whereas for the English teachers in the sample, the relevant domain of knowledge has to do with proper use of linguistic forms.

The structure of school writing tasks seems to derive quite directly from this emphasis on evaluation of subject-area learning. We have already noted the lack of attention to prewriting activities. This becomes reasonable when the body of relevant information has been presented and synthesized through lectures and textbooks. In such a situation (if the students have done their work), it should be enough to simply state an essay topic. The topic will cue the relevant information, which students will essentially repeat back from memory. If the information has been well learned, the performance will be routine and writing should pose little problem.

In looking at samples of writing provided by teachers in the national sample, the topic in fact proved to be a good index to this view of the relationship between the writing task and subject-area learning. In many cases, students were asked to write on topics that were in a real sense impossible:

Western Europe on the eve of Reformation was a civilization going through great changes. In a well-written essay describe the political, economic, social, and cultural changes Europe was going through at the time of the Reformation. (23 points)
                                                                 —ninth-grade Social Studies

In a well-organized essay of 200–500 words, answer the question which follows: Homer considered that Odysseus was a hero, a representative of Greek ideals. How is Odysseus a model for youths of all times?

                                                                 —ninth-grade English

Write a one-page report on one of the following topics. Please be neat with your work. Check for spelling and sentence structure.
    1. the diesel engine
    2. the gas engine
    3. supersonic flight
    4. sound

                                                                 —ninth-grade Science

Write a paragraph on solving quadratic equations.

—ninth-grade Algebra

Books could be written in response to such questions; they become possible topics for school writing only because they serve to index bodies of previously presented information. (In the science report, it is unclear whether the information has been previously presented, or whether the student is being directed to a textbook or encyclopedia entry; the basic principle remains the same, however.)

To the extent that school writing is really concerned with received bodies of knowledge, we would expect that teachers' marking practices would focus on the accuracy of that information. And this indeed seems to be the case. When science teachers were asked which responses were most important in reacting to student writing, they focused on assessing accuracy of conclusions and pointing out errors of fact. English teachers, for whom the subject matter to be learned seems to be defined in part in terms of language skills, chose improvements in style, logic, organization, and writing mechanics for the focus of their responses. Neither group placed much emphasis on responses related to the development of ideas or new knowledge. Only 21% of the science teachers, for example, felt it was important to pose counterarguments, 7% to respond with their own views, and 19% to suggest related topics that a student might wish to explore.

Knowledge of Audience

The third body of knowledge which a writer draws on has to do with the audience to whom the writing is being addressed. In the school situation, this is virtually always the teacher. This in itself is neither good nor bad; the factors that will shape the text continue to involve such things as the overlap in knowledge between student and teacher and the effect that the student wants the writing to have.

To the extent that school writing tasks are used to evaluate subject-area learning, the writer–audience relationship in school writing is atypical. Where we might ordinarily visualize the situation in terms of overlapping areas of knowledge, in the typical school situation the student's body of relevant knowledge is COMPLETELY CIRCUMSCRIBED by the teacher's knowledge of the subject area.

We have already noted that when author and audience share a common knowledge base it is usual to leave much of the argument unspecified; formalization is no longer necessary to understanding, and is in this sense unmotivated. This would lead us to expect that contrary to the usual notion of the essay as highly rigorous and formal, the nature of the task is one that might lead to loosely organized, unexplicit writing. The teacher, drawing on a larger and better-articulated background of relevant information, may well make more sense of the essay than could the writer who prepared it. This is an hypothesis that can be tested systematically. In the meantime, results from work already completed provide strong indirect support for the hypothesis.

As we have seen, marking practices tend to stress the accuracy of information presented, rather than the arguments that can be built up using that information. (Indeed, essays in the content areas are sometimes scored against a rubric that specifies credits to be allowed for various items of information.) In the writing samples that we collected, we found many examples of essays that were little more than catalogs of important facts, related to one another primarily in the teacher's vision of the subject area. The following essay, judged by the teacher to be a "good" response to a question asking students to relate architecture to the culture of the times, is quite typical:

> Throughout history there have been many buildings built that tell a lot about the people, their beliefs and the technology they had established during this time. One building that was built during the Middle Ages was Saint Mark's Cathedral. The Cathedral of Saint Mark in Venice, Italy, is an outstanding example of Byzantine architecture. The church is decorated with beautiful carvings, mosaics, and religious statues. The church was built in A.D. 1050 when architecture was very advanced. The building is in the form of a Greek cross, 250 feet long and 220 feet wide. There are domes as large as 42 feet in diameter. The architects of the time utilized the pendative to support these giant domes.
>
> If historians were to look back 500 years now to a building that would represent our beliefs and our technology the building would probably be the Smithsonian Institution in Washington D.C. The Smithsonian Institution was opened in 1846. Activities of the Institution include scientific research, exploration into the field of space travel and the growing field of computer sciences. This building is very appropriate because the people of the world are always looking for easier and better ways of life. The Smithsonian Institution also has exhibits dealing with subjects such as art, historical objects, technological inventions of the world today. Because the Smithsonian Institution deals with many of the problems of todays world and how they can be solved through the use of modern technology it is the right building that will tell historians 500 or 1000 years from now the peoples of the 1980s culture.

We also found that at least some students were aware of the oddities of writing to the teacher-as-examiner. Commenting on social studies essay exams, Sarah told us:

> Normally it will be a compare essay when we're supposed to compare two periods with several different things. I don't write an introduction to these, 'cause I rarely have the time. So I'll just go in and I'll show the differences in very short paragraphs. For everything, for every topic that he gave us, I'll show the differences and if I have time I'll add a little conclusion at the end which will tell what I really think.

Sarah was in fact a very successful student; her essay-writing strategy, though surely leading to oddly shaped writing, was highly appropriate for the situations in which she found herself.

In English classes where the "content" is writing skill itself, a different kind of distortion is introduced. Here when the teacher acts in the role of examiner, what the student writes about becomes (within certain limits) irrelevant: The task becomes one of demonstrating language skills rather than extending a shared knowledge base. The kind of writing that Ken Macrorie (1976) has called "Engfish" is the natural result—writing in which there is no commitment from the writer, no purpose or direction to bring the writing to life. The following essay on summer illustrates what happens; on an earlier draft of the same essay, the teacher's remarks focused entirely on spelling.

> The proof has finally come that summer has arrived. The warm rays of the sun stretch like fingers to smother the imprisioned cold of the winter.
> The flowers begin to appear and the sweet perfume of the roses drifts by hanging on the breeze. The scent of freshly cut grass mingles in the air with all the other fragrances.
> The white sand, warm to the touch, is crowded with people playing or just taking in the sun. The radios blare their voice over the beach while the people sit and enjoy. The frizbees fly gracefully through the air. People swim in the cool waters to quench their parched skins from the burning sun.
> The coconut of the tropical lotions engulfs you like a wave as you approach the once not so long ago desolate area.
> In the evenings, the cicadas are singing their song, blending with all the other sounds.
> But summer does not bring all good things either, for the screaming voices from the all-night parties down at the point drifting over the evening air spoil the mood at the close of a day.
> It will all soon begin. The roses have buds and the beaches have already been full. The sun beats down its warmth to send the message that summer has arrived.

Though "Engfish" is easy to ridicule, and Macrorie does a masterful job of it, the pressure toward such writing within the school situation is a powerful one. It gets institutionalized in a concern with mechanical skills and "correctness," and has recently received added impetus from the minimal competency movement. In New York State, for example, a writing test was instituted as part of a state-wide competency-testing program. To help ensure common standards in marking and interpreting students' responses, the state department undertook to provide "exemplary" models—papers that should get full marks on the grading scale. Though prepared with the best of intentions, the models distributed in connection with the tests given during the early rounds were committee efforts— adults writing as they thought students would write, all in turn edited by committees of adults to ensure the models were really exemplary. The following sample is typical; it was offered as an exemplary model for a report-writing task on the preliminary competency test given in 1979 (New York State Education Department, 1979, p. 25):

> Henry Fuller, who teaches in the social studies department of our school, had an exciting trip to Egypt last summer. Because he found Egypt so fascinating, he was happy to tell me about his trip for my report to our class.

Mr. Fuller said that his three weeks there in July taught him many things, among them the fact that summer is not the best time to go there. The temperature reached 100°F or more every day, and as a result, he got up at 3 a.m. to do his sightseeing before the worst heat of the day. By 10 a.m., he was back at his hotel to rest.

Although he was bothered by the heat, he said the sights and the experiences were well worth the discomfort he endured. "The tomb of King Tut was exciting to see, as well as the many interesting historical places," Mr. Fuller said. "One unforgettable experience was climbing the largest pyramid during the early dawn hours, but I think I enjoyed the ancient temples the most."

During his time in Egypt, Mr. Fuller traveled in several different ways, including a ride on a camel, a sail on the Nile River in an Egyptian sailboat, and travel by air to Abu Simbel. We have an opportunity to see what Mr. Fuller saw, as he is willing to show movies of his trip to social studies classes.

Inevitably, any sense of person or of engagement with the task was lost in the process of writing-by-committee. This model, like the others that were offered, is true "Engfish": a triumph of form over content.

THE KNOWLEDGE THAT MATTERS

In discussing the types of knowledge that students draw on in school writing, we have taken each type in turn. From this step-by-step analysis, we can provide the following conclusions about what types of knowledge are stressed:

1. Language skills at the word and sentence level.
2. Routine recital of previously organized subject-area information.
3. Knowledge of how to relate to an audience whose body of relevant information is both larger and better articulated than the writer's own.

Conversely, we can list the types of knowledge that might be stressed but are typically (though not necessarily intentionally) downplayed:

1. Language skills at the text level, including metacognitive strategies for monitoring and revising the evolving text.
2. Heuristic activity in which subject-area knowledge is examined and extended.
3. Knowledge of how to assess and then extend a reader's relevant knowledge.

The situation reflected in these two lists is hardly likely to seem ideal to anyone. The language skills students are being asked to exercise are ultimately narrow, and the level of knowledge required within the subject area is limited.

It is at this point that our attempt to deal separately with the various realms of knowledge breaks down, for the present situation is the result of the interactions between students' knowledge of subject area, knowledge of language, and knowledge of audience; we cannot effectively broaden our attention to one without altering the others.

Consider audience alone. If a student is to learn to share information or experiences with audiences for whom the information is new, the writing cannot be based on routine recital of subject-area information. The student must learn how to share information in the role of expert with others who do not know. We found some such activity in our study of secondary schools, though not a great deal of it. One source was science projects, where the students carried through their own work at some length, using writing to share results with their teacher (and sometimes with classmates). Using writing in this way involved more than a shift in audience, however; since they were writing about their own experiences, they were using writing as a heuristic tool. It became a sorting-out process for the writer as well as the reader, a process of interpretation and synthesis very unlike the routine recital of previously ordered bodies of information.

Reports on science projects are rooted in students' own experience, and that grounding turns out to be fundamental to most shifts in audience. In school contexts, the role of teacher implies an asymmetrical relationship between the student-as-writer and the teacher-as-reader; the reflection on personal experience, whether of subject-area exploration or of out-of-school experience, is one of the few ways that the balance in the rhetorical situation can be shifted to confront the writer with the situation of having to communicate with someone who does not know what should be said. (The adult will still be more skilled in many relevant areas, but those skills become available as resources to help student writers extend their repertoire, instead of making formal and effective argument unnecessary.)

Implicit in what we have just said is a shift in the language skills being called into play. The way in which a writer builds from knowledge that is already shared toward new insights is through coherently organized text, whether that organization is achieved through expository or literary form. To the extent that the text is not well structured, the communication will begin to break down and the audience will not be effectively addressed. Here, metacognitive skills are necessary to monitor the evolving text, testing what has been written against such criteria as consistency, relevance, and reasonableness, cycling back when deviations become too great.

Beginning with the intention of broadening the kinds of audiences students must learn to address, we have been led to changes in the role of subject-area information and in the nature of the language skills called into play. We would prompt the same chain of reactions whichever area of neglected knowledge we turned toward first. Because writing does involve the interaction among various kinds of knowledge, improving writing instruction will have ramifications throughout the curriculum. Simply asking for more writing is not enough: The essay test will continue to be ill-structured by the very nature of the rhetorical situation we create. Neither will it be productive to place more emphasis directly on writing skills; we will produce an epidemic of "Engfish" such as that now threatening New York. We have to broaden the range of rhetorical situations, to ask students to share information that they possess with others who need to be persuaded of its interest and importance. And at that point we will have altered the nature of subject-area learning as well as broadened our teaching of writing.

ACKNOWLEDGMENTS

The research reported in this chapter was supported in part by Grant NIE-G-79-0174 and Grant NIE-G-80-0156 from the National Institute of Education, Department of Education. However, the opinions expressed do not necessarily reflect the policy or position of the National Institute of Education, and no official endorsement should be inferred.

REFERENCES

Applebee, A. N. The elaborative choice. In M. Nystrand (Ed.), *Language as a way of knowing.* Toronto: Ontario Institute for Studies in Education, 1977.

Applebee, A. N. *Writing in the secondary school.* Urbana, Ill.: National Council of Teachers of English, in press.

Applebee, A. N. *The child's concept of story: Ages two to seventeen.* Chicago: The University of Chicago Press, 1978.

Bereiter, C., & Scardamalia, M. From conversation to composition: The role of instruction in a developmental process. In R. Glaser (Ed.), *Advances in instructional psychology, Vol. 2.* Hillsdale, N.J.: Lawrence Erlbaum, in press.

Britton, J. N. *Language and learning.* London: Allen Lane–The Penguin Press, 1970.

Britton, J. N. Talking to learn. In D. Barnes, J. Britton, H. Rosen, & the London Association of Teachers of English, *Language, the learner, and the school.* Harmondsworth, England: Penguin, 1969.

Britton, J. N. What's the use? A schematic account of language functions. *Educational Review,* 1971, *23,* 205–219.

Brown, A. L. Knowing when, where and how to remember: A problem of metacognition. In R. Glazer (Ed.), *Advances in instructional psychology.* Hillsdale, N.J.: Lawrence Erlbaum, 1978.

Brown, A. L. Metacognitive development and reading. In R. J. Spiro, B. Bruce, & W. F. Brewer (Eds.), *Theoretical issues in reading comprehension.* Hillsdale, N.J.: Lawrence Erlbaum, 1980.

Flavell, J. H. Metacognitive development. In J. M. Scanduran & L. J. Brainerd (Eds), *Structural process theories of complex human behavior.* Leyden: Sijthoff, 1978.

Flower, L., & Hayes, R. The cognition of discovery: Defining a rhetorical problem, *College Composition and Communication,* 1980, *23,* 2–32.

Halliday, M. A. K. *Learning how to mean.* New York: Elsevier, 1977.

Halliday, M. A. K., & Hasan, R. *Cohesion in English.* London: Longman, 1976.

Macrorie, K. *Telling writing.* Rochelle Park, N.J.: Hayden, 1976.

New York State Education Department. *Preliminary competency test in writing. Form A. Directions for Administering and Scoring.* Albany: University of the State of New York, 1979.

Polanyi, M. *Personal knowledge.* London: Routledge and Kegan Paul, 1958.

Rosenblatt, L. M. *The reader, the text, the poem.* Carbondale, Ill.: Southern Illinois University Press, 1978.

Subject Index

Cloze procedure, 62–63
Code, 150
  switching, 11
Cognition, 10, 270, 274–276, 284
Cognitive processes, 203
Cognitive science, 229–235
Cognitive structure, 21
Coherence, 94, 122, 185, 194–203, 205, 207,
    213, 366
  versus cohesion, 94, 197–200
Cohesion, 65, 68–69, 94
Combinatorial explosion, 235
Communication, 16, 22, 58, 65, 69, 83,
    88–89, 102, 105–106, 125–126, 156–157
  breakdown, 64–66, 72, 89–90, 106, 379
  failure, see Communication breakdown
Communicative act, indirect, 112
Communicative dynamism, 94, 96
Communicative homeostasis, 9
Communicative intention, 224
Community of readers and writers, 134, see
    also Print community; Speech
    community; Writing community
Competence, 294–295
Competency testing, 377
Composing process, 24, 131, 174, 182, 187,
    see also Writing process
Composition, 66
Comprehension, 21, 22, 65, 73, 76, 79, 89,
    232–233, 236, 366
  as construction of meaning, 76
  as constructive act, 81
Conceptual dependency, 326
Conceptual knowledge, 271, 286
Consciousness, 174
Consolidation, 249
Constraint, 17, 18, 21, 22
  audience as, 62
  contextual, 65
  graphic, 64
  linguistic, 19–20
  semantic, 65
  situational, 19–20
  syntactic, 64
  textual, 21, 65
Context, 17, 87, 150, 157, 227
  extralinguistic, 88
  interpretation, 79
  linguistic, 79, 87, 88
  relation to text, 9–11, 105–126
  role in written communication, 105–126
  of situation, 9
  situational, 87

of use, 11, 68
visual, 79
Contextualization, 159–160
  global 159, see also Poetic
  piecemeal, 159, see also Transactional
Contingency, 219
Convention
  cultural, 105
  discourse, 160
  genre, 105, 111, 118, 167, 366
  linguistic, 105, 111, 368
  narrative, 120–126, 366, see also Narrative
    structure
  superordinate genre, 19
Conversation, 41, 176, 177, 186–187, 189, 192
  as cooperative endeavor, 112
Conversational act, 116
Conversational presumption, 303
Cooperative principle, 112
Coreferencing, 94–102, 245, 354
Cue, 82, 110
Cueing stimuli, 177
Curriculum, 4, 208, 377

D

Dartmouth Seminar, 152
Decentering, 347
Decisions, high-level, 184
Decoding, 81
Decontextualization, 32, 159
Deletion, 249
Delivery, 5–6
Derivation rules, 222
Detection and identification processes in
    revision, 355
Developmental changes, 199
Dialect, 120, 124, 242
  interference, 242
Dictating versus writing, 8
Dictation, 179
  versus slow dictation, 185–208
Differentiation, 135–136, 251
Discoordination of language production,
    177, 187
Discourse, 270, 271, 274, 275, 277–283
  analysis, 72
  literary and nonliterary, 149–151
  pointer, 97–98
  processing, 313–319, see also
    Comprehension
  processing, theory of, 315–316
  production 233, 235–240, see also